# Task-Based Instruction in Foreign Language Education

## Practices and Programs

**BETTY LOU LEAVER**
**and JANE R. WILLIS**

*Editors*

GEORGETOWN UNIVERSITY PRESS
Washington, D.C.

Georgetown University Press, Washington, D.C.
© 2004 by Georgetown University Press. All rights reserved.
Printed in the United States of America

10 9 8 7 6 5 4 3 2 1 2004

This book is printed on acid-free paper meeting
the requirements of the American National Standard
for Permanence in Paper for Printed Library Materials.

*Library of Congress Cataloging-in-Publication Data*

Task-based instruction in foreign language education : practices and programs /
Betty Lou Leaver and Jane R. Willis, editors.
    p. cm.
  Includes bibliographical references and index.
  ISBN 1-58901-028-0 (alk. paper)
  1. Language and languages—Study and teaching (Higher)   I. Leaver, Betty Lou.
II. Willis, Jane E. (Jane Rosemary), 1944–
  P53.T344 2004
  418′.0071′1—dc22                                          2004005619

# Contents

# Preface

This book has been compiled for teachers of foreign and second languages who are in the process of implementing task-based instruction (TBI), have been using it, or would like to. The intent of the book is to provide examples of programs and courses that are fully or partially task-based and that can, therefore, serve as models to teachers and administrators. Although some programs described here could be used with adolescent learners (and in some cases, have), most cater for the adult professional learner and students in tertiary education.

Much has been written in the past twenty years on the theories underlying the use of tasks in language teaching. Chapter 1 of this volume reviews some of the milestones in this literature and puts forward the case for TBI. We aim to help the reader to understand some of the beliefs that underpin current practices but do not try to add to the theory-making that is associated with task-based instruction. Rather, the intent of this volume is to present case studies of successful TBI programs in a number of languages including Arabic, Chinese, Czech, English, French, German, Korean, Russian, Spanish, and Ukrainian—representative programs from all levels of language difficulty and from real beginner level upwards. Most, if not all of these, can serve as generic models suitable for any foreign language. Programs in this volume range from those which use tasks as supplementary materials to fully fledged task-based syllabi and to Internet delivery. In addition to these applications, authors in this volume address issues of task-based testing and faculty development. The settings include two U.S. government schools, three private schools in Brazil and Moldova, six highly respected U.S. universities, and an international Web-based program. The concerns of this volume are the nitty-gritty everyday decisions that are made in task-based classrooms: the how-to, when-to, and with-whom-to pedagogical questions that teachers must constantly address. Challenges are faced, and a wide range of solutions are proposed.

In assembling this volume, we sought out highly experienced, respected, and successful practitioners, as well as faculty developers, with recent experience of TBI. These teachers and administrators of successful TBI second language and foreign language programs and consultants to them come from a number of countries. Although the shared experiences in using TBI are very much parallel among the authors, terminology can vary from country to country. Therefore, we have standardized upon American English usage and terminology and have included a glossary of terms at the end of the book to help interpret among the many international variations.

We have divided this book into four parts. Part I provides the theoretical underpinning for the rest of the book. It gives a history of TBI, as well as provides a discussion of task-based theories, presents models and typologies of tasks, and sets forth some of the issues that will be discussed in other chapters. Part II contains the case studies, which are frankly discussed from the point of view of course contents, course success, and challenges encountered in implementing TBI in the classroom. Part III presents versions of TBI on the Internet. All these programs are available for reader use. Finally, part IV discusses two issues often unmentioned in the literature on TBI: (1) difficulties in designing task-based tests and ways to overcome them and (2) issues in developing faculty for successful teaching in TBI programs. Taken together, we think that these experiences and contributions will be of benefit to teachers, administrators, and curriculum developers in all areas of second language and foreign language education and teaching.

The references at the end of this volume combine the general references from all thirteen chapters. A glossary defines terms used in the book. An appendix provides an overview of the two scales used in the United States for measuring foreign language proficiency (proficiency almost always being the catalyst for and goal of task-based instruction): the Interagency Language Roundtable scale and the American Council on Teaching Foreign Languages scale.

There are many books and papers about research into tasks and theories behind TBI. We offer this book as a practical resource of real-life TBI experiences for language teachers who want to add more task-based instruction to their own classrooms; in other words, as a pragmatic volume whose examples show various ways of applying the research and theory on TBI in a wide range of settings. We hope that it will inspire you to innovate and try new tasks.

# Acknowledgments

We would like to thank the following individuals who read various chapters of the prepublication draft of this volume and provided useful comments and helpful insights: Maurice Funke, Mirian Resende, Tatiana Rusu, and Tamara Turcan. Their comments served to improve this book; any errors and omissions are those of the authors and editors alone.

We would also like to thank Dr. Elvira Swender of the American Council on Teaching Foreign Languages for providing updated information about the council's proficiency scale and tests.

Jane Willis would especially like to thank the following people. First and foremost, her husband, Dave Willis, who read and made detailed suggestions for several drafts of chapter 1 and also for chapter 4. In addition, members of the Aston University Language Studies Unit WRAP group (WRiting for Academic Purposes) read and made some excellent suggestions for chapter 1. Last, acknowledgment is given to Ramon Ribe, whose book *Tramas creativas y aprendizaje de lenguas* greatly inspired her.

Very important, we who were involved in the early stages of the book wish to thank Gail Grella and Georgetown University Press for their patience in waiting to see the finished manuscript—and for not giving up on it.

We also want to thank Carl Leaver, who converted many of the graphics for this book to publication format. In many cases, that required remaking the tables and figures, and for that the editors are very grateful.

# Part I

## An Overview of Task-Based Instruction: From Theories to Practices

# 1

## PERSPECTIVES ON TASK-BASED INSTRUCTION: UNDERSTANDING OUR PRACTICES, ACKNOWLEDGING DIFFERENT PRACTITIONERS

Jane R. Willis

EDITORS' NOTE: This chapter presents an overview of task-based instruction (TBI) from its earliest days, including the changing ideas in foreign language education that led up to it, to its recent incarnations. Commonly accepted principles of TBI are discussed, as well as illustrated with examples from the chapters throughout this book and in other sources. Because TBI has taken a number of different shapes since its first appearance on the foreign language and second language teaching scene, definitions and frameworks are provided for understanding the global concepts. This chapter serves as the theoretical foundation of the rest of the book, and chapter authors refer to its contents in explaining their programs.

### TBI in Use

Beginning learners of English in Brazil complete a family tree for their partner's family, leading on to a class survey on family structures; in a joint U.S.–Russian training program, early intermediate learners of Russian, together with their counterparts learning English, in the United States work out a set of procedures for handling a fire at a space station; learners of Japanese discuss their draft texts for a "voice-over" commentary for a video of their home town to send to their future host families in Japan; advanced learners of Spanish search the Spanish press for information on "rights to privacy" before writing a piece for a local Spanish paper; and learners of German peer edit and upload to their Web site another episode from the life story of their German-speaking interview partner.

One thing unites all these learners: As participants in programs that use TBI, they are all making a real effort to communicate as best as they can in the target foreign language. As you will see from the programs described in the chapters in this book (from which the above examples are drawn), TBI is not monolithic; it does not constitute one single methodology. It is a multifaceted approach, which can be creatively applied with different syllabus types and for different purposes. Within TBI, programs vary tremendously worldwide, as do practitioners' assumptions about the nature of language learning, but they all share the same basic philosophy. Ribe (1997, 17) defines this well: "Comparten el mismo enfoque de aprendizaje de lengua por la accion, en el que la atencion y el enfasis se centran en el processo y el contenido de la tarea."[1]

TBI is happening worldwide. Ribe, based in Barcelona, but with links to schools in other European countries, led a large-scale investigation into the use of tasks for foreign language teaching, exploring both theoretical and practical aspects during the period 1992–95 (Ribe 1997). In 1999, the Education Department of Hong Kong launched their Target-Oriented Curriculum, which as Candlin (2001, 233) describes it, is "underwritten by a task-based approach" whose philosophy is broadly similar. International conferences are revealing a growing interest in TBI (or task-based learning, TBL, as it is called in Europe).[2]

So how is it that we, as practicing professionals, have come together to share this philosophy? What influenced us to move through grammar translation and audiolingual methods to communicative language teaching (CLT) and TBI? To answer these questions, we begin with a brief historical overview.

## The Swing toward Communicative Language Teaching: A Historical Perspective

The CLT movement developed partly as a reaction against the rigid control of the behaviorist audiolingual methods of teaching of the 1960s and partly because such methods failed to have the desired effect of helping learners to communicate in the target foreign language. Bloomfield (1942) had already convinced language teaching practitioners of the primacy of speech in language acquisition. This led to the development of an audiolingual approach with more emphasis on spoken language (Lado 1957a, 1964).[3] However, the behaviorist methods on which audiolingualism was based treated language learning primarily as habit formation and automatization. It was believed that if language patterns were presented, imitated, and practiced intensively, avoiding error, learners would be able to assimilate them and use them accurately in contexts outside the classroom.

There were, however, many problems with audiolingual approaches. Syllabuses consisted of an inventory of structural patterns illustrated by contrived dialogues. This meant that the limited language to which learners were exposed in the classroom bore very little resemblance to the spontaneous interactions they would hear outside it. In class, teachers did their best to restrict their talk to the items they had taught, and learners had little chance to experiment with language and express their own meanings. This was because the emphasis was on eradication of error and accurate production of the target forms, not on communication of meanings. Vocabulary was often selected on the basis of what words could best fill the slots in drills and substitution tables designed to practice grammar patterns, rather than the words learners needed to express themselves and socialize in the foreign language.

Chomsky (1959) launched a scathing attack on behaviorist views of language learning. He demonstrated convincingly both that language learning and language use must be creative processes and that they cannot be accounted for by behaviorist theories. Chomsky saw language as rule-governed creativity. He believed that a basic rule system that underpins all languages is innate and that, given exposure to a specific language, children will naturally create the specific rules of that language for themselves. Learning is thus seen as a process of discovery determined by internal processes rather than external influences.

These doubts about behaviorism were reinforced by research into second language acquisition (SLA) by Corder (1967), who studied learner error in an attempt to gain insights into the learning process. Corder found that errors were systematic, rather than random, did not generally stem from the learners' first language, and showed positive evidence of learners moving through specific stages of language development. Selinker (1972) coined the term *interlanguage* to describe these developmental stages.

The most striking finding by Selinker and Corder was that language learning, even in a classroom setting, seems to develop independently of instruction (which is *not* to say that instruction is superfluous). The way language developed did not always reflect what was taught in the classroom. Research into the sequence of acquisition of morphemes, such as Dulay and Burt (1973, 1974) suggested a "natural order" hypothesis, and this and subsequent research (e.g., Pienemann 1988) showed that learners acquire language according to their own inbuilt internal syllabus, regardless of the order in which they are exposed to particular structures and regardless of mother-tongue influences. In other words, it is unlikely that learners will acquire a new pattern unless they are developmentally ready for it, no matter how many times they practice it. In English, the third person *s* is a good example of a pattern that is easy to explain and easy to get learners to produce when the linguistic focus is on the forms of the present simple tense, but that is often omitted in spontaneous speech because it is typically acquired late in the developmental sequence. In Romance languages, gender agreement in adjectives and past participles is similarly late acquired.

At the same time, Hymes (1972) showed that there was a good deal more to language use, and therefore to language learning, than simply grammar and lexis. He drew attention to the need for *communicative competence*. Brown (1994, 227) defines communicative competence as

> that aspect of our competence which enables us to convey and interpret messages and to negotiate meanings interpersonally within specific contexts. . . . [T]he knowledge that enables a person to communicate functionally and interactionally.

Paulston (1974) added to this the concept of *linguistic competence*, that is, knowledge about language forms. More definitions and further analysis of communicative and linguistic competences continued over the next decade or so (Canale and Swain 1980; Bachman 1990), and the important swing toward CLT was well under way.

This move to CLT drew on a number of influences. First, it drew on the work of Halliday (1973, 1975), who views language as a system of meaning rather than simply of wordings. Halliday's (1975) study of his young son acquiring the first language is significantly titled *Learning How to Mean*. Once we view language as a meaning system, we are obliged to accept that grammar and lexis are a means to an end, rather than an end in themselves. Another influence was the work of the linguistic philosopher, Austin. Again, the title of Austin's (1962) work, *How to Do Things with Words*, reveals a particular view of language. We use language to achieve communicative goals, to make requests and suggestions, to persuade and entertain. And, as Grice (1975) demonstrated, even when language is used to make factual statements, these statements are interpreted in the context of purposeful use.

In 1971, the Council of Europe set out to identify a common core of communicative functions for all foreign language syllabuses, and Van Ek's functionally based "threshold syllabus" was published in 1973. It was Wilkins who outlined a notional syllabus for English in 1976. Both Van Ek (1973) and Wilkins (1976) were concerned with language *functions*, what language users are doing with the language, and *notions*, the meanings users wish to communicate. The notional-functional syllabus took as its starting point the questions *What do learners need to do with the language?* and *What meanings do they need to communicate?* It began by specifying functions and notions and then went on to ask what language is needed to achieve these communicative goals. Notional-functional syllabuses began to supplement the grammatical syllabus in foreign language teaching, the emphasis being on using language for social and transactional purposes. Syllabus descriptions began to be expressed in terms of communicative situations.

In this context, more and more classroom time was spent in developing learners' communication skills. After presenting and practicing language items (grammar patterns or functional dialogues), more importance was given to a third stage—that of free production, with learners interacting in pairs or groups, often to complete a communication task. There was generally greater tolerance of error at this "free" stage. This three-stage presentation–practice–production cycle is known in Europe and Latin America as PPP (Littlewood 1981).

Materials and textbooks also changed. A less rigid dependence on structural grading meant that more naturalistic texts could be used in the classroom. These changes meant that learners had exposure to a richer diet of natural language and more opportunities to express what they themselves wanted to mean.

However, much of what went on under the label of CLT still had a primary focus on practice of form (the second stage in the PPP cycle) rather than expression of learners' own meanings. For example, pair-practice of set dialogues, manipulation of functional dialogues, role-plays with cue cards, games using routinized or preordained language patterns, and similar activities aimed to give learners a chance to practice particular structures or realizations of functions and notions in realistic but carefully controlled situations. These activities are helpful in highlighting and automatizing useful expressions and patterns in particular situations, but only the third phase (free production) offers learners opportunities to control the interaction themselves and express their own meanings. It is in this third phase, however, that learners are encouraged to use the new forms. In functional CLT, then, there is still the belief that acquisition follows immediately on teaching. It still rests on the belief that what is learned can be assimilated and become an established part of the learners' language repertoire without any lapse of time.

However, SLA research (Ellis 1985, 1994, 2003) has established that "teaching does not and cannot determine the way that the learner's language will develop" (Skehan 1996b) and there is much research to show that learners do not necessarily learn what teachers teach. Even in programs where patterns are drilled and practiced in an attempt to help learners to use them correctly from the very beginning, learners fail to develop high levels of accuracy and lasting linguistic knowledge (Lightbown and Spada 1999; Ellis 1985). They may be able to reproduce the new items when their attention is on form in a monitored situation, but there is no guarantee that they will be able to use them in meaning focused communication, or that they have stored them for future use. In other words there is no guarantee that what is taught and practiced will be learned; rather, this will depend on the developmental stage of the learner's interlanguage, which is internal to the learner.

It is not surprising, then, that the above approaches to CLT, which Howatt (1984) called the weak version of CLT, still did not seem to offer a significant improvement on the structural approach in terms of the achievement of communicative competence. In fact, Skehan (1996b), referring to the findings of J. B. Carroll (1975) and H. H. Stern (as quoted in Skehan), states that

> levels of attainment in conventional foreign language learning are poor, and students commonly leave school with very little in the way of usable language. In other words, most language learning is associated with relative failure. Only the gifted learners achieve impressive levels of proficiency. (p. 18)

A strong version of CLT can be seen in action in the "natural approach" put forward by Krashen and Terrell (1983). This strong version rests on the belief that language can be acquired naturally simply through exposure and communication (Howatt 1984). Ellis puts this more forcefully; he reports that SLA research now shows that

> learners do not first acquire language as a structural system and then learn how to use this system in communication, but rather actually discover the system itself in the process of learning how to communicate. (Ellis 2003, 14)

This process is more akin to what happens when people go and live or work in a foreign language environment, that is, where they acquire the language naturally without formal tuition.

It was this belief—that learning is driven by communication and exposure to purposeful language use—that led to the use of foreign language immersion programs—or the near-exclusive use of foreign language in cross-curricular contexts. Examples are French for English speakers in Canada (Swain 1985) and English for Science and Math teaching in Turkey (Aytan 1994). It also led to content-based language instruction (CBI), which is based on a subject-matter core with authentic materials on core topics, in both English as a foreign language and English as a second language (Snow, Brinton, and Wesche 1989), and in foreign language programs (Leaver and Stryker 1989). It also inspired Prabhu (1987) in Bangalore, India, to begin his Communicational Teaching Project in which sequences of tasks were used (with no explicit grammar teaching) to give secondary school learners experience of English in use. Thus TBI evolved as a branch of CLT.

## The Emergence of TBI

Some practitioners, for example, those teaching on CBI programs, adopted TBI out of a desire for a meaning-focused approach that reflected real-life language use. Of importance was the concept that language (as indeed any subject learned in a classroom) needs to be transferable to real-world activities and that is best accomplished by doing some of these activities in the classroom (Brown, Collins, and Duguid 1989). In other words, the cognition, knowledge, and/or skills—however one wants to classify language performance—need to be "situated" not in a location (the classroom) but in an activity (the task). In this way, language that is used in the classroom becomes truly communicative rather than pseudo-communicative. Authentic materials, that is, texts taken from real-life sources, play an important part in such programs.

Other practitioners, like Prabhu (1987), adopted tasks because they firmly believed that task-based interaction stimulated natural acquisition processes and were less concerned with real-life situations per se.

Most teaching practitioners would agree that TBI rests on three basic premises, though not all practitioners would give equal importance to each. These premises are:

1. Language learning does not proceed in a linear additive fashion but is a complex organic process (Long 1985a; Lightbown 2000). In other words, teaching a discrete language item does not lead to immediate mastery of that item.

2. "Language form is best learned when the learners' attention is on meaning" (Prabhu 1982, cited in Brumfit 1984, 234). The effort put into "grappling" to understand and to engage with meaning will, in time, lead to the subconscious acquisition of form. This means that learners need a lot of comprehensible input, that is, exposure to the foreign language being used in a variety of contexts, both spoken and written, that is just slightly above their current level of comprehension (Krashen 1985; Long 1983, 1996; Ellis 2003). This is often referred to as the "Input Hypothesis."

3. In addition to exposure, learners need opportunities to use the target language for a real purpose in order to learn it (Swain 1985; Swain and Lapkin 2001). This is sometimes referred to as the "Output Hypothesis," the details of which follow below. Output of course normally occurs in the context of interaction. Proponents of the "Interaction

Hypothesis" (Long 1996; Gass and Varonis 1994) argue that interaction provides opportunities for negotiation of meaning, which in turn facilitates second language acquisition.

Let us take these three premises one by one and explore them more fully.

### LANGUAGE LEARNING AS AN ORGANIC PROCESS

Language learning is a gradual and complex organic process. This has been well documented over the years, from Corder's research into learners' errors (1967, 1981) to subsequent research on developmental sequences. Skehan (1996b, 18) explains: "Learners often go through a developmental sequence which does not go directly to the target form, but involves a number of errors on the way."

With each language feature—possessive adjectives and pronouns, the negative system, the article system, relative clauses, question forms—learners pass through a series of transitional stages, restructuring their interlanguage to accommodate a new form as they become aware of new evidence in the input they receive. Sometimes they even seem to take a step backward (see Lightbown 1985 for research on variability). A lot of grammar, then, is acquired subconsciously from the input that learners are exposed to. A useful role for the teacher is to make this input both engaging and accessible and then to highlight useful patterns in it and draw them to their students' attention. As this book shows, this can certainly be done through the use of TBI.

There has always been a focus on grammar in SLA research, but recently more attention has been paid to lexis. With the advent of corpus studies, linguists have begun to explore in depth the relationship between grammar and lexis (Sinclair 1991; Hunston, Francis, and Manning 1997; Willis 1990, 2003). This work has borne out the findings of Bolinger (1975) and Pawley and Syder (1983), who stressed the importance of lexical chunks in communication. Much of the language we use comes in readily accessed phrases rather than being composed one word at a time by applying grammatical rules. Both Widdowson (1983) in his definition of communicative competence and Hunston and Francis (2000) view language as a series of lexically based patterns rather than as created by the application of a system of abstract rules.

Ellis (1997, 123) suggests that different aspects of words are learned in different ways. The form, collocational partners, and grammatical class of a word are best acquired subconsciously through "implicit" learning (Carter 2001, 44–45), whereas meaning—the semantic properties of a word—can be learned in "explicit" ways, that is, through teacher explanation, dictionary use, use of bilingual word lists, word cards, and so on. An overview of researched techniques for deliberate learning and direct teaching of words (suitable for both TBI and independent learning) can be found in Nation (2001) and Nation and Meara (2002). However, it is generally agreed that extensive reading and listening are necessary for deepening learners' knowledge of the meaning, forms, and use of each word. Yet this reading and listening must be purposeful; for example, in chapter 3 of the present volume, Van Altena illustrates ways of integrating it into her TBI program for Spanish learners.

### THE ROLE AND NATURE OF INPUT IN TBI

We have seen above that both grammar and lexical items can be acquired through learners processing the input that they receive for meaning. This brings us to the second premise, that learning must be primarily meaning-focused rather than form-focused. This can be attained through setting tasks that provide opportunities for learners to "grapple" with meaning. The key to success is the provision of sufficient suitable language data to serve as input, lack of which was one reason for the failure of audiolingual methods.

So what constitutes suitable input? Krashen (1985) talks of providing "comprehensible input plus 1," often referred to as $I + 1$. The $I + 1$ is, in practice, a somewhat vague and immeasurable concept, but a basic interpretation would be texts (spoken and written) that provide a challenge to learners without frustrating them. It is also possible to grade the tasks rather than the texts and also to prepare pretasks that will mitigate the difficulties inherent in the language of the text itself.

Most TBI instructors believe that carefully selected authentic materials can be used as the basis for tasks that require learners to process the text for meaning. The texts can come from the kind of real-life contexts that students will be facing and can be about topics and themes that interest them. Even with beginners, in addition to teacher-led listening tasks, very short texts and recordings of short interactions can be made accessible by pretask preparation, a graded sequence of tasks, and subsequent study of linguistic features of transcript or text. This is illustrated by Leaver and Kaplan (chapter 2 of this volume) and Lopes (chapter 4).

There is much research to support the Input Hypothesis. Research carried out in French immersion classrooms in Canada (which provided rich comprehensible input through subject matter instruction from beginner levels upward) showed that learners developed good comprehension, confidence, and fluency in French, but in some aspects of grammar did not achieve the high levels of accuracy expected (Harley and Swain 1984). Swain ascribed this partly to the fact that certain grammatical features appeared very rarely in classroom settings and, therefore, might need more direct instruction (Swain 1988) and partly to insufficient opportunities to speak or interact in the target language, as the classes were large (Swain 1985).

### INTERACTION AND OUTPUT IN TBI

The third premise—that interaction and output are also necessary for learning—has been confirmed by other research. In early experiments, Montgomery and Eisenstein (1985) added "real-world" communication activities to a grammar-based course for one of two similar groups of learners. The results showed that the group who had had this addition made greater improvements not only in accent, vocabulary, and comprehension but also, and most of all, in grammatical accuracy. Long (1976, 1996) investigated learner-centered communication activities and found (not surprisingly) evidence of far richer interaction than that which occurs between teacher and learners. He holds that negotiation of meanings is essential for acquisition, a view supported by more recent studies using tasks, including Gass and Varonis (1994) and Mackey (1999). Since then, there has been further research on learner–learner interaction as reported in both Lightbown and Spada (1999) and Tsui (2001) that points to the same conclusions. However, Ellis (2003, 80–83) outlines some limitations of the interaction hypothesis and Poupore (2005) reports evidence suggesting that other types of negotiation in addition to that of meaning—for example, negotiation of form, of procedure, of task content—might also be beneficial.

Shehadeh (1999) reports research showing support for Swain's Output Hypothesis (1985); this and other work in this area is described in more detail in Gass (2003). Skehan (1998a), building on the Output Hypothesis and taking account of other research findings, outlines six reasons why communicative output can contribute (either directly or indirectly) to acquisition. Below, I have both summarized these and elaborated on them, exploring, where possible, their potential for both spoken and written discourse. In short, opportunities for communicative output can help learners

1. to generate more finely tuned input from an interlocutor that renders the subsequent input more comprehensible, for example, as a result of requesting a clarification or an explanation. This is part of the process of the negotiation of meaning alluded to above.

2. to direct their attention to syntactic processing of input—if learners hear the teacher and another person rehearsing in the target language a task (or a task recording) that students will do later, they are more likely to listen for forms and expressions they can use themselves. Syntactic processing also happens when learners are planning to speak the foreign language in a more public situation, or to write for others to read.

3. to test hypotheses about language, to try out new expressions and patterns that they are not certain about, and to see if they are readily understood in that context and, if not, to get help in generating a more appropriate wording. This involves an element of risk taking, and this, too, is something learners need to gain confidence in.

4. to develop automaticity which leads to fluency. For example, to prepare for speaking in real time, a learner needs to generate a stock of already assembled (or at least partially assembled) chunks, instead of having to compose each utterance one word at a time. The same is true for most genres of writing, especially those that contain a high number of formulaic or genre-related wordings, as found in thank-you letters or specific sections of academic research papers or term papers.

5. to develop discourse skills, for example, turn taking, introducing or changing a topic, holding the floor, or, when writing, signaling stages in an argument. Practice is also needed in organizing and composing more sustained talk and writing, for example, thinking ahead when mustering an argument, or narrating a story so as to keep the hearer's/reader's attention.

6. to develop a personal voice, for example, to find ways of expressing individual meanings, to give and justify personal opinions, to steer conversations on to preferred topics, to narrate or describe from a personal point of view, to make jokes and perhaps even play with words and language.

There are then many arguments in favor of interaction and output in stimulating learning. But this does not mean that a focus on form and explicit language instruction have no part to play in a TBI approach.

## An Explicit Focus on Language Form

There is now quite a large body of research carried out with different ages and levels that suggests a focus on form at some point within a TBI or CBI course can help learners achieve greater levels of accuracy. Summaries of this research can be found in Long (1991), Lightbown and Spada (1999), Lightbown (2000), and Ellis (2003). Instruction and correction can highlight points of language that may otherwise go unnoticed in the input; in other words, explicit learning helps learners to recognize patterns and to notice them in subsequent input (Schmidt 1990). This is likely to contribute to their acquisition at a later stage when learners are developmentally ready. Research to date does not indicate that formal instruction can change the order in which learners acquire forms, but overall language development seems to be accelerated and learners seem to reach a higher standard of attainment when given direct instruction. A comprehensive study of fifty language learners who had reached native-like proficiency, as judged by a U.S. government test, indicated that all, without exception, considered that without direct instruction they would have stagnated at a lower level plateau (Leaver and Atwell 2002).

TBI practitioners and learners have a range of opinions about the desirability and format of instruction in TBI courses. In Prabhu's Bangalore program, there was no direct teaching of grammar; teachers did, however, correct and recast learners' errors. However, Nicholas, Lightbown, and Spada (2001), who analyzed the effects of teacher recasts, report that learners often fail to perceive these as corrections of form, and recommend more explicit corrective feedback.

In this volume, in the Web-based writing program described by Stevens (chapter 10) and the language improvement courses run for teachers (Cozonac, chapter 13), the study of grammar is not overtly treated in lessons but left to the individual student. Error correction does, however, play a part in both programs; for example, students' work is corrected before being displayed on the Web page (Stevens) and grammar references and other forms of assistance may be provided outside regular classes (Cozonac).

There are also variations of opinion regarding at what stages in a task cycle or in a TBI course an explicit focus on language is most effective. Several practitioners, for example, Leaver and Kaplan (chapter 2 of this volume), Van Altena (chapter 3), Antokhin and her colleagues (chapter 9), and Lys (chapter 11) deal with grammar within the context of the task itself, as the need for it arises, and/or during a subsequent review session. Others, notably Lopes (chapter 4) and Passos de Oliveira (chapter 12), prefer to prepare learners lexically for the task and go into the grammar later. Still others, for example, Alosh (chapter 5), Saito-Abbott (chapter 6), Macías (chapter 7), and Hager and Lyman-Hager (chapter 8), use an approach where new language, both lexis and grammar, that might be useful for the realization of particular function is introduced in advance of the task and followed up later. When and how an explicit focus on form is tackled will also depend on the level and prior language experience of the learners concerned, the kind of language being learned, and the goals of the course.

To understand the specific choices made by each of the contributors to this volume, as well as the nature of choice in presentation order of task and schemata (grammar, lexicon, even cultural knowledge) needed to accomplish the task, it is first necessary to understand the nature of tasks themselves.

## Defining the Term "Task"

The discussion that follows attempts to organize the multiple ways in which tasks are currently viewed by practitioners of TBI around the globe. We begin by discussing aspects of tasks as defined in the literature on TBI, and then we go on to compare interpretations of the term "task" in practice.

### DEFINITIONS FROM THE LITERATURE

The term *task* can mean different things to different people. Just as there are weak and strong forms of CLT, there are different interpretations of the word *task*. Given the six representative definitions from the literature on TBI below, teachers or administrators about to embark on the development of task-based courses or programs might consider (1) the common elements among them and (2) which definition best suits the requirements and needs of their particular learners.

Most of the six definitions proposed in tables 1.1 through 1.6 include mention of achieving or arriving at *an outcome*, or attaining *a goal* or *an objective*. Table 1.1 is an exception to this, but it does state that the teacher must specify what will be regarded as the successful completion of the task, in other words the expected outcome would be specified beforehand. This concept of completion occurs several times. Nunan's definition (table 1.3) says that a task should have a sense of completeness, and Skehan (table 1.6) mentions task completion in addition to task outcome.

Implied or stated in most definitions above is that tasks are *meaning focused*. In other words, learners are free to use whatever language they want in order to convey their intended meaning and to sustain the interaction. When doing this, they are trying to understand things they need to find out about or explain things they need to tell someone else. They are not simply displaying their control of particular patterns or structures or phrases, which would be a linguistic objective. To support this view, the first definition above includes the phrase: "a task

TABLE 1.1. **Definition of Task: Task as Response**

"An activity or action which is carried out as a result of processing or understanding language, i.e., as a response. For example, drawing a map while listening to a tape, listening to an instruction and performing a command may be referred to as tasks. Tasks may or may not involve the production of language. A task usually requires the teacher to specify what will be regarded as successful completion of a task. The use of a variety of different tasks in language teaching is said to make teaching more communicative . . . since it provides a purpose for classroom activity which goes beyond practice of language for its own sake."

*Source:* Richards, Platt, and Weber 1985.

TABLE 1.2. **Definition of Task: Task as Derived Outcome**

"An activity which required learners to arrive at an outcome from given information through some processes of thought and which allowed teachers to control and regulate that process was regarded as a task."

*Source:* Prabhu 1987, 2.

TABLE 1.3. **Definition of Task: Task as Focus on Meaning**

"A piece of classroom work which involves learners in comprehending, manipulating, producing, or interacting in the target language while their attention is principally focused on meaning rather than form."

*Source:* Nunan 1989a, 10.

provides a purpose for classroom activity that goes beyond practice of language for its own sake."

Task performance may entail the use of any number of *skills*, from one single skill to all four. A task need not entail actual production of language, although many do. Listening tasks (table 1.1) may have a nonverbal outcome, like a completed map, drawing, or pictures arranged in a particular sequence to follow the story another person is telling. A TBI course for beginners may well start with whole sets of listening tasks with the aim of rapidly building up a large receptive vocabulary and giving learners a "feel" for the language. A reading task may simply involve identifying information of a particular type (e.g., increase or decrease in sales over a half-year) to be put into a table, graph, or flowchart, in which case the completed table, graph, or flowchart would be the end-product. Such tasks are largely receptive, but tasks can promote the use of all four skills, receptive and productive. Ellis (table 1.5) underlines this point. In fact, it is quite possible to design one single task with conditions that encourage learners to use all four skills as well as microskills, such as skimming or scanning a text. Task design depends on the procedures selected for the work plan and the format of the end-product.

The *real-world* theme is taken up in the final two definitions. Ellis (table 1.5) states that a task is intended to "result in language use that bears resemblance, di-

**TABLE 1.4. Definition of Task: Task as Goal-Oriented Activity with Real Outcome**

"A goal-oriented activity in which learners use language to achieve a real outcome. In other words, learners use whatever target language resources they have in order to solve a problem, do a puzzle, play a game or share and compare experiences."

*Source:* D. Willis 1996, 53.

**TABLE 1.5. Definition of Task: Task as Workplan with Content-Oriented Outcome**

"A workplan that requires the learners to process language pragmatically in order to achieve an outcome that can be evaluated in terms of whether the correct or appropriate propositional content has been conveyed. To this end, it requires them to give primary attention to meaning and to make use of their own linguistic resources, although the design of the task may predispose them to choose particular forms. A task is intended to result in language use that bears resemblance, direct or indirect, to the way language is used in the real world. Like other language activities, a task can engage productive or receptive, and oral or written skills, and also various cognitive processes."

*Source:* Ellis 2003, 16.

**TABLE 1.6. Definition of Task: Task as Focus on Meaning with Assessment of Outcomes**

"An activity in which: meaning is primary; there is some communication problem to solve; there is some sort of relationship to comparable real world activities; task completion has some priority; and the assessment is in terms of task outcome. . . .

"Tasks:

—do not give learners other people's meanings to regurgitate;

—are not concerned with language display;

—are not conformity-oriented;

—are not practice-oriented;

—do not embed language into materials so that specific structures can be focused on."

*Source:* Skehan 1998a, 95.

rect or indirect, to the way language is used in the real world." With reference to the definition in table 1.4, Willis (1990), calls tasks *replication activities* because they replicate "aspects of communication in the real world." Here both Ellis and Willis are talking about *language use* in tasks, not the tasks themselves. Skehan (table1.6) mentions that tasks bear "some sort of resemblance to the real world" but fails to say how, though later he says that, in most classroom contexts, interactions that truly reflect real-life interactions outside the classroom are very difficult to set up, given the norms in classroom interaction and its rituals and routines that stem from the recognition of status and power differences between teacher as "knower" and students as learners (Skehan 1999).

Role-playing real-life situations may be the closest that one can come in terms of task authenticity; however, these would, in their basic form, involve acting out scenarios with "pretend" outcomes (*simulations*; Willis 1990), rather than learners exchanging real meanings to reach a real outcome. For example, booking a hotel room in the foreign country can be easily role-played in class; different hotel-booking scenarios with various problems can be rehearsed and practiced through role-play simulations. A truly authentic hotel-booking task would involve actually telephoning a real hotel in the foreign country to book a room, and, unless students were actually going to that country to stay on those dates, they would then have to cancel it. Although this, too, would be an authentic task, it is somewhat unethical to mislead hoteliers! However, it would be possible to upgrade the initial role-play *simulation* to a *replication*, that is, a true task, thus:

a. List the information you would need to give and request when booking a hotel room. List also the problems that might arise.

b. Then, with a partner, compare lists and compose and script a short telephone conversation between a tourist and a hotel reception desk that includes one of the problems, resolves it, and results in a hotel booking.

Here, the outcomes are the lists and the scripted dialogue, which can then be recorded and/or acted out to the class. However, the process of achieving them would have involved real communication and led learners to consider a range of potential language realizations. This would thus count as a replication or a true task.

In the classrooms described in this book, TBI writers have devised some ingenious ways of introducing the "real world" of the target foreign language into the learning program. For example, in the Defense Language Institute's classrooms (Leaver and Kaplan, chapter 2 of this volume), students often prepared tasks that replicated their future job requirements (e.g., carrying out car searches), and in the French program described by Hager and Lyman-Hager (chapter 8), students in situ carried out real-life purchases of needed supplies following pretask preparation that provided them with the necessary linguistic schemata. Others have used a mix of *simulation* and *replication* activities to do this. This mix is typical among programs that motivate the development of classroom tasks on the basis of grammatical and lexical features being studied, as in the Arabic program, described in chapter 5 by Alosh, and the Spanish program, described in chapter 7 by Macías.

Some kind of resemblance to real life is important for learners' *motivation*; adults especially like to know they are not wasting time by learning things they may never need. However, motivation can also result from having real outcomes to achieve in the target language and the feeling of success in achieving them and sharing the results with others, as described in the outcomes-based Japanese program (Saito-Abbott, chapter 6 of this volume). Increases in motivation and student engagement have been reported in the vast majority of task-based programs. In this book, Antokhin and her colleagues (chapter 9), Cozonac (chapter 13), Leaver and Kaplan (chapter 2), Lys (chapter 11), and Passos de Oliveira (chapter 12) provide details.

### INTERPRETATIONS OF "TASK" IN PRACTICE

When reading about research into TBI, appraising or planning a TBI program, or selecting a text book, it is important to identify how the term *task* is used in that particular context. The six definitions above were formulated by researchers and practitioners writing about tasks. In practice, however, many kinds of activity bear the label of *task* even though they have no obvious outcome. The three-way distinction offered by Willis (1990) and mentioned above is useful here. Classroom activities can be classified as *citation, simulation,* or *replication.* All these activity types can be found throughout the chapters of this volume.

*Citation activities* involve form-focused practice, from repeating and drilling, to using the target form in controlled response to teacher elicitations, and practicing scripted dialogues in pairs. In the citation activities described in this book the intent is, typically, to provide opportunities for repetitive practice of form within a specified context related to life outside the classroom.

*Simulation activities* also focus on form but bear a semblance of, or "simulate" real communication, for example, role-plays where learners are given roles to act out and are encouraged to use the language forms they have just been taught. Games like "Find someone who . . . likes classical music/plays the piano/goes cycling" can be used to practice "Do you . . ." questions and reporting the findings using the present simple to practice third person verb forms. Learners may be asked to write an essay about "The happiest day of my life," or, having watched a cartoon-strip video, to retell the story, but the intended purpose is generally not to entertain or amuse or even inform the teacher (who will have seen the cartoon and heard the story before) but to show how accurately they can write or speak and whether they can incorporate new patterns. These examples are language display activities: learners know they are displaying their control of language form and are not primarily concerned with trying to express their own personal meanings or to find out things they really need to know about.

*Replication activities* are so called because "they replicate within the classroom aspects of communication in the real world" (Willis 1990, 57–58). Language forms are in no way predetermined. Learners are free to use any language they can muster to interact with each other or with a text, with the teacher or other speakers of the target language in order to solve problems, reach decisions, compare real-life experiences, conduct surveys in or out of class and subsequently present their findings (in writing or in spoken form) using whatever language resources they wish to achieve their purpose.[4] Replication activities would also include out-of-class activities like interviewing native-speakers or fluent speakers of the target language as described in the German writing program (Lys, chapter 11 of this volume) and the media-based Spanish course (Van Altena, chapter 3), as well as the French shopping trip described by Hager and Lyman-Hager (chapter 8).

Many TBI practitioners (Prabhu 1987; D. Willis 1996; and many of the contributors to this volume) would argue that only replication activities count as tasks, since the focus is predominantly on learners understanding and conveying meaning and achieving goals through using, as best as they can, whatever language they have at their disposal, rather than on displaying their control of language form.

Use of replication tasks does not preclude a focus on language form at some stage in the TBI instructional sequence (as Alosh points out in chapter 5 of this volume) and most TBI courses do make use of citation activities, but distinct from the task. However, according to D. Willis a perceived disadvantage of a preliminary focus on specific forms is that it predisposes learners to a display of language, leading to a simulation rather than a replication activity.

There are nearly always ways to upgrade simulation activities to give them outcomes and turn them into replication activities. The hotel-booking task was one example. And if the video cartoon strip story had been shown in two halves, with half the class (A students) watching the first part and the other half (B students) watching the last part, students could have been placed in pairs, asked to reconstruct the whole A–B story telling their version to the class, and the class could see if there were any differences of interpretation. Here there is a genuine reason for giving and hearing this information—to achieve the outcome of a cooperatively constructed whole story.

To illustrate the importance of "outcome" and of the *citation, simulation,* and *replication* distinctions made above, I will give an example from my personal experience of learning Spanish in a two-hour-a-week evening course for second-year adult learners. Our textbook included a number of activities labeled *tarea* (literal meaning: *task*), which we did in class.

The rubric for a speaking task about a beach scene was similar to the one below. To determine whether it constitutes a *citation, simulation, replication,* activity (i.e., task), one should ask: (1) Is there a specified outcome that can be shared? (2) Is there a real need to listen to and understand the person talking, other than just politeness? (3) Are students required or expected to used prespecified language forms in their interaction or responses?

> Look at this picture of a beach scene. Work in pairs. Take turns to make sentences about what is happening in the picture.

There was a distinct feeling of unease as we did this task. There was no real need for me to communicate anything to my partner who could, after all, see the same beach scene picture as me; so what was the purpose of my telling him things he knew already? We realized this *tarea* was, in fact, designed as a language practice activity, calling for language display. So, as dutiful learners, we simply kept on making sentences, trying to remember and use the sample patterns on the previous pages until we ran out of things to say. There was no real sense of task completion. Further, because there was no outcome to work toward together, there was no need for us even to listen to each other talking. In fact, I can remember rehearsing my next sentence in my head while my partner was saying his sentence to me. There was no real interaction or engagement with meaning, except when I made a mistake or did not understand a word and my partner explained it to me. This, then, is an example of an activity that comes closer to *citation* than *simulation*; it bears no resemblance to a communicative or real-life situation at all.

If the teacher had adapted this *tarea* slightly and added some kind of communicative goal and outcome, it could have been made into a task that created a need for us to communicate and a reason for us to interact and to listen to each other. This would have motivated us to try a bit harder to express what we wanted to mean. We would have known when we had finished the task because we would have had a product to share with other learners.

Tables 1.7 through 1.9 give three examples of ways that the beach scene picture could be made into a more engaging task with outcomes. The first two tasks, suitable for elementary learners, contain two alternative versions (bulleted) that could be set depending on the language level or type of learner.

Note that the task in table 1.8 can be made easier linguistically by allowing learners to point at the object and simply say the color they remember.

The task in table 1.9 can be done at a number of levels, from elementary upwards. Instead of describing a beach they know, students could be asked to draw and then describe the features of their ideal beach and use this as the basis for the rest of the task. The first stage—drawing a rough sketch and making a list—is important as it gives learners a chance to decide and plan what they will talk about, and later they have the security of their drawing to fall back on if they need to.

All three tasks above have clear outcomes that provide a degree of challenge. They are more likely to be fun and engaging than simply making sentences about a picture. Note that in the lower level tasks the rubrics are specific, giving a number or setting a time limit. This helps learners know when they have completed the task. They also know what they have to do after the task so they can start planning an improved version to present to the whole class.

---

TABLE 1.7. **Task: Memory Competition I: Identifying People**

a. Look at the picture for twenty seconds without drawing or writing anything.

b. Close your books. Then, in twos, without looking again at the picture, do one of the following:

- Write, in note form, one list of the people you could see in the picture and explain exactly where they were. You have four minutes.

- List four people from the picture and include where they were, what they were wearing and doing.

c. Take turns describing people from the picture to the class. Do the others agree with the details you remembered about each person?

d. Listen as the others speak. At the end, think which two characters from the picture were the most often described? Why do you think this was?

e. Finally look at the picture again and try to judge whose description (or which of your descriptions) was the most accurate. Which pair remembered the best?

---

TABLE 1.8. **Task: Memory Competition II: The Colors**

a. Look at the colored picture carefully for twenty seconds, remembering the colors.

b. Close the book. Now, look at your black and white photocopy and

- In twos, try to remember the colors of at least ten things. Make notes if you wish.

- Using crayons, without showing your partner, color in at least ten things so they are the same as the picture. Then compare the colors in your picture with your partner's and find how many similarities and differences there are. What other colors can you both remember?

c. Plan how you will describe the colors you remember to the class without pointing to the picture (e.g., *the T shirt of the boy playing in the sand on the left is blue and green*).

d. Take turns telling the class your colors, without pointing to the picture. Do they agree? If you hear someone else talking about one of your things, and if they say the same color, cross it out.

e. Evaluation: Did you have any colored things that nobody else had? How many? Who had the most? Finally, look at the colored picture again and check how many you all remembered correctly.

It can be seen from the examples above that language display activities (*citation* or *simulation*), such as the original one based on a picture, can often, with a little thought, be turned into a *replication* activity with a specific outcome to achieve,[5] providing an opportunity for truly communicative interaction, a far richer use of language, and a basis for further tasks. There are two examples of longer, more complex tasks in appendix A to this chapter.

TABLE 1.9. **Task: Comparison—Comparing Beaches**

In this task, you will be comparing the beach in the picture with a beach you knew and liked as a child or a beach you like to visit now.

a. On your own, draw a rough sketch of the beach you know. Write a list in note form of similarities and differences between your beach and the beach in the picture.

b. Ask your partner about their beach and compare your two beaches. Find whose beach is the most similar to the one in the picture. Decide which beach is the best for a family day out (*or* a romantic day out) and give your reasons.

c. Choose one of your beach drawings. Plan how you will describe it to the class so that everyone can draw it. Also tell the class why you chose this beach for the day out.

d. Listen to the others describing their beaches. Draw them as best you can. Note down the reasons people give for choosing their beach. How many different reasons were there?

e. Finally, show each other your beach drawings and compare them. How accurate are they? Who in the class would make the best artist?

### TYPOLOGIES OF TASKS

Various classifications of tasks have been put forward, both by researchers (e.g., Duff 1993; Pica, Kanagy, and Folodun 1993) and practitioners (Prabhu 1987; D. Willis 1996). These and others are clearly summarized in Ellis (2003). Here we will concentrate on some of those drawn up for pedagogic purposes, to help teachers design tasks for classroom use. These can be divided into three categories according to the basis upon which they were drawn up: (1) the gap principle, (2) reaching a decision or solution, and (3) cognitive processes.

### The Gap Principle

The information-gap principle was probably one of the earliest used by task designers. The idea was that one learner held information needed by another learner in order to fulfill a task or that a text held information that the learner needed, for example, to complete a flowchart. For the gap to be bridged (and the outcome achieved), some kind of communicative interaction had to take place. Prabhu (1987) extended this idea and in his Communicational Teaching Project in Bangalore he identified three types of gap tasks:

- information gap (e.g., transferring information from a text to a table or from one pupil to another);
- reasoning gap (e.g., deducing a teacher's timetable from a set of class timetables or working out an optimum course of action given different variables); and
- opinion gap (e.g., completing a story and comparing endings, or giving opinions on a social issue).

Many ingenious materials have been devised to create such gaps: pairs of maps, pictures, charts, etc., each one containing only part of the information required to achieve the task outcome (see Pinter 2005 for research on these). Learners could only complete the task by sharing and collating the information as in the video cartoon story reconstruction task above. This type of task is also known as a "jigsaw" activity (Pica, Kanagy, and Folodun 1993).

Memory challenge tasks or competitions are also based on the gap principle. They rely on the fact that, given only a very short time limit to commit the picture/text/story to memory, different people will remember different things about it, so the gap occurs naturally. To complete a summary or a list or a full description of items, students need to assemble information based on what they can each recall. These could, in fact, be called "memory gap" tasks!

### Reaching a Decision or a Solution

The principle here is that there is a decision or solution to be reached through interaction of some kind. Decision-making and problem-solving tasks are either based on a set of data given to the learners at a "pretask" stage or on information already known by the learners (e.g., parking problems in a local town). These are mainly convergent tasks, as participants work together to find possible ways forward, justifying their points of view, evaluating each others' ideas, and finally coming to a conclusion or a solution cooperatively.

Such tasks could, however, be set up as divergent or debating tasks, where some learners are given one or two possible solutions to argue for, with others being asked to argue against them. Duff (1986), however, found that divergent tasks produced far less negotiation of meaning than convergent tasks (i.e., where learners have to agree on a solution, rather than defend their position against their partner's) and so were judged less effective for language learning. Long (1989) explored this more deeply but others, like Ellis (2003), feel that more research needs to be done in varying circumstances to substantiate this.

### Cognitive Processes

Willis (1996a) offers a classification based on six major cognitive processes in order to help teachers devise a set of tasks around one topic or theme. Her task categories, in approximate order of cognitive challenge, from simple to more complex, are:

- Listing (of things, people, actions, processes, reasons, requirements, etc.) through individual or group brainstorming or fact finding, reading, and/or the use of reference materials.
- Ordering and sorting. This can entail sequencing, ranking, classifying, prioritizing, etc., and then justifying the agreed-upon order. This type of task can nearly always follow a listing task (e.g., listing the parts of a lathe and classifying them according to their function), and often includes elements of decision making.
- Comparing and contrasting. Subsets include matching and finding similarities or differences (in texts, diagrams, pictures, etc.).
- Problem solving. Subsets range from logic problems, puzzles, and responses to advice-column letters to more complex case studies. These often involve expressing hypotheses, describing experiences, comparing alternative courses of action, and evaluating and agreeing on a conclusion.
- Sharing personal experiences. This type involves the speaker in producing longer, more sustained discourse (e.g., anecdote telling or describing a terrible journey) and the listeners in reacting to the discourse and comparing it with their experiences. It is more akin to social talk and useful for casual conversation.
- Creative tasks and projects. These can entail creative writing, recording a news report or interview, carrying out and reporting a survey, producing a brochure or video. Depending upon the topic chosen, it may involve carrying out some initial research and writing interim reports.

These six types are not intended to be watertight categories; in practice, the second three types will often include elements of listing, prioritizing, comparing, and so on from the first three types. The actual degree of cognitive challenge can be raised or lowered by changing any one of the design features or parameters mentioned in Ellis's Framework below.

Tasks based on these cognitive processes can be designed around any theme or topic, selected to suit learners' lexical and discourse needs, whether general or specialist. Topics used for courses in this book include: weather forecasts, my hometown, my ideal home, dating, first aid assistance, kidnappings, women in parliament, and a host of others. Each topic can give rise to several types of tasks that can be done as a series; this allows topic lexis to be recycled within the context of different tasks that involve different cognitive operations and different discourse genres. This approach proved very popular with students on the Spanish media-based program (Van Altena, chapter 3 of this volume). Of course, not all task types will prove equally suitable for all topics.

In addition to the six types given here, J. Willis (1996b, 74–81; drawing on Willis 1983) also lists five text-based task types: prediction, jigsaw / split information, jumbles / sequencing, restoration, memory challenge. For these, a variety of cognitive processes will be engaged, together with detailed interpretations of meaning. The first three are particularly suited to specific genres of text. For example, narrative texts and news stories with headlines lend themselves to prediction, listing, and sequencing tasks. (As Van Altena points out in chapter 3, news stories are often not reported in chronological sequence, so learners can be asked to list the events in the order in which they happened.) Expository texts of a descriptive nature make good jigsaw tasks. Memory challenge and text restoration tasks are suitable for any text after an initial reading task, i.e., as a second task. For text restoration, words or phrases or sentences are either removed or added, and the learners' task is to recall or work out what was in the original text. Memory challenge can include tasks like dictogloss, where learners in pairs try to reconstruct a text after a very fast dictation, during which they take down as much as possible, but there will inevitably be gaps they need to fill from combined use of recall and lexical and grammatical knowledge.

Bygate (1987) suggested genre analysis as a broad basis for a syllabus of tasks (e.g., narrative, descriptive, expository), and a way of selecting and ordering texts is touched on by Antokhin and her colleagues in the description of the online reading program in chapter 9. However, a task typology like one of those above would still be useful when one designs specific tasks based on individual texts from the selected genres.

As they approach task design from different angles, these ways of classifying task typologies naturally present some overlapping categories. There are also some omissions. Many additional task types are presented in the subsequent chapters of this volume.

## PARAMETERS IN TASK DESIGN

The literature on TBI has proposed four main parameters in task design, each of which can be seen as a cline between two features, although the features themselves are commonly expressed as "either–or" distinctions. There can, in fact, be varying degrees of each attribute. It is, therefore, more useful to think of each parameter as a continuum.

### Parameter 1: Open or Closed Tasks

*Closed tasks* have very specific goals, are often highly structured, and have only one right answer or solution (J. Willis 1996b, 28). A good example would be a "Spot the Differences" game, where two pictures have ten differences and learners work in pairs cooperatively to find a specific number of differences, say seven, and write a list of them to show to other pairs in the class. This is illustrated by Lopes in chapter 4. The beach scene memory challenge tasks above are also specific enough to be described as closed. The first one, recalling the people, is slightly less closed than the color memory task, in that learners have slightly more choice about which specific features of each person to write statements about. The language used in closed tasks tends to be more predictable than that used in more open tasks.

*Open tasks* include experience-sharing tasks, or anecdote telling, where the content and style of the end-product are likely to vary quite widely between individual learners, even if they are on a specific topic like "A Childhood Memory." The fourth beach task, planning a party (see appendix A to this chapter), would need to be split into stages, for example, doing the survey, and then deciding the budget. Each stage would fit somewhere toward the open end of the cline with some being more predictable than others.

SLA research (Long 1991; Ellis 2003) is generally reported as favoring closed tasks on the grounds that they generate more interaction, more negotiation of meaning (including clarification requests, confirmation checks, self-expansion, and greater sentence complexity) than open tasks. As we saw above (Long 1983), it is believed that interaction with negotiation of meaning promotes language acquisition. However, as Skehan (1998a), points out, when expanding Swain's Output Hypothesis, there are good arguments for using open tasks, too, as open tasks give learners more opportunities for taking longer, more sustained turns and managing their own discourse (Bygate 1987).

Open tasks are likely to give opportunities for learners to control the topic, and they create a greater need to explain the relevance of contributions to the discourse. Skehan (1998a) makes the point that learners cannot acquire these skills passively; they can only gain experience and achievement of these skills by actually participating in discourse themselves. Open tasks give them the opportunities to do this.

When planning a TBI program, teachers would need to decide which kinds of tasks best reflect target language use or which kinds best help students achieve an established language-acquisition goal. In the case of language for academic purposes, this is certainly likely to involve open tasks.

### Parameter 2: One-Way / Two-Way Tasks

These terms (Pica, Kanagy, and Folodun 1993) refer to the conditions set for the task and describe the direction of information flow among learners. They correspond roughly to the terms reciprocal or nonreciprocal tasks used by Ellis (2003). Ellis explains that reciprocal or two-way tasks involve interaction between two or more learners to achieve the task outcome where both learners have equal rights to speak.

In a nonreciprocal or a one-way task, just one participant controls the flow of information. Other participants are involved in listening and doing something; an example is identifying which person is being described, listening and arranging a sequence of pictures, or listening to a mini-lecture and labeling a diagram. The listener may or may not be allowed to ask for information or clarification, but his or her role is certainly subordinate. Yule and Macdonald (1990), as reported in Lightbown and Spada (1999), experimented with adult mixed ability pairs in one-way tasks and found if the weaker learner is placed in the speaker's or sender's position, giving the required information for the listener to complete the task promoted far richer interaction than if the stronger learner was the sender. Other research suggests that two-way reciprocal tasks generally provide more opportunities for negotiation of meanings, unless the subordinate partner is allowed to ask for clarification in order to complete the task. However, this research is very preliminary and needs to be replicated with different student populations and in varying conditions.

### Parameter 3: Focused and Unfocused Tasks

These terms are used by Ellis (2003) and refer to whether or not the task has a specific and predetermined linguistic focus. An unfocused task is one that encourages the learner to use freely any language he or she can muster, without concentrating on just one or two specific forms (i.e., a replication activity). A focused task (Ellis 2003) can be either

- a consciousness-raising activity, where the focus is on examining samples of language to explore particular features of it (these are sometimes called "meta-cognitive" activities); or
- a task used because it is likely to encourage the comprehension of, and/or the use of, particular language forms (i.e., a citation or simulation activity).

Examples of the first type of focused task include classifying the uses of a verb plus -*ing* forms that appear in a reading text or identifying from a spoken transcript phrases containing the preposition *in* and putting them into three categories: time, location, other. If, in addition, learners do this type of consciousness-raising activity using the target language, they will not only gain insights into these language features by classifying them but will also gain experience in talking about language itself, which is a very useful skill for a language learner. Examples of other consciousness-raising activities are given by Lopes in chapter 4 of this volume. Examples of the second type of focused task can be found in chapters 5 (the Arabic course by Alosh) and 7 (Macías's Spanish course).

Because of the unpredictable nature of spoken task interaction, the second type of focused task lends itself more readily to receptive tasks. Long (1999) provides an example. He used a split-information quiz with facts taken from a written report of company sales over the last half year. This report contained a large number of noun and verb expressions of increase and decrease, including the use of past simple and present perfect verb forms. Learners had to obtain information from each other in order to complete the graph representing sales trends. The follow-up entailed reading the full report in detail in order to check the figures in their graph. Most of this work plan involved receptive skills of listening to others reading out their information and reading the text to check results. In doing so, students were obliged to focus on the meanings of the expressions of quantity and increase and decrease.

Some texts, such as the ones Long used above, naturally contain a number of similar patterns or phrases expressing a particular function; others do not. In the latter case, teachers may need to search for examples in previous texts learners have read. Another way round this problem is described by Ellis (2003), who talks about "seeding" the text with target structures, in order to deliberately "enrich" the text with these forms. This is referred to as "enhanced input" in Lightbown and Spada (1999), who review the research on this and conclude that even if the frequency and salience of correct models are increased in input data that they process for meaning, learners still do not discover what is ungrammatical in their own interlanguage without a specific focus on form.

Productive tasks designed with the aim of encouraging productive use of specific language forms, however, are less likely overall to succeed in their aim, especially with open tasks, where learners have more personal choice of what to say. In a closed task like "Spot the Difference," which is set up so that learners cannot see each other's pictures, teachers might expect learners to use phrases like "Have you got a . . . / Is there a . . . ?" and then add expressions of location. However they may well use other forms to accomplish the task successfully, saying, for example, "My picture has a . . . —what about yours?"

In practice, the only way of discovering if the task is likely to encourage the targeted language features is to record and transcribe pairs of fluent speakers doing precisely the same task in similar conditions and then examining the language they use to achieve the outcome. The language forms that fluent speakers typically use for the task may well be more useful to the learner than those targeted in the textbook. Cox (2005) showed a group of teachers three sets of typical textbook task instructions (unfocused or open tasks) and asked them to predict the language features their students would need to do the tasks. He then recorded twenty pairs of fluent speakers doing the same tasks and found that teachers had not had been very successful in their attempts to predict typical language items that would occur naturally.

### Parameter 4: "Real-World" Target Tasks or Pedagogic Tasks

For Long and Crookes (1992), target tasks are everyday tasks that learners may need to do in the real world, like buy a train ticket, read and follow instructions in a technical manual, take lecture notes, or watch television. Some people refer to these as "authentic" tasks. These would be identified through a needs analysis and then broken down into target task types, from which pedagogic tasks are derived and worked on in the classroom. Examples abound in chapter 2 of this volume.

As we have already seen, some tasks may be carried out in a real-life location, rather than in the classroom, as is the case when a class plans a party, then goes shopping together for the ingredients. Chapter 2 describes how students of Czech put together a Czech-language tour of a local aquarium and then led a tour there for Czech teachers (and, unplanned, Czech-speaking visitors to the aquarium who happened to be in the vicinity, overheard the students, and joined the tour).

A somewhat similar approach is taken by Jennings and Doyle (1996; personal communication, 1995), who, having identified real-life tasks with which their learners in Ireland needed to cope (e.g., applying for a temporary job), broke them down into units and set "real-life rehearsal" tasks for the classroom, involving learners in imagining, scripting, and acting out their own versions of these interactions before comparing them to transcriptions of recordings made of parallel real-life transactions.

Other researchers (D. Willis 1996; Ellis 2003) would argue that any task interaction (whether spontaneous or planned) will contain features of language that are useful in real-life and so the need for this distinction is less obvious. In the recording used by Lopes in chapter 4 of native speakers doing a collaborative version of a "Spot the Difference" task (highly unlikely to be a "target" or "real-world' task in the sense used above), much of the language that was used could be extremely useful in real-life contexts, both in and outside the classroom. Phrases such as *What do you think?* or *Doesn't matter, so what shall we say?* or *So what shall we put?* or *Anything else?* or *How many have we got to get?* are useful in spontaneous social and academic discourse; and similarly, patterns, for example, with "*-ing,*" like "*a young woman sitting at her desk,*" and frames like "*depending on whether it was . . .*" "*a pen in one hand and a diary or something in the other.*" The last example also contains a useful example of vague language ("*or something*"), very common in spoken language. Focused consciousness-raising tasks can be used to draw learners' attention to these, and learners can be encouraged to learn the more formulaic utterances by heart. These utterances are all likely to appear again in spontaneous interactions and may well be acquired naturally.

For a closer parallel between real-world task and classroom task language, consider the language and discourse skills needed by the military police in a peace-keeping force where one of the target tasks will be questioning suspects. This situation could of course be rehearsed and reenacted as a classroom *simulation*, but there would be no real communicative purpose or outcome to achieve, other than rehearsing a possible scenario. However, there is a classroom game called Alibi. In this game, two learners have to provide a false alibi for one another for a specific date and time. In order to do this, they have to get together and concoct a convincing story. Other members of the class then question one of the two. After this, they plan their strategy for questioning the second person. Then they interrogate the second person and try to find discrepancies in the two stories. This entails a questioning routine with language features very similar to the language needed for investigating suspect stories in the real world, more similar, in fact, than a role-play or simulation of the situation, because in Alibi there is a real purpose for the questioning routine: to try to crack the alibi. One-off questions will not do; questions need to be carefully planned, as in a real-life interrogation. The game of Alibi may be considered a pedagogic task, but it is, in fact, a replication task, in that it involves real communication and purposeful negotiation and replicates the language use of the real-world target task far more closely than a role-play simulation would.

The four parameters above affect the early stages in TBI program design. At the later, more detailed level of task implementation, there are other design features that can be adjusted and adapted. Some of these variables are shown in table 1.10 in the section below.

### A FRAMEWORK FOR DESCRIBING TASKS

The features in this framework adapted from Ellis (2003, 21) can help us achieve a more systematic way to describe, design, and grade tasks. Formulating clear and concise instructions for tasks is not always easy but the table here identifies features that could usefully be addressed in task instructions. In adapting the table I have kept the main headings and definitions but added some examples taken from the tasks illustrated so far in this chapter. Immediately noticeable is Ellis's use of the word "goal" here with a different meaning from its use in the definitions above, where it was synonymous with outcome of task or communicative purpose. And his use of the term "conditions" is somewhat similar to the use of the term "parameter"' above (see table 1.10).

In the last two sections, we have looked at parameters of tasks and specific features of task design. We now go on to look at ways of designing whole syllabuses, using tasks and TBI.

## TBI and Syllabus Design

The case studies in this book illustrate several different types of syllabus. In most of the programs here, tasks are central in each teaching cycle; in others, tasks are the culminating point, following on from language focused activities designed to prepare learners for some of the linguistic demands of the task. Ellis (2003) distinguishes between these two practices, referring to the former as task-based learning and to the latter as task-supported learning.

### SETTING PROGRAM OBJECTIVES

The factors that instructors and program designers in this book have taken into account when setting their objectives include the following:

- the starting level of the learners;
- their background and general linguistic sophistication;

TABLE 1.10.  **A Framework for Describing Tasks**

| Design Feature | Description |
| --- | --- |
| Goal | This is the general purpose of the task in terms of aspects of communicative competence and possibly in terms of linguistic skills or rhetorical mode—for example, to practice the ability to identify people from oral or written descriptions, to provide an opportunity for the use of post-modifying phrases, such as "the boy on the left in a blue T-shirt," to give directions, to narrate and react to stories, to put forward and jointly evaluate possible solutions to a problem in a formally chaired context. |
| Input | The verbal and/or nonverbal information supplied by the task materials—for example, task instructions, a story or experience recounted by the teacher, a written text, a recording, a picture, a map. |
| Conditions | The way in which information is presented, or the way in which it is to be used—for example, information seen by both partners for a limited time (as for memory tasks), *or* split between partners (e.g., comparison tasks), *or* held by one partner (story to be told while the listener arranges pictures), *or* shared (statement of problem to be solved cooperatively, the first part of a story for discussion of possible endings). Note that comparison tasks can also be done in a collaborative mode, with two learners helping each other and composing a list together. Even slight changes in the conditions will of course result in a different type of interaction. |
| Procedures | The methodological procedures to be followed in performing the task—for example, individual/pair/group; with/without pretask planning time; note taking allowed / not allowed, time limit / other limit; posttask report spoken/written. |
| Predicted outcomes | *Product:* The "product" that results from completing the task, for example, a completed table, a route drawn on a map, a solution to a problem, a list of differences / things in common / things remembered, a sequenced or prioritized list, the ending of a story, a personal anecdote, the enacting of a scenario. |
| | *Process:* The linguistic and cognitive processes the task is hypothesized to generate, for example, sifting, selecting, ordering, sorting, matching, comparing, reasoning, evaluating, justifying, hypothesizing. |

*Source:* Adapted from Ellis (2003, 21).

- their target language needs in terms of knowledge objectives (what words, patterns, types of discourse, etc., will they need to handle?);
- their performance objectives (what they will need to do in the language: the target tasks, possible contexts, and levels of accuracy needed within each context);
- their motivation for learning and willingness to study, including outside class; and
- the time and resources available for the course as well as for its planning.

Long-term objectives among the programs described in this volume are varied. Four of the programs cater to students whose precise purpose for learning the language is as yet unknown: Spanish in chapter 3, English in chapter 4, Arabic in chapter 5, and Japanese in chapter 6. Such programs are obliged to aim at a general overall competence in the target language. Both the teachers' and learners' English courses in chapter 13 also aim at overall competence.

Three chapters concentrate on general programs directed at specific skills: reading programs for many languages at the Defense Language Institute, chapter 9; writing for those interested in Web technology in chapter 10; and an Advanced German writing course in chapter 11. Chapter 12 on task-based assessment (TBA) keeps in mind the need to assess all main curriculum objectives but focuses primarily on productive skills.

Three chapters describe programs for students with slightly more specific purposes: Spanish for professionals in real estate and medicine working in a bilingual environment (chapter 7), French for engineers going to study in France (chapter 8), and various Slavic languages for professionals like peace-keeping forces (chapter 2).

In the case of the Japanese program, the long-term objectives were specified in terms of major learning outcomes, from which were derived specific learning objectives and motivational learning goals—for example, make an instructional video about your own school to send to a school in Japan.

For many languages, the general curriculum objectives relate to levels on the general proficiency scales used in the United States. These scales can be found in the appendix at the end of this volume.

The next few sections will briefly touch on some key concepts in syllabus design that are common to all kinds of courses, namely, specification of syllabus items, coverage, accountability, grading, and testing. We begin by looking at ways in which TBI courses can be organized and specified.

## FROM TOPIC AND TEXTS TO TASKS

Tasks have to be about something, and most practitioners in this book have found that a practical way of organizing and sequencing a language program is to start from a list of topics or themes that will engage students.

The Czech course presented in chapter 2 of this volume was topically driven for the first twenty-four weeks of study. The topics were selected by both teachers and students. The course itself was based almost exclusively on current authentic materials, including newspapers from Czechoslovakia, Voice of America radio broadcasts, films, television news and documentaries, observed interactions among native speakers, and interactive software programs. Therefore, the topics were to a great extent controlled by what the media was presenting at the time, along, of course, with information from classified advertisements and the like. The Spanish higher-level writing course (chapter 5) was also based on topics that could be readily found in the media, but also used literary sources.

Yet another topically driven TBI course is the engineering program at Pennsylvania State University (see chapter 8), which prepared learners for studying engineering in France. In this case, there was one main topic, engineering, and related subtopics. There were also tasks that students themselves decided upon in preparation for living in the French environment, such as planning of tourist itineraries and preparation for chance encounters with native speakers of French. This shows how learners can take part in setting their own personal objectives with the help of a teacher, especially over the short term.

One question here is: If there is no suitable course book, who selects the topics and materials? Teachers? Students? For the online reading programs described in chapter 9, the topics were selected in advance by instructors. In a course for beginners, as Leaver and Kaplan (chapter 2) show, it will be very much up to the teacher to find suitably accessible texts and tasks (filling out a visa application form was one), although students may request specific topics of interest or perceived need.

Some chapters show how learners can be given choices once a general framework for course design is established. Lys, in chapter 11, shows how one broad theme "Geschichte, die das Leben schrieb" (translated literally, "stories written by life") was chosen by the teacher for a writing project, but within that broad topic area, students were free to choose who to interview and write about and what to include. In chapter 10, which describes an online writing course, topic-based Web pages were set up. Stevens describes how one online teacher started by giving out a list of possible topics for students to select from, to contribute to a Web page. As the course evolved students began to choose their own topics through online discussion. So new Web pages were formed, with links back to students' previous work. Two themes introduced by students in this way were carnivals around the world and national dishes. The latter later evolved, through student suggestions, into an online cooking school!

In cases where student motivation has been low, learners often feel a sense of empowerment if they are allowed to choose their own topics and their mode of contribution. They often begin to engage better in the learning process as a result (Williams and Burden 1997). This has certainly happened in courses in this volume, for example Van Altena's media-based Spanish course (chapter 3 of this volume) and Lys's German writing class (chapter 11).

For general learners with no fixed purposes for learning the language, a broad range of topics and task types might be the most suitable. Ellis (2003) provides a circle-shaped "theme generator" (Estaire and Zanon 1994). This generator contains general themes working outwards from the center of the circle, starting with the students themselves, moving on to home life, school life, community, and the world around them and finally to imagination and fantasy. Also valid, especially for adults, are topics arising from cross-linguistic exploration, on aspects of language itself, like forms of greeting in different countries, or the use of common metaphors (Lakoff and Johnson 1980). Social issues and cultural practices can stimulate engaging tasks, for example, identifying questions that are taboo in the foreign language culture.

Finally, it is worthwhile remembering that there may be specific topics and tasks best avoided with some groups. For example, in second language teaching across Europe, in classes attended by political refugees and asylum seekers, it would be insensitive to introduce personal topics such as families—when a significant number of learners may be the sole surviving member of their family group.

A syllabus for a TBI program can have several strands. So far, we have illustrated a topic strand. From these topics, it is possible to generate a more detailed task strand, offering a variety of types of tasks for each topic, as we saw above. These tasks and texts chosen for them could in themselves cover an appropriate range of cognitive processes, discourse genres, functions and interaction types, and so on to suit learners' needs.

### FROM FUNCTIONS TO TASKS

Some programs, like that of Alosh in chapter 5 of this volume, begin with functions as the main organizing feature and move from functions, via their grammatical and lexical realizations, to tasks. Examples of functions given by Alosh are (1) describing the location of objects in a picture, (2) describing the people in a picture, and (3) speculating on the type of event or on participants' future actions. This list is essentially content free but, by subsequently adding a topic or theme, for example, through a visual of a hotel wedding reception, which gives learners a context, each function can then engender a task, based on the data illustrated in the picture. For each function, words and useful patterns are preselected and taught in a pretask stage.

However, there is the danger—pointed out by D. Willis earlier—that when tasks follow explicit grammar teaching they may become simulation activities rather than replication tasks, as learners struggle to display their control of the forms rather than concentrating on meaning what they say. Repeating and recycling similar tasks at a later stage may well reduce this tendency.

### SPECIFYING LANGUAGE COVERAGE

Some TBI programs make no attempt to specify language in any way and, like Prabhu (1987), feel justified in leaving linguistic coverage to chance. Stevens's Writing for Webheads program in chapter 10 is one such program. Students have the choice to write about what they want to, and take part in discussions on any topics that interest them and obviously feel their language needs are fulfilled.

If language for specific purposes (LSP) program materials are carefully chosen from real-life sources to reflect accurately a representative sample of the kinds of written and spoken language used in the learners' target discourse community, it could be argued that this careful selection will ensure adequate language coverage, even though no actual items were prespecified. Based on this principle, many Defense Language Institute TBI programs (Leaver and Kaplan, chapter 2 of this volume) have simply taught the grammar and lexis that emerged from the texts and other materials selected for the course. The same approach is used in the advanced Spanish course (Van Altena, chapter 3), which is based on a wide variety of materials selected from different kinds of media. The same applies to the online reading courses described in chapter 9. This means that most of the appropriate grammar will have been covered by the end of the course but in a different sequence from that found in most grammar books. This approach is sometimes referred to as a data-driven approach.

However, others argue that program designers should be more directive, and that it helps all stakeholders (teachers, management, assessors and testing bodies, inspectors, employers, parents, and the learners themselves) if they have an inventory of the language items that will be focused on in class during the course. Knowledge of these items can then be assessed at the end. The Arabic course in chapter 5 is prespecified in this way. This is touched upon, too, in chapter 12 by Passos de Oliveira in the context of TBA.

A more objective method of drawing up an inventory that ensures thorough coverage of the language needed can be achieved through assembling a research corpus in advance of the course. This corpus should contain a representative sample of written texts and transcripts of spoken language from the learners' target discourse community. An initial needs analysis is carried out to identify the most typical contexts in which the target language will be used. This helps to identify possible sources of language samples. For example, for studying engineering in France (chapter 8), texts might include textbook chapters used by students in the department, sample exam scripts and student assignments, transcripts of recordings of lectures, tutorials, coffee breaks, plus local tourist information and whatever else that is common in the engineering students' target language environment. The language samples collected are then analyzed, and the most frequent words, phrases, patterns, and discourse structures can then be identified and listed to form a checklist of the most commonly used language items. This can be used, alongside materials to be used in class, to check language coverage over a period of time (Kirkgoz 1993; Willis 1990).

This was the process used for writing the Collins Cobuild English Course adopted by Lopes (chapter 4 of this volume). The early Cobuild Research corpus (a mix of spoken and written data) was consulted and from frequency lists and concordance evidence from this a list was derived of the most common 2,500 words of English, their meanings, uses, and patterns. Next, the course materials of suitable authentic texts and task recordings were assembled electronically, unit by unit, thus becoming a *pedagogic corpus*, and this was searched for the words and phrases identified by the research corpus findings. Hence, a lexical syllabus was born (see D. Willis 1990, 1996). Such a *pedagogic corpus* can in theory become the vehicle for almost any kind of syllabus: functional, notional, lexical, structural, skill based.

In circumstances where a research corpus cannot be compiled, either through lack of funding or availability of staff or too little time for precourse planning (the situation that exists with many, if not most, of the target language communities in this volume), teachers can keep a retrospective record of language covered explicitly with the class, for example, language features arising out of the authentic materials used or from student project work. This record can be used to show other teachers joining the team when they are planning revision or setting tests. It can be checked by inspectors and assessors, and it can then be adapted and used as a preplanned syllabus for the next TBI courses.

Individual learners can also be encouraged to keep their own records of words, phrases, and patterns covered during each lesson or homework session. Such personalized dictionaries can contribute to their sense of progress and help maintain motivation. By examining these records, teachers can learn what words, phrases, and patterns students have considered important enough to write down for review.

### How to Specify Language? And When?

Studies of second language acquisition suggest that beginners learning in a natural environment start by noticing useful words and stringing together lexical items (words and phrases) to get their messages across. They first make sense of things lexically and then go on to perceive how the grammar is used to make meanings more precise and explicit. In a classroom context, this would mean specifying the language syllabus lexically to begin with.

This is the reason why Ellis (2003) argues strongly that syllabuses should begin with a communicative task-based module with an emphasis on rapid vocabulary gain and then later, at an intermediate level, incorporate a code-based module. By this time, learners will have already acquired a rich vocabulary along with many basic structures and patterns. Since learners will have already had experience of grammar in use, the teacher can gradually start helping them to identify their gaps (e.g., patterns they avoid using or have never noticed, endings they omit or confuse), to notice these features in their input, to build up systems, and to find acceptable ways to express the nonstandard forms in their output. By the time students reach advanced levels of proficiency, the tasks can become more complex and sophisticated, with outcomes that require a strong need for attention to form as demands for precision and succinctness of expression increase. For more discussion on this, see Van Altena, chapter 3 on media-based Spanish, and Lys, chapter 11 on the need for precision when writing in German.

Skehan (1998a) also acknowledges that learners begin naturally with lexicalized language, but he does not clarify at what level an explicit focus on language form should start. He does, however, suggest that rather than introducing and practicing one pattern at a time thoroughly during TBI courses, we should teach useful lexis and a range of structures lightly at a pretask stage in the hopes that there will be something useful for everyone and that one or two may just trigger learning or recall in some learners. However, Skehan fails to say on what basis this range of structures should be selected.

Starting with a lexically driven TBI module for beginners is however still far from standard practice in most foreign language teaching contexts. In most cases, publishers and teachers feel that grammar and lexis need to go hand in hand, with an emphasis on grammar.

Some published TBI courses do have topic and task strands as a distinctly separate entity from the language syllabus strand, but running in parallel. This is justified on the grounds that learners need (and like) some focus on language form. The textbook titled *Cutting Edge* (Cunningham and Moor 1996–99) is an example of this. It combines elements of a TBI approach with a strong emphasis on vocabulary, alongside a separate grammar and skills syllabus. The latter, however, was seen as the most important by the publishers and comes first in each unit, although the writers themselves emphasized the importance of the TBI strand.

Finally, in this section on language specification, it is worth adding a note of clarification. Itemizing the linguistic syllabus in a detailed list does not mean that each item is taught on its own in an additive, linear fashion. The list serves simply as a means of checking coverage. Normally, in TBI courses, learners gain a holistic experience of language in use before focusing on particular items, which will already be partly familiar and which they will already have processed for meaning. There are also plenty of chances for natural recycling, as additional tasks and texts are used, and words and meanings from the checklist can be ticked off each time they are covered in class.

So the TBI watchword for learners is "First experience the target language in use, and then examine the language you have experienced and learn from it." This, of course, is also the rationale for content-based instruction (a syllabus design based on subject matter), and it is no accident that TBI is frequently the teaching approach of choice in content-based programs.[6]

## Grading in TBI Courses

There have been many attempts to find systematic ways of assessing task difficulty and grading and sequencing tasks (Skehan 1998a). Factors to take into account include such things as familiarity of topic and text type, cognitive complexity of task, length of text, syntactic complexity of text, number of known/unknown words or cognates, cultural accessibility of content, clarity and precision of intended outcome, and in addition to these, the conditions under which the task is done (e.g., number of interactants, time pressure, level of accuracy required). There is also the need to provide a variety of task and text type, learner activity, and so forth. If we take into account the possible effects of the interaction of all these variables, it is no wonder that teachers and course designers tend to fall back on more intuitive means of sequencing tasks, as most of the contributors to this volume seem to have done.

Prabhu's judgment was that as long as most of the class could achieve the outcome of the task in their own way, to an acceptable level without too much frustration, and so long as the task was sufficiently challenging to engage learners' attention in the first place, it was probably pitched about right.

Finally, Ellis (2003, 228) reassuringly makes the point that even with traditional structural syllabuses, we still "cannot grade linguistic structures to ensure their learnability" and since TBI syllabuses do not generally "seek to dictate what linguistic forms a learner will learn at any time, the need to ensure a precise match between the teaching syllabus and the learner's syllabus no longer arises."

## Testing and TBI courses

It is generally agreed that similar activities should be used for testing as for teaching and that topics chosen for achievement tests should be familiar to learners. In other words, test methods and inputs should be closely linked to teaching and learning experiences. For example, learners could be asked to repeat, with a new partner, two of the tasks they had done at some point during the course, and then to summarize their findings on one task. This way, both interaction and sustained talk could be evaluated for both learners. Their task performance could be audio-recorded in the presence of the teacher or examiner and the cassette made available for markers or modifiers. Various methods of assessment are described in this volume. Lopes in chapter 4 uses class visitors for assessing student progress on a monthly basis and emphasizes the need to find a public examination that is true to the philosophy of TBI.

Initially it can be challenging to introduce task-based testing. Passos de Oliveira (chapter 12) illustrates how TBA procedures were introduced and implemented in his institution. New testing methods were needed in order to reflect recent curriculum changes where aspects of TBI had been implemented alongside more traditional methods. This chapter illustrates how changes can be implemented gradually and how new TBA testing procedures can help teachers adopt and come to terms with TBI.

## TBI Methods and Options

As this book reveals, a rich variety of practices exists within a broad TBI approach. Practices will vary in order to accommodate learners' language levels, their needs and wishes, and in order to make the most of the social context in which they are learning, both face to face and online, and the resources and materials available, both inside and outside the teaching institution.

Tasks can also vary enormously; Alosh (chapter 5 of this volume) and Macías (chapter 7) describe simple tasks for Arabic and Spanish beginners that can take less than two minutes. More complex tasks may take a whole lesson to do, and creative tasks or projects may be achieved in stages over a week or even a term (Saito-Abbott, chapter 6; Lys, chapter 11).

But TBI is not just a matter of getting learners to do tasks. It is more a matter of working out how tasks can be used to create optimum conditions for learning, to engage students interest, and to stimulate target language use—both receptive and productive.

In this final section, I will draw together common practices used by practitioners in this volume and highlight alternative methodological options, giving some brief underlying rationale so that instructors and program designers can make principled choices.

### A TYPICAL TASK CYCLE

Most contributors to this volume appear to use a three-phase task cycle. In its very basic form this consists of

- *a pretask phase*, where teachers set up relevant topic schemata, explain the task and clarify the intended outcome, the main aim being *"to let the language relevant to (the task) come into play"* (Prabhu 1987, 54).
- *the task itself*, where learners, on their own, or in pairs or groups, work toward the task outcome. Here the focus is principally on meaning. Various skills and strategies may come into play. Since they are with peers, the situation is generally nonthreatening and conducive to taking risks, and learners may experiment with language forms they are not yet sure of.
- *a posttask phase*: drafting, finalizing, and presenting the outcome or finished product to others. Making the outcome public creates a natural sociolinguistic context where a prestige variety is the norm (Labov 1972a; Willis and Willis 1996, 55).

Generally speaking, the task phase stimulates exploratory talk and encourages real-time composing and fluency (and often a dependence on a lexical mode of communication), while the processes involved in the posttask phase, as learners aim at more formal, planned, and concise language for the presentation of their product, stimulate greater linguistic processing and syntactic development. In Willis's terms, this posttask activity is called the report stage and is preceded by a planning stage, where the learners are helped to improve and upgrade their language as appropriate for a more public report or presentation of their findings (see appendix B to this chapter). Learners cooperate to check, improve, and polish the language they will use and make an effort to eradicate mistakes so as not to lose face. This is sometimes referred to as "pushed" output (Skehan 1998a) and can help to prevent fossilization, driving learners' interlanguage development forward. The process of learners working on accuracy of form in the context of meanings that they want to express is likely to give them further impetus for developing their language; research by Long (1991), Doughty and Varela (1998), and Johnston (2005) bears this out and Doughty (2001, 227) stresses the importance of the teacher "determining optimal language processing intervention points" in her pedagogical recommendations.

In all these three phases of the task cycle, conditions for natural learning have been created: there are several opportunities for learners to hear and/or experience the target language in use, as well as chances for different types of output, spontaneous talk or writing at the task stage (as in the online meeting room in chapter 10) and more formal, planned talk or writing at the posttask phase when outcomes are shared with an audience or published on a Web page.

It is quite possible to include some explicit language instruction and focus on specific language forms during or after these phases. As we have seen above, there are differing views on this among chapter writers and more details are given in their respective chapters.

## METHODOLOGICAL OPTIONS WITHIN THE TASK CYCLE

At more or less any time, the conditions or parameters mentioned earlier in this chapter can be manipulated to set up better learning opportunities. Here are some examples that have been used in the programs in this book:

### Pretask Options

- The task or a similar task can be rehearsed by a teacher with the class, or demonstrated with a helper or played on video or audio cassette. This provides support for those students who feel more secure if teachers or others show them how to do things.
- Pretask planning time was found by Foster and Skehan (1996) to be helpful for learners and seemed to increase the learners' engagement with the task. It can increase the quantity and quality of the language used during the task because it reduces the overall mental load during the task performance. This is especially important if the task is complex or creative, as it releases learners' attentional capacity for composing language. This is borne out in recent research (Essig 2005; Djapoura 2005).

### Main Task Options

- In some cases, teachers interact quite closely with pairs and groups during the task interaction, providing useful language, ensuring that the target foreign language is being used, analyzing student deficiencies, and correcting errors (see chapter 2). This also gives learners individualized time with the teacher and the teacher a chance to assess individual learner progress.
- Alternatively, teachers can let their learners get on with the task by themselves (this will be inevitable when the task happens out of class or online). Learners can talk to each other about the task, use dictionaries, or refer back to previous texts and "borrow" language (Prabhu 1987, 60). This can promote a higher degree of learner independence.
- To ensure target language use and/or to increase learners' attention to accuracy of form, a cassette recorder can be placed on students' tables and the task recorded and parts of it played back to the class. Alternatively, a student "observer" can sit a little apart from the pair or group

and can write down notes of main points or useful phrases or examples of learners' use of their mother tongue. These can form the focus of a subsequent language focus session.

## Posttask Options

- The planning of the final product could be done at home, individually, or in groups with peer editing, or in class with the teacher acting as a linguistic adviser.
- The format of the product can vary widely. It may be written and displayed, like a brochure or advertisement for a local holiday resort or entertainment area, spoken (e.g. a report on the solution to a problem) or written to be read out loud, like a short story or notes for a mini-lecture on a subject known to the student; it can be recorded on audiotape or videotape as with news broadcasts and played back to the class, or learners could introduce a recorded interviews with local native speakers. It could even be a Monopoly game produced in a new language for other learners to play. Many more examples of products and outcomes are given in the chapters that follow. For longer, more complex tasks, there may also be interim progress reports.
- Learners can listen to a recording of fluent or native speakers doing the same task as they have just done. Learners enjoy this, as they can compare their results and see how others did the task and learn from it (Leedham 2005). They generally have little difficulty with comprehension, since, having already expressed similar meanings when doing the task themselves, they have detailed expectations. Learners have a chance to read the transcript of the recording and identify useful language they could have used themselves during the task phase. This is illustrated in Lopes (chapter 4).
- The same or a similar task (depending on whether it was a closed or open task) can be repeated with different partners some time later. Researchers have found marked improvements in the quality of learner interaction on a second or third time round, even without interim language instruction. (Bygate 2001; Lynch and MacLean 2001; Pinter 2005; Essig 2005).
- The task and the outcome can be evaluated by students, either as individuals or in pairs or groups (see Ozdeniz 1996 for ways of doing this). As a result of such appraisals, subsequent tasks can be adapted slightly, for example, by changing the conditions to better meet students' needs or wishes. A variety of kinds of appraisal sessions are reported in this book, for example, the feedback sessions in the Czech program in chapter 2.

Other options are illustrated in the chapters of this book. Knowing about a range of options is like having a wide repertoire of music. It is an advantage to have something for every occasion. The options that instructors choose or recommend to others will naturally depend on their own teaching context.

## Conclusion

In this introductory chapter, I have attempted to give an overview of different aspects of TBI in foreign language teaching and have begun to reveal something of the variety of approaches to TBI. The following chapters will reveal even more. They illustrate a range of types of language courses and describe how these courses were implemented and assessed. The writers discuss the problems and the constraints they faced, and they explain how they attempted to overcome them. They touch on controversial themes, such as error correction and the place of grammar teaching. Finally, they appraise their efforts and allow us to share their ambitions and their successes.

The aim of this collection is not only to illustrate a range of foreign language teaching contexts and TBI methods but also to help you, as the reader, to open up your views and reflect on your own practices. It is not easy to design tasks and implement TBI. The writers in this volume hope to support the efforts of others by sharing their own experiences. We hope readers will enjoy reflecting on these experiences and find the process rewarding.

## Appendix A: Sample Community Tasks

### 1. PLANNING A CLASS PARTY

a. Conduct a survey with your classmates to find out what kinds of activities they might like to include in a beach party for your class. (If a beach party is not suitable in your context, plan a different kind of party or outing.) Begin by considering the activities shown in the picture and then add your own ideas. Arrange them in order of popularity.

Find out what food they would like to take for a picnic, taking into account cost, convenience, and so on.

b. Make more detailed plans deciding who will do what in terms of preparty preparations. For example, write lists of which group will organize each activity, and who will bring what, and how to share the costs to buy what is needed. You may need to make a budget. Can you find some native speakers to invite, so you can practice speaking?

c. Finalize your arrangements and have your party.

d. The next day, in class, everyone can write some feedback on the party, and make suggestions for the next one. Collate this information to produce a short report that might be useful for another class to use when planning a party. You could divide the sections of the report up between groups. When the final draft is ready, decide who to circulate it to.

This task would be suitable for intermediate learners and above. It could last over several lessons and will need careful management so that everyone can be involved in its planning and execution, and also so that use of the target language can be maintained throughout. For example, the inclusion of brief written progress reports or other writing tasks or recording some of the decision-making proceedings may help reduce the amount of L1 spoken.

The original inspiration for this task came from Legutke and Thomas (1991). A task very similar to this was carried out by Spanish secondary school learners of English at the Barcelona airport and is reported in full in Ribe (1997, 222–27).

a. Find out when there are flights departing to a country where your target language (TL) is likely to be spoken. Find out what time check-in procedures open on the day you choose to go.

b. Organize how your class will travel to and from the airport. Make sure each person has a small cassette recorder, a cassette to record on, and a notebook. Buy one disposable camera for everyone in the class to use.

c. Go to the airport. In pairs, find people in the check-in queue who are willing to talk to you in TL for two or three minutes. Explain you are doing a project for your TL course. If they agree, put both your cassette recorders on *record*.

d. Ask them where they are going and why, and find out as much about their traveling habits (and the reasons for them) as you can in the time allotted.

If they allow you to, take a photo of them. If you get along well, you could also ask them where they live / work locally and whether you could get in touch with them again at a later date and, if so, get their names and contact details. After the interview, write in your notebooks any details about them you want to remember, so you can describe your person / people to the class.

e. Take your recorded cassettes home and listen to your recordings. Each of you choose a different one-minute section to transcribe. Leave gaps for any bits you cannot catch and ask your teacher to help you in class.

f. Plan together how you will present your interview to the class. For example, describe the people, summarize what they said in the interview, and pick out one particularly interesting point to expand on. Choose a short section of the cassette to play to the class and prepare a transcript for that section on an overhead transparency (OHT). Finally, list on a separate OHT four or five useful samples of the target language (TL) that was used in the interview: (expressions, patterns, and phrases with new words, etc.), that you can introduce to the class.

g. By this time, the photographs should be developed. Present your interviews to the class, as above, with the photo. The class should take notes on people's reasons for travel and ask questions afterwards. At the end, work out which were the most common reasons for travel. Then discuss (and vote) to decide which were the most interesting people interviewed.

h. Write up a summary of your interview and put in a portfolio with the transcripts of the recordings you both did. Hold a display of the portfolios.

i. Hold a short meeting to appraise the whole task. In your pairs, decide what the two best things about it were, and suggest one improvement. Tell the class and then discuss your next project. If some of the people gave their contact details, plan how you can involve them in a future project once they have returned.

## Appendix B: Components of a TBL Framework

**PRE-TASK PHASE**

**Introduction to topic and task**
Teacher explores the topic with the class,
highlights useful words and phrases.
Helps learners to understand task instructions and
ensures the intended outcome is clear. May give learners some silent
time to think what to say. May play learners a recording of a similar task
or read part of a text as a lead-in.

**TASK CYCLE**

| Task | Planning | Report |
|---|---|---|
| Students do the task, in pairs or small groups. Teacher circulates, checking progress on the task, helping if necessary, encouraging all attempts at communication, not correcting. Since this situation has a "private" feel, students feel free to experiment—mistakes don't matter. | Students prepare to report to the whole class (orally or in writing) how they did the task, what they decided or discovered or created. Since the report stage is public, students will naturally want to be accurate, so the teacher visits pairs/groups to give language advice. | Some groups present their reports or products to the class, or exchange written reports, and compare results. Teacher acts as a chairperson, summing up at the end. |

**LANGUAGE FOCUS**

| Analysis | Practice |
|---|---|
| Students examine and then discuss specific features of the text or transcript of the recording (consciousness-raising activities). Teacher reviews findings with the class; brings other useful words, phrases, and patterns to learners' attention. May pick up on language items from the earlier task cycle. | Teacher conducts class practice activities for new words, phrases and patterns occurring in the data, to build confidence. Students can enter new words, phrases, and patterns in their language notebooks. |

FIGURE 1.1. **Components of a Task-Based Learning Framework**
*Source:* Adapted from Willis 1996b.

## Appendix C: Four Tasks for Teacher Development

### TASK 1: DEFINING THE TERM "TASK"

Write down your own definition of what you mean by the term "task" in your teaching context. Compare it with other colleagues. How far can you agree?

### TASK 2: WRITING INSTRUCTIONS FOR A TASK

Select a simple task suitable for a class you teach. Write the instructions for it, addressing the features in Ellis's framework (presented in this chapter). Suggest a time limit (not more than two minutes.) Ask two people to record it, following your instructions. Listen to the task recording. Was the interaction what you expected? Ask the speakers for their feedback. Do you need to revise your instructions?

### TASK 3: RECORDING AND TRANSCRIBING

Record two fluent speakers doing a task you could use with your class. (Suggest a time limit of two or maximum three minutes.) Select a two-minute section of the recording—a part that would be useful for learners to study—and transcribe it roughly. Look to see what useful phrases and language features occur in it. Design an activity that would focus learners' attention on these. If you are interested in how far it is possible to predict the language generated by a task, read Cox (2005).

### TASK 4: DESIGN A TASK SEQUENCE

Steps 1 and 2 involve task design. Steps 3–5 involve recording and creating TBI materials. Step 6 involves sequencing and grading

1. Choose a topic your class might be interested in. Try to design one of each type of task for it, beginning with listing, ordering, etc. You may well find that some types are easier to think up than others for your current topic. (See D. Willis 1996, 149–54, for examples.)

2. Choose two or three of the best tasks, write the instructions for each one on a separate card.

3. Ask two people (fluent speakers of the target language) to record themselves doing the tasks, following the instructions on the cards. Set a time limit of about two minutes for each task. Also ask one of each pair to record a summary for each task, saying how they did the task and what they decided.

4. Transcribe not more than two minutes' worth of each recording.

5. Compare the language used for the task and for the report in the two recordings. What language features can you find in the transcripts that it might be useful to draw learners' attention to?

6. Decide in what order you would use the recordings in class and make a note of your reasons.

Note that steps 3–5 above can be used for collecting spoken material for any TBI course.

## Notes

1. They share the same focus—that of learning a language through actively using it, where attention is directed toward the content of the task and the process of task implementation.

2. Among these are the Regional English Language Center seminar held in Singapore in 2002, the International Association of Teachers of English as a Foreign Language (IATEFL) conference held in Brighton, England, in 2003, and the last dozen annual meetings of the American Council on Teaching Foreign Languages (ACTFL).

3. The situation, of course, was not quite this simple. The "look and feel" of the audiolingual method, the most common embodiment of the audiolingual approach, was significantly influenced by the structural linguists of the time, especially those working in the area of tagmemics (Pike 1959), and behavioral psychologists (Skinner 1957).

4. Note that decision-making activities based on scenarios or case studies are sometimes labeled *simulations* (e.g., in English for business courses), but in Willis's terminology these would count as *replication* activities if learners are free to interact as in real-life contexts and so long as there is an outcome for them to achieve.

5. In the United States, this term has in the past been associated with the audiolingual method and the mechanical practice ("replication") of model dialogues (i.e., form-focused rather than meaning focused). Here replication activities refer to meaning focused tasks, ones where the language used in the task "replicates" language used in real life, naturally.

6. Such courses are often called CBI-TBI courses.

# Part II

## TBI in Classroom Instruction

# 2

## TASK-BASED INSTRUCTION IN U.S. GOVERNMENT SLAVIC LANGUAGE PROGRAMS

Betty Lou Leaver and Marsha A. Kaplan

EDITORS' NOTE: This chapter outlines U.S. government foreign language programs that use task-based instruction. They cover a range of languages and proficiency levels, from very low to very high. Despite the challenges, it is clear that (1) task-based instruction can be used successfully for nearly any language and proficiency level and (2) the nature of the tasks assigned to students and the relationship between task and linguistic knowledge will vary with the proficiency level of the students.

An important difference between U.S. government foreign language programs and U.S. university programs is that government teachers and administrators are held accountable for results of their teaching. This means that students *must* acquire foreign language proficiency—and do it at a rather rapid pace. It is a tribute to the efficacy of task-based instruction (TBI) that this method has become the one of choice in the best government programs. Since the 1980s, nearly all government institutions have used TBI in their foreign language programs.

This chapter describes representative courses in Czech, Ukrainian, Russian, and English for speakers of Russian, as taught at the Defense Language Institute (DLI) and the Foreign Service Institute (FSI). TBI has also been used at most other government language schools, including the National Aeronautics and Space Administration, the Marshall Center, and other government training facilities, for nearly every language family (see, e.g., chapter 10, this volume).

### Defining TBI

All the programs described below define TBI simply and similarly. A task, in these programs, is an activity conducted in the foreign language that results in a product with a measurable result such that students can determine for themselves whether or not they have adequately completed the assignment. Most often, the product is tangible (e.g., a schedule), but it can also be intellectual (e.g., a resolution to a problem).

Tasks, as used in these government programs, occur in two varieties: pedagogical tasks and authentic tasks. Pedagogical tasks are those that do not necessarily reflect an activity that the students will be accomplishing in real life with their language skills after graduation; an example might be giving students two different pictures, in which they are required to find the differences. In contrast, authentic tasks do reflect work that students will be accomplishing after graduation and are based on authenticity of task as well as authenticity of language use. Examples include conducting car searches and interviewing specialists to make films.

## Representative Programs

As was mentioned in the introduction to this chapter, examples of TBI in government programs include Czech, Ukrainian, Russian, and English, among many language programs. Details of these four representative programs are given below.

### BASIC COURSE: CZECH (DLI)

The first TBI course to be offered in a Slavic language at the DLI was the forty-seven-week intensive (thirty hours a week) Basic Czech Course. The TBI curriculum was introduced in 1991 with little advance preparation time. Only two people on the team (the dean and the academic coordinator) had experience in TBI and they each taught at least one lesson a day with a junior instructor together in the same classroom, often in a four-handed combination. This configuration meant that the teachers quickly became comfortable with and proficient in task-based teaching and it became the preferred and highly successful method of training new teaching staff within the Slavic School. It could perhaps serve as a model for any TBI program that is periodically infused with new faculty unacquainted with a task-based approach.

Because the TBI course was a radical change from other courses being taught at that time, teachers suggested a liaison approach as a mechanism to help students make the transition from more traditional experiences (and expectations) in language learning to TBI. Students chose an academic representative who served as liaison between teachers and students, and met with instructors in planning sessions. This entailed describing student needs to teachers and explaining the curriculum choices to the students.

### Curriculum

The curriculum had several components. It had a bifurcated syllabus design, using a theme-based syllabus for the first half of the course and a content-based syllabus for the second half. Activities were principally authentic tasks based mainly on authentic materials. The curriculum was influenced by the work on TBI by Prabhu (1987) and Nunan (1989a), instructional principles advanced by the Proficiency Movement (Hancock and Scebold 2000), higher-order thinking skills (Bloom 1956), and adult learning theory (Knowles 1990).

*Theme-based syllabus.* For the first twenty-four weeks, themes related to daily living and specific areas of student interest were used for lessons. Initially, instructors selected the themes. After the twelfth week, students themselves selected them, choosing topics such as dating, dreams and goals, international affairs, military strategy, and fashion.

On a daily basis, teachers found appropriate authentic materials on the current theme, developed accompanying real-life tasks, and produced lessons for the next day. These lessons were labeled by topic and proficiency level and alphabetized into an archive that became available to all Czech instructors.

Grammar and vocabulary were taught in context, with the introduction and explanation of specific grammar points and lexical items determined by what students encountered in the authentic materials. In order to progress to the next theme, students had to master the structures and lexicon necessary for managing the current theme in reading, listening, and speaking.[1] Using authentic materials and authentic tasks to present the theme meant that students often encountered what would be considered highly complex grammar very early in the course. For example, on the first day of class, students learned how to present biographical information. This lesson was followed immediately by one on how to obtain a visa, in which teachers, in a skit, requested a visa from an embassy consular officer (played by a teacher) and students filled out the information along with the "consular officer." Then, students filled out the information for themselves. The information requested by the visa required a number of sophisticated grammatical structures, such as verbs of motion (not found in Lesson 1 of any grammar textbook!) and the prepositions required for use with them versus the prepositions (and noun case endings) used with verbs denoting location. The instructors found that "this contrast was slight and was not confusing because it was introduced in a variety of meaningful tasks in all four skills" (Maly 1993, 39). Likewise, the genitive case, a complex structure typically taught much later in traditional Slavic-language courses, was among the first cases acquired by students in the TBI course because of its frequency in authentic materials.

*Content-based syllabus.* Halfway through their Czech course, students expressed a desire for a change from the theme-based syllabus to a content-based one. They felt that they could handle most authentic media materials on the range of daily themes and wanted something more challenging. At that point, their language skills were already, for most, at Interagency Language Roundtable (ILR) Level 2 proficiency in reading and listening and close to that in speaking— the graduation goal of most DLI programs (see the appendix to this volume for proficiency level descriptions).

In the content-based instruction (CBI) portion of the course, students took required and elective subjects. Required subjects included grammar (using a book for native speakers of Czech) and military affairs. Electives, on which all members of the class had to agree, included physics, zoology, children's stories, history, and geography. As a group, the students decided how long they would study each elective. Textbooks for teaching these subjects were obtained from the State Publishing House in Prague; these were the same books used by students in Czechoslovakian public schools.

*Tasks.* Tasks were devised to reflect real-life, meaningful activities. Most tasks required the integration of all four skills—reading, writing, listening, and speaking. Since authentic materials were, especially in the beginning, well above the heads of students, tasks were adapted to ask students for an achievable product, one that required them to use and develop a range of learning strategies in coping with extensive amounts of linguistically complex materials. For example, teachers introduced Voice of America broadcasts intended for a listening public in Czechoslovakia on the third day of class. As a prelistening activity, students made a list of current political and social topics. For each of these, they elicited key words from their instructors. Then, they listened to the information that had been broadcast to Czechoslovakia to determine which topics the U.S. government considered important enough to broadcast. To do this, they listened for the key words that they had earlier elicited. Later in the course they returned to these broadcasts and studied them in more detail. Some language exercises were also used in the Czech classroom to prepare students linguistically to handle the lesson's task(s) but these comprised a very small percentage of class time.

To the extent possible, all tasks incorporated higher-order thinking skills, such as analysis, synthesis, and evaluation (Bloom 1956). Lower order activities, such as memorization, comprehension, and application—that is, those not focused on meaning-making—were, for the most part, avoided. In designing tasks, teachers strove to devise ones that would facilitate students' ability to transfer the new knowledge to a new environment (Brown, Collins, and Duguid 1989). Typically, application activities, such as role-plays, are attempts at transfer. However, most are inauthentic and simulated (like those classified as *simulation* activities; Willis, chapter 1, this volume) where language is not being used for real purposes, and, therefore, transfer is rarely realized.

Higher-order thinking skills, on the other hand, can help students develop language skills inside the classroom that they can later use outside the classroom[2] when they are combined with authentic tasks. Analysis activities require students to disassemble incoming information in order to understand its components, determine details, and discover the writer's or speaker's intent. In synthesis activities, students must make use of new and already-held information in order to assemble a new idea, propose an original concept or construct, or make a unique object. Evaluation tasks ask students to develop an opinion based on subjective and objective criteria (including research undertaken and data collected by themselves) and critical thinking.

Most tasks used in the Czech course, even those assigned at novice levels of proficiency, required students to produce a product that required analysis, synthesis, or evaluation, or some combination of these. For example, a lesson about weather forecasting that required all three higher-order thinking skills was used quite early in the course. This lesson is in appendix A to this chapter.

Some tasks were easily accomplished during one lesson (one hour). Others were far more elaborate and took several lessons to complete. Students also had a long-term project. Examples of projects included making a television broadcast in Czech (current news, weather report, and an interview with a Czech immigrant working as a boat mechanic at the Monterey harbor), researching and reporting on a wide range of local scientific phenomena, and creating a Czech version of monopoly that reflected locations, transportation services, and other aspects of Czech culture. For the latter project, students also wrote instructions for players and produced currency that looked like the Czech koruna (crown).

Students typically completed the tasks working in small groups. The teacher(s) circulated among the groups, keeping them in the target language (although, given the immersion atmosphere, students rarely tried to use English), helping with just-in-time grammatical or lexical explanations, and providing guidance on time management. The small-group format provided several benefits. One was to lower the affective filter of students. Another was to afford students the opportunity to share learning strategies. Yet a third was to free the instructors to interact with individual students and groups, assess student progress as an observer of group interactions, and otherwise act as facilitators, rather than deliverers of instruction.

*Authenticity.* Authenticity of material, language, and task was achieved in two ways. First, instructors obtained newspaper and magazine articles from Czechoslovakia for use in the classroom. In addition, several times a week, they sent students to the institute's library to find information on the theme among the library's Czech collection of newspapers, magazines, audiocassettes, and videotapes and realia. Letters, maps, and other materials produced by native speakers for native speakers were used as well.

Second, four-handed instruction was used in cases where written texts or broadcasts were not available with two teachers working together to create semi-authentic communication situations, such as discussing a topic or presenting a model of interaction for student emulation. Even in cases where authentic materials were available, four-handed instruction was often used to bring life to these materials. Usually the students were given a task to accomplish during this presentation. Examples include deciding who argued more persuasively in a presented debate or, at an earlier level of proficiency, jotting down the differences between ordering food in the United States and Czechoslovakia. Students were allowed to tape these presentations so that they could listen to them again at home in order to increase the amount of exposure to the language, consolidate what they had learned, and enhance the possibility of language intake.

*Immersion.* Immersion is not necessarily a component of TBI. However, it was prevalent in Slavic School programs, and this set of instructors had developed a preference for it. Initially, students were allowed to ask questions in English although teacher responses and all teacher talk was generally in Czech. Students quickly adjusted to an all-Czech environment, and after the first few weeks rarely, if ever, reverted to English. When non-Czech-speaking visitors came to the classroom, one or other student would immediately volunteer to interpret. When visited by their English-speaking commandant they found it hard to revert to English. Over time, they had developed greater comfort with Czech in their classroom than with English.

*Error correction.* Error correction was carried out principally by students, who corrected each other, more or less naturally, during the completion of a task.

Instructors felt that such an approach helped to lower students' affective filter. Help was however provided, as necessary, by the instructor.

## Testing

Testing of students occurred both informally and formally. Testers came from outside the Slavic School. Informal tests were conducted by speakers of Czech working in other (nonteaching) divisions at the institute (similar to the "class visits" arranged by Lopes, reported in chapter 4). Formal tests were conducted by the institute's testing division. More importantly, the quality of task completion gave teachers a good understanding of what students did and did not know—often, a better understanding than most tests could provide. Facilitative teaching in which the teachers were able to spend a fair amount of time observing students in small groups (and helping them with their tasks) provided even more information about students' progress.

Periodically, students took a task-based "prochievement" test (a test integrating proficiency and achievement) upon completion of each theme (approximately every two and a half weeks). In prochievement tests, by definition, students completed a series of tasks on the familiar topic (achievement) but using unfamiliar scripts (proficiency). Students self-corrected these tests, and in the process, could raise their grades. The corrections were then reviewed by the teacher and additional errors pointed out. The purpose of the prochievement tests was to help students learn from their own errors.

Proficiency tests for speaking, listening, and reading skills were conducted at eight-week intervals. The purpose of these was to document and track student progress and identify any developing weaknesses. Proficiency scores were the basis of student grades.

### "BEYOND-THREE" RUSSIAN COURSE (FSI)

The Beyond-Three course began life as the Russian Advanced Course, which ran successfully from 1983 to 1989 at the FSI. It had the goal of bringing students to Level 4 proficiency, or what is often called a "near-native" level (Leaver 1997).

Developed by two Russian instructors in the mid-1980s, it was the first high-level course taught at the FSI. The students were for the most part senior-level diplomats or military attachés. Nearly all had already served a tour at the U.S. embassy in Moscow or the U.S. consulate in Leningrad and would be deployed there once again after course completion. All had achieved Level 3 proficiency (a prerequisite) before enrolling in the six-month intensive course, and those who completed it all reached the Level 4 goal.

The advanced course was designed as a content-based course by choice but many of the essential activities of the course were elaborate, real-life tasks. It was the tasks that assisted in making this course highly successful—and unique among government language programs.

After a couple of years of dormancy in the early 1990s, the Russian Advanced Course was revived as the Beyond-Three Course with some changes unrelated to TBI. This new course, as its name implies, aimed to take individual students up to whatever level is feasible in the time available. It lasts one year full-time and has the same entry requirements as its predecessor. The name and goal change is a result of a new conviction that not everyone is a candidate for Level 4.

### Curriculum

The curriculum of the Beyond-Three Course is composed of a content-based syllabus, in-class exercises, and extramural tasks, all requiring the near-exclusive use of authentic language. The students are not taught in classes per se but carry out activities individually with the assistance of the teaching staff. Many of those activities are self-selected. A number of them are accomplished via the Internet.

The syllabus for each student is individually tailored, offering an eclectic approach to teaching and learning that is highly learner centered. The approach is that of a "salad bar," where students, with teachers' help, choose what language nourishment they need and like.

There are seven dimensions, or elements, to the program. These include:

- vision,
- linguistic profile,
- extensive reading,
- "push the performance" exercises,
- public appearance modules,
- in-country internship, and
- community outreach.

*Vision.* A major challenge, in working over the years with highly proficient speakers, is helping them become aware of ways in which they are not "near native" and where they need to focus in order to attain Distinguished Level (Level 4) speaking and reading skills. Speakers at the 3 or 3+ level are, by definition, already quite effective using their language skills in most everyday professional, social, and personal contexts. Moreover, they rarely get negative feedback from native speakers, who are often impressed and encouraging. Their confidence may hinder their ability to notice their deficiencies at the outset. Thus, students entering the program are helped to envision what a Level 4 can do. This helps the student focus on what he or she needs to do to reach that goal.

In addition to self-assessment questionnaires and re-reading the ILR skill level descriptions of the Level 4 criteria for speaking and reading, students do exercises intended to help establish, in concrete terms, skill at this level. An example of one such exercise is based on an excerpt from a widely read and quoted eighteenth-century play. Students are encouraged to use Google's search engine, which supports the Cyrillic alphabet, to find references to the title of the play and to certain lines and names of characters. They will inevitably call up numerous references to the title and lines in newspaper headlines. This exercise exposes students to an archaic style of literary discourse which they may have difficulty reading but which a Level 4 reader should be able to handle. At the same time, it helps them to discover such cultural references in ordinary, everyday news articles which they may have previously missed.

*Linguistic profile.* Basic course instruction (covering Levels 0 to 3) typically emphasizes compensatory strategies, such as paraphrase and guessing from context, in order to facilitate fluency and communication. In contrast, advanced instruction subordinates (at least temporarily) fluency to help the learner attain nuance and precision. In establishing a linguistic profile of the learner, the teacher records several samples of the learner's planned and unplanned monologic and dialogic speech and performs a detailed analysis or profile of the learner's speech, underscoring salient features of pronunciation, syntax, word choice, collocations, intonation, and conversational style—which deviate from that of an educated native speaker. In a sense, the student's performance is defined in negative terms—from the point of view of what gives this person away as a nonnative speaker. On the basis of this analysis, student and teacher together design a syllabus that identifies their deficient areas and guides the learner to developing nuances and precision in speech that are needed at high levels of sophistication.

*Extensive reading.* Students are expected to read voraciously. They can, however, build their own reading lists. In addition to the canon of Russian literature, student reading lists encompass newspaper and journal articles, postings to Internet sites, and books on a wide range of topics, including history, diplomacy, philosophy, cultural studies, politics, sociology, art, religion, and numerous other areas of individual interest. A wide range of genres is also included: biography, memoirs, general science, songs, essays, speeches, lectures, Russian Ministry of Foreign Affairs briefings, reference works, movies, fiction (thrillers, detective stories, and mysteries), and various literary genres, and even well-known works of American literature in translation. Popular novels, particularly those with dialogue, are useful for exposing the learner to colloquial speech registers.

*"Push the performance" exercises.* Over the years, teachers have developed a compendium of exercises (informally called "Pushing the Performance") that force the students to refine their language use. Their purpose is to help the learner to avoid the kinds of strategic competence, such as compensation strategies, that allow students to deal with everyday situations comfortably at lower levels of proficiency (Skehan 1998a, 1998b). Through these exercises, students are taught to notice subtle differences between English and Russian and, in this way, to continue to refine their speech. Pushing the performance entails coaching the learner to avoid paraphrasing to bypass, using structures and vocabulary the learner may not be sure of. Here, it is not always the teacher who has responsibility for intervening or correcting. For example, the learner might record his or her performance and, during the debriefing or playback session, may stop the recorder to say "this is what I really was trying to express." Some traditional approaches are useful for helping the learner to "notice the difference":

1. close translation of short passages from Russian to English and from English to Russian; and
2. transcription of radio broadcasts, recorded conversations, and other types of authentic audio materials.

Other useful exercises include the following:

- discussions of readings—authentic topics, in contrast with a thematic approach, based on predetermined themes;
- multiparty discussions enhance interactional skills and the learner's ability to cope with unplanned, spontaneous talk; and
- working with American literature and speeches in translation, focusing, with teacher guidance, on useful expressions.

*Public appearances modules.* In the federal government there is an increased need for individuals with high-level language skills who are able to take part in unscripted debates on current policy issues or appear on television and explain America to host country audiences. Modules have been developed to help learners cope with using Russian in public and media contexts—from prepared performances of the ribbon-cutting ceremony, to the less scripted and more confrontational interactions characteristic of televised policy debates and press conferences. Teachers help learners prepare and rehearse for such activities. Videotaping performances and debriefing are essential tools in such training. This is a simulated real-life task-based component.

*In-country internship.* Students spend two weeks in Tver, Russia, working with companies or schools, depending on their areas of interest. One student, for example, did her internship with the Tver Oblast Department of Agriculture and visited several large cooperative farms, an independent goat breeder, and private horse breeder. Another met with local political, religious, and business leaders. This is a real-life, task-based component.

*Community outreach.* The most significant task-based portion of the course entails the community outreach activities. Thanks to the presence of a large Russian émigré community in the Washington, D.C., area, where the FSI is located, community-based real-life tasks are possible. Beyond-Three students are matched with senior citizens who want companionship, need help with motor vehicles or citizenship issues, or need an interpreter for court or with doctors. These émigrés are generally not used to nonnative speakers and do not act as tutors. Rather, the students use their Russian to provide them with the service they need, and also to build personal relationships. Thus, students can perfect their knowledge of language and culture.

*Authenticity.* Since there is no textbook for the course, nearly all materials are by necessity authentic. In the earlier Advanced Course, students, in consultation with teachers, determined the topics that they wished to explore during the course. Specific students or groups of students were responsible for researching newspapers, journals, and other authentic sources of information in their areas of expertise and for leading the discussions on them. Teachers brought in articles, as well; a number of these served as models of speech for students to acquire for either formal or informal use, depending on the topic and nature of the article.

## Testing

Upon departure a formal proficiency test is administered. Periodically, depending on the duration of the training, an interim proficiency test might be given for diagnostic purposes. Assessment tools are used throughout the training to help the learner ascertain areas on which to focus.

In early 1993, in conjunction with the expansion of video-teletraining courses (the term used for distance education using videoconferencing facilities) at the Defense Language Institute, a group of eight linguists (four military students and four civilians) at the National Cryptologic School began training in Ukrainian at the DLI. Proposed as a cross-training course for students with Russian language proficiency ranging from Level 1 to 2, the Ukrainian course aimed to develop Level 2 Ukrainian linguists in a four-hour-a-day, twelve-week video-teletraining course. Six of the most successful Russian teachers, who were also native speakers of Ukrainian, were assembled for this project.

### Curriculum

In developing the Ukrainian CBI-TBI curriculum, experience in the DLI Czech Basic Course was used, along with experience in several of the Russian courses that had been using CBI-TBI as supplements to the textbook. No Ukrainian textbook was available for this kind of course so teachers gathered authentic materials and wrote tasks to accompany them. Since the course was taught through satellite dish, it was difficult to individualize instruction. Therefore, a writing component was added to the course, even though writing was not a tested skill. Students kept journals in which they reacted to the course, wrote compositions, and otherwise communicated with instructors in writing. The instructors responded to the content and form of these written communications, correcting them as necessary. (This type of learner-teacher interaction can be considered authentic communication in its own right.)

*Syllabus design.* The content-based framework for the course opened with a lesson on the history of Kiev, using an authentic documentary in Ukrainian. Students were expected to rely on keyword cognates and parallels in grammar and vocabulary with Russian in order to understand the main ideas in the documentary. Each topic occupied at least two weeks of students' time. History was followed by geography, culture, politics/political systems, and military affairs.

*Tasks.* Tasks varied in length and complexity, although most were accomplished in dyads in ten to fifteen minutes. Examples include drawing up a chronology of Kiev's history, making a map, or determining opinions of a peer on a specific topic. Sometimes results were shared with the full group, sometimes not. While some task activities could have been recorded for subsequent student analysis and/or listening, most were not. Given four hours of "contact" each day, two teachers in the "classroom," and a set of teachers who were also trained proficiency testers, most teachers were capable of near-instant diagnosis of learning difficulties.

*Authenticity.* All materials used were authentic. They included videotapes, audiotapes, and publications. Prior to the start of the course, reading packets were mailed to the students. During the course, materials were sent by mail or faxed or shown via satellite (where the use was immediate).

*Immersion.* The course was conducted entirely in Ukrainian, including dyadic and small-group work. Correspondence with teachers was in Ukrainian. Students never heard their native language spoken in the classroom, not even on the first day.

## Testing

After completing each topic, students took a prochievement test on the topic. At the end of the course, students took a proficiency test in three skills: reading, listening, and speaking. For other examples of cross-training courses, including Croatian and Serbian (DLI), see Corin (1997).

## Challenges in Government TBI Language Programs

A wide range of challenges was reported by the teachers and administrators of the U.S. government TBI language programs. These included:

- significant investment of time,
- lack of predictability,
- need for faculty development,
- obstacles related to student teaching expectations,
- obstacles related to student testing expectations, and
- paucity of materials.

### SIGNIFICANT INVESTMENT OF TIME

As in other programs in this volume (e.g., the Japanese program in chapter 6), a significant obstacle to implementing TBI in government programs has been the amount of time required to prepare lessons. Indeed, until instructors learn to think in terms of tasks, lesson preparation can take considerable time. A number of ways have been found by creative teachers and administrators to overcome the obstacle of time. These include:

- increasing experience in task-based teaching,
- direct assistance from administrators and others,
- paid development time, and
- use of an archive.

### Experience in Task-Based Teaching

In planning the first day of class, the DLI Czech instructors spent five hours of preparation time for each hour of class taught. Very quickly, as instructors became proficient in TBI, the time dwindled to just a few minutes per class—considerably less than that of those teachers who elected to supplement the textbook with their own activities and lessons, but not tasks. This savings in preparation time has been the typical experience of teachers who move into task-based teaching.

## Direct Assistance

The DLI Serbian and Croatian teachers had two full-time coordinators to work on curricular issues with them, do much of the research work, and locate authentic materials on the topics of study. Direct assistance in obtaining such resources can significantly reduce the amount of preparation time required for a teacher.

## Development Time

The Russian teachers at the FSI found that they needed four hours of preparation time daily in order to teach the other four hours. In this case, a different solution was found. Administrators reduced the teaching load to allow for the amount of development time needed. In addition, two teachers were granted six months full-time leave from teaching in order to develop a basic set of materials for the content-based aspects of the CBI-TBI advanced course. While this option worked for the various government institutions, it is not likely to be a possibility for high schools and universities where less flexibility is possible.

## Use of an Archive

In all the programs described in this chapter, teachers and program administrators developed archives of materials in order to cut down on the amount of search time for locating authentic materials and task preparation. Successful lessons, in most cases, were filed by proficiency level and topic.

The use of and sharing of archives is a model that can easily be emulated by non-government language programs. In fact, several such programs have done this, including an English-language program in Moldova (chapter 13) that began with a strong base, thanks to a sister program in Uzbekistan sharing its already-developed archive.

### LACK OF PREDICTABILITY

Where TBI was used with a student-centered curriculum, it was difficult to predict how much time students would need with each topic. Therefore, preparing a syllabus for the TBI courses was very tricky. Specific dates set in advance were not likely to coincide with the way the course played out. If students were allowed to participate in the theme-generation process, as they were in the Czech course at DLI and the Russian course at FSI, the curriculum became fully unpredictable, and new syllabi had to be periodically regenerated. This is not unusual for courses that are based on a process syllabus, whether or not TBI is the method of choice (Breen and Candlin 1980).

The FSI's Beyond-Three program in French addressed this problem of lack of predictability through the Learning Contract. The student, together with the teacher-consultant, draws up a set of personalized objectives for a specific period of time. The contract specifies activities, learning resources, and self/other assessment tools to help the student attain these objectives. The contract is modified in the course of training as the learner progresses and his or her needs change. The contract serves as a way to help the learner set priorities. It provides focus and structure and is a useful tool for helping the learner to manage his or her expectations.

Lack of predictability is not always a learning problem. In fact, most students appreciated the opportunity to participate in designing their own instruction, and while they may have spent more time on one task than anticipated and less on another, their overall progress was not impeded.

Lack of predictability, surprisingly, has turned out not to be much of a teaching problem, either. Most teachers have found that topics rise naturally, as reading and speaking are integrated. In the FSI Russian course, teachers found that the curriculum evolved readily and comfortably, as they engaged students in what they were reading.

However, lack of predictability can be an administrative and affective problem. Higher-level administrators often want to see a set schedule of syllabus that is followed and does not change on a rolling basis. Students also often feel the need for something "printed in stone" to help them organize their learning. The resolution to these problems is generally a matter of educating both administrators and students. Most of the TBI programs described here spent time on student manuals and newsletters, informational packages for administrators, and open-door policies.

## NEED FOR FACULTY DEVELOPMENT

TBI is still relatively new. Therefore, the deans and department chairpersons at the U.S. government language schools that adopted TBI as a teaching method found that they needed to set aside a significant amount of time for faculty development. This need is shared with many of the programs in this volume. Lopes (chapter 4) and Cozonac (chapter 13) describe this problem in some detail. How the government schools accomplished faculty development differed in some important aspects from typical private and university faculty development, and depended very much on the circumstances of the moment. With a little creativity there is much in these programs that could be emulated. The DLI Czech instructors learned on the spot with the help of the dean and the academic coordinator, who each devoted at least one to two hours daily to team teaching. The DLI Ukrainian teachers had developed TBI skills during earlier stints in teaching Russian, where many hours had been devoted to familiarization of the teaching staff with this method. The two FSI teachers of the first advanced Russian course prepared the course and accompanying materials themselves but were allowed six months of full-time effort to do so.

TBI, at both FSI and DLI, has now been institutionalized. Leading experts are regularly brought in for ongoing faculty development. In addition, more experienced faculty can share their experiences with younger faculty. In both institutions, four-handed instruction is common, so teachers can learn the practices of TBI from each other.

Faculty development in the FSI Beyond-Three course has taken a very different turn. Because of the individualized nature of the course, each time the course is run it looks somewhat different. At the end of each course, teachers undertake a course evaluation, examining possible reasons why some students did not reach the desired proficiency level. The nature of staff development, then, is more re-search-oriented and exploratory. The analyses, conducted individually and jointly, lead to improved practices with the next set of students, but not in the traditional sense, for the next set of students may have very different programs and learning styles than the current set.

## OBSTACLES RELATED TO STUDENT EXPECTATIONS

A few of the programs described above met with initial student dissatisfaction (albeit ultimate satisfaction) because students had never before experienced a TBI approach. In fact, often the greatest resistance came from students who had had the most experience in studying foreign languages in high school and college. While in many cases they may not have had much skill in the studied foreign language, especially those taught in non-communicative ways, they were comfortable with and "were expecting rote memorization, daily quizzes, grammar explanations, and extrinsic motivation" (Maly 1993, 40). Not surprisingly, "they did not feel that they were learning, *unless it hurt*" (p. 40). These government students are not unique; other TBI teachers have met with similar surprises (see Lopes, chapter 4, this volume).

DLI Czech students, for example, did not feel they were learning unless they could recite discrete pieces of information from a vocabulary list or set of grammar rules. Instructors periodically asked students to list all the things they had learned. Initially, the last hour on Friday was set aside for this purpose, and students usually needed the full hour to do this, producing very long lists. As the course progressed, the need for this activity lessened, and students became strong advocates of the program.

FSI handles these problems in a different way. The institute has a student consultation service to which teachers and supervisors may refer students who are experiencing difficulties in learning or frustration with teaching methods (Ehrman 2001). The consultation service is staffed with learning consultants who are trained in learner differences, learning strategies, and teaching methods.

## OBSTACLES RELATED TO STUDENTS' TESTING EXPECTATIONS

Students' previous experiences in high school and college foreign language classrooms also create obstacles to the implementation of task-based testing, not unlike those reported in Brazil by Passos de Oliveira (see chapter 12, this volume). Students often prefer tests of knowledge over achievement tests. They can prepare for knowledge tests through cramming and memorization and receive good grades whether or not they can actually use the language in real situations. Preparation for prochievement and proficiency tests is much more complicated and requires students to apply what they have learned, as well as use the language on a regular basis.

While some programs have reported difficulties in student acceptance of task-based tests, the courses described above escaped this problem in many instances simply because students were not tested during the course. The DLI Czech and Ukrainian courses, which did include task-based tests, did not encounter any student resistance.

## PAUCITY OF MATERIALS

Few textbooks are truly task-based. None of the programs described above had a task-based textbook in the first few years of teaching via TBI, and some chose not to use a textbook. As a result, most of the teachers and administrators who desired to add tasks to their classrooms found that they had to find appropriate authentic materials and then develop their own tasks. Sometimes even authentic materials were difficult to obtain.

In some cases, building a shared archive of materials helped. In other cases, teachers went to great lengths (and to great distances—including all the way to Prague) to obtain materials for their students. With more commonly taught foreign languages this is less of a problem, and even in some less commonly taught languages, the problem is less today, thanks to the Internet.

## Outcomes of Government TBI Language Programs

Outcomes of TBI in government language programs are not totally clear because TBI is a purely a method, and the syllabus design also influences the success of the program. In some cases, the content-based syllabus design might have explained the success of the course as well as the conversion to TBI. Keeping that consideration in mind, among the reported benefits of TBI were:

- greater motivation,
- opportunity for repetition without boredom,
- greater curricular flexibility,
- promotion of learning how to learn,
- an opportunity for natural error correction,
- promotion of risk taking,
- higher proficiency results,
- increased student satisfaction, and
- better program evaluation results.

### GREATER MOTIVATION

Many teachers who use tasks in their classrooms find that their students exhibit greater motivation. When students entered the DLI Czech program, for example, instructors noticed that they were primarily extrinsically motivated, if they had much interest at all. The TBI program changed the nature of their motivation. Students found the tasks to be interesting, and the program became even more interesting when they introduced their own favorite themes. Student-generated themes are highly motivating, "allowing the students to be responsible for their own learning and allowing the teacher to become the 'manager of student learning'" (Maly 1993, 41). Often, students refused to take the Institute's scheduled breaks between class hours, as they became intensely involved in completing a complex task.

A unique situation is that of the FSI Beyond-Three Russian students. Students in that program are motivated in a different way. Part of the motivation comes from the ability to individualize their programs. Many, if not most, are also instrumentally motivated by the opportunity for receiving a 15 percent pay increase through the Language Incentive Pay Program.

### OPPORTUNITY FOR REPETITION WITHOUT BOREDOM

In TBI, themes can be explored at length, with new twists; a range of different task types can be generated from one theme, as J. Willis (1996b) shows. Teachers can continue working on one theme until students acquire the preestablished goals without becoming repetitive because the tasks themselves can differ. In other courses, teachers are often forced to repeat the same or a similar set of exercises over and over, which students generally find boring. Both the DLI Czech and DLI Serbian and Croatian teachers noted this advantage of TBI (Maly 1993; Corin 1997).

### PROMOTION OF LEARNING HOW TO LEARN

The DLI Czech instructors noticed that "when a student is involved in a meaningful activity and is tasked to higher levels of mental activity beyond memory and understanding, he or she processes and stores information in the cognitive domain and actually learns how to learn" (Maly 1993, 41). In fact, attention to learning how to learn (i.e., development of strategic competence) is an important component of most of the courses described above.

### OPPORTUNITY FOR NATURAL ERROR CORRECTION

When students are completing tasks, the teacher has an opportunity to facilitate learning by circulating among the learner groups, pairs, or individuals working on tasks to help them understand the task instructions, eavesdrop on progress (both linguistic and assignment), and to discuss the task as the students work on it. Such discussions allow for students to hear differences between their own speech and the teacher's and to receive a natural form of error correction. Since students at lower levels of proficiency do not always recognize when they are being corrected (Lightbown and Spada 1999), teachers used to correcting errors in natural settings will not allow the student to get by without making the adjustment to his or her speech and will continue to interact on the same topic in ways that cause natural repetition. In some cases, overt correction may be needed for individual students and the individualization that accompanies TBI permits this.

In addition, students can be taught natural error correction strategies. They can learn to listen to how native speakers react to what they say, hear any differences in usage of vocabulary or grammar, and then, adjusting their own usage, practice the correct version without the interlocutor

In the FSI Russian Beyond-Three Course, students are deliberately taught to take advantage of another kind of natural error correction—and to provide their own error corrections through skilled noticing of the differences between English and Russian. Through audiotapes, videotapes, and comparison of the tapes, students learn to do what native speakers do. For example, J. Willis (1996b) advocates recording fluent target language speakers doing the same tasks that learners will have done, transcribing them and letting learners analyze the transcripts, noting down any new expressions. If learners also record themselves doing tasks, they can compare their task performances with those of fluent speakers even more directly (Leedham 2005).

## PROMOTION OF RISK TAKING

The lowered affective filter associated with task-based activities generally means greater risk-taking (Maly 1993). Learning to take risks in language use and trying out new language in the classroom are important because very often they translate into comfort in taking risk in the target language environment. Goodison (1987) found that U.S. Embassy employees who took risks in the classroom at the Foreign Service Institute continued to take those risks abroad and became more proficient by the end of their assignment to the Embassy duties. Conversely, those who had been reluctant to take risks in the classroom spent more time in expatriate communities abroad and often returned from their Embassy assignments with less proficiency than they had upon arriving at post.

## HIGHER PROFICIENCY RESULTS

The results from the pilot course in TBI Czech (and for the latter half of the course, CBI-TBI) were considerably higher than any ever achieved to date in the Czech language program. Up until that point, a typical class would lose more than a third of its students to attrition and average 44 percent of its graduates achieving an ILR Level 2 in reading and listening and ILR Level 1 + in speaking. The pilot TBI course lost only one student to attrition (a student who had been diagnosed by the public schools as dyslexic) and graduated all of the rest of the students at Level 2 or higher in speaking, reading, and listening, exceeding the DLI graduation standard at the time. Eighty percent of the students achieved a proficiency level one-half point above the graduation standard for each of the three skills. Further, nearly two-thirds of the class reached Level 3 (Professional Proficiency or, on the scale of the American Council on Teaching Foreign Languages, Superior-Level Proficiency) in one or more skill, and 20 percent of the class reached a Level 3 in all three tested skills, an unprecedented achievement in the history of the Czech program. Similar results have been reported on other TBI programs.

In the pilot Russian-to-Serbian conversion course, 90 percent of the students reached Level 2 or higher in one or more skills in eight weeks. The Ukrainian distance education course also achieved unprecedented results. In twelve weeks of half-time study, 88 percent of the students reached a Level 3 in one or more skills (and no one achieved less than a Level 2 in any skill), for a course in which students would typically expect to spend forty-seven weeks to reach Level 2. Class size did not make a difference; the class size of the distance education program was significantly larger than the ordinary class size (maximum of ten students) at DLI.

## INCREASED STUDENT SATISFACTION

One of the common positive attributes of the TBI courses described above was the overall student satisfaction with the courses. This is especially remarkable, considering that some of these courses typically enrolled the kinds of students who had the potential to be highly critical of the courses—those taking languages that they had not selected, those being forced into "emergency" language training, and, in several cases, experienced learners (who often second-guess classroom teachers).

The Czech students quickly came not only to appreciate the TBI course but to be strong advocates of the program. Typical comments are in appendix B to this chapter; perhaps the most telling of the comments was that they thought their experience was unfair: they had learned more than their peers while having much greater fun and far less stress (Duri 1992). Student satisfaction was bolstered by feedback questionnaires administered every eight weeks, following which instructors made course corrections.

Feedback from the Ukrainian students was likewise positive. In an interesting twist on feedback procedures, learners provided weekly evaluations of the course and their progress in the journals that they kept in Ukrainian.

### BETTER PROGRAM EVALUATION RESULTS

Not all programs described above have been evaluated by anyone other than the administrators' immediate supervisors. Two programs, however, were formally evaluated, and in both cases, the introduction of TBI into the programs contributed to an increase in instructional effectiveness.

Better program evaluations are not unusual for TBI courses, especially those that occur in conjunction with content-based instruction. All the programs described in this chapter have enjoyed a reputation as being among the leading programs in the respective institutions.

### INTRINSIC REWARDS

A unique aspect of the FSI Beyond-Three Russian Course is that the task-based portion of the course (the community outreach activities) results in psychic rewards beyond anything associated with language learning itself. Students gain the satisfaction of knowing that they are using their language skills to help someone.

## Conclusion

One must note that not all the improvements noted in the courses described in this chapter can be credited to the introduction of TBI. In all cases, TBI was introduced together with CBI. Often, learner-centered instruction also accompanied the new CBI-TBI format. Authentic materials were extensively used by all, and immersion was preferred by most. In several cases, four-handed instruction was the norm, and in one case, course administrators were trained to understand better the principles of managing a language program. All of these factors could account for the improvements these courses showed over previous courses or the excellent results in terms of proficiency outcome that most received.

Some advantages, though, are clearly TBI related. These include student satisfaction, greater risk-taking, promotion of how to learn, opportunity for non-boring repetition, and for natural error correction. Student feedback has confirmed that students *like* tasks, and the course results confirm that students *learn* from tasks.

When all is said and done, TBI as a method can provide effective instruction to students in a wide range of program types. Moreover, it can be fun and interesting for students—and for teachers.

## Appendix A: Sample Czech Task: Weather

This task, from Eugene Maly's "Task-Based Instruction from the Teacher's Perspective" in *Dialogue on Language Instruction*, was originally written in Czech and students did not receive the English-language instructions.

### A. BRAINSTORMING EXERCISE

Students brainstorm concepts, lexical items, and phrases already acquired and write them on the board.

### B. PREREADING EXERCISE

Tasks: (1) Match weather charts with written passages.

(2) Compare American and Czech weather newspaper format.

### C. READING EXERCISES AND DISCUSSION (NEW MATERIALS)

Tasks: (1) Separate into small groups. Read and discuss the forecasts (each group has a different forecast). Which seasons are the forecasts for? Support your answers.

(2) Find out by discussion which group has the best forecast.

(3) Listening exercise. Fill in a chart—European Weather Report. (Students were not provided with the translations; these are given for the convenience of the reader who does not speak Czech.)

(4) Task: Create a weather map, using the information in your chart.

### D. COMPREHENSION CHECK

Match weather symbols and corresponding lexical items by placing the number of the symbol next to the correct lexical item.

### E. HOMEWORK ASSIGNMENT

You are a meteorologist. Prepare a written long-range weather forecast for next week based on data from last year.

## Appendix B: Typical Comments of Czech Students in the DLI CBI-TBI Course

1. I like the use of magazines and getting ideas across by figuring out things for ourselves.

| město (place) | teplota (temperature) | počasi (weather) |
|---|---|---|
| Londryn | | |
| | 18°C | |
| | | zataženo |
| | | |
| | | |
| | | |
| | | |
| | | |
| | | |
| | | |

TABLE 2.1. **Data Collection Chart for Western Forecasts in European Cities**

2. I like the fact that our teachers don't speak English with us, and when we don't understand, they simplify or compare to things we do understand.

3. Being placed in situations where the only outlet is through oral communication, one begins to listen for words and look for gestures and facial expressions, which is merely the rehearsal for the real-life drama.

4. The relaxed atmosphere created an atmosphere I like more; I feel I will not burn out.

5. I feel I would not be as far as I am now if taught in a more stringent manner as in some other schools.

6. . . . making us offensive rather than defense learners. (From Maly 1993, 43.)

## Notes

1. Although writing is often used as a supportive skill, writing per se is not taught at DLI.
2. In some TBI courses, tasks were frequently carried out in a real environment outside the classroom.

# 3

# USING MEDIA-BASED TASKS IN TEACHING SPANISH

Alicia Mora van Altena

EDITORS' NOTE: In this chapter, Alicia van Altena presents a course that she designed for use by advanced students of Spanish at Yale University. The course is both content-based and task-based. The tasks are designed to teach linguistic (specifically, discourse) and paralinguistic skills to students—an area of study very infrequently taught in university foreign language programs. The materials for study are about contemporary media and are designed for students who are content specialists in other areas, who have plans for travel, and who are especially interested in connecting their language study with their overall major (hence, the CBI-TBI combination). This program is not dissimilar to the programs described by Leaver and Kaplan in chapter 2, yet the student body is quite dissimilar. The success of this course provides evidence that CBI-TBI can work as well in a university environment as it can in a specialty school or government agency.

The objectives of the Spanish Language Task-Based Instruction programs at Yale University are to improve the language competence of the students by concentrating on a specific field of study: the linguistic and paralinguistic discourse that pertains to journalism. We identify its basic characteristics as precision, clarity, and coherence. The attainment of these fundamental objectives is also essential to achieving proficiency in a foreign language. It was in this context that a decision was made in 1998 to introduce content-based, task-based instruction (CBI-TBI) into the Spanish language program's course offerings.

Having made and implemented that decision, we have found the response of students to be overwhelming, forcing the department to limit the enrollment in virtually all of these content-based courses. This article provides some details of the rationale, organization, and implementation of this course.

## Rationale for CBI-TBI Coursework

The Language Director of the Spanish and Portuguese Department at Yale University, Professor María Crocetti (2003), has described the rationale for CBI-TBI courses as follows: "If we already face a challenge in identifying the essential characteristics of a 'native speaker,' how much more complex can it be to determine foreign/second language students' proficiency level and use that information for program guidance!" For that reason, we carefully analyzed how to determine level boundaries in our foreign language program. In so doing, we took into account ACTFL's generic proficiency guidelines (ACTFL 1999a; see the appendix to this volume) that are used nationwide plus the specific local conditions, motivation, and potential of the Spanish student population at Yale. The result was Yale's own Spanish-language proficiency test that is used for placement, as well as measuring instructional outcomes.

## THE DECISION FOR CONTENT-BASED INSTRUCTION

The definitional levels we developed for the Spanish-language proficiency test used for the full range of assessment requirements can be refined and/or adjusted, as the need arises, based on careful observation of boundaries, continuity, and course content. Proficiency level criteria require the valid specification of context, function, and accuracy in a specific curriculum content.

This was just one of the issues we had in mind in 1996–97, when, under the direction of Professor María Rosa Menocal, Georgina Dopico-Black, and I reviewed the third-year level course which at that time included only advanced grammar, advanced conversation, and writing in Spanish (composition). We wanted to offer students new choices by opening the door to a series of content-based, third-year language courses that would be taught at the Advanced/Superior Level of the American Council on Teaching Foreign Languages scale. At that point, I conducted a survey to determine if other universities were using such an approach to third-year language courses. The search included Brown University, Harvard University, Princeton University, and the University of Washington, among others. The survey results showed that the following courses have been offered at the Intermediate/Advanced level): Cultura Urbana Actual (Contemporary Urban Culture), Spanish for the Bilingual (multiple levels), Language and Culture, and Film.

As the world economy moved into the globalization era and the Spanish-speaking population in the United States was rapidly increasing, many of our students majoring in medicine, law, business, or with aspirations toward public policy careers began to realize the importance of high proficiency levels in Spanish to success in finding employment in an increasingly difficult job market and increasingly Spanish-speaking population.

Relying on the specific interests and backgrounds of our Spanish-language instructors, we began to organize courses that used current topics in specific fields to develop the advanced language competence of students enrolled in courses in law, medicine, ethics, and film. Examples of related language courses include Theater and Poetry Workshop, Legal Spanish, Spanish in Film, Spanish in Politics, International Relations and the Media, Spanish for the Medical Professions, The Unity and Diversity of Spanish, Creative Writing, and Advanced Spanish for Bilingual Students. This chapter explores the media as discourse in the course, called Spanish and the Press: Journalism on the Web, in Television, Radio, and Print.

In my thirty-eight years of teaching experience, twenty-two of them in Argentina, I have used the direct method, the audiolingual method, and functional and communicative approaches (see chapter 1, this volume). As Willis points out in chapter 1, each of these methods developed as a reaction to the method in vogue, when it failed to fulfill the expectations for competence in a foreign language. Nevertheless, each method has contributed to the development of certain skills better than others, and as a consequence, the summation of "the parts that work" from each method are what I now use. It is the content-based and task-based approaches that allow me the freedom to incorporate strategies from the various methods when needed.

In the 1960s, authentic materials available for teaching included only a few records, primarily songs, and tapes for pronunciation and intonation. In the 1970s, videos became available, and finally came the explosion of authentic multimedia materials that the Web and satellite television now provide. At the same time, technical advances have made it possible to use computers, camcorders, and other instruments as tools for the creation of one's own material. Each of these methods and aids has influenced the way I teach, and as result I see myself applying strategies that best suit the students in each class. Most recently, I have incorporated large measures of task-based instruction into this eclectic mixture. As Stevens writes in chapter 10 of this volume, technology can be used to assist the teacher in cost-effective ways and at the same time be task-driven and student-centered: "Technology is a vehicle through which the most viable pedagogical principles can be delivered so as to optimize their impact and success."

## THE DECISION FOR TASK-BASED INSTRUCTION

One of the definitions of content-based instruction suggests that an important component of CBI is adapting the program to the needs and interests of students (Stryker and Leaver 1997). The nature of Yale, the types of students it enrolls, and the need for learner-centered instruction in Yale's upper level Spanish classes prompted the selection of TBI as the teaching approach.

### The Institution

Yale University is a private institution with approximately 5,000 undergraduate and 5,000 graduate students. The undergraduate students are randomly divided into twelve residential colleges on their admission, while the instruction is concentrated in traditional departments. The curriculum is oriented toward all students achieving a broad-based education in contrast to a heavy specialization in one topic. Yale admissions policies are designed to ensure a racially diverse student body. Prospective students have outstanding academic records and wide-ranging interests.

### The Nature of the Spanish Language Program

In describing the pedagogical and philosophical rationale behind the program, Crocetti (2003) says:

> The Spanish Language Program at Yale University endorses a humanistic approach to foreign language teaching, which is interpreted as the holistic development of the student through language learning. Humanistic strategies imply the internalization of language through the application of

cognitive and affective principles of human learning. The program uses an eclectic approach via a multiplicity of teaching modes in order to facilitate the learning process of each particular individual. Instruction is planned to be meaningful and interactive while considering students' needs and interests. A communicative approach is emphasized in developing student foreign language proficiency, establishing guidelines, and defining objectives. At Yale, language teaching goes beyond a pragmatic view of service, and the Department of Spanish promotes a holistic approach to teaching as a way to know oneself and others better. Careful selection of authentic linguistic, audiovisual and multimedia material occurs at all levels. Further, the body of literary works is considered to be within the paradigm of foreign language instruction. It is also a goal that the literary language be used correctly and appropriately.

To accomplish all this, foreign language learning and teaching includes more than linguistic competence and informal discourse alone, bringing the "real world" into the classroom, as described by Willis in chapter 1 of this volume, where she refers to tasks as *replication activities*.

### Students

Some students arrive with their two-year language requirement already fulfilled as a result of receiving an Advanced Placement test score of 4 or 5. The Yale Spanish-language proficiency test generally places these students at a mid-intermediate level, where a wide range of tasks, including authentic ones, are possible to use in the classroom. Because the proficiency test sets high standards for third-year students, TBI was seen by them as a vehicle to facilitate the achievement of such standards.

Among undergraduate students are individuals interested in expanding the study of Spanish to subjects related to their majors, such as international studies, law, or medicine. In addition, these students are generally interested in traveling abroad, whether for a summer program or semester. For these students, the ability to handle specific subject matter in authentic ways is important.

## Development and Implementation of CBI-TBI

The materials selection as well as the teacher's preparations for TBI courses poses many difficulties because there are no suitable textbooks and teachers must do extensive research to be able to collect relevant documents, newspapers, magazines, videos, or radio programs for the course.

### MATERIALS SELECTION

TBI courses typically require the use of authentic materials, as noted by all of the authors in this volume. Such materials are generally available for Spanish. However, in the selection process for the new CBI-TBI courses, certain considerations were important. These included (1) an appropriate level of textual and contextual difficulty, (2) an appropriate reliance on background knowledge (i.e., only a moderate amount of unknown schemata), and (3) the extent of technical language and knowledge used by the author.

Consequently, for my course on journalism, in addition to linguistic, literary and traditional materials, I chose Latin American and Spanish articles from newspapers, magazines, radio, television and the Internet that convey useful information in a field and do not state the obvious. This approach permitted selection from a wide range of media resources, not only in twenty-two countries where Spanish is the dominant language, but in other countries where some communities publish in Spanish (e.g., in the United States, France, Italy, and elsewhere).

## FACULTY PREPARATION

To prepare for teaching this course, I researched manuals on journalism and textbooks used by the Schools of Journalism in Argentina, Mexico, and Spain. My interests were to study (1) the characteristics of journalistic discourse; (2) how to write news, chronicles, columns, editorials, and interviews for a newspaper; and (3) how to write a radio or television script, and then how to produce and deliver the outcome. Keeping in mind that the goal of TBI is to advance the students' command of the language, I selected those activities that would provide an effective source of relevant activities that would involve all four language skills.

## TOPICS AND ASSIGNMENTS

If we are to capture the students' interest and stretch their minds, then the material needs to elicit strong responses and generate controversy so that they can develop their critical thinking skills. Journalistic discourse is ideal for this subject, since it offers a wide range of styles and registers that can be explored in other fields of studies.

Though the media provides up-to-date information, the content topics need to be selected carefully for several reasons. It is not practical to change the syllabus in its entirety every year nor should students be presented with dated material that is no longer relevant for discussion in class. Additionally, as mentioned earlier, the material should reflect student's interests. Many of the well-known and prestigious Spanish writers such as Gabriel García Marquez, Mario Vargas Llosa, Arturo Pérez Reverte, and Rosa Montero are, or were, very successful journalists who contribute columns, editorials, chronicles, and short stories to the principal newspapers in the Spanish-speaking world. Moreover, their literary works sometimes are journalistically formatted.

Materials were selected in accordance with the guidelines recommended by Lazar (1993). Texts that were selected were based on content with universal interests that go beyond everyday concerns. These include topics such as globalization, corruption, violence, life, death, hate, and love (see Antokhin et al. in chapter 9, this volume).

The articles should be well written and relevant to social and political issues that are of common interest in the Spanish world (e.g., corruption at different levels of society or government). These topics are then contrasted and compared in the different Spanish-speaking countries. Some materials that I select are specifically related to journalism, such as libel, yellow journalism, censorship, and right of privacy. These topics are frequently reported in the media and are an invaluable source to exemplify the impact caused by the choice of words, gradation of adjectives, and lexical distinctions. Other topics include the power of the press, hackers, cloning, and globalization—up-to-date topics that generate a lot of discussion and can be easily updated.

### TASKS BASED ON MEDIA GENRES

In chapter 2 of this volume, Leaver and Kaplan point out that "a task is an activity conducted in the foreign language and results in a tangible product." In my class, the "tangible product" is a journalistic work. As mentioned earlier, students in this course are generally at the intermediate midlevel of proficiency. At this level, they are able to ask and answer questions, participate in conversations about their most immediate needs, narrate, and describe in a simple way. Their errors are evident; their vocabulary is limited; and they struggle to find the correct language forms. It is essential that the text not only conveys useful content and forms, but also that it lends itself to a pedagogical purpose or has the "capacity for didacticization" (see Antokhin et al. in chapter 9).

### Task Preparation

To organize the learning tasks, I start by analyzing the functions that, in addition to describing and narrating, would enable to students to identify the different types of journalistic writings. To accurately interpret the intention of the writer in a chronicle, column, editorial, advertisement, or interview, the student should be able to identify when the language is used to argue, inquire, request, persuade, advise, praise, condemn, doubt, deny, and the like. These activities require the ability to synthesize information in the case of the news and analyze or evaluate for a column. This involves the use of some grammatical element, such as the subjunctive mood, sequence of tenses, lexical distinction, position, gradation, and connotation of adjectives.

The tasks are presented in a gradual way, generally in the form of detailed tables or charts that help in the identification of the different kind of texts, elements, organization and then proceed to the creative production. The intention is to integrate skills and discourse features divided into tasks that involve a variety of reading skills such as skimming, scanning, extracting points for summarizing, titles, captions, introductory paragraphs, and other journalistic features (see Antokhin et al. in chapter 9 of this volume). The final task is the preparation of news, narrative, descriptive, commentative, and argumentative segments, as well as dialogue scenes for a chronicle, column, editorial, or interview. These evaluation tasks involve the student in developing an opinion based on subjective and objective criteria and critical thinking, as well as collecting research data, as described by Leaver and Kaplan in chapter 2. In addition, choices need to be made for the appropriate headings, captions, and visual materials. In each journalistic task we stress the importance of the use of the appropriate language for a written or broadcast presentation on a given topic with preparatory exercises to highlight the specific vocabulary and grammar needed for the topic in hand.

With respect to news format, we study the relationship among the heading, news, graphics, and content, as well as the treatment of flowcharts, maps, plans, and diagrams. We start with an analysis of the news to determine whether an event pertains to the public domain or constitutes a private issue. We establish the sources of information, their reliability, and the impact that they might have on public opinion. When reporting news, it is necessary for students to understand the importance of precision, clarity, coherence, impartiality, and integrity. Those aspects are also indispensable tools in advancing language students to a higher level of competence and accuracy in all four skills.

A news story can be presented in three alternative forms of chronological order: (1) Chronological Pyramid, in order of relevance of the major points; (2) Inverted Pyramid, a summary of the major points told in the first sentence or paragraph with details expounded in chronological order; and (3) Modified Pyramid. The media most commonly use the latter approach. News is written as concisely as possible by responding to the questions—who, what, when, where, why, and how—and avoiding the obvious. Long sentences and adjectives that may be viewed as biased should be avoided. The language should be clear and the number of words minimized. Again, these are also key elements in learning a second language to a higher proficiency level and involve striving for precision and elimination of paraphrasing.

To prepare for the news tasks, students are expected to do the following:

1. read the journalistic explanation from a manual;
2. identify the characteristics in papers or on the Web;
3. give the appropriate heading to a given text; and
4. change a song, a historical text, an advertisement, or a novel into news.

For example, students read the prologue and first chapter of the novel by Gabriel García Márquez, *Noticia de un secuestro*, which is based on a real kidnapping of journalists and politically influential people in Colombia. They then prepare a news article as it might have appeared in a paper in Colombia or the United States at the time. This leads to discussions in class about the present situation in Colombia, research on the latest conflicts and debates over social and political issues related to safety, freedom of speech, personal guarantees, putting the news in the context of previous events, and listing the possible reasons that led to the kidnapping. All these items help with the analysis and understanding of the events by creating an informed perspective of the issues.

Generally the debates are conducted in what we called *mesa de redacción* (newsroom), and they would constitute what Willis (chapter 1, this volume) would call "a replication activity." The students bring the information they have found on the specific topic "kidnappings in Colombia," and they discuss it as if they were journalists on an assignment, devoting some time to talk about similarities and differences in other regions, while the teacher goes from group to group helping them with the task, correcting errors in a natural way, or providing the appropriate lexical item, a process similar to that described by Leaver and Kaplan (chapter 2). Finally, in groups or pairs they give a short oral report based on the analysis of the stories, bringing together the news and their views while trying to distinguish both clearly. This involves moving from narrating and retelling to expressing opinion, which requires more complex grammatical features. Macías (chapter 7, this volume) describes the role of the teacher as "being a bridge which helps facilitate communication and learning in this new language." At higher levels, the teacher continues being that "bridge" when presenting the journalistic conventions, while the students rearrange the content and meaning.

### Chronicle

When reading chronicles, the students identify the category of each chronicle, (historical, war, travels, etc.) and determine whether or not it follows chronological order. The various segments—narrative, descriptive, commentative, and dialogue—are identified. The connectors that have been used must be recognized, as well as the role that the title, photos, captions, and other graphics play as resources to present the information in a better way. We concentrate on the study of the commentative segment, that is, how the writer or presenter introduces his own comments on the story that has been told, the journalist's resources when including the summary, the role-played by photos, infographics, and so on. For example, we discussed the story of a young hacker. The students searched for information on the latest occurrences of hacking in Spanish newspapers, such as *El País* or *La Jornada*, and reported on them to the class. On the basis of students' readings, we made a list of vocabulary needed to explain the subject: (1) the different kinds of hackers and their actions, (2) the consequences of their actions, (3) the hackers' motivations, and (4) the publics' reactions or opinions. The students explore and debate the moral and ethical concerns and the damage caused by the hackers to determine whether they would justify or condemn the hackers' behavior. The next step is to write a commentary segment that would be added to the story based on the class debate, incorporating the vocabulary and the expressions used in class. For a sample lesson based on a "chronicle," see appendix A to this chapter.

The final work is an interview that the student prepares during the last month of classes. Each earlier assignment is designed to fulfill a specific partial objective. The combination of these constitutes a complex task that involves all of the skills in this final interview project. I have explored this genre by videotaping interviews of professional journalists in Argentina, Chile, and Uruguay. These serve as an important visual component of the class throughout the semester, because it is authentic material designed for the classroom and used for improving comprehension, instigating debate about the interview topics, and providing models of interviews.

The native speakers who are accessible to Yale students for interviews come from the Yale University campus, professors, graduate students, and even foreign undergraduates or members of the local community. I divide the interview project into three stages.

*Stage one.* The students choose professionals or relevant native people in the subject of their major or field of interest and assemble the résumé of the person to be interviewed, related material, and a bibliography on their subject. Each student must bring the materials to a meeting with the instructor where they justify their selection. Each week in class, the students make a short report of their work in progress and gather ideas from the other students.

*Stage two.* The students prepare questions for the interview and then meet with the interviewee and tape the responses using tape recorders and cameras for the visual component that are provided by the Center for Language Study at Yale University. This process constitutes a real-life transmission of information in the target language from person to person (see information-gap principle, Alosh, chapter 5, this volume).

*Stage three.* The students select, transcribe, and organize the interview following appropriate journalistic conventions.

*Stage four.* Students write the introduction, descriptive and narrative segments, conclusion, and choose the heading and visual components.

This interview project has many similarities to that used by Lys for her Advanced German course (chapter 11, this volume) and is supported by a similar rationale.

For an example of a sample assessment paper for the interview task, see appendix B to this chapter.

### HANDLING GRAMMAR AND VOCABULARY

At the intermediate midlevel of proficiency, the speech of many students contains fossilized errors. In some cases, their fluency results in their inability to recognize their errors (see Leaver and Kaplan, chapter 2), while in others their lack of confidence in language skills slows down their performance. Although students have been exposed to most of the important grammatical aspects of the language system by this time, they frequently ignore the rules of syntax. They also lack vocabulary, or use it in an imprecise way, which makes it even more necessary to devote time to lexical distinctions, as well as to increase the active vocabulary related to specific topics. We generally review those grammatical aspects needed to fulfill a task-related function. Examples include the following:

- the sequence of tenses needed to narrate news;
- the use of the subjunctive to express an opinion or reaction to information or text as would be needed to write a column;
- the use of the conditional to "spread rumors" or to indicate that something is not confirmed by reliable sources;
- the use of an adjective, and how its meaning changes according to its position and its intensifiers—this especially helps them to understand yellow journalism;
- the use of the present tense, instead of the preterit or the preterit perfect in Spanish television to narrate events; and
- the use of gerunds, active or passive voices (*pasiva con se*) when giving a title to an article or a presentation.

In all cases, the grammar point is not presented in isolation, but rather examples of it are extracted from the passage or article that is being read and are focused on in the related tasks and exercises.

One of my main concerns is that most of the time the students seem to have good fluency in the language but continue to make the same basic mistakes. Up until now, I have found that self-correction, peer correction, and the keeping of a journal do work to some extent, but only when these are monitored by the teacher and the students are highly motivated. In some cases, the strategy is to subordinate fluency to accuracy in order to push a higher level of sophistication in the use of the language (Leaver and Kaplan, chapter 2).

As mentioned earlier, the class becomes a newsroom, where the students work in pairs or groups on a project. They write a title for an editorial, transform a story into news for a radio program, or make a questionnaire for an interview. To help with reviewing and correction in this environment, I prepare evaluation forms that call their attention not only to the grammatical aspects but also to the format and style of the particular exercise (news and column).

The teaching of vocabulary depends on the purpose that the lexical items fulfill. Some vocabulary is extracted from the readings and is only presented for the purpose of understanding the article. Some is selected because of its frequency, and students are encouraged to put this to active use. In addition, the journalistic terminology that is needed to work with the specific subject is provided through technical journalistic readings. (See Antokhin et al., chapter 9, for language and discourse forms.) Using exercises on synonyms and antonyms, noun and adjective formation, and idiomatic expressions enhances the student's awareness of grammatical correctness. If the students are forced to avoid paraphrasing and use the appropriate term, they are likely to become more accurate in the use of the language (see Leaver and Kaplan, chapter 2, this volume).

### GRADING

The system used for grading is as follows:

1. Attendance and participation          20 percent
2. Two group workshops (*debate de prensa*, 10 percent each)    20 percent
3. One short paper (*formato prensa escrita: entrevista*)    20 percent[a]
4. One oral presentation (*programa de radio*)    10 percent[a]
5. Written (*noticia y columna*, 5 percent each) and workbook homework    30 percent[a]

[a]Written and oral production of your own journalistic texts.

Testing in TBI poses a number of difficulties, because the students are asked to apply what they have learned to create and express meanings, instead of being tested on memorized items. The preparation of these proficiency tests involves more complex processes (for ideas on task-based testing, see Passos de Oliveira, chapter 12, this volume).

## Evaluation

It is noticeable that the challenge carrying out specific tasks in the second language gives the students self-assurance and at the same time triggers an awareness of details that fosters language proficiency.

### LANGUAGE IMPROVEMENT

The results of TBI have been very rewarding in our program. Creative tasks, such as writing a chronicle or a column after debating issues, presenting an opinion, recording a radio program, or conducting an interview, are implemented within the journalistic framework, which helps to improve language proficiency. The rehearsing required to speak in real time with the correct diction and appropriate intonation, for example, for a radio program, develops "automaticity which leads to fluency" (Willis, chapter 1). In my personal experience, I have seen students' increased awareness of the connotative and denotative language, as well as the understanding of the need for precision in the choice of words and expressions when dealing with a particular function.

### STUDENT SATISFACTION

There has been positive feedback from the students. They see the tasks as a tool that helps them carry out specific real-life activities, such as interviewing professionals or relevant people for their final essays in other subjects.

By learning some of the principles of journalistic discourse, students develop an awareness of the incredible amount of material that can be found in newspapers, broadcasts, Web sites, and archives. They begin to understand that they provide useful ideas, different points of view and thoughts on a variety of issues, and that they help to identify reliable sources of information. Furthermore, journalism helps the students to delve deeply into other disciplines such as history, political science, and the arts, to name just a few. Therefore, this course is interdisciplinary because we research, read, write, and debate about different topics that are part of several disciplines. All these benefits appeal to students.

The students participate enthusiastically in group projects, such as writing scripts for television scenes that they later perform. They enjoy the preparation and recording of radio programs in the professional studio at the Yale Center for Language Study, which is done with the support of the technical and professional staff. At first, they feel a little intimidated by the fact that each of them has to interview a native speaker (generally a professional) for their final work, but as the work progresses, they become engaged, generally because they feel comfortable once they meet the person they are going to interview. They report learning a great deal about the particular subject and having very interesting experiences. For example, one student interviewed an Argentine dancer in New York and was invited to the rehearsal of *Aida*, while others interviewed a Spanish CNN reporter in Atlanta, an adviser to the New Haven mayor, the dean of the faculty of psychology, a historian, and a graduate student working on a dissertation on Cuban religions.

Some of the comments of the students on the course evaluation for this class were:

- I would absolutely recommend it (this class). It helps writing and verbal skills in Spanish, but also teaches more universal lessons about the press and current topics of debate.
- This course is engaging and informative.
- The final project was really fun and very helpful in terms of practicing language skills.
- I feel I learned more about newspapers and the different types of articles featured. My favorite part of the course was that there was a lot of group work, which I feel is an effective way to learn without putting too much pressure on each individual.
- The subject matter was very interesting. I think I definitely learned a lot and improved my Spanish. I thought some of the projects were a bit too time-consuming, like the radio project. And at times, there was too much reading, but overall, the reading was interesting.
- It is an interesting way to improve your Spanish and learn a little about journalism.

## Next Steps

It is very difficult to keep the materials updated for a course on the media when the content is continuously changing. However, there are some very useful textbooks on journalism that can be adapted for teaching second languages.

### IMPROVED MATERIAL SELECTION

I was very concerned at the beginning about the selection of readings, and I am still researching the field of journalism to improve on them. I have been experimenting with different journalistic formats that might be suitable for language practice and help with accuracy and competence. I am satisfied with the use of news, columns, opinions, radio debates, magazines, and interviews because they demand precision, clarity, and coherence and involve all the skills.

### PUBLICATION OF STUDENT WORK

I have also made contacts with several small Latin American newspapers trying to publish some of the students' works in a real paper, in addition to looking for students of journalism that would correspond with our students. During the summer of 2002, with a grant and support from the Center for Language Study at Yale University (CLS), I made a DVD with interviews of Latin American journalists and professionals. I use the CLS template Vision to put the DVD material on the Web and plan to use the CLS Craft template to access the media.

## Conclusion

My observations are that when trying to fulfill a real-life task, students acquire a deeper understanding of the language, which as a result leads to higher proficiency. When completing a task outside the class, they become aware of their strengths and weaknesses. For example, in preparing the questionnaire for the interview, some students realized that they needed help in formulating specific points that were critical for their task. Other students brought their recorded interviews to me because they were unable to understand the nuances of a specific expression used by the interviewee. I found that students were able to attain higher levels of sophistication and precision in the use of the language as well as gaining deeper content knowledge when they were dealing with subjects related to their major.

This combination of TBI and CBI lets the students work at their own pace and focus on their weaknesses and at the same time it allows the teacher to give attention to the individuals who most need the help. The use of authentic material has the advantage of dealing with current issues as well as new language expressions that appear in response to social, economic, and political issues. In other words, the language and content are alive instead of being dated. The analysis of journalistic discourse helps to identify not only the organization of the text, radio, television, or video presentation but also the specific linguistic devices and the lexical and grammatical elements. Finally, the integration of language and discourse obliges the student to distinguish journalism from other types of discourse and this is conducive to better proficiency.

## Appendix A: Sample TBI Lesson: Chronicle

### RESUMEN "LA CRÓNICA" (TENEWICKI 1995)

La crónica es el género más específico cuando se relata un acontecimiento con desarrollo. Da la ilusión de un desarollo cronológico. Es el más literario de los géneros. Tiene procedimientos típicos del discurso narrativo. Se usaba para la noticia hasta que apareció la pirámide invertida en Estados Unidos pero todavía se usa cuando ésta se hace insuficiente.

### PARTES DE LA CRÓNICA

¿Qué partes puede tener una crónica y cuáles son las características principales?

a. narración: Usa el pretérito o el presente histórico.

b. descripción: Proceso, espectáculo, justifica los hechos y la psicología de los personajes.

c. comentario: Nexos (sin embargo, además) transición de la narración al comentario coherentemente. Aparece como síntesis, da idea que el periodista está allí. Adjetivación subjetiva.

d. diálogo: Menos frecuentes. En estilo directo/ indirecto o narrativizado.

### CRÓNICAS VARIAS

Hay crónicas según el enfoque, el tema, y el estilo. Puede ser crónica urbana, sentimental, especializada, de interés humano, de humor, de color, de deporte, etc.

**Recursos gráficos que se utilizan**

Título, volanta, copete, destacado, foto, y epígrafe.

**Tasks**

  I. Responda el cuestionario sobre la crónica siguiendo la guía del paquete.
 II. Identifique elementos y partes de la crónica en Antoni Masso, *Diario de un cibernauta*.
III. Identifique tipos de crónicas según su formato y contenido en periódicos y revistas.
 IV. Identifique segmentos narrativos, descriptivos, comentativos y dialogados.
  V. Analice los recursos gráficos.
 VI. Torbellino de ideas (para trabajar en clase). Leer la informacíon extraíde del *New York Times*:

En julio de 1998 el grupo L0pht se presentó ante el comité de asuntos gubernamentales del Senado e informó sobre una cantidad de errores o fallas en el sistema de seguridad de oficinas públicas y privadas. El senador Lieberman calificó el hecho como "acto de patriotismo y los comparó con el servicio prestado a la nación por Rachel Carson y Paul Revere."

Según el *New York Times* del 26 de mayo de 1999 grupos como Global Hell y Masters pusieron en aprieto a los expertos en computación. Los piratas llenaron de insultos y obscenidades el sistema como venganza por la investigación del FBI, el Senado y la Casa Blanca y tuvieron que cerrarlo. Probablemente los adolescentes expresan de esta manera su rebelión como antes lo hacían con el graffiti.

**Debate sobre el tema y práctica de vocabulario**

¿Existen piratas buenos y malos en la realidad?

¿Qué puede hacer un pirata informático? robar información; cambiar archivos; interferir en operaciones bancarias; espionaje; desconectar el sistema operativo de una central eléctrica; otros.

¿Cómo se autodefinen, se describen o justifican sus acciones los distintos grupos?

¿Cuáles son sus propósitos? (moral, ético, ambiguo, destructivo, educativo)

¿Qué tipo de trabajos que desempeñan?

¿Cuál es su futuro? (¿Inventores como Jobs and Wozniak de Apple?)

¿Quiénes son los piratas informáticos? ¿Ególatras? ¿Gente con una moral muy particular? ¿Genios del bien o del mal? ¿Delincuentes? ¿Rebeldes o inadaptados sociales?

VII. Busque una noticia sobre los hackers en la red y escriba un segmento comentativo de no más de 80 palabras. Siga las indicaciones de los modelos analizados (pp. 114 y115) y *Organizadores discursivos* de la pág. 113. (Lorenzini and Ferman 1988)

## Appendix B: Final Paper (Sample)

### Guía para el trabajo final del curso: *La entrevista*

   I. Traiga su bosquejo a la oficina de la profesora en la semana del 3 de noviembre (nombre y CV del entrevistado, justifique su selección, tema, y bibliografía).

   II. Fecha de entrega: 6 de diciembre.

   III. Extensión: 1.200 palabras en columnas de 8 o 10 palabras cada una (ver modelos).

### Recomendaciones para el momento de la preparación

Elija una persona y fundamente por qué la ha elegido. (Agréguelo en su trabajo la reflexión o comentario personal.)

Busque todo el material disponible para conocer su vida y obra.

Pídale con anterioridad su curriculum vitae y le servirá para organizar su cuestionario.

### RECOMENDACIONES PARA EL MOMENTO DE LA ENTREVISTA

Sáquele o pídale fotos y material ilustrativo use una grabadora para registrar toda la conversación.

Siga su cuestionario pero tenga en cuenta aquellos aspectos en los que la persona se extiende.

### Recomendaciones para el momento de la escritura

Consulte fuentes de información en la red.

Determine qué clase de entrevista va a escribir y docuséntese.

Elija el título, el formato y la sección en la que puede aparecer su entravista.

Seleccione el material que irá en la introdución, el cuerpo y la conclusión.

Dele el título con una frase textual del entravistado que refleje el tema de la nota o bien escoja un título sugestivo.

No se olvide del material gráfico que ilustrará su entravista.

Seleccione los procedimientos que va a usar conforme a los ejemplos que ha escogido.

Elija el léxico y las formas gramaticales más adecuadas.

Tenga cuidado con los tiempos verbales, uso de pronombres, género y número de los sustantivos, secuencia de tiempos, etc.

No escriba lo obvio ni repita conceptos.

   IV. Incluya en su entrevista (table 3.1)

TABLE 3.1  **Diagrama de la entrevista**

**Tema central de la entrevista**

Título; bajada; copete.

Foto; epígrafe; destacados.

Datos biográficos o descripción provistos por el entrevistador en la introducción y los segmentos narrativos.

**Segmentos**

Narrativo; comentativo; descriptivo (dos procedimientos argumentativos).

Estilo de la presentación de las palabras del entrevistado (lenguage directo o indirecto).

Explicaciones, referencias o reflexiones del periodista.

**Conclusión**

Para la evaluación se tendrá en cuenta:

| | |
|---|---|
| —La documentación y precisión de datos expuestos | 30 |
| —El estilo y formato | 10 |
| —La selección del título y el lenguaje apropiado | 10 |
| —Los actos de habla del procedimiento argumentativo | 20 |
| —El uso de expresiones adecuadas, tiempos verbales y corrección gramatical | 20 |
| —Originalidad | 10 |
| | 100 |

# 4

## INTRODUCING TBI FOR TEACHING ENGLISH IN BRAZIL: LEARNING HOW TO LEAP THE HURDLES

Juarez Lopes

EDITORS' NOTE: In this chapter, Juarez Lopes describes how an English-language program structured in accordance with the principles of task-based instruction (or, in that case, task-based learning) was introduced and implemented in a private school in the south of Brazil. The result of this change in approaches met with extraordinary success: a small program grew to more than 1,000 students. The details of the process, the problems, and the solutions that Juarez Lopes discusses here are remarkable. We anticipate that other programs will be able to use the details provided to help structure their own programs in task-based instruction and generate the same kind of enthusiasm among their students.

This chapter describes the introduction of a task-based instruction (TBI) approach to teaching English in a private language school in the south of Brazil, where teachers had been used to following a presentation–practice–production (PPP) approach. (The PPP approach to teaching English rests on a behaviorist theory of language learning; for more on PPP, see chapters 1 and 12 in this volume.) The school began life in two small classrooms, but, due to the success of TBI among the English student community, it grew into a school of 1,000 students over a period of five years.

The chapter records the process of change during the introduction of the new courses. It illustrates briefly the types of tasks that were well received and those that were less popular with students. It outlines the problems that occurred while introducing a TBI method, what caused them, and how they were overcome. To the extent possible, it shows how deeply and extensively TBI was accepted by the end of the project. Finally, it summarizes recommendations for teachers considering the adoption of a TBI approach.

## Description of Institution and Student Population

The project took place in a private English school, called British House. In Brazil, as a whole, students study English in their regular (public) schools. However, the teaching is not always very efficient, so students who are highly motivated and recognize the importance of English to their future career or other plans look for a private English school. Such schools, of which British House is one, have proliferated in Brazil in response to high demand.

At the time, most of our students were either adolescents who were forced to study English by their parents, or young university students who needed English for academic purposes. We also had adults who needed English for professional reasons. Most students had previously encountered frustration and even lack of success in learning English and were willing to try something new.

The teaching team consisted of a group of highly trained teachers who had just finished their third teacher development course using PPP. This chapter will show how they were able to change their teaching practices and adapt their instruction to a TBI approach.

## The Beginnings of Change: Making the Decision for TBI

The decision to change from the PPP approach to TBI was taken when we (the institute's director and I, as director of studies), concluded that the former approach was ineffective. Two reasons were posed for dissatisfaction with the previous approach. These were the following:

- PPP did not produce the desired enrollment statistics; and
- PPP did not produce the desired learning outcomes.

Enrollment statistics was a serious problem for a for-profit school. PPP was not attracting new students. Students at other schools were not inclined to change schools because the curriculum was essentially the same.

Learning outcomes were also disappointing with PPP. Students tended to behave like parrots even in the "free" production stage where they would only repeat what had been drilled in the practice stage. We felt that PPP students would never have the opportunity, nor develop the ability, to express themselves "freely" in English. Because of this, we set out to look for something new—something that would attract new students who were interested in something different, and once they were with us, would feel that they were learning to communicate.

In our search, we came across a series of textbooks that used TBI as its basic methodology. The series had just been launched in Brazil, and we saw in it the marketing differential we were seeking. Although we had had no experience with it, the principles of TBI seemed to meet the requirements we had established for selecting a new teaching approach. However, PPP and the audiolingual method (ALM) were the approaches in vogue (and deeply entrenched) in local language programs. Introducing TBI into a community with this profile involved a high degree of risk; it was a radical decision, but we felt courageous enough to take it. The fact that no competitor knew that TBI existed, let alone how to use it, could turn out to be to our advantage.

Our main goal, then, was to provide our students with something new and different from what they were used to. It was not difficult to convince them to give TBI a try. Despite serious teething troubles, the new TBI courses proved to be popular with the students and soon became a very effective marketing differential in our town.

### The New Materials

The course we had selected was the Collins Cobuild English Course (CCEC) three-level series: books 1 (elementary), 2 (pre-intermediate) and 3 (intermediate). This series was chosen for the following reasons:

- It used a task-based methodology that rested on the principles that people learn a language most effectively by using the language to do things—to find out information, to solve problems, to talk about personal experiences, and so on.
- It had a lexical syllabus based on the 2,500 most common words of the English language. CCEC 1 introduced the first 700 words, CCEC 2 recycled these words and introduced another 950, and CCEC 3 recycled the previous words and introduced another 900 words. The recycling of words was accomplished through meaningful tasks.
- It was based on authentic material. All the reading texts were from authentic sources (e.g., see the text-based task activity in appendix A to this chapter) and the recordings were unscripted, which gave a very rich input of natural language (see the transcript in appendix B to this chapter).
- It approached grammar in a communicative, rather than structural, way. The titles of all the units are related to a topic, not to a grammar feature. The lessons first required students to speak and then finally to analyze grammar. The textbooks followed the principle that grammar features can be learned holistically (through exposure to and practice with the language), rather than taught explicitly as separate items.
- The tasks were interesting and would be meaningful to students.

The books were divided into the following hours of teaching: CCEC 1 was done in 120 hours, CCEC 2 in 120 hours, and CCEC 3 in 150 hours. The methodology used was similar to the Willis task-based learning (TBL) framework shown in chapter 1 appendix B. It included the following elements:

1. Pretask (introduction to topic and explanation or rehearsal of the task).
2. Task cycle: Learners do task > plan their report > report to class on task results (learners may then listen to a recording of fluent speakers doing the task).
3. Language focus: analysis and practice (based on transcripts or texts).
4. Optional repetition of the same task with a different partner.

## The Process of Change: Initial Stages

In the beginning, we were aware that TBI existed as an approach, but we did not really know how to use it. We accepted the challenge of starting to use a task-based book and devised an initial familiarization course for TBI teachers.

Despite our best efforts and planning, the first semester was rather chaotic. We started the semester with eighty students, and by the beginning of the second semester we had already lost fifty of them. In assessing the needs of the thirty students who remained enrolled, along with another forty who joined the group later, and the issues related to implementing TBI during the first semester, we found ourselves at a crossroads: we could either abandon our innovation and retreat to PPP, or we could stay with TBI and treat the problems as a challenge for teaching and as a business risk. We chose to continue with TBI and never regretted that decision. In retrospect, we all realized how much we benefited from our decision to take that risk.

At first, the program was used with adult learners. Later, we introduced it into courses for adolescents, some as young as twelve years old. Teachers from other programs in Brazil whom we subsequently met at conferences could hardly believe we were using TBI successfully with adolescents. So, we finally took a video recording of a class using Collins Cobuild 3 to one of these conferences and showed colleagues what we were doing.

### TASKS USED

The most popular tasks among students were ones they could relate to their own lives. For example, elementary students really enjoyed a set of tasks where they had to talk about their families. At the pretask stage, teachers would tell the class about their own families, maybe drawing their family trees on the board and talking about them, and also writing up useful words and phrases. The first task the students did in this series was to ask their partner questions and create a family tree for their partner's family, after which they reported their findings to the rest of the class. This, in turn, led into a class survey where they found out what proportion of families had more boys/men than girls/women. After completing these tasks, students listened to recordings of native speakers doing the same task and comparing the size of their families. The transcripts from these recordings provided the data for a "language focus" phase, where students looked for and classified verb phrases with got or words ending in "s." See appendixes A and B to this chapter for samples of transcripts and consciousness-raising exercises.

Level 1 students also enjoyed tasks that involved an element of competition or challenge, such as "Find the Differences." Two students were each provided with a picture. The two pictures were basically the same but had a number of differences in the details. At the task stage, students had to find seven differences between their pictures but they were not allowed to look at each other's pictures; they had to speak to one another in English to establish the differences. The teacher provided students with a model at the pretask stage. After the task, at the planning stage, students planned, with teacher guidance, how to report their differences to the whole class. At the report stage, students told the rest of the class about the differences they had found, listening to each other to find out how many differences there were in total (there were always more than seven differences, so each pair would find different ones). After this, they would listen to two native speakers performing a similar task, and they would have to tick off the differences in their pictures, determining whether they had missed any. Students then analyzed specific features of the language used by the native speakers, both listening to the recording and studying the transcripts, and practiced useful phrases and patterns. (See samples in appendix C to this chapter.)

Both task types described above were popular among the students, as they were able to see the relevance of the language they used for the tasks to the language needed in their own lives. The kind of tasks that were not popular at all with the students were the ones they were less able to relate to their own lives. An example of this is the task in CCEC 3 in which students had to listen to someone talking about a leopard in a game park in Africa that almost attacked his family, and subsequently talk about leopards from the point of view of conservation. Students did not see any reason for talking about leopards since they regarded the situation as too far removed from their own lives. They were also unhappy about tasks based on the texts of "funny" stories and jokes from sources in popular magazines like the *Reader's Digest*. The stories were far removed from their own lives and even with careful advance preparation they often found them a frustrating experience as they could rarely guess the punch lines or understand when teachers were obliged to explain the joke.

## Problems and Solutions: Change of Focus—From Grammar to Meaning

Students were not used to having to speak first and then analyze grammar. They all came from a tradition in which they were presented with a grammar item first, then practiced this item in a controlled way, and finally had a "free production stage" where they would, in theory, have the opportunity to practice that item of grammar in a less controlled way. Not only were the students used to this PPP approach, but so were the teachers. Consequently, teachers were tempted to insert a grammar presentation stage into the lesson before doing the task from the book. We realized that this was contrary to the intentions of the coursebook writers and that we had to convince our teachers of the value of TBI, as well as to teach them to use TBI in the way it was intended. Without this, they would be unable to motivate their students.

A solid theoretical background in TBI was needed by the teachers. A week's intensive teacher development course was devised, with three hours in the morning for input and three hours in the afternoon for teaching practice and feedback. The first session of the course was dedicated to reading about the approach. We used an article called "TBI: Is It PPP Upside Down?" (Willis 1994). This title provided teachers with their first question which would need to be answered at a later stage.

If we were to be successful in converting our teachers to a TBI approach, we also needed to use a TBI approach in our teacher development sessions. The task we devised for teachers reading this article consisted of comparing what happens during the three steps of the PPP cycle (presentation, practice, production) with the three main phases of the Willis TBL framework, (pretask, task cycle, and language focus) with its three- or four-step Task Cycle (task, planning, report plus listening). This would help them to answer the question *Is it PPP upside down?* Our aim in comparing the steps of both approaches was to focus on the differences between these approaches and show teachers that we would have to start planning our classes in a different way—and that it was entirely possible for them to do so.

Possibly the most difficult thing at this stage was to convince teachers that there was a change in focus. PPP starts by introducing language, for example an item of grammar, which is practiced by students following the explanation. The TBI model that we used starts by introducing the topic of the task. Taking the structure "have got" as an example, PPP provides a grammatical explanation of the structure, then has students practice using its affirmative, negative, and interrogative forms in drill-like exercises, and, in the final stage, asks students to talk about their families, using "have got," as in "I have got a sister and two brothers." PPP first breaks down the new language and then expects students to put it into practice. TBI is the opposite. The language students will need to perform in the task stage is introduced by teachers talking about the topic holistically and in a less formal, more lexicalized, way. Taking the example of the family, the teacher would introduce the topic by telling the students about his or her own family, introducing useful words and phrases. Students would then follow the teacher's example and use the same kind of language to talk about their own families. Students first use the language to mean things and then analyze and practice the language used by fluent speakers doing the same task. This new focus was made very clear to teachers through examples using both approaches and by analysis of textbooks.

## COPING WITH ANXIETY

Another difficulty that we had was the feeling of anxiety, in teachers as well as in students. Teachers were not able to hold back and allow students to express themselves freely. They believed that accuracy must come before fluency, so they felt they should interrupt if students made errors. On the other hand, students were not used to this amount of freedom and felt anxious about performing the task. They thought they would not be able to perform the task without being taught a particular grammar item beforehand.

The students' problem was overcome by explaining to them on the first day of classes how the approach worked. We listed all the steps of a TBI cycle on the board and provided details about each of them. For example, we pointed out which steps promoted fluency and meaning-focused communication, where mistakes did not matter (pretask and task stages), and which steps needed more emphasis on accuracy in addition to fluency (planning and report stages). This explanation needed to be constantly recycled in order for students to assimilate and accept it. We began to use the name of the stage when we introduced the activities associated with it. At certain points during our classes, we would stop and ask students at which stage they thought we were. At first, they could not tell, but through constant recycling, there came a point when students were able to pinpoint the exact stage of the lesson. This made them feel more secure in class and trust the teacher, as they began to feel confident that the teacher knew what he or she was doing. Interestingly, Moser (2005) in Japan had the same problem. His solution was to give out to each learner, at the start of each new task-based lesson, a blank TBL framework diagram (called a "learning journal") with headings: pretask, task, planning, report, language focus. His learners had to identify what stage they were at, and then write language notes in the appropriate blank section. This also formed a partial record of their learning.

The problem of teacher anxiety took longer to be eliminated. Teachers were not used to watching their students struggling to find a word or to convey meaning in their own way. They were used to spoon feeding their students with language at all stages. This habit gradually decreased with the help of class observation and by videotaping classes for subsequent analysis. This meant we could take a good-humoured approach to our successes and failures, and gradually move in the right direction.

## VOCABULARY LEARNING

Students also complained about the fact that they were exposed to useful language at the introduction (pretask) stage, but when they got to the task stage they could not remember the vocabulary and phrases they needed. In order to overcome this problem, teachers were asked to write the phrases and words on the board so that students would be able to refer to them. Teachers would also leave a space on the board for new words or phrases that might appear during the task or planning stages. Using this aid, students felt more confident and performed better during the task stage. This has now become a commonly used technique. We also tracked vocabulary learning, introducing systematic vocabulary recycling, emphasizing words students had difficulty in remembering.

## PERCEPTIONS OF LONG-TERM PROGRESS

With TBI, learners are constantly acquiring new language. However, much of this is learned subconsciously, so learners are simply not aware of how much English they are learning. They get the feeling that they are not making progress and lose confidence. (See Leaver and Kaplan's description of a similar problem in their basic Czech course in chapter 2.)

To increase students' confidence in their rate of learning we came up with the idea of "class visits." Students at elementary and pre-intermediate levels were usually taught by teachers who had Portuguese as their first language. So, every three weeks, these students would receive a visit from one of our British teachers. The visit lasted forty to forty-five minutes. The British teacher would walk into the classroom, and the class teacher would simply sit down and observe the visit. The visitor would sit down with the students and get the students to talk about the topics they had covered in their tasks. For example, if they had learned how to talk about families, the visitor would ask students to tell him or her about their families. The visitor would also tell students about his or her own family and encourage questions The class visits were carefully prepared, and the visitor had a structured framework to follow. This framework was produced based on the syllabus of each level.

We had four aims for the class visit. First, to expose students to "real English" as spoken by a native speaker. Sometimes students are only used to listening to native speakers of English on tapes or CDs and never get a chance to talk to a real native speaker of the language. Second, we wanted to show students that they were learning more and getting better. By being able to communicate with a native speaker, they were able to confirm for themselves that they were making progress. Third, we wanted to check how much learning was taking place. At the end of the visit, the class visitor would fill in a form giving names of particularly weak learners and any who had specific problems with grammar or pronunciation. This form would go the director of studies who would discuss the notes with the visitor. The director would decide whether the group needed extra practice or was learning as expected. We were also able to identify students who needed extra help outside class time, and these students would be called for special tutorials. In this way, we were able to identify weak students at the very beginning of the course and not just at the time of the tests. Our fourth aim was to promote the school. We were the only school in town that was able to offer this kind of activity; it was, in marketing terms, "a unique selling point."

The class visits, in addition to raising students' awareness of their progress, also produced invaluable information about our students, information that sometimes we would not be able to get from the oral tests. We were able to find out what grammar items had not been acquired, what pronunciation mistakes were commonly being made, and which students needed extra instruction. Students usually performed well in the oral examinations due to the fact that they were already used to talking to native speakers and had been exposed to similar situations before.

### "TOO LITTLE GRAMMAR"

Some students also felt that there was no focus on grammar. As the grammar analysis sections in the book came as the last stage of the cycle and were mainly consciousness-raising activities, some students had the impression that they had not learned any grammar at all. Even when students had performed successfully at the task stage, some of them were not satisfied that they had learned the grammar. What they had learned did not meet their expectations. In order to counter this negative perception, we instructed teachers to get learners to repeat the task at the end of the whole cycle. By redoing the task, students would be able to see for themselves that they were able to perform better. There is much recent research on the benefits of task repetition—see Pinter (2005), Essig (2005), and Lynch and MacLean (2001). Also, we began to provide students with a controlled practice activity, following grammar analysis, to help them feel that they had begun to acquire the new grammatical items.

Another activity we provided for students was the "Grammar Marathon." This was a long class (usually three hours) that took place every two weeks on a

Saturday morning. The teacher responsible for this activity would compare English grammar with the Portuguese equivalent. These Grammar Marathons were carried out in Portuguese so students could clarify doubts they had from their lessons using their own language. We held Grammar Marathons at Elementary, Pre-Intermediate, and Intermediate levels and did not aim at adding to the grammar to which students had been exposed in class but to revisit it using different teaching techniques. Grammar Marathons were thus based on the syllabus and prepared taking into account the language that students had been using in class. They were extremely popular with our students. They certainly helped to banish students' perceptions about the lack of focus on grammar.

## Evaluation

The seven solutions to the problems described above had a twofold effect. First, students became happy because they recognized they were learning how to mean things in English and to express themselves. Second, they began to change their beliefs about what learning a language entailed. Teachers, too, became more confident. Those who were new to TBI methodology not only felt confident that they had helped students to become more fluent in English and able to communicate but also that they had provided students with grammar and vocabulary that they considered important for students' language development.

After the initial problems were resolved, TBI was a constant success with our students. They became far more fluent in English than they had been before. When the Collins Cobuild series went out of print, we had to begin using a course book with more of a PPP approach, and so we were able to compare students who had used TBI with students who had been taught through PPP. Students who had used TBI were much more fluent and had more strategies to convey meaning than the others. However, students who had used a PPP approach, though less fluent, appeared to have a higher level of accuracy.

Perhaps this was the only remaining problem with using TBI: a lower level of accuracy. Due to lack of time in class, teachers were not always able to repeat the task or analyze language sufficiently. Looking back now, I realize we tended to skip a very important stage. Our students were very fluent but not very accurate. But there may be another reason for this.

Was it simply because, as a result of their greater fluency, our students were using far more language and attempting to express more complex ideas and thus exposing themselves more to the possibility of error? Students taught by PPP tend to talk much less, take more time to express their ideas, and, therefore, appear to make fewer mistakes.

Whatever the reason, this lower level of accuracy initially posed a problem as far as international exams were concerned. We had to look for exams that tested students' ability to communicate in English, so we switched to the Certificate in Communicative Skills in English (CCSE) offered by Cambridge University. Our students were no longer prepared for exams like the UCLES First Certificate in English where accuracy was very important. We geared our students toward the

CSE exams as they were more similar to what they were doing in class and placed a higher value on fluency and ability to communicate. We achieved an 85 percent success rate in the CCSE exams.

Nowadays, we still use TBI in our classes. However, we take grammar more seriously than we used to. We analyze grammar in more depth and do controlled grammar exercises in order to practice a grammar feature. More important, we still leave grammar analysis and practice to the last stage. We still believe that accuracy derives from fluency, not the contrary. This way, we are able to cater to students who just want to be fluent and able to communicate in English, as well as to students who have a more formal goal in learning the language, such as doing international examinations like the Cambridge Certificates and TOEFL.

## Conclusion

We came to the following conclusions:

- People using TBI learned English more effectively because they were using the language to do things—to find out information, to solve problems, and to talk about personal experiences;
- Students who are exposed to real language are able to deal with real-life situations when they encounter them outside the classroom;
- A focus on accuracy at some point is vital. Students need time to think about the language they are learning and see what its linguistic system looks like;
- The approach tends to lead students to learn grammar for themselves instead of waiting to be taught grammar. It is an excellent principle; however, there are times when students need to look at grammar in a more formal way. Teachers should not be ashamed of resorting to "old" techniques when everything else has failed. Students' "wants" should also be taken into account; and
- Teachers who come from a different background, as far as teaching approaches are concerned, should be trained before using TBI in the classroom.

Overall, we found that TBI is a very efficient approach to teaching English as a foreign language. Students leaving other language schools were able to make only very limited use of their English, partly because they were afraid of making mistakes and partly because they had very little experience in using the language. Students leaving British House were fluent, confident about using English, and able to understand and express far more complex meanings, even if they did make mistakes. They had reached a level where they were able to socialize with confidence, enabling them to go on learning, and to build on their accuracy by using English in real life.

## Appendix A

*Sample of a set of short text-based tasks for near beginners based on extracts from the* Guinness Book of Records 1986. *The original task was illustrated with photographs of the three houses.*

**Theme: Where we live**

**The largest . . . the smallest . . . the most expensive . . .**

*Pretask Discussion*

How many rooms does a typical family house or flat have in your area? How much does a typical town house or flat cost?

*Reading Task*

Read about the following houses. Which one is the most expensive house in the world? the largest private house in the world? the smallest house in Britain? Write the words (*The largest / The smallest / The most expensive* ) in the appropriate gaps and then compare with a partner.

---

_____ is Biltmore house in Asheville, North Carolina, USA, belonging to the Vanderbilt family. It was built in 1890 at a cost of US$4,100,000. It has 250 rooms and stands in an estate of 48,100 hectares.

---

_____ is the Hearst Ranch at San Simeon, California. It was built for the newspaper owner William Randolf Hearst in 1922-39 at a cost of US$30,000,000. It has over 100 rooms and a garage for 25 cars.

---

_____ is a cottage in North Wales built in the nineteenth century. It is 10 feet (309cms) high and measures only 6 feet (182cms) across the front. It has a tiny staircase and two tiny rooms.

---

*Writing Task*

Look at the photographs of the houses above. Write one or two more sentences about each of the houses. Begin: It . . .

Give your sentences to other students to read. Can they say which house each sentence is about?

## Appendix B

Extract from transcript of a recording of native speakers performing a Spot the Difference task where both speakers could see both pictures. They were asked to write a list of seven differences.

DF: Okay? Another difference is the number of the house.

BG: Yes

DF: In picture A it's thirty, in picture B it's thirteen . . . That's right, the number of the house is different.

BG: –is thirty. Oh.

DF: Oh. Okay.

BG: Oh. Do you think – ?

DF: Doesn't matter. Thirty in picture A and thirteen . . .

BG: Thirteen in picture B. And this number's different.

DF: What number?

BG: The phone number of Paul Smith and Sons.

DF: Oh yeah. So, the phone number of Paul Smith and Sons . . . is—what—in picture A is six three one nine o—six three one nine o—in picture A.

BG: Mhm.

DF: And, six three three nine o, in picture B.

BG: Okay.

DF: Okay. How many have we got? That's three.

BG: Three. How many do we have to have? Seven. Mm.

DF: How about the television? Is that on? Yes. Oh no, the television is on in—is it? in the first picture –

BG: Yes, it is.

DF: And it's not on in the—picture B. . . . That's—what have we got?

BG: The television is on in picture A but off in picture B.

DF: Okay. Right. . . . Anything else? Oh yes, the man's carrying an umbrella.

BG: Okay.

DF: So, what shall we put? The man –

BG: Yes, he's got an umbrella in picture B but not in picture A.

DF: Okay. So the man in picture B has got an umbrella, or is carrying an umbrella I don't know, yes . . . but not in picture A.

BG: That's right . . . And then there's a cat –

DF: One, two, three—

BG: Oh yes.

DF: So he's sitting—

BG: Well the cat's in a different place in picture A.

DF: Right. So what shall we write?

BG: Yes, okay. The cat in picture A is on the right of the "Sold sign."

DF: Okay. So in picture A the cat is sitting on the right of the—of what?—the—

BG: "Sold sign"

DF: "Sold sign, but in picture B it is sitting on—What? What shall we say?

BG: On the left of the "For sale" sign.

DF: Sitting on the left, next to the tree.

BG: Oh. "Sold" in picture A and "For Sale" in picture B.

DF: Ah. Oh yeah. Hang on—next to the tree. So, the sign—what shall we say for that? The sign's different?

BG: We've got enough now—I think—haven't we? We only have to have seven. We've got—I've got four.

DF: How many have we got to do? Seven. I've got one, two, three—okay, that's seven. Good. . . . All right?

BG: Mhm.

## Appendix C

Figure 4.1 shows a sample consciousness-raising activity using examples of language taken from tasks and texts earlier in the course book that were already familiar to learners.

| 73 | *Language study* |

**a** Read transcript 70, and find the following:

1 fifteen questions

Do any of the questions have the same words or phrases in them? Put the questions in groups (for example, put all the questions with the word *shall* together) and write them all down.

2 five phrases with **and** and four phrases with **but**

Read these to your partner.

3 seven examples of Yes or Yeah

Write down the words that come after them (for example, *Yes, it is*).

4 five examples of the word *so*

Where does *so* come in most sentences?

**b** Useful idioms

Match a phrase from the left with a phrase from the right that means the same thing.

| *Doesn't matter.* | *Wait a minute.* |
| *Anything else?* | *Never mind.* |
| *Hang on.* | *Any other things?* |

BG: Oh. Do you think –?
DF: Doesn't matter. Thirty in picture A and thirteen . . .
BG: Thirteen in picture B. And this number's different.
DF: What number?
BG: The phone number of Paul Smith and Sons.
DF: Oh yeah. So the phone number of Paul

FIGURE 4.1. **Consciousness-Raising Activity**

*Note.* All appendix samples are extracts from the original *Collins Cobuild English Course*, Level 1 (Willis and Willis 1988).

# 5

## LEARNING ARABIC: FROM LANGUAGE FUNCTIONS TO TASKS IN A DIGLOSSIC CONTEXT

### Mahdi Alosh

EDITORS' NOTE: This chapter discusses issues relating to the design of lower-level courses in Arabic, in which pedagogic tasks form a significant portion of the learning activities. Alosh uses a functional, communicative, and task-mediated approach to teaching that places emphasis on process over product. Therefore, the kinds of tasks presented here are somewhat different from those in other chapters of this book that emphasize product and outcome. In Alosh's system, both meaning and form are important, and activities are interwoven with tasks in developing both the ability to communicate thought and intent, as well as to understand and (re)produce the linguistic phenomena underlying communication.

Until recently, designing and implementing learning tasks have not been considered an integral part of language curriculum design. However, a growing number of second language specialists believe that methodological practice goes hand in glove with theory—and theory is leading teachers toward task-based learning. Practice, though, lags behind for two reasons. First, a teacher's prior experience in language learning and teaching has an important impact on his or her teaching techniques, and few teachers were taught in a task-based mode. Second, when there is lack of guidance about how to teach communicatively, the textbook tends to become the source of language material and its texts the object of linguistic analysis.

This chapter describes how classroom tasks are structured and implemented in the Arabic Language Program at Ohio State University (OSU). As part of the Department of Near Eastern Languages and Cultures, this program offers courses at all levels of proficiency to students in two tracks: (1) the regular classroom track, and (2) an individualized track. The latter track allows learners to learn at their own pace without having to come to class at prescribed times. Instead of attending class, they work on their own at the Arabic Learning Center, before seeking the assistance of the instructor there, thus taking more responsibility in managing their own learning. Not only do students have flexible hours, but they also receive variable credit, which allows them to cover as much material as they are capable of learning.

It is important to note that the type of tasks described here not be construed as the only effective kind for the classroom. Nor should noncommunicative tasks always be avoided. In the Arabic program, tasks are usually sequenced such that structural tasks precede communicative ones, providing the learner with the linguistic tools required for communicative tasks. The primary aim of engaging learners in communicative tasks is to take them beyond manipulating language forms and to enable them to put these forms to actual use.

## Arabic Diglossia

Diglossia has been defined as the existence of two varieties of the same language side-by-side in a speech community, each variety having a specialized function (Ferguson 1959). In Arabic, one variety of language, usually a specific regional or local dialect, is used for everyday, informal oral interaction. Local dialects are collectively known as Colloquial Arabic (C). They are largely mutually intelligible, but they do vary from one speech community to another. The degree of variation usually parallels geographical proximity, and, indeed, there may be more than one dialect in a speech community. The other variety of language exists alongside the spoken dialects and is superposed, mostly written, with limited oral use (restricted mainly to highly formal situations).[1] This variety is Modern Standard Arabic (MSA), which is based on Classical Arabic, and is more or less invariable throughout the Arab world. It is the language of instruction, government offices, the media, literature, and scholarship. It is used orally on radio and television (e.g., news broadcasts, commentaries, formal interviews) and in political speeches, courts of law, and the like. Although the distinction may sound much like a matter of register, in fact the difference involves substantial phonological, lexical, morphological, and syntactic variations.[2]

Diglossic differences are neither fixed nor permanent. Much depends on who is speaking, to whom, and in what context. I have proposed a model (Alosh 1991, 1997) with eight possible combinations, each one representing interaction among three different variables: situation, event, and setting. The situation can be either formal or familiar. The event in a formal situation may be public (e.g., many people involved, as in a ceremony), or private (e.g., two department heads having a meeting). In a familiar situation, the event can be either public (e.g., a party) or intimate (e.g., two close friends, man and wife). The setting can be local or nonlocal (local being within the dialectal speech community of the interlocutors).

According to this model, speech is conditioned by these three variables, resulting in output that ranges along a continuum from pure Standard to pure dialect, with most utterances occurring at some point on the continuum, rather than at either end. In real life, however, language performance is affected not only by the three variables (i.e., situation, event, and setting), but also by a host of other factors, such as age, education, status, topic, and gender, creating ever finer distinctions in the Standard-dialect "mix." Figure 5.1 depicts this model.[3]

### DIALECT

The term "dialect" refers to local casual speech within a distinct geographical/social area. This area does not necessarily correspond to political boundaries. The

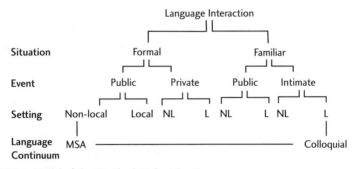

FIGURE 5.1. **Model of the Standard-Dialect Continuum**

differences observed between a given dialect and MSA are caused by the influence of indigenous languages that existed before the introduction of Arabic, the influence of the languages of the colonial powers that occupied parts of the Arabic-speaking world, and deviations caused by extended isolation and geographical distance. Most speakers of Arabic perceive their dialects as deformed versions of MSA (which is linguistically untrue) and regard MSA with great respect.

### THE IMPACT OF DIGLOSSIA ON ARABIC INSTRUCTION

In light of the model above, learners of Arabic ideally are expected to receive instruction that reflects this linguistic situation. However, given the constraints of time and opportunity of exposure to the language in its context of situation, many programs teach MSA only. As Alosh (1992a) indicates, the rationale for not incorporating a C component is threefold. First, the MSA content of the course is presented not with the assumption that the student will have to use the same MSA items in communicative situations, but rather because the student would develop the necessary strategies of oral communication. Thus, a course may not necessarily contain C items if it enables the students to develop the necessary skills that facilitate the acquisition of any dialect in its social context. Having first developed oral skill using MSA, students would be able to use it later as a springboard to acquire a specific dialect in the social context where the dialect is spoken. (The classroom is not seen as an effective environment in which to produce highly proficient speakers. It is generally accepted that students who wish to acquire Arabic language skills similar to those possessed by an educated native speaker must travel to the target country.)

Second, the use of MSA in an academic setting, such as a university classroom, is perfectly appropriate from the sociolinguistic point of view, though not appropriate for all topics that might come up within the classroom. Third, at advanced levels of instruction, students are expected to perform at higher levels of abstraction, which makes the use of MSA appropriate in both speaking and reading. I may add another reason for excluding C from formal instruction. Many educators believe that exposing learners to two varieties of Arabic at the same time would be confusing.

## The Arabic Language Program at OSU

The Arabic language program includes only the language courses. The Arabic literature and culture courses are offered under the literature and culture programs, respectively.

### STUDENTS

Student demographics have changed significantly over the last decade. Growing numbers of heritage students are taking Arabic. Their exposure to Arabic ranges from none or very little and from some comprehension of colloquial Arabic to a low level of proficiency in speaking one of the dialects. As most Arabic programs in the United States teach mainly MSA, these students are, in fact, at a disadvantage because they have the perception that they "know" Arabic, but this knowledge does not contribute positively to their learning as it is of another linguistic code. Muslim students from India, Indonesia, Iran, Malaysia, Pakistan, and other Islamic countries enroll in Arabic classes with the purpose of developing the ability to read religious texts (mainly the Koran) and understand them. Many of them come with a rudimentary ability to "read" Arabic, that is, to sound out the words, but generally they do not understand what they read. Even this ability is, in most cases, defective. Muslim Americans constitute another category. The vast majority has no ability in Arabic whatsoever, but they do have the same motivation as other Muslim students, and many of them excel thanks to that. Caucasian Americans, who used to be the dominant category in the 1980s and earlier, enroll in Arabic classes for various reasons: a relationship with a boyfriend or a girlfriend, academic interest, or preparation for professional pursuits. This variability in background and interest of students of Arabic has prompted some programs to create separate sections for heritage and Muslim students if their enrollments allow it.

### THEORETICAL ORIENTATION

In 1987, the Department of Near Eastern Languages and Cultures at Ohio State University shifted to a function-based, proficiency-oriented curriculum. This shift entailed drastic changes in methodology and instructional materials. The new, expanded curriculum is designed around language functions (e.g., expressing possession, describing location, narrating an event, expressing opinion). Structures that are needed for the performance of these functions are presented and practiced as pattern drills. Information about the linguistic system is provided in lucid explanations for the students to read outside of class. These grammatical explanations are viewed as an intermediate stage between the presentation of new input and actually using it in contextualized situations. Since classroom time is reserved for teacher–student and student–student oral interaction, attention to effective teaching methodology has become an important part of curricular development. The description of the activities below elaborates this component.

### CURRICULUM

The Arabic curriculum includes five categories of courses: (1) language courses, (2) literature courses in translation, (3) literature courses in Arabic, (4) linguistics courses (historical and applied), and (5) Arab culture and folklore courses (taught in English). Below is a more detailed description of the language courses.

### Language Courses

The Department of Near Eastern Language and Cultures offers eight five-credit-hour language courses in addition to two grammar courses. The first four satisfy the foreign language requirement. They emphasize oral interaction in class designed around the language functions listed at the beginning of each unit in the textbook as objectives. Oral interaction involves the students in carrying out tasks, or communicative activities, in pairs or groups. Out-of-class work consists mainly of reading, writing, and structural exercises designed to reinforce the abilities being developed in the classroom and expand on them. While it retains focus on the four skills, the fifth course represents a transition from edited reading passages to authentic material. The sixth course focuses on reading comprehension and strategies, in addition to continuing to develop the four languages skills. The seventh course has a writing focus, and the last, most advanced language course, is designed to develop advanced language abilities in all language skills. Students who take this sequence of language courses are expected to reach at least the Advanced level, according to the scale of the American Council on Teaching Foreign Languages (see the appendix to this volume), in all language skills. However, the unstated goal is to develop the ability to cope with literary and other texts successfully. This may not be a realistic goal for classroom instruction alone unless majors and graduate students in particular devote some time to studying abroad.

### Evaluation

Two formal means of evaluation are used. Every week for the first six weeks of a given quarter, students complete an anonymous formative evaluation form during the first three minutes of class. This form contains three questions:

1. What aspects of class work were most useful and interesting to you during this week?
2. What parts of the material or class activities were unclear to you?
3. What can I do to help you learn better?

The responses help the teachers modify the syllabus, methodology, tasks, or other aspect of instruction immediately, before the course is over.

At the end of each course, two summative evaluation forms are given, one developed by the department and one for campuswide use developed by the registrar's office. The feedback from these forms may be used for modifications of subsequent courses and for evaluation of teaching performance.

### Language Assessment

Informal assessment is accomplished daily whenever teacher and student are in contact. In these private settings, students often relay to teachers their concerns and their challenges with their language program; teachers likewise have an opportunity to elicit feedback from students casually and naturally.

Formal assessment has several forms. The most familiar are written quizzes and tests. The quizzes range from daily to weekly, and they focus on one or two points covered the day before (e.g., vocabulary, grammar, reading comprehension). The tests, including midterm and final tests, are more integrative and comprehensive. They comprise vocabulary, reading comprehension, writing, and grammar. Oral proficiency interviews are conducted the last week of classes (and sometimes at midterm). Function-based skits developed and performed by students are also an assessment tool in beginning classes.

### Teachers

The majority of teachers are graduate students. All of them take a two-week intensive training workshop. In addition, they take one course in methodology and one in language acquisition. Higher-level language classes are taught by faculty members, whereas elementary and intermediate courses are normally, but not always, taught by trained graduate teaching assistants.

### Instructional Materials

The instructional materials used are a series of textbooks initially designed and developed by the author (1989–91, 1991–93). Additional textbooks were later written to meet the program needs (Alosh 1996, 1999, 2000a, 2000b, 2000c). Textbook content is organized according to language functions with a functional, pragmatic orientation, where doing rather than knowing is the focus.

### Study Abroad

Through an agreement with Damascus University, Syria, students can study Arabic in an immersion, intensive fashion. They are placed with Syrian families in order to maximize their exposure to the culture. Through home stay, shopping, using public transportation, visiting sites of cultural and historical importance, meeting with dignitaries and spiritual leaders (both Christian and Muslim), and interacting with young Syrian students of a similar age, they can get a first-hand knowledge and appreciation of the culture and language. Preliminary reports received from OSU students on their experience attest to the beneficial effects study abroad has on their language proficiency and cultural awareness.

### LEARNING TASKS

The language courses are structured in a manner conducive to achieving the targeted proficiency levels in the four language skills. The students perform in-class and out-of-class tasks. Classroom tasks can best be summarized by the instructional cycle described below. They show what students and teacher do in the classroom in order for learning to occur. Such tasks are mostly oral, but they do include some reading and writing tasks as well. Out-of-class tasks are mainly reading and writing tasks, in addition to some listening comprehension tasks. The writing tasks include daily journals and reaction papers.

### CHARACTERISTICS OF A COMMUNICATIVE-FUNCTIONAL APPROACH

A communicative-functional approach does not preclude such activities as practicing phonological, morphological, and syntactic points that have traditionally been associated with structural, form-based approaches. The focus of instruction and activities, however, is on meaning and the function to which the language is put and practice with structure has a direct connection with development of understanding of form and automaticity in its use in applied contexts. Some salient characteristics are:

### Focus on Meaning

Focus on meaning is highlighted, especially at the beginning level, by asking the learners to elicit simple, yet genuine, information from their partners, as in the following tasks.

1. Find out who in the classroom walks to school.
2. Describe three activities that you usually do over the weekend and compare these with your classmates' activities.

### Student-Centered

In a task-mediated, communicative-functional approach, most activities involve pair and group work. The teacher's role is one of guiding these activities. The presentation of the material is broken down into small segments (i.e., one language function at a time with the necessary vocabulary and structures). Presentation of new material and interactive activities alternate at a brisk pace so that the students remain engaged. A task similar to the following may be used immediately after the presentation.

Find out from your partner how far from school he or she lives and how he or she comes to school. Report your finding back to the class. (If appropriate and the teacher desires, students can then use that information for some purpose, such as completing a transport survey.)

### Proficiency Goal

The guiding principle in the OSU Arabic task-mediated communicative-functional approach is the development of specific language abilities. The long-term goal of instruction is the achievement of Advanced-level proficiency. Two sample tasks follow:

1. Find out from your partner which foods he or she prefers, where he or she gets them, and who prepares them for him or her.

**2.** Describe how your favorite dish is prepared (orally or in writing). Following this, students could produce a class recipe book, try out some dishes outside of class, and report back on them. These tasks give practice in using everyday functions such as expressing likes and dislikes, making recommendations, giving instructions, and specific language abilities like listing stages in a process and reaching a decision within a group.

### Interrelatedness of Function and Form

Another characteristic of the task-mediated communicative-functional approach is the focus on the relationship between form and function, in which functional tasks are used for reinforcing grammatical features. (Using tasks for pedagogic purposes has received some support in recent days, especially from teachers of linguistically complex languages; see, e.g., Samuda 2001.) The purpose of instruction is obviously the development of pragmatic control, accomplished by providing comprehensible input and expecting students to produce output in relation to context-specific sociolinguistic requirements realized through the correct application of grammatical rules. What seems to be one process is, in fact, two—one pragmatic and the other psycholinguistic. Garrett (1991) makes this distinction, noting that using language knowledge, or grammatical rules, to perform communicative functions is a sociocultural, sociolinguistic phenomenon, whereas using language knowledge to comprehend and produce language is a cognitive, psycholinguistic phenomenon.

Further, research conducted by Swain and Lapkin (2001) determined that regardless of task type—real-world or pedagogic—students paid much attention to learning form, as needed for required output. Alosh (1997) contends that separation of form and meaning under any pretext would deny grammar its mediating role between these two sources of knowledge. For instance, learners of Arabic find it difficult to master the subjunctive when it is presented as a set of structural relations because they are unable to associate the form with the various functions that require its use. If they know, however, that in order to express obligation or indicate reason, they need to use certain expressions (which necessarily include the subjunctive form), they can focus on meaning/intent, as well as relate the form to something they already know (i.e., the concept of expressing obligation).

### Use of Authentic Materials

To most foreign language teachers, authentic materials are those produced by native speakers for native speakers. This is, in my opinion, a limited view of authenticity. A broader interpretation of authentic that includes authentic function and communicative activity can provide a better base for student learning, while still adhering to the principles of proficiency-oriented language teaching and learning (Alosh 1991).

### Processing Information, Not Manipulating Form

The focus here is on the kind of memory (declarative or procedural)[4] the learners must access and the manner in which they are trained to view and use language. Students are encouraged to focus on processing information, with the teacher keeping an eye on form so that any gaps in structural knowledge may be addressed later. The following tasks exemplify this concept.

1. Use figure 5.2 to write a paragraph on the hypothetical import-export activities in the United States in the year 2001. The purposes of this task are to enable learners to transform numerical data into meaningful information and to use Arabic (and the pertinent grammatical structures) to make decisions about export-import activities, for example, to determine whether the United States is in good or bad shape economically, using the import-export data to make and support a case for either opinion.

2. Read the following paragraph and then fill in the chart to illustrate the imports and exports of the United Arab Emirates (UAE) in 2001:

   Comprehension of expository texts with factual information and demonstration of comprehension by filling out a chart with data based on this information entail the use of the underlying knowledge and transferable skills that are developed in doing tasks on the basis of this authentic input. The kinds of tasks that can be done are myriad, depending on students' proficiency levels: (1) hold a debate, write an essay, or argue in pairs over whether the United States or the UAE has the better economy, (2) list actions that the government might take in the following year to change the ratios, and (3) decide whether or not the government needs to take any action, among others. The generic task, which can be implemented in these and many other ways, is to find out something about imports and exports in the UAE and to do something ana-

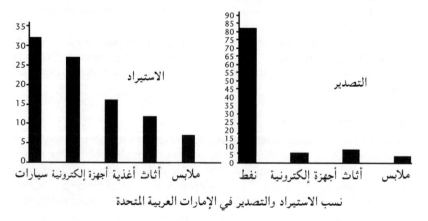

FIGURE 5.2. **U.S. Import-Export Activities, 2001**

lytic, evaluative, or reactive with that information. Learners read the Arabic passage and, in figure 5.3, fill in the chart accordingly.

### Treating Errors as Part of the Learning Process

Error correction is accomplished by modeling, repetition, or other forms of feedback after the communication is over so that it will not interrupt the message. Errors are viewed as a dynamic aspect of the learning process. Some of them may not simply go away by correction alone. They might linger until the learner reaches a particular developmental stage. There are written and oral errors. The instructor notes them and focuses on them through form practice in class at appropriate moments. At the beginning level, most errors are pronunciation errors. These are developmental errors, particularly when they pertain to sounds and phonological processes that do not exist in the English linguistic system (e.g., pharyngealization). Students are encouraged to repeat certain sounds intensively, but with the understanding that learners will not be able to produce them until they can perceive them (Alosh 1987).

### Process versus Product

By its nature, a task-mediated communicative-functional approach is based on the *process* of learning, that is, the "how" of student learning. A course of this nature is, in a sense, performance based because learners are expected to perform language functions in the process of learning. A speaking task that concentrates on the process (i.e., elicit, negotiate, evaluate, and report meaning) might be the

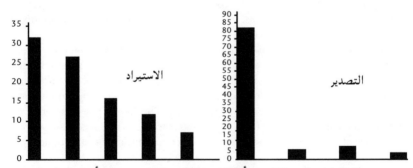

تستورد دولة الإمارات العربية المتحدة أصنافًا مختلفة من السلع من جميع أنحاء العالم. فهي تستورد السيارات مثلاً من أوروبا واليابان والولايات المتحدة وكوريا. وتشكل السيارات حوالى ٣٢ بالمئة من إجمالي الاستيراد تليها الأجهزة الإلكترونية والكهربائية والتي تصل إلى ٢٧٪ من قيمة المستوردات ثم الأغذية ١٦٪ والأثاث ١٢٪ والملابس ٧ بالمئة٪. أما بالنسبة للتصدير فيحتل النفط المرتبة الأولى حيث يصل إلى ٨٢٪ من قيمة ما تصدره الإمارات. وتساهم المنطقة الحرة قرب دبي في تنويع السلع المصدرة ومنها الأجهزة الإلكترونية والملابس والأثاث.

FIGURE 5.3. **Imports and Exports of the United Arab Emirates**

following: Find out from your partner two things he or she prefers to do on Saturday morning, compare these with those chosen by other pairs of students, and vote on who has the most exciting life.

The above characteristics make it abundantly clear that teaching and learning activities according to a functional approach are centered on the learner, are task based, and occur in context. Not only do classroom exercises meet these basic conditions but so also does the Arabic language curriculum as a whole in order to ensure consistency between instructional design and application.

### COMMUNICATIVE TASKS IN PRACTICE

An oral communicative task, as used in the OSU Arabic program, is a series of structured actions in the target language that (1) elicits new information, (2) processes oral language input and output, and (3) is specified in relation to the components of a speech event (i.e., learners are aware of the role they are playing, the setting, the topic, and the purpose of the interaction). Tasks can be focused or unfocused, as shown in table 5.1.

The context is set by giving precise instructions in English. A communicative task is part of an instructional cycle. A class is made up of a series of instructional cycles.

*Instructional cycle.* An instructional cycle may be defined as a series of classroom procedures, the purpose of which is to provide learners with meaningful input that facilitates interpreting, negotiating, and constructing meaning in the target language (see figure 5.4). Each cycle begins with a presentation of a new item by the instructor in context. The context for the presentation of the new material (e.g., one function, one structure, or a few vocabulary items at a time) is set either by pictures, charts, props, gestures, or by explanation or description, depending on the topic and the level of the students.

*Example:* The instructor uses pictures to teach the words for bicycle, car, and computer in a four-phrase approach. The first phase focuses on getting students to learn the new lexical items. The second phase involves practice of the new items. In the third phase, learners do things with the new language input that require understanding the meaning of the items. The fourth phase is application and entails a communicative task; this allows learners to use in context what has been presented, practiced, and learned. The communicative task is basically the

TABLE 5.1. **Sample Communicative Tasks**

| *Unfocused Tasks* | *Focused Tasks* |
|---|---|
| Tell your partner something about yourself. | Find out from your partner if he/she studies at the library, at what times, and for how long. |
| Write about a day in the outdoors. | Find out who in the class lived in this town before becoming students at this university. |

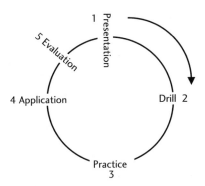

FIGURE 5.4. **An Instructional Cycle**

execution of a language function or functions. Below are two examples from different stages in the OSU Arabic program:

1. Find out if your partner owns a bicycle and report your finding back to the class.
2. Find out which of your classmates have traveled or lived abroad and for how long and report your finding back to the class.

The fifth, or evaluation, phase allows the instructor to assess how well the learners have learned by checking for their recognition and production abilities.

### Components of a Communicative Task

The central component of a communicative task is context. As seen in figure 5.4, context influences all other components since it involves participants, setting, topic, purpose, and so forth. Figure 5.5 illustrates the relationship among the components of a communicative task.

A. *Context.* The context is set by props, pictures, or precise instructions. At the beginning level, the latter are in English and prepared in advance because slight changes in the formulation of instruction can result in different actions and outcomes. Instructions specify, among other things, participants, their roles and relationships, the setting, and the purpose of interaction. Here are some examples of context from the OSU Arabic program:

(1) Examine this picture of a hotel and read the description next to it. Imagine that you are staying at this hotel and write a description of your stay, including the hotel location and facilities, the time when you arrived, by which means of transportation, with whom, for

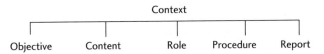

FIGURE 5.5. **Components of a Communicative Task**

what purpose, how long you are planning to stay, and what activities you expect to do.

(2) Examine this driver's license and fill out the blank form with information about yourself.

B. *Objective.* The task objective is always functional, unlike unit/lesson objectives, which may be specified in structural terms. Even if a task objective, for example, is designed to make learners use the perfect, it is specified in functional terms. Objectives related to the tasks above are:

(1) Structural: using perfect and imperfect verb forms; spelling basic words.

(2) Functional: describing physical surroundings and activities in the past and future; providing biographical information.

C. *Content.* The content refers to language items and structures learners are expected to use in a given task. It is specified indirectly by describing the actions the learners are expected to perform, which would call for the use of particular words and structures. The content of the tasks described above is:

(1) Vocabulary related to hotels, living areas, travel, entertainment, exercise, and food.

(2) Vocabulary related to biographical information.

D. *Student role.* The students' role in a communicative task is an active one. They draw on their own resources to interpret, negotiate, and construct meaning. The learner plays the role of a conversational partner or a participant in a survey or an opinion poll. For the two tasks described above, the students' role is as follows:

(1) To draw on previous input in order to express meanings describing their own experiences.

(2) To emulate written input and modifying it to fit their own situations.

E. *Teacher role.* The teacher's role in a communicative task is not a dominant one. He or she acts as a guide, consultant, facilitator, or feedback provider. The teacher's behavior during the initial stages of the two tasks (cf. the pretask phase described in chapter 1 above) would look something like the following:

(1) During task 1, the teacher would show the picture of a hotel preferably with some action going on and do some brain storming to elicit from the students vocabulary related to hotel, vacations, travel, food, exercise, entertainment, and so forth in addition to structures used in describing such activities.

(2) During task 2, the teacher would show a drivers license (his or her own) and try to have the students provide the words necessary in describing biographical information.

F. *Procedure.* Procedure refers to what learners are expected to do in order to achieve the objective. It could be exchanging information with one classmate or more, or filling out a form with reference to the learner's own background. Specifically, for the two tasks described in this section, the following procedures are used.

(1) In carrying out task 1, students are expected to be involved in a collaborative fashion with the teacher and with one another in order to produce a list of relevant words and structures, sort out the items, organize them, and develop a text to fulfill the task.

(2) In carrying out task 2, students are expected to work with one another and the teacher to produce the items needed for this task such as the names of the months, spelling of foreign names, and names of professions.

G. *Reporting*. If the activity involves elicitation of information, students may be asked to report the information back to the class, thus they use the third person in addition to first- and second-person forms. In the instance of the two tasks in this section, students are asked to report specific information, identified below, to the class.

(1) Report about the hotel where their conversation partner stayed, the occasion for the stay, the duration, and the activities he or she performed.

The second task is not amenable to elicitation and reporting.

## CONDITIONS OF COMMUNICATIVE TASKS

The communicative tasks in our program have a number of distinct features. The checklist in table 5.2 provides a guide for teachers to ensure that they address all the potential conditions of communicative tasks wholly or at least partially in designing and giving instructions for a task.

Here is an example of the checklist in use from the OSU Arabic program.

Task: You have been invited to a classmate's house for a party but you do not know the address. Call your classmate and get the directions to their house. Write them down as he/she gives them to you. (The students sit back to back to avoid overreliance on gestures.) The items in table 5.3 help the novice teacher to ensure adherence to the components of a communicative task.

## PRINCIPLES OF COMMUNICATIVE TASKS

In order for a task to be "communicative" and to produce the desired functional outcome, at least one of three basic principles must obtain: (1) the information transfer principle, (2) the information gap principle, or (3) the functional principle. These principles are described below.

### The Information Transfer Principle

In applying the principle of information transfer (Johnson 1982, 164), students' attention is focused on the ability to understand and convey the informational content in a form different from the original (e.g., from text to graph, letter to application form, and vice versa). Information transfer is particularly useful in writing tasks. It is not really communication, but it is communicative in the sense that the focus is on pragmatic meaning and information. The student is not

TABLE 5.2. **Communicative Task Characteristics**

| Yes?/No? | Task Characteristic |
|---|---|
| | Does this task involve all students? |
| | Is this task based on pair or group work? |
| | Does this task require learners to interact in context? |
| | Are the materials aural/oral, visual, or both? |
| | Are the materials interesting to this group of students? |
| | Do they introduce an element of fun? |
| | Do they allow students to interact with one another and to elicit genuine information from each other in Arabic? |
| | Is length of performance appropriate to the nature of the task (e.g., pair work vs. group work; question-and-answer technique vs. poll/survey; two vs. multiple exchanges)? |
| | Is language specified in relation to speech event components (i.e., who is speaking/writing, to whom, about what, with what purpose)? |
| | Are learners engaged in this task with the full understanding of the roles they and their partners are playing in the interaction and the reason for communication? |

TABLE 5.3. **Checklist**

| Yes?/No? | Task Characteristic |
|---|---|
| Y | Does this task involve all students? |
| PW | Is this task based on pair or group work? |
| Y | Does this task require learners to interact in context? |
| BOTH | Are the materials aural/oral, visual, or both? |
| Y | Are the materials interesting to this group of students? |
| Y | Do they introduce an element of fun? |
| Y | Do they allow students to interact with one another and to elicit genuine information from each other in Arabic? |
| Y | Is length of performance appropriate to the nature of the task (e.g., pair work vs. group work; question-and-answer technique vs. poll/survey; two vs. multiple exchanges)? |
| Y | Is language specified in relation to speech event components (i.e., who is speaking/writing, to whom, about what, with what purpose)? |
| Y | Are learners engaged in this task with the full understanding of the roles they and their partners are playing in the interaction and the reason for communication? |

required to comment on any structural point or lexical meaning. Here is an example of transfer from the OSU Arabic program: Read this letter from Adnan to his family about his life and study in the United States, then fill out his daily schedule based on the information in the letter.

### The Information Gap Principle

The information gap principle involves the transmission of information, or the conveying of a message, from person to person (Johnson 1982, 166). The receiver does not initially possess the information, and he or she receives it via spoken or written communication. Tasks designed in this manner create the condition of unexpectedness, with Student 1 not knowing in advance what Student 2 will say. Here is an information gap task from the OSU beginning Arabic program:

Task 1: Find out your conversation partner's favorite color and report this information back to the class. (The reports can be used then, if desired, for comparison or other activities such as a survey.)

Task 2: Find out your partner's telephone number. If she or he agrees, report this information back to the whole class. (Each class member could listen to the report and make a complete list of class phone numbers.)

### The Functional Principle

There is a type of social interaction that has little or no informational load, yet it is genuine and communicative. Examples include greeting, apologizing, excusing oneself, and so on. Language is used in these expressions to perform a specific function. Tasks based on functions may be limited to an elementary level of language. Here are some functional tasks from the OSU Arabic program:

1. You enter a room with several individuals talking together. Would you say anything upon your entrance? If so, what would the phrase be?
2. You pass by an acquaintance on the street in the morning. How would you greet him or her?
3. Your best friend is wearing a new shirt, how would you express your admiration?

As we saw above, communicative tasks in the OSU Arabic program are conducted after other components in the instructional cycle have been completed. We have found it to be extremely important to strike a balance between prior practice and the opportunity for genuine information exchange. For example, if students have already practiced the functions of telling time and describing activity—using the verbs "to eat" and "to drink," the phrase "at x o'clock," and several relevant nouns—there is still room for real information flow because in pair work one student knows neither the time when an activity usually takes place nor which foods have been consumed by his or her conversation partner.

### TASK TYPES, LEVELS OF PROFICIENCY, AND LINGUISTIC COMPLEXITY

At OSU, we have found that one of the advantages of a proficiency-oriented approach is that it describes what learners can and cannot do in the language at each step in the process of language acquisition. When designing tasks, teachers are conscious of their students' levels and design tasks that are appropriate for their levels (see the appendix to this volume and the Arabic proficiency guidelines, 1989). Although linguistic complexity is not a major consideration in designing a communicative syllabus and its accompanying materials, it makes sense to select exponents of functions for beginning students that are less complex. Davis (1997) recommends that task type be commensurate with proficiency level and with what learners can do or are expected to do at that level.

In addition to taking into consideration proficiency levels, course designers also consider task types. Figure 5.6 illustrates the choices available.

The sample communicative tasks described in this chapter are divided into oral and visual tasks. The latter are further subdivided into writing and reading exercises. The Arabic curriculum also includes integrative communicative tasks.

### Oral Tasks

A distinction is made between pair work and group work on the basis of the time the task requires and the intensity of language use. Before describing the task, the teacher takes the following preparatory steps: (1) The instructions given to the students (perhaps in English for beginning students) prior to conducting the task are very carefully formulated because they determine the outcome of the activity and the kind of language forms used during its performance. (2) After the instructions have been clearly stated, the instructor, in preparation for the task, elicits from the students the forms of the language necessary to execute it, including both the initial statement or question and the response, assuming that the proper question word or words, the necessary verb, and lexical items have already been presented and practiced. Examples for beginning students might be: How do you ask someone in Arabic what he or she eats for breakfast? How do you describe to someone what you eat for breakfast?

The students then make individual attempts at providing suitable responses. With guidance and help from the teacher, they ultimately produce something like the following: What do you eat for breakfast? I eat such and such for breakfast.

If the language program emphasizes grammatical accuracy, this emphasis may be reflected in the preparatory phases of drill and practice, as well as in the conduct of the task itself. Students may, in this case, be expected to produce verbs and nouns with the appropriate inflectional markers.

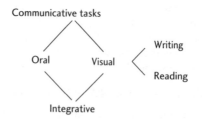

FIGURE 5.6. **Types of Communicative Tasks**

TABLE 5.4. **Task 1**

*Novice Mid*

*Instructions:* Ask your partner for his/her telephone number.

*Follow-up:* Time permitting, students may be asked to report their findings back to the class.

*Pair work.* Pair work involves two partners, and the content of the activity reflects a language function. Students perform a language function whose exponent(s) have been previously presented and practiced. Table 5.4 shows an oral task accomplished through pair work. (When one or more variations of the task are possible, they are listed after it.)

*Notes on task 1.* The reporting back serves two purposes: (1) reinforcement of the forms used in the activity, and (2) the chance to transfer the elicited information to a third person. The teacher decides if reporting is called for, and if so, how much of it, as described in table 5.5.

*Notes on task 2.* This information may be elicited by two different Arabic structures: a nominal sentence (What's your address?) and a verbal sentence (Where do you live?). Variation is determined either by the student or the instructor if he or she wants the students to practice verb forms, for instance. Tables 5.6 and 5.7 list two oral tasks at two different levels of proficiency.

*Group work.* Group work differs from pair work not in the language content, but in the intensity of practice. It often takes the form of class opinion polls and student surveys, thus requiring the student to repeat the same questions over and over and the respondent to give the same response as many times as there are students participating in the survey. Like pair work, it is highly communicative since the students' attention is focused on the information they are collecting or providing and how to process it in order to give the right report (e.g., the number of students in the class who own bicycles). Group work, however, requires more time to complete. The instructor uses his/her own discretion in deciding on pair

TABLE 5.5. **Task 2**

*Novice Mid/High*

*Instructions:* Find out your partner's address.

*Follow-up:* Students report their partner's address to the class and locate it on a map, with the result being a map with marks where everyone lives. One possibility is the use of the words for "many, few, none" to describe where most of the students have chosen to live.

*Note:* This information may be elicited by two different Arabic structures: a nominal sentence (What's your address?) and a verbal sentence (Where do you live?). Variation is determined by either the student or the instructor if he or she wants the students to practice verb forms, for instance.

TABLE 5.6. **Task 3**

*Novice High*

*Instructions:* Find out what school subjects your partner studies.

*Follow-up:* The students write the different school subjects on the board and compare the subjects taken by various members of the class by listing them under categories such as science courses, music courses, etc. It might be interesting for them to see what the class profile is in terms of the kinds of courses being studied.

or group work, based on how much practice is needed and how much time is available.

The sample tasks demonstrate the versatility of communicative tasks in terms of the language forms practiced, the information elicited, variations of the same activity, and the different levels of proficiency at which they may be conducted. They are used on a regular basis in the OSU Arabic program as part of instructional cycles to promote aural comprehension and speaking ability. Types of group work follow.

*Interviews.* Interviews may be of two kinds: staged and real (Harlow 1998). The staged ones, in which a student assumes the role of a celebrity, for example, may be used when access to a celebrity is not possible. They are appropriate because the background knowledge is shared by most students. Interviews can be conducted at several levels of proficiency, depending on whether the questions are provided in full (student reads from script), suggested (student is told what to ask about), or only the type of information sought is suggested (e.g., biographical information, work, hobbies). Students ask about personal biography, foods, drinks, hobbies, sports, and the like. This provides an opportunity to introduce cultural and/or historical information. Real interviews can be conducted with real people from the community, such as classmates, teachers, and native speakers. This is a more complex task given the amount of new information obtained from the interviewee. In this case, several students may interview the same person.

*Class opinion polls and surveys.* Selected students are assigned different tasks that involve obtaining information from the other students and then reporting it back to the teacher or class. Some topics from opinion polls and surveys include the number of students planning to study Arabic abroad, which students are taking science courses, the students who go away for the summer vacation, and the number of students who work and study.

TABLE 5.7. **Task 4**

*Intermediate Low*

*Instructions:* Ask your partner about the number of languages he or she speaks, which languages these are, and how well he or she speaks them.

*Follow-up:* The students compile a chart with a list of all the languages spoken by members of the class and how many members speak each.

*Information search.* Different identification cards are distributed to all students. The task is for students to go around the class and ask questions to identify the person assigned to them.

### Writing Tasks

Certainly, proficiency is not only oral. Communicative writing tasks can be designed to develop proficiency in the literacy skills even at low levels of competence and in an unfamiliar language like Arabic. Once students master the Arabic script, they may be exposed to written texts so that they can perform reading and writing activities. Communicative task types include activities that involve providing, transferring, or replicating new information. These classroom tasks come in different formats, some of which are described below.

*Communicative sentence builders.* Communicative sentence builders are used at the Novice level and are usually a meaningful activity. They can be easily modified to serve as integrative activities. To render them communicative, names of students from the class, their attributes, facts about them, or actual activities done by them may be used. Teachers develop fresh exercises for every course or modify previous ones. The student's task is to form sentences from the table that have a high degree of truth value about the other students mentioned. The students are required to verify the truth value of the sentences they form by consulting orally in Arabic with the other students whose names are listed. Table 5.8 is used as the basis of a number of tasks, for example those in tables 5.9 and 5.10. (Note that English is not provided in the original task.)

*Notes on Task 5.* The five sentences may include the daily schedule of some students or some other set of facts. From experience and observation, this kind of task has many advantages. First, it makes writing fun. Second, it promotes oral

TABLE 5.8. **A Communicative Sentence Builder**

| سكـن <br> live | لسلي <br> Leslie | — <br> 0 | الكيـمياء <br> chemistry | ذا/هذه <br> this | (ال)يـوم <br> day |
|---|---|---|---|---|---|
| عمل <br> work | مـايكل <br> Michael | فـي <br> in, at, on | شـارع هـاي <br> High Street | الفصل <br> term | الماضي <br> last |
| درس <br> study | ميليسـا <br> Melissa | مـع <br> with | الجبن <br> cheese | مرارا <br> often | (ال)سـنة <br> year |
| سـافر <br> travel | هوب <br> Hope | إلى <br> to | مـطعم <br> a restaurant | كل <br> every | (ال)صبـاح <br> morning |
| غنـى <br> sing | ستـافورد <br> Stafford | | تـونس <br> Tunisia | الليـلة <br> night | الفصل <br> term |
| أكل <br> eat | كارولاين <br> Caroline | | الحمـام <br> the shower | الصيـف <br> summer | — <br> 0 |

TABLE 5.9. **Task 5**

*Novice High / Intermediate Low*

*Instructions:* Construct five sentences from the table, paying attention to the truth value contained in each one. Verify the truthfulness of your sentences in Arabic with your classmates whose names are used.

TABLE 5.10. **Task 6**

*Intermediate Low / Mid*

*Instructions:* Construct five sentences from the table, providing the correct forms of the verbs and paying attention to the truth value of each one. Verify the truthfulness of your sentences with your classmates whose names are used. The table includes facts about some students.

and literacy skills simultaneously. Third, it creates a genuine opportunity for purposeful and meaningful interaction among learners. The teacher may control the amount of time needed to do the task by increasing or decreasing the number of names used in the table or by limiting the number of sentences required. At a higher level of difficulty, the task may be made more demanding by providing infinitives rather than conjugated forms so that the students use verbs with the appropriate tense, number, and gender as well as true information about their classmates. In this manner, they pay equal attention to the accuracy of the language and its functional use and strike a balance between form and meaning.

*Filling out forms.* This task can be performed at several levels, starting with simple imitation at the Novice Mid / High level. Learners make minor changes in the information pertaining to biographical information but not to language forms. At higher levels of proficiency (Novice High and above), students can replicate a form, which means that they have first to understand the content in the model provided, make some factual changes, and provide language forms with changes demanded by the suggested context.

*Imitating a form.* Students examine and understand a model, then provide a replica, following the same format, but with different information, as requested in the task given in table 5.11.

*Notes on Task 7.* In transferring information from text to form and vice versa, the student level may be Intermediate Low or above, depending on the complexity of the reading passage and assigned task. The text may be in a letter format or

TABLE 5.11. **Task 7**

*Novice Mid / High*

*Instructions:* Examine Rami's driver's license and then fill out your own driver's license with information about yourself.

ولد سالم الخالد في مدينة بيروت عام ۱۹۷۸ في الخامس من شهر آب. يسكن سالم الآن في مدينة طرابلس في شارع الأرز في الدار رقم تسعة وتسعين. يعمل سالم محاسبا في شركة هندسية ورقم هاتفه في العمل هو ۳۷۸٥٥۳۰ أما في المنزل فهو ۳۷۸٤٥٦۳. حصل على شهادة القيادة لأول مرة في التاسع من نيسان سنة ١٩٩٦. ينتهي مفعول الشهادة خلال ست سنوات لذلك فهو يريد تجديدها في هذه السنة.

FIGURE 5.7. **From Text to Form**

an expository passage. Figure 5.7 provides an example, and table 5.12 contains a task based on that example.

*Salem Elkhaled was born in Beirut on the fifth of August 1978. He lives in Tripoli now on Elarz Street in house number ninety-nine. Salem is an accountant at a construction company. His work number is 3785530 and his home number is 3784563. He got his first driver's license on the ninth of April 1996. His license expires within six years of its date of*

TABLE 5.12. **Task 8**

*Intermediate Mid*

*Instructions:* Read the passage above and fill out the blank driver's license provided with appropriate information about the person described in the passage.

*Variation:* Provide the students with the filled out driver's license in figure 5.7 and have them write a descriptive biographical sketch in one paragraph of the person whose driver's license is used.

TABLE 5.13. **Task 9**

*Intermediate Mid and Above*

*Instructions:* Examine the charts in figure 5.2 and then write a short passage in which you compare and contrast the imports and exports of the United Arab Emirates. Note that all the percentages are hypothetical.

*issue. Therefore, he wants to renew it this year.* Table 5.13 represents a writing task at the Intermediate Mid level.

*Transferring tabular, numerical, or graphical information into verbal description.* The exercise in table 5.12 is especially information- and meaning-based. Students' attention is primarily on constructing a text that conveys the information properly. It does not require reading comprehension as much as writing ability. Students are expected at this level at least to have mastered the formation of meaningful sentences with reasonable accuracy.

*Transferring textual information into tabular or graphical form.* This is the reverse of the writing task. It is made up of a text and a blank chart (figure 5.8) that the student is asked to fill out with numerical information according to the text. This type of task serves also as a test of reading comprehension.

Variation: Based on the passage about the exports and imports of the United Arab Emirates, students fill in a blank chart with the names and percentages of the different commodities mentioned in the passage.

*Replicating text and providing additional new information.* This task involves reading and understanding a model text (table 5.14) and then providing a similar text that differs from the model shown in figure 5.9 in content only. Students are preferably given inferential comprehension questions prior to writing their own texts, postcards in this case. For the writing task, they are provided with a blank form of nearly the size of the model postcard so that the task is a realistic one.

### Reading Tasks

Reading is not restricted to reading literary or textbook passages. In real-life situations, one reads signs, menus, schedules, business cards, memos, forms, invoices,

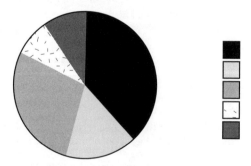

FIGURE 5.8. **Blank Chart to Be Filled Out on the Basis of a Text**

TABLE 5.14. **Task 10**

*Intermediate Low and Above*

*Instructions:* Read the postcard in figure 5.9 and write a similar one to a hypothetical Arab pen pal about a trip you have made, using the blank postcard provided.

maps, recipes, shopping lists, brochures, messages, charts, graphs, and the like. Such short, functional texts are especially suitable for elementary learners. Ervin (1988) describes communicative activities based on using 4x6 cards. He defines "communicative" as the exchange of new, unpredictable information for the purpose of these activities, since students, in order to complete the activity, have to interact orally with other students. The activities are divided into four types: matching, grouping, arranging, and discovering.

1. "Matching" activities require students to go around the room with two or more cards, reading them to one another in order to find the matching cards. Students may match word and definition, question and answer, words and their antonyms or synonyms, and sentence halves.

2. The "grouping" task is actually a categorization activity ideal for reviewing and retaining vocabulary. Categories suggested by Ervin include things one keeps in a refrigerator, things one finds in a student locker, things one takes on a trip, things one does outdoors, and things one sees at the zoo.

3. The "arranging" task addresses the discourse level of meaning. Students work in small groups to reconstruct a piece of discourse. It may be a text they have studied or a modified version of it. In such an activity, students have to negotiate meaning in the target language in order to find

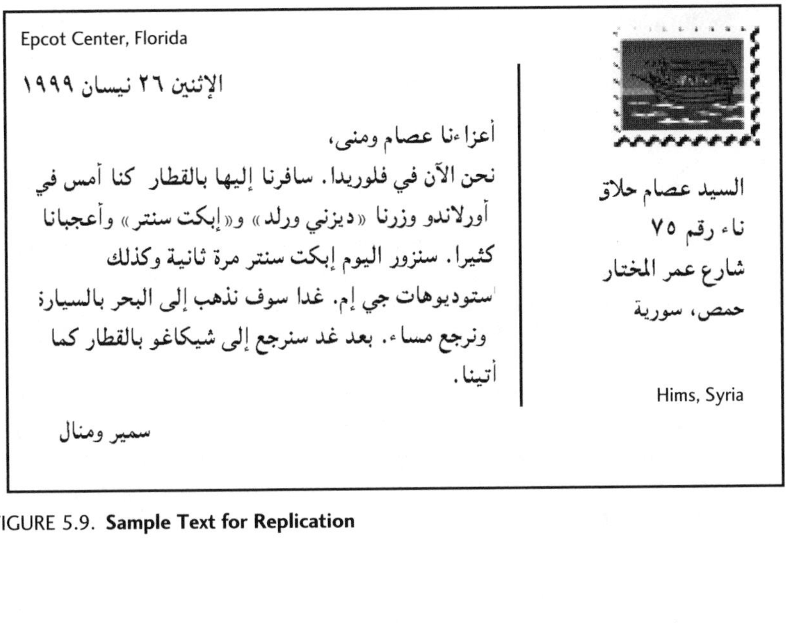

Epcot Center, Florida

الإثنين ٢٦ نيسان ١٩٩٩

أعزّاءنا عصام ومنى،

نحن الآن في فلوريدا. سافرنا إليها بالقطار  كنا أمس في أورلاندو وزرنا «ديزني ورلد» و«إبكت سنتر» وأعجبانا كثيرا. سنزور اليوم إبكت سنتر مرة ثانية وكذلك ستوديوهات جي إم. غدا سوف نذهب إلى البحر بالسيارة ونرجع مساءً. بعد غد سنرجع إلى شيكاغو بالقطار كما أتينا.

سمير ومنال

السيد عصام حلاق

ناء رقم ٧٥

شارع عمر المختار

حمص، سورية

Hims, Syria

FIGURE 5.9. **Sample Text for Replication**

out who has which part and to put them in the right order. They may arrange lines of a dialogue, a story, events in history, or a sequence of pictures.

4. "Discovering" activities integrate reading, writing, and speaking skills. They involve a large group of students (e.g., the whole class). Ervin describes two kinds. In the "cocktail party," each student first writes an unusual fact or attribute about himself or herself on a card. Then the cards are collected and redistributed randomly. Students go around the room to find those with the characteristic on the card.

### Variable-Level Tasks

The following tasks are ones that can be used with a picture depicting an event, such as one that shows people in a restaurant, at a wedding in a hotel, at the airport, or in similar locations. The tasks are arranged in order of complexity and level of proficiency.

a. List the names of objects in the picture.
b. Describe the location of objects, using prepositions of place.
c. Describe age, appearance, disposition, relationship, status of the people, activities they are engaged in, etc.
d. Construct a paragraph from jumbled sentences, describing the picture.
e. Complete a paragraph about the picture.
f. Anticipate future events for the people in the picture (i.e., what they would do after this event).
g. Describe where, when, and why the event is taking place.
h. Write about the event as if it were a story reported in the newspaper.
i. Pretending that the picture is that of a hotel room, for example, prepare an advertisement, describing a stay at the hotel.
j. Write a letter to a friend about the event from the point of view of one of the participants in the event.
k. Speculate about the place, people, weather, time of day and year, etc.

### Conclusion

Most students learn a foreign language in order to use it for practical purposes. It is incumbent on those of us in the field of foreign language instruction to see to it that this goal is achieved. With the existence of conflicting approaches and goals, it is important to ensure that the meaning-form controversy does not polarize us and undermine our efforts to deliver effective instruction. Although knowledge about the system of the language is useful at a later point during the students' course of learning it, in earlier stages the Arabic program at OSU has found it useful to focus attention on ways of using the language. Function and form are viewed as elements that support each other or as two facets of the same phenomenon. It is not a matter of either form or function, but rather of role and priority of each. Focus on function and focus on form are not two different approaches or methodologies to choose between. Focus on one to the exclusion of the other retards students' ultimate progress. Both are simultaneously present and significant in the language. Each component plays a specific role. In my view, accuracy in form is essential to achieving successful communication. Using the language functionally in the classroom through well-designed communicative tasks will ultimately help learners to develop not only communicative abilities but also knowledge about the language that contributes to the learner's emerging linguistic (structural) competence. Although students perhaps spend as much time drilling the forms as using them, creating a mindset in students in which they perceive that the purpose of language study is functional use in both the oral and visual modalities may be beneficial in developing their proficiency.

## Notes

1. In fact, MSA is gaining in prestige and in potential for oral use. Many television and radio programs, historical films, and some songs that used to be in the domain of dialects are now produced in MSA, particularly in the eastern part of the Arab world. The Arabic adaptation of *Sesame Street* is a case in point (see Alosh 1984). It scored considerable success in the Arab world, triggering an influx of programs that are produced in MSA for both children and adults.

2. To illustrate diglossic shifts, the MSA statement in example 1 below may be rendered in different possible forms in different dialects, exhibiting phonological morphological, syntactic, and semantic changes.

   (1) *yataqaaDaa al-muhandisuuna fi-ddawlati rawatiba mutadanniya.*
   Literal: receive the engineers in the state salaries low
   Meaning: State-employed engineers receive low salaries.

   In Damascene Arabic, for example, one possible rendition of the above statement may be as follows:

   (2) *le-mhansiin bil-Hukuumeh b-yaakhduu ma'aashaat aliileh.*

3. Nonetheless, given the imprecision of language interaction, the proposed model may need further refinements to account for language behavior in specific situations. For instance, in attested samples from formal interviews conducted by the author, the speech of some native-speaker interviewees from the same dialectal speech community as that of the interviewer (i.e., local) tended to be closer to the MSA end than that of other interviewees who come from another dialectal speech community (i.e., nonlocal) contrary to what the model suggests. Of course, this discrepancy may be attributed to other factors. Obviously, therefore, the situation is certainly neither simple nor static.

4. Declarative knowledge refers to knowledge of facts, such as the chemical elements in the Periodic Table. Procedural knowledge refers to knowledge about how to do things, such as riding a bike.

# 6

## DESIGNING AN OUTCOMES-BASED TBI JAPANESE LANGUAGE PROGRAM

Yoshiko Saito-Abbott

EDITORS' NOTE: In this chapter, Yoshiko Saito-Abbott describes a task-based Japanese course in which specific proficiency outcomes are the focus for teaching and course development. Given carte blanche by the university system in developing a foreign language program, the Japanese Department at California State University, Monterey Bay, decided on a task-based approach. The advantages and difficulties of using tasks in programs where teachers are held accountable for the results of their teaching are detailed here. In some ways, this university program is reminiscent of some of the U.S. government programs described by Leaver and Kaplan in chapter 2: the accountability, the emphasis on outcomes, the use of task-based instruction at very beginning levels of instruction, and the periodic assessing of student proficiency.

Creating a new program, an ideal program, can be any educator's dream. If you were given a tabula rasa, what would you draw on it? California State University, Monterey Bay (CSUMB), was established in 1994 as an innovative campus to experiment with new ideas for the California State University (CSU) system; the university opened its doors to students in 1995. It was the twenty-first campus built in the CSU system. I arrived at CSUMB with the opportunity to be the architect of a new Japanese program at a new university. CSUMB was envisioned as an outcomes-based university, tasked with preparing students for the twenty-first century. The university has a unique vision of higher education that emphasizes multicultural, multilingual, and technology-infused outcomes-based education (OBE). In this chapter, I describe a program designed to prepare students with language competence to meet targeted outcomes that were established specifically for the lower division Japanese Language Program and were delivered through task-based instruction (TBI). First, I discuss the background and the overarching structure that has influenced program design. Second, I explain the processes of implementing TBI and assessing program effectiveness, as well as describe the challenges and benefits of using TBI in a four-year college language program setting.

### The Background

CSUMB was established as a result of converting a military base to civilian use. The university sits on the grounds of the former Fort Ord, a vast U.S. Army base located near Monterey, California. The campus opened its doors in 1995. Approximately 28,000 people once lived and worked at the military post, an area about the same size as the city of San Francisco. When the decision was made to close Ford Ord, the state of California acquired some of the land and built a new university, known today as CSUMB. The founding faculty met to articulate a vision for an ideal, twenty-first-century university. This vision was based in part upon educational theory and in part upon a needs analysis of the local community that CSUMB would serve; that vision guided the creation of the university and the design of the language program. Preparing ethical, multicultural, and multilingual graduates who can communicate effectively in the world is one of the university's core visions.

OBE is a paradigm shift that addresses the issues of how well learners can perform relative to standards that have been established for a given field of learning (Braskamp and Braskamp 1997; California State University 1989). Whereas the traditional system of education counts students' seat time in a number of classes to determine successful completion of a curriculum, in the language-learning context, we seek to determine how well students can perform (demonstrate) against the standards we have established as Outcomes for the University Learning Requirement for Language (Language ULR) at CSUMB. TBI is employed throughout the lower division Japanese language program, which is designed and developed to achieve the requisite outcomes that, in turn, derive from the university vision statement to meet the needs of the population being served.

## TBI in an Outcomes-Based Institution

Implementation of TBI at CSUMB was strongly influenced by the institution's guiding vision and students' demographic characteristics. From this foundation performance outcomes were defined and the TBI curriculum was developed.

### POPULATION BEING SERVED

The state of California has a highly diverse population and is dedicated to providing quality education for all. CSUMB is a residential college. As such, it attracts many students from around the state of California, as well as those from the local area. There are a relatively large number of Hispanic or Chicano students, which reflects both the population and the needs of the central coast communities. These communities are primarily agricultural and are host to a significant Chicano population.[1]

Based on the Vision Statement, we developed a set of academic goals to ensure higher-order learning outcomes, more effective service to historically under-served populations, greater public accountability, and higher development of electronically distributed education. A set of academic values and focuses were identified: technology infusion, multiculturalism, globalization, ethical reflection and practice, interdisciplinary, applied learning, service learning, and collaboration. We were charged with the task of infusing these elements into every field of study including language learning.

The ULRs[2] are a set of learning outcomes designed to ensure that all CSUMB students, regardless of major, acquire a broad range of basic skills and knowledge to help them live and function effectively in our complex, information-intensive, global community. The ULRs consist of thirteen diverse competencies that students must demonstrate before graduation. Among these, effective and ethical communication in at least two languages is a basic requirement for all students.

The vision statement also informs us that students should prepare for a high technology global society of the twenty-first century. Given our location, it is only natural that we are also focused on the countries of the Pacific Rim as the probable working environment for our graduates. For that reason, too, a high degree of competency in foreign language is a major objective of the university.

### Setting the Learning Outcomes, Standards, and Evaluation Criteria

Prior to designing curriculum and syllabus for language courses, we set language learning outcomes, standards, and criteria for evaluation. As an OBE institution, we were charged to design comprehensive learning outcomes for communication to the learning community, as well as to set clear standards and evaluation criteria. For this, we chose the proficiency guidelines (ACTFL 1999a) and National Standards (ACTFL 1999b) developed by the American Council on Teaching Foreign Languages (ACTFL) as the source for CSUMB's Language ULR Outcomes. Thus, to fulfill language requirement, students must demonstrate the following three Learning Outcomes.

- Outcome 1: Students will be able to communicate in a designated language other than English with native speakers of that language.
- Outcome 2: Students will be able to describe and appreciate cultural customs, practices, products, and perspectives.
- Outcome 3: Students will be able to compare their own culture with another culture with respect to customs, practices, products, and perspectives.

Initially, Outcome 1 was the only learning outcome for the Language ULR. We added the two other learning outcomes to align with the 1998 National Standards.

These outcomes are published along with criteria and standards, described below, on the university Web site and in publications to communicate the requirements to students before they enter the university since not all CSU campuses require foreign language study for enrollment or proficiency for graduation; each campus sets its own foreign language requirements. It is also important to inform incoming students of university expectations. This prepares them psychologically for the learning environment they will encounter (Saito, Horwitz, and Garza

1999) and guides them in connecting their chosen foreign language to their major field of study while enrolled at the university.[3] Such practices typically have positive effects on retention rates.

### Criteria and Standards

The criteria and standards described below were established for the language requirement and published on the student academic advising Web site and elsewhere. These criteria and standards have been revised twice, based on the internal and external evaluation and from analysis of student feedback.

*Communicative competency (criteria for Outcome 1).* Students entering CSUMB as freshmen or sophomores must successfully demonstrate Intermediate-Mid proficiency levels on the ACTFL scale in speaking, listening, reading and writing for languages such as Spanish, Italian, or Portuguese, which is in keeping with national achievement levels (Brecht and Rivers 2000). Students who study languages such as Japanese, Chinese, or Korean that have traditionally been more difficult for native speakers of English to acquire[4] must demonstrate a proficiency level of Intermediate-Low.

Students who enter CSUMB as junior transfers with at least fifty-six transferable semester units and who have completed the General Education program must demonstrate an Intermediate-Low level of proficiency in the first set of languages or a Novice-High level of proficiency in the second. These outcomes were initially set one level higher and then subsequently adjusted to a realistic proficiency level for exit language requirements for transfer students.

*Cultural appropriateness (criteria for Outcome 1).* Students may achieve one of three levels of proficiency in exhibiting the cultural appropriateness of their speech. These include:

- *Exemplary:* Consistently uses respectful, accepted, and appropriate vocabulary, expressions, and body language for individuals and situations and can explain the reason for use.
- *Satisfactory:* Usually uses respectful, accepted, and appropriate vocabulary, expressions, and body language for individuals and situations and can explain the reason for use.
- *Unsatisfactory:* Rarely uses respectful, accepted, and appropriate vocabulary, expressions, and body language and does not understand the reason for use.

*Depth of understanding (criteria for Outcomes 2 and 3).* Students may achieve one of three possible levels of understanding cultural practices. These include:

- *Exemplary:* Consistently describes extensive examples of cultural practices and comments in detail on the historical origins and significance to the culture and does so with sensitivity/respect (lack of bias and stereotype).

- *Satisfactory:* Usually describes multiple examples of cultural practices and comments on the historical origins and significance to the culture, and does so with sensitivity/respect (lack of bias and stereotype).
- *Unsatisfactory:* Can provide few examples of cultural practices with very limited comments on historical origins and significance to the culture, and does so with a lack of respect for the culture.

#### EVIDENCE FOR ULR COMPLETION

Whether an individual student meets the three Language Learning Outcomes or not is evaluated, using the criteria and standards described above. Evidence of student proficiency is collected in various forms: participation in class conversations, portfolios, oral presentations, papers, oral interviews, projects, audio/video tape recordings, exams, reading responses, student journals, and performance on Classroom Writing Competency Assessment (CWCA) and Classroom Oral Competency Interview (COCI) assessments.

## TBI Curriculum in OBE

In order to help students to meet the targeted ULR Outcomes, each course in the sequence has been carefully designed to nurture students' growth in language ability. The curriculum is planned to articulate across (vertical alignment from beginning to advanced level courses) and among (horizontal alignment of courses at each level) courses. With clear outcomes for each course, instructors are free to design tasks to achieve the outcomes based on the characteristics of the particular class and to provide evidence (student work) that demonstrates that students have achieved the outcomes.

Vertical articulation is particularly important to help students who plan to major or minor in Japanese after the completion of the language ULR and need to fulfill the higher level Major Learning Outcomes (see figure 6.1). TBI instruction is very well suited for use with both low- and high-performing students in the same class. After establishing outcomes for each level of instruction (see table 6.1), we set specific outcomes for each course related to topics to be covered in class (see table 6.2). The specific course outcomes and ULR Outcomes are evaluated annually to ensure student mastery of learning objectives using evidence of students' work as described in the section on program effectiveness (see figure 6.2).

#### LANGUAGE INSTRUCTION TIME CONSIDERATIONS IN CHOOSING TBI

CSUMB is a semester-based institution (one semester is fifteen weeks) and each course is four units/credits. In other words, students receive four hours instruction per week, for a total of sixty hours per semester. TBI seems to be an effective way to achieve the desired learning outcomes while maintaining high learner interests through various types of tasks sequenced to engage and involve them in meaningful ways and challenge their language capacity through negotiation of

TABLE 6.1. **The Process of Establishing Articulated Outcomes for Lower Division Language Programs: Japanese Lower Division Curriculum**

*Japanese Lower Division Curriculum*

| Semester | Theme | Overall Semester Outcome | Overall Year Outcome | Language University Learning Requirements (ULR) Outcomes / Minimum Proficiency Level |
|---|---|---|---|---|
| Semester 1 | Outcome Theme a | Outcome A | Target outcomes for year 1 | Language ULR for junior transfer students: Outcome 1 • Novice-High Outcome 2 Outcome 3 |
| | Outcome Theme b | | | |
| | Outcome Theme c | | | |
| | Outcome Theme d | | | |
| Semester 2 | Outcome Theme e | Outcome B | | |
| | Outcome Theme f | | | |
| | Outcome Theme g | | | |
| | Outcome Theme h | | | |
| Semester 3 | Outcome Theme i | Outcome C | Target outcomes for year 2 | |
| | Outcome Theme j | | | |
| | Outcome Theme k | | | |
| | Outcome Theme l | | | |
| Semester 4 | Outcome Theme m | Outcome D | | Language ULR Outcome 1 • Intermediate-Low Outcome 2 Outcome 3 |
| | Outcome Theme n | | | |
| | Outcome Theme o | | | |
| | Outcome Theme p | | | |

TABLE 6.2. **Samples of Theme Outcomes and Semester Outcomes**

| Semester | Theme | Overall Semester Outcome |
|---|---|---|
| Semester 1 | Theme: Useful Expressions:<br><br>Outcomes: Students will act out spontaneously based on highly likely situations<br><br>Evidence: Role Play | Tasks:<br><br>1. Create and present a short video/QuickTime Movie to send to their perspective host family in Japan introducing:<br><br>a. Themselves,<br><br>b. Their hometown, and<br><br>c. Highlights of their daily activities.<br><br>2. Write an accompanying letter to the host family.<br><br>Evidence:<br><br>1. Short video/QuickTime Movie.<br><br>2. Letter. |
| | Theme: Self Introduction:<br><br>Outcome: Introduce yourself using various visual aids to support presentation.<br><br>Evidence: Scrapbook, oral presentation<br><br>Theme: My Town:<br><br>Outcome: Introduce your hometown and make a short promotional video to revitalize your city for economic development (3 to 5 minutes)<br><br>Evidence: Promotional video, flyer<br><br>Theme: My daily Life:<br><br>Outcome: Create a slide show of your daily routine and choose one unusual day and make a presentation.<br><br>Choose the most unusual day among the presentations.<br><br>Evidence: Slide show (PowerPoint), Oral presentation | |

meaning. We have found TBI to be time-efficient in that students acquire more transferable learning experiences in the same period of time when they work with authentic materials and authentic tasks.

### RATIONALE FOR IMPLEMENTING TBI IN OBE

Liskin-Gasparro (1982) reports that the Foreign Service Institute (FSI) found 480 hours (eight weeks) of intensive instruction to be needed in order for students to reach Level 1 proficiency (Intermediate level) for languages like Japanese, with an additional four weeks or a total of 720 hours of instruction to achieve Level 1+ (higher level of Intermediate level). This is for students with average language learning aptitude. This data, however, is based on teaching languages to mature, highly motivated students at the FSI where students have specific goals, study in an intensive language learning environment, often have high language aptitude, and frequently have studied other languages.

CSUMB is different from U.S. government language programs in that it is a public, four-year university where students typically learn language over two years, taking a sequential series of courses as a part of a language requirement along with their other university course work. In this learning environment, the students demonstrate Intermediate level competency with 240 hours of classroom instruction spread over two years. In other words, the learning is extensive, not intensive, in nature—and the total number of in-class hours is much lower than at government institutions (see Leaver and Kaplan, chapter 2, this volume, for details of TBI at government institutions). The number of students in one university class is relatively large, ranging from twenty to thirty students, so it is critical to design tasks that ensure all students have the opportunity to engage in using language in this learning environment.

Although a majority of students are able to achieve the targeted level of proficiency (Intermediate-Low), for those students who want to major or minor in Japanese, instruction must be designed to achieve a higher level of proficiency than the targeted minimum language ULR requirement level for all skills when they complete the two-year sequence.

In other words, students who major in Japanese must demonstrate a minimum proficiency level of Intermediate-High by the time they graduate; students who minor in Japanese must demonstrate foreign language proficiency at the Intermediate-Mid level. Progressing from Novice to Intermediate-Low, in our experience, has been easier than progressing on through Intermediate-Mid to Intermediate-High. This means that Japanese majors should reach Intermediate-Mid before the end of their second year in order for them to be able to reach Intermediate-High in time for graduation. In order to bring students to higher proficiency levels, the curriculum and syllabus are designed to develop each learner's ability as much as possible through TBI.

### THEME-BASED SYLLABUS

The curriculum for lower division Japanese starts with a dynamic, theme-based syllabus and gradually shifts toward content-based instruction for upper division courses. Course outcomes are established for each of four courses (101, 102, 201, and 202) and are derived from the themes needed by students in order to reach the ULR Outcomes, as well as themes that are particularly relevant to incoming students. In order to determine the latter, we conducted surveys of students' interests, their hobbies, experience, and other topics of interest, including their reasons for studying Japanese language.

We then evaluated the textbooks being used in the Japanese program to determine if the themes and content therein reflected the National Standards (ACTFL 1999b), as well as students' interests, and displayed the potential to facilitate students' achievement of the Language ULR Outcomes. Where textbook themes were determined to be inappropriate, those themes were modified or replaced by more appropriate themes.

In each course, four themes are typically introduced over one semester. Although the textbook has a list of learning objectives, we develop additional motivational learning goals for each theme to cover the language elements (vocabulary, grammar, and culture information) in the units. Those goals have to be engaging, and students need to perceive that they are authentic and useful. Since the majority of students are still preparing for unknown purposes, outcomes need to be somewhat closer to their current experiences and expectations. We established motivational and authentic outcomes, such as creating an introductory video about a student's own school or family to send to an exchange school in Japan or writing stories to present to local high school students of Japanese. Where more appropriate, we established motivational and pedagogical outcomes such as creating an infomercial about products or "designing your own dream house or town." At the same time, we also develop evaluation rubrics so that students know what they are expected to do and why.

After we choose themes in each course, we identify minimum vocabulary, grammar, and cultural knowledge to be introduced in the theme. When the language elements of the textbook are not appropriate or sufficient, we add, delete, or modify accordingly. Students use a course packet prepared by instructors that contains various practice sheets for learning kanji, vocabulary practice quizzes, and task sheets to use in class. The textbook is treated principally as a reference for students to use in studying outside of class.

The final unit outcomes for the unit "My Home Town" are to (1) create a promotional video and flyer to introduce a student's hometown or a facility within it (e.g., the Monterey Bay Aquarium) and (2) make a short promotional video to revitalize a city or facility for economic development. The videos are three to five minutes long, and students are expected to share their products with the local community. In preparing the production of the videotapes, students complete the series of tasks shown in table 6.3.

### LEARNING-SEQUENCED TASKS

We have found that a seamlessly sequenced series of tasks is critical to successful learning and sustained motivation. This five-step sequence can be seen from the sample task sheet of "My Home Town," in figure 6.1.

TABLE 6.3. **Task Cycle for My Home Town**

*My Home Town: Sample Tasks*

A:  View video introducing Monterey Bay:

- Brainstorm lexical items and phrases already learned and write them on the board.
- Introduce new lexical items, phrases, and Kanji and write them on the board.
- Various input activities to learn new lexical items, phrases, and Kanji.

B:  View the video again:

Tasks:

1. Draw a conceptual map after viewing the video.
2. Retelling to group using the drawing.

C:  Tasks:

1. Draw a conceptual map of (your) hometown (homework).
2. Make pairs. Students will ask for information from their partners and complete a drawing based on the information obtained from the partner.
3. Then share the drawing with the partner. The partner provides more information when needed.
4. Then introduce the partner's hometown using the drawing.

D:  Tasks: Make a promotional video and flyer

Share evaluation rubrics

1. Make pair or small groups to discuss and choose a city or building facility as the subject for a promotional video and flyer.
2. Make a story line for the video of the chosen city or facility to revitalize the economy.
3. Take digital camera or video camera and capture images of the city or facility (outside class).
4. Using iMovie or PowerPoint, create a promotional video (class and outside of class).
5. Students work as a group and prepare for the presentation of the video.
6. Students can get help from instructor or language facilitators.
7. Students do a rehearsal and get feedback.
8. Students make a presentation orally. Submit short video, and flyer.
9. Students, community participants and instructors, language facilitators participate on evaluation and provide feedback.
10. Students submit the final products in portfolio.

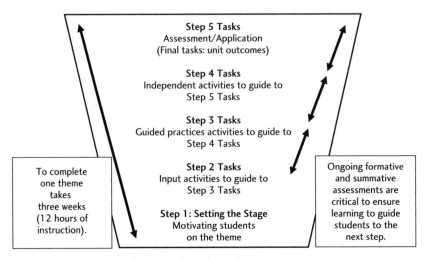

FIGURE 6.1. **Sequential Tasks to Reach Final Unit Outcomes**

*Step 1: Setting the stage.* First, the instructor entices student interest in the theme by showing a promotional video that the teacher or other students have made about Monterey. The reason for this is that students will usually engage in tasks more readily when it is something to which they can relate.

*Step 2: Input activities.* Using the same materials, prior to expecting students to use the language productively, the instructor then provides simple receptive tasks (comprehensible input) for acquisition of new vocabulary and grammar. For example, students engage in learning new vocabulary through graphically organizing tasks or drawing a visual outline of a story that uses the new language elements.

*Step 3: Guided practice.* Following these tasks, the teacher encourages productive activity. In the second and the third stage, we focus on students' learning of new lexical items and forms of the items that are more likely to be needed to perform the outcomes.

*Step 4: Independent activities.* As students approach Step 4 the instructor provides tasks similar to the final assessment tasks with minimum help from the instructor to prepare for Step 5.

*Step 5: Assessment application.* In this stage students demonstrate the outcomes of the unit.

If students need extra practice or assistance, they are able to work with language facilitators or tutors at the Academic Skills Achievement Program. At the end of the course students are expected to present their final projects, which reflect the overall outcomes of the course and include all four themes. For example, students are asked to create and present a short videotape or QuickTime movie accompanied with a letter to send to their perspective host family in Japan introducing themselves, their hometown, and highlight of their daily activities. This task is realistic and motivating for students since CSUMB has an active exchange program with a Japanese university. Exchange students from Japan, returning students from the exchange program, and independent Japanese students work in the Japanese Program as language facilitators, and they participate in various stages of tasks and assessment. Students are encouraged to be creative. One student, for example, who loved the topic of Ninja played the role of a Ninja in his video to illustrate daily life, or pretended to be a famous historical hero who talked about his daily life. In a sense, it is not a situation that students are likely to encounter in real life, but it is clearly motivational for students and that is what matters at this stage to keep them involved and learning.

### AUTHENTICITY

Both semiauthentic (realia simplified to fit the lesson and students' language level) and authentic materials (realia taken from the culture and used without adjustment) are used in the tasks. Due to the students' limited knowledge of *kanji*[5] during the first year, we use semi-authentic materials when it is more appropriate, especially during the first semester. For example, authentic written Japanese may include an unlimited number of *kana* and *kanji* characters, whereas semiauthentic materials will use only characters to which students have been introduced.

Recently, more and more resources are becoming accessible through the Internet, making it easier to find resources and authentic materials for tasks. The Japanese government, especially, has made a significant effort to fund and develop an archive of authentic materials for Japanese teaching professionals; this archive is easily accessed through the Internet at no cost.

Instructors have also collected materials, such as pictures and videos, and realia, such as advertisements, magazines, restaurant menus, maps, and travel timetables, in Japan and developed resources such as Web sites and digital archives. In addition, we use materials collected by students who have visited Japan during school breaks or studied in exchange programs. Those materials capture students' interests and provide useful insights into the culture and cultural behaviors. Returning students, for example, have created their own multimedia presentations and Web sites that show their interests, often on topics teachers had never anticipated.

### ACCURACY

Over the past two decades, communicative approaches have swept the language-teaching profession. In the process, the role of grammar has been deemphasized to the point where some instructors have become concerned that learners are not developing the ability to produce accurate oral and written communication. Consequently, a new call for attention to linguistic elements, a focus on form within communicative instruction, has emerged (Doughty and Williams 1998). When new forms are introduced and followed up with some activities, we focus on accuracy, but while students are engaging tasks with pair or group activities, we focus on meaning and interaction, providing some corrections where meaning is compromised. During the presentation phase, we do not make corrections; rather, we provide comments on feedback sheets and students are encouraged to make appointments with language facilitators to work on the specific form to develop accuracy. Instructors meet once a week with language facilitators and go over the list of students and areas to develop outside of class.

When an instructor notices that there is a special need to bring students' attention to a particular form for greater accuracy, the instructor spontaneously creates some activities or tasks for reinforcement.

### ASSESSMENT

Both formative and summative assessments are conducted in class, in addition to proficiency testing using COCI and CWCA a few times during the course.[6] We also conduct Oral Proficiency Interviews (OPI) at the end of the third and fourth semesters.

The results of these assessments determine the type of facilitation sessions that will be conducted by the language facilitators outside of class. In terms of formative assessment, the quality of task completion gives teachers a good understanding of what students can do and cannot do and guides teachers in preparing for the next lesson. Since we established specific unit outcomes and course outcomes to be evaluated for grades, students compile the evidence in their portfolio at the end of the course. Students' evidence is reviewed during summer by faculty and the director of teaching, learning, and assessment to evaluate how well students have met the ULR Outcomes and to make recommendations for refining the ULR Outcomes and strategies of effective and successful instruction.

## Challenges in Implementing and Sustaining TBI Language Programs

Although TBI has a powerful logic and is well suited to OBE, it is still challenging to implement and sustain a TBI program. CSUMB is a new university and has a commitment to OBE. In that sense, there is no struggle in terms of shifting from an already existing traditional structure to a new one. As the university has grown, new teachers who were not involved in the initial curriculum design process have entered this new learning community in which there are ongoing review processes to find the appropriate structure for implementation of TBI and its infrastructure. In some cases, some artifacts from teachers' backgrounds and previous experience have impeded adaptation to the new paradigm. In addition, OBE is still unique in higher education; it is somewhat challenging and contentious for students who transfer into this university without a sufficient number of remaining classroom hours to achieve the levels required on the proficiency assessments. Specifically, challenges we have identified in using TBI are the following:

- articulation within the program;
- meeting a wide variety of student backgrounds;

- teacher commitment;
- discrepancy between teacher and student expectations;
- professional development;
- materials development;
- program evaluation;
- materials development; and
- insufficient instruction time.

### ARTICULATION WITHIN THE PROGRAM

In order to achieve the outcomes, it is desirable for students to move smoothly through a four-semester sequence that is essentially a series of integrated tasks, with each set of tasks building upon the previous set. Achievement of seamless transitions from semester to semester requires an ongoing process for evaluating students' progress and subsequently fine-tuning the program. While it is relatively easy to achieve the targeted outcomes in the first year of instruction, it becomes increasingly challenging to do so after that point due to language attrition during summer breaks and the "marathon effect" in which the learners, over time, spread out across the lower proficiency spectrum like actual marathon runners at the eight-mile mark. A class of beginning language learners is much like a group of marathon runners at the starting gun. As soon as the gun fires, they start off in their own way and soon the field of learners spreads out, as students learn at their own pace. Over time, some tire and drop back (by some, this is called a language learning plateau), while others continue to move along steadily. This analogy is limited because we want all of the learners to finish the marathon. However, teachers are assigned a specific course to teach and may not be familiar with each student's pace of development, making it difficult to see the student's progress easily within the larger picture of an articulated curriculum.

Further, although task-based instruction can facilitate working with different levels of language by pair or group activity, it is nonetheless challenging, depending on the tasks chosen, to conduct effective TBI with a large numbers of students in only fifty minutes of class per day and to ensure that all students ultimately achieve the outcomes.

### DIVERSE STUDENT BACKGROUNDS

At a public university with a language requirement, a wide range of students enroll in language programs. Some of the differences among students include previous language learning experience, prior exposure to Japanese language and culture, preferred learning styles, areas of interests and major fields of study, and motivations and goals for studying Japanese. In the academic setting, there is also the reality that time is limited and students are expected to make a certain amount of progress each semester.

Designing tasks to meet this variety in students' backgrounds is a time-consuming process. Tasks prepared last year may not work with this year's students. In addition, all students are expected to achieve required outcomes during the same time frame, regardless of ability, experience, or motivation. These outcomes are tied to specific topics, but scheduling of the topics is difficult to regulate because TBI is unpredictable in terms of the time it takes for various students (or small groups of students) to complete the same tasks.

## TEACHER COMMITMENT

Typically, language instruction at CSUMB, as in many large universities, relies on the services of many part-time instructors/lecturers. Those instructors come with various degrees of professional training and notions about education. It is critical that they have a personal commitment to ongoing professional development and a willingness to adapt and work with an innovative curriculum. This is especially so in light of the fact that TBI requires a considerable amount of time for preparation and revision of materials. Like others who are committed to TBI as a teaching method, we have found that teachers with experience or education in TBI can usually develop materials relatively quickly, but while developing a sense of the essence of TBI most teachers spend longer periods of time not only than their counterparts in the TBI program but also than they themselves would expend if they were using other methods (Maly 1993). Developing a teaching and learning community for the purpose of sharing task-development and teaching strategies can be critical to the success of a task-based program, yet securing financial resources, space, and time to do so in a public institution is always challenging.

## DISCREPANCY AMONG STUDENT EXPECTATIONS

Due to the large number of community colleges in California, a major feeder source for the CSU system, we need to consider how to serve a rather sizable transfer population that has usually not been prepared for a content-based, task-based instruction (CBI-TBI) learning environment. Additionally, our students who want to study or work in Japan usually must take Japanese government tests or Japanese university tests that emphasize knowledge of vocabulary, the ability to read and write *kanji*, and grammatical knowledge rather than overall language proficiency. Students in a CBI-TBI program may initially doubt that they are adequately prepared, but they soon realize that they can prepare on their own for such assessments. In other words, TBI develops overall proficiency and as students continue they gain confidence in their abilities.

## PROFESSIONAL DEVELOPMENT

Lower division language teaching relies heavily upon part-time faculty and lecturers. Their primary duty is to teach assigned courses. The CSUMB foreign language programs conduct voluntary (optional) professional development workshops for all full-time and part-time faculty. While, in fact, part-time faculty may well need these workshops more than do their full-time counterparts, the reality is that they often cannot attend them. Typically, these faculty members are combining work with multiple employers in order to piece together a living wage. In these situations, the part-time faculty members' work schedules rarely permit them to take advantage of professional development opportunities. Moreover, faculty development time becomes a workload issue especially for the part-time faculty who are expected to do their own course preparations but who are not supported for professional development time.

The irony is, of course, that as an OBE institution, it is critical that all faculty be familiar with the overall program structure and assessment instruments and procedures such as OPI, COCI, CWCA, and Classroom Receptive Competency Assessment (CRCA). To cope with this challenge, periodically we must allocate time and budget to organize mandatory workshops with stipends. In addition, the CSUMB Center for Teaching and Learning provides small grants and seminars to sustain ongoing teaching/learning community and support the implementation of OBE. These workshops, for example, include alignment projects and biannual outcome reviews during the summer. Alignment projects assist faculty members to analyze their syllabus and their course components to ensure that each component and all components combined achieve the desired outcomes. The biannual outcome review provides opportunity to examine actual students' products relative to outcomes and standards. In the case of languages we examined the tasks and students' products and samples to determine if indeed desired outcomes are being attained.

### PROGRAM EVALUATIONS

In order to ensure the success of TBI in OBE, we conduct alignment projects in which the instructor builds a matrix listing all tasks, quizzes, tests, and homework assigned to students in daily classes along one side and lists the outcomes of the ULR across the top. Then, the teacher matches work performed with desired outcomes and checks the boxes to see if all elements of teaching events are in fact achieving the ULR Outcomes. The same grid is provided to students and they are asked to evaluate each element of teaching events is meaningful to achieve the outcomes. Surprisingly, the majority of students' responses matched with the instructors' intent.

Collected samples of student work from each category (exemplary, satisfactory, unsatisfactory) are analyzed biannually with the director of teaching and learning, in sessions where faculty meet and study the students' evidence. The process includes informed checks of reliability and validity as well as a reflective review of pedagogy. This valuable process allows faculty an opportunity to analyze and reevaluate their teaching effectiveness and to compare the final proficiency assessment and final tasks to be sure they match the skills to be measured.

### MATERIALS DEVELOPMENT

In recent years, communicatively oriented textbooks for Japanese have began to appear, and these are a great improvement over more traditional textbooks. Yet, since a task-based approach should be adapted to the students' needs and interests, if one wishes to develop a task-based approach, it is necessary to develop many of one's own materials. This can be a challenge: it is quite time consuming to develop tasks for the classroom. Not only do seeking and identifying appropriate authentic materials require time, but also developing tasks takes some creativity. Using the Internet capability, even with the Japanese government and educational institutions providing some resources, and selecting appropriate materials, especially for lower division classes, takes time, and adjustment for and in the classroom is almost always necessary. In addition, due to budgetary reasons, most tasks need to be planned well ahead in order to prepare a course packet for students to purchase through the bookstore; this is quite complicated, given that tasks or themes still need to be tailored to students. If we want to include proprietary materials in the course packet, we have to allow additional time for obtaining copyright permissions, which may require overcoming barriers from language problems, legal practices, or cultural notions about intellectual property ownership.

### INSUFFICIENT INSTRUCTION TIME

With only four hours of classroom instruction time each week, there is simply never enough instruction time to cover all themes and language elements (functions, grammar, vocabulary, cultural knowledge) considered essential to the lower division curriculum. Tasks require time for negotiation of meaning, and, therefore, it is sometimes challenging to cover planned materials. At CSUMB, we attempt to manage this challenge within a sequenced course through the careful selection of teaching materials based on ongoing evaluation of students' interests, needs, and language levels.

## Benefits of TBI in OBE Institution

TBI is outcome oriented, which is the principal reason we selected it for our programs, which are also outcome oriented. Tasks are a means for students to engage in and use language to reach outcomes or goals. In this sense, TBI is a very logical instructional approach for OBE. At CSUMB, we have observed the following benefits of TBI:

- great motivation for students,
- high rate of achieving outcomes, and
- an emerging collaborative learning community for both teachers and students.

### GREATER MOTIVATION AND DEVELOPING CONFIDENCE

Since students, through the selected topics and tasks, can see an immediate application of language, they are very motivated in learning Japanese. Various authentic and pedagogical tasks give them confidence in communicating in Japanese. Many students who enter beginning Japanese are fresh out of high school. Some of them have not yet attained the discipline to study in college. TBI provides greater motivation and promotes effective study habits. Choosing interesting topics is very important for sustaining student interest in learning Japanese. Through various topics, students also see a connection to their future career field or their major field such as computer/technology, business, teledramatic arts, and science. As the evidence accumulates in their portfolios, it is easy to see students' developmental stages and, more than anything else, students have something they are proud to share.

## HIGH RATE OF ACHIEVING OUTCOMES

As mentioned earlier, at the end of the third and fourth semesters, students take assessment tests. The majority of students have met their ULR requirement but have found it challenging to attain higher levels of proficiency, particularly in writing. Additional, voluntary, two-unit-per-semester courses, focusing on developing reading and writing skills, are offered, but since other language courses require only the four-unit courses, it is difficult to require students to take the extra courses.

## COLLABORATIVE AND SUPPORTIVE LEARNING ENVIRONMENT

Whenever possible we create or seize upon opportunities for students to become involved in activities outside the classroom that will expand their language learning experiences. For example, through expanded task activities, groups of stu-

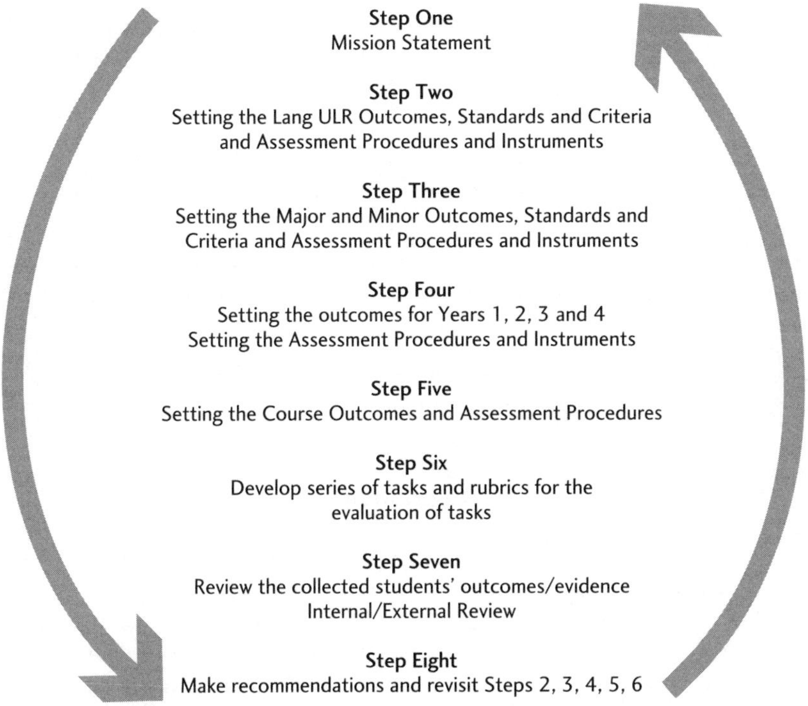

**Step One**
Mission Statement

**Step Two**
Setting the Lang ULR Outcomes, Standards and Criteria
and Assessment Procedures and Instruments

**Step Three**
Setting the Major and Minor Outcomes, Standards and
Criteria and Assessment Procedures and Instruments

**Step Four**
Setting the outcomes for Years 1, 2, 3 and 4
Setting the Assessment Procedures and Instruments

**Step Five**
Setting the Course Outcomes and Assessment Procedures

**Step Six**
Develop series of tasks and rubrics for the
evaluation of tasks

**Step Seven**
Review the collected students' outcomes/evidence
Internal/External Review

**Step Eight**
Make recommendations and revisit Steps 2, 3, 4, 5, 6

FIGURE 6.2. **Internal/External Review Process**

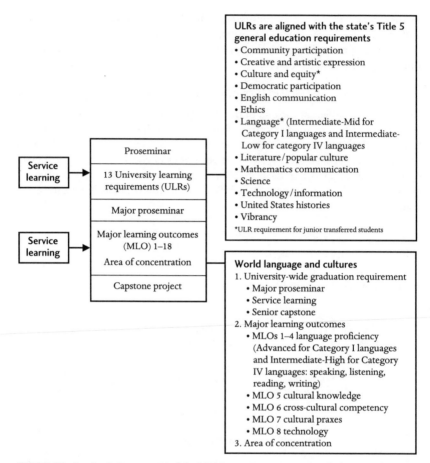

FIGURE 6.3. **Academic Program Model of California State University, Monterey Bay**

dents have started to develop movies on their own. From writing scripts to acting, filming, and editing, students enjoy creating movies in Japanese.

## Conclusion

Implementing TBI in an outcomes-based program was a natural choice to prepare students with language competence to meet the ULR Outcomes. TBI is an excellent approach to motivate students and promote higher levels of proficiency. It also creates a low-anxiety learning environment where students can try out ideas and practice their language to develop confidence. Since it becomes evident how students are learning through the process and completion of tasks, teachers can provide timely guidance, which leads to higher retention rates. Despite the fact that TBI is labor intensive and high maintenance, it develops a cooperative learning community among students and faculty. For that reason, the Japanese faculty at CSUMB is committed to continuing the TBI orientation in their language classrooms (see figures 6.2 and 6.3).

## Notes

1. Current demographics show the breakdown of the local population as 46 percent Caucasian, 26 percent Hispanic/Mexican American, 4 percent Asian American, 4 percent African American, 19 percent other or unknown, and 1 percent American Indian (CSUMB 2002).
2. The University Learning Requirements are the equivalent of California's General Education Requirements.
3. Students who are diagnosed as having a learning disability can petition to take an alternative pathway that allow students to take foreign culture courses instead of language courses.
4. CSUMB language programs use the U.S. government categories for classifying languages. The first set (Spanish, Italian, etc.) are considered Category 1 languages and relatively easy to learn by American students who are native speakers of English. Japanese, on the other hand, falls into Category 4 and is considered one of the more difficult for American students. The higher the number of category, the longer the time required for achieving any particular level of proficiency, hence the lower exit requirements for Category 3 and 4 languages.
5. The Japanese writing system includes ideographic characters (*kanji*) and two phonetic syllabaries (*hiragana* and *katakana*). Students first learn the *hiragana* and *katakana* first and then begin to learn the *kanji*. To be considered literate, Japanese high school graduates must master about 2,000 *kanji*.
6. COCI, CWCA, and Classroom Receptive Competency Assessment (CRCA) are California's state-recognized proficiency tests similar to OPI developed by the California Foreign Language Project (1993, 1996) and the California Language Teachers Association is more sensitive to the incremental learning of beginning to advanced language levels of high school and lower division college students.

# 7

## TASK-BASED INSTRUCTION FOR TEACHING SPANISH TO PROFESSIONALS

### Clemencia Macías

EDITORS' NOTE: This chapter presents task-based instruction at the beginning level in teaching Spanish to professionals and appraises its effectiveness in the author's personal experience in teaching at Hartnell College, American Global Studies Institute, and in private classes. The approach in these cases was to use task-based instruction (as method) together with content-based instruction (as a syllabus design). Most Spanish students were in Language for Special Purposes (LSP) courses, such as real estate and health care. Some were taught in classes; others were taught as tutorials. The courses took place in a location where Spanish is as much the primary language of communication as English, and in some ways, these courses were a cross between second language and foreign language education.

Teaching a foreign language as a set of grammar rules, separate from any practical application of that language, often prevents students from acquiring the deep foundation they need to use that language in a larger context. It is dangerous to assume that the ability to perform written and oral repetition drills is an indication that students have mastered the language. Typically, students in such structurally oriented programs, where learning a new language focuses on such immediate goals as passing an examination based on knowledge of discrete linguistic elements, are unable to transfer discrete items of knowledge to the practical needs of everyday life outside the classroom. Indeed, there is research to indicate that language, taught structurally, can result in knowledge "situated" in the classroom rather than skills situated in the individual (Brown, Collins, and Duguid 1989). They need to realize that language is principally a tool for facilitating communication and for understanding a different culture.

If a language is taught within a real-world context, it builds a bridge between the real world and the classroom so that the student can pass easily from the classroom to other environments in which the foreign language serves as lingua franca in various kinds of communication. This is especially true in the case of professional people, such as doctors, lawyers, and businessmen, living in bilingual environments, such as the many areas in California where Spanish is either a very prevalent second language or, in many cases, the first language of the majority of the population. For these individuals, daily schedules are filled not only with the opportunity to use the foreign language in the workplace but also with the need for good language skills in order to perform their jobs successfully.

This chapter discusses task-based Spanish for Special Purposes (SSP) programs designed for professional language learners who live and work in bilingual environments like those found in California. The difficulties and successes of teaching this kind of student body are addressed, as well as the nature of the task-based instruction used.

## The Professional as Language Learner

When a student is already engaged in a profession, the acquisition of a foreign language becomes more difficult. Time constraints, office distractions, and fatigue all negatively influence the ability to make adequate progress in the language. Fatigue affects the ability to attend to and to notice details, which are necessary ingredients for the adequate functioning of sentient memory. As a result, sentient memory, which opens the door to memory storage, is significantly decreased.

Finding time to attend class, let alone to study and review outside class, can pose nearly insurmountable problems. Emergencies, unplanned meetings, and a myriad of other obligations, together with family considerations, can prevent students from attending class and completing assignments.

Distractions also cause problems in the workplace, where ideally students will be putting into practice what they have learned in class. Professional obligations come first, and often incoming new mother-tongue information from the rigorous professional world competes with new information in the target language, to the detriment of language acquisition.

However, the student's desire to apply the lessons learned, whether in conversation or as an integral part of his or her professional life, determines ultimate success. Retention of memorized information decreases with age; adult students do not recall information as easily as a young adult or child, unless a strong association is built in their minds. Language learning, while not less effective or efficient at older ages, does occur in different ways (Shleppegrell 1989). Adults, in fact, have an advantage in the "binding" of new vocabulary and grammar to cognitive constructs already present in the mind (Terrell 1986) because they already possess a large number of constructs, including that of their first language. Where the difficulty occurs is with information retrieval, especially under conditions of cognitive overload—something that happens quite routinely with professionals who are also students. Thus, retrieving information often takes more effort for them than it does for children. Psychologists now think that information storage takes place in pieces: sound is stored in one part of the brain, meaning in another, and grammatical form in a different place. Since we store information in pieces, we cannot recall information as one whole piece. The process of reconstruction in language learning implies that (1) a missing piece can create a distorted image and (2) one piece might be retrieved easily one day but not the next (Leaver 1999). These attributes of information retrieval are a common frustration for the student working in a professional setting. Altogether, these elements create obstacles, which the student needs to surpass and over-come in order to learn the language.

These particular circumstances make it very important that the instructor be aware of the constraints on these students and tailor his or her program accord-ingly. Task-based instruction is an excellent option for the professional in all these respects. Why? Because "a task provides a purpose for classroom activity that goes beyond practice of language for its own sake" (Willis, chapter 1, this vol-ume). Exposure to a foreign language, using a method in which the student ap-plies the target language in real situations, facilitates learning. This is because the student begins using "new words" or "new sounds" in known contexts. The im-mediate link to a familiar environment creates comfort and ease. The memory does not need to work overtime since it already recognizes a structure (the envi-ronment in which the lexicon will occur) and absorbs it unconsciously. Fluency evolves from working with the word, sound, and meaning not in an isolated world but in its typical context.

## The TBI Spanish Program at Hartnell College

Hartnell College, located in Salinas, California, is one of the State of California's community colleges. It is unique in that it is located in an area where the lingua franca is as much Spanish as it is English, and the college caters both to Span-ish-speaking students and to professionals who work or will work locally—and, therefore, will need Spanish language skills for working with many, if not most, of their clients.

The "Conversational Spanish for Professionals" course at Hartnell College that is described in the main part of this chapter uses task-based instruction from the very first day. The syllabus design is content-based and follows the definition suggested by Stryker and Leaver (1997) in that it is based on a subject-matter core, uses authentic books and other materials, and takes into account the needs of this specific group of students, who are mostly beginning Spanish learners and profes-sionals from a variety of fields.

### TASKS AND ACTIVITIES

On the first day of class, students are asked to introduce themselves to each other in Spanish. They tell the group their names and their occupation as if they were in an English professional setting with new colleagues. This is accomplished with two simple sentences, *Yo me llamo . . . (My name is . . .)* and *Trabajo en . . . (I work in . . .)*. As a group of professionals representing various occupations, the students begin to acquire the new word, *trabajo*. Both sentences are practiced contextually; they will need these sentences to introduce themselves in a Spanish-speaking professional environment, within an office setting. The message expressed by all students is im-mediately understood. At the same time, they begin to learn about various profes-sions. This is an environment with which the student is familiar, so it is easier for the learner to assimilate the language.

Grammar rules are interwoven from the beginning in a simple, effortless, and unconscious way. Even though the pronoun *"Yo"* is not absolutely needed from a grammatical or conversational standpoint (since one can say *"me llamo"*), it is taught and practiced so the student can identify with its correspondent English pronoun, *I*. The subject doing the talking identifies him/herself with *Yo*, which helps make the connection to and facilitate the retrieval of information on verb conjugation in the first person singular. By using the word *Yo*, its ending *"o"* aids recall through sound. The first person singular ending of verbs in the present tense is *-o*, as in *como* (I eat), *llamo* (I call), and *trabajo* (I work). A sound–meaning connection begins to build inside the student's ear and mind. By speaking and hearing a word, they understand it not only when they speak it but also when it is spoken to them—therefore making the emphasis on communication.

Following personal introductions, the alphabet is presented and then connected to a task. First, letters are given phonetically to train the students' ears. Afterwards, the students meet these sounds in context. They read a basic children's alphabet book, about thirty pages long, in which the narration follows the story of an animal's journey through a country town. The book presents the letters of the alphabet consecutively; each letter is reviewed a page at a time with simple vocabulary and sentences that students can easily read aloud. Translation of the text is provided in a very small, gray print above each sentence, almost imperceptibly, so the students can choose to read it or not in order to understand the content better, while learning new vocabulary and cementing the sound combinations of the language. Different elements of language learning intertwine. Even though a short basic meaning is sometimes given in the students' native language, the focus remains on the text itself as communicating meaning. While many foreign and second language teachers have vehemently questioned the efficacy of reading aloud, it has been my experience that many students do want to do this, do benefit from doing this, and, if not allowed to do it in class, do it on their own at home, anyway. In recent days, elementary school teachers are returning to reading aloud, although it was once considered not to be an indication of understanding and a difficult combination of two different kinds of skills. These teachers are finding that reading aloud not only improves reading comprehension, but listening, speaking, and writing, as well (Reading aloud 2003). Following in their footsteps, ESL teachers have reported similar findings (Staley 1997; Smallwood 1992).

In the instance described above, the students are being exposed to simple text, but the fact that they are reading a whole book, albeit a book for Spanish children, is motivating in itself. Students gain a sense of real accomplishment when they have finished reading the entire book while reviewing a new alphabet. New words and meanings are grasped by deciphering the text through picture and word connections, and/or by consulting the translated text if necessary. Through reading, a foundation for decoding the written word is being built effortlessly. Deep, not shallow, cognitive processes are required, with their accompanying better connections to acquisition, memory, and recall (Leaver 1999). Both conscious and subconscious learning may occur. In addition to the new language knowledge and cognitive skills that come from this reading, they receive implicit cultural information that can be discussed in more detail at a later date and that will definitely assist them in their interactions with the local community.

A secondary activity, based on the reading, would be to build communicative tasks. For example, students could do a memory challenge task after completing the reading. Students take turns and tell the others what part of the story she/he remembers the most. Or what object, or word, in the story caught the student's attention and why. Likewise, exercises pairing the students and asking them to say what were the objects, or words, beginning with B. Finally, sequencing and classification tasks, in which the whole class participates, where the first outcome is to list all the objects they can remember and write them in alphabetical order on the blackboard. These could then be classified into sets, for example, animals, buildings, etc. Some tasks might well resemble what Spanish-speaking children are assigned to do when they are first developing literacy skills in their own language. They are useful for adults learning language because they recycle the same words and phrases in different ways and thus aid retention.

### DEVELOPING TASKS FOR THE COURSE

In creating tasks that help students develop automaticity and accuracy in using specific forms, the authentic contexts in which a given form is used and the real-life tasks that would normally accompany its use were explored. One example of tasks used in authentic contexts for adult professionals is learning numbers. There are many ways in which students may need to use numbers in their professional work; numbers can be very important aspects of Spanish for medical and real estate professionals, in particular. The following questions were used as a guide in shaping tasks:

- Where would students use this grammar feature?
- How would they use it?
- When would they use it?
- How often would they use it?

Below are examples of tasks for learning numbers, devised by using the above approach. Most are language display activities (equivalent to what Willis, in chapter 1 above, terms *simulation* activities) but some (e.g., asking prices of things) could be carried out outside the classroom for real and turned into a survey (which Willis, in chapter 1, would term a *replication* activity). Possible answers to the posed questions are shown in table 7.1.

### Role Playing

Using the learning of numbers as the example of how role playing can be used at very beginning levels of proficiency, the teacher first gives instruction in English to make sure students are very clear about the task at hand. The students, in pairs or small groups, ask and answer the questions in Spanish of a specific character, in a specific role, in each given situation. For example, the context may be a bar, where students are playing the roles of waiter and customers. The waiter's questions might be *"¿Qué desean tomar?"* (What would you like to drink?). One of the

TABLE 7.1. **Questions for Developing Tasks with Numbers**

| Where would they use numbers? | How would they use numbers? | When would they use numbers? | How often would they use numbers? |
|---|---|---|---|
| Supermarket, corner store, coffeehouse, bakery | Asking prices of items | Buying fruits, vegetables, or drinks in any food establishment | Daily |
| Real estate office | Exchanging information on house values | Buying a house / Discussing house's market values with friends | Weekly Daily (if buying a house) |
| Bar / entertainment location | Ordering a number of drinks | Paying a bill or ordering drinks | Weekly |
| Government agency | Filling out applications | Talking to government representatives | Monthly |
| Bus / train stop | Asking street numbers, addresses | Asking for fare prices, departure or arrival times | Daily |

possible student answers might be *"Queremos dos cervezas, una coca-cola y tres vinos tintos."* (We would like two beers, one coke, and three glasses of red wine.) The members of each small group take turns performing the roles of the various characters. The teacher prepares a list of questions for each situation and gives it to the group as a guide; alternatively, the role-play could be preceded by a pretask activity that included key line elicitation from the students themselves. When the questions are prepared by the teacher, they can be "doctored" to ensure the use of basic vocabulary learned (fruits, vegetables, drinks, objects inside a house, etc.) and the need to use numbers.

There are many different kinds of role-plays that can be used. The nature of the role-play is to simulate real life where the use of telephone numbers, addresses, and social security numbers become familiar as information commonly used in the English-speaking business context. Below are several examples of role-plays for teaching various forms of numbers.

- *Telephone Numbers*
    (1) Exchanging personal information with new friends
    (2) Calling a dental office to make an appointment
    (3) Calling a financial institution to ask for a car loan
- *Addresses*
    (1) Ordering from an e-business site on the internet
    (2) Calling a utility company to inform it of a change of address

> (3) Setting up an account for a mobile phone
> (4) Calling a cable service company to install a new system
- *Social Security Numbers*
> (1) Filling out medical records
> (2) Calling and asking for credit card balance
> (3) Filling out an insurance claim
> (4) Opening an unemployment claim
- *Prices*
> (1) Car rental inquiry
> (2) Home rental inquiry or exploring cost of new houses
> (3) Asking for cost of items in a flea market, or prices of fruit, vegetables, eggs, and cheese at a farmer's market
> (4) Bill payments: at a restaurant; at the utility company; at the phone company.

### Time of Day Task

One task that has enjoyed classroom success in teaching students the time of day is to ask each student to prepare a daily schedule, showing his or her routine activities for each day of the week. Once done, students compare their schedules in a small group for the purpose of finding a time that they can meet for a professional discussion. Alternatively, they could plan a joint weekend activity, conference attendance, or anything that would require manipulation of the times and, thus, discussion and use of time expressions. (Sometimes, depending upon who is in the class, these tasks can be actual requirements, not just classroom activities.)

A follow-up task is for students to make actual appointments that are needed in the next few months: medical, dental, vision, court, and the like. In Salinas, all of these can be done in Spanish because nearly every professional office is staffed with Spanish-English-speaking bilingual assistants. All these would count as replication activities (see Willis, chapter 1).

In preparation for the last task, a pretask activity can be done in which one student takes notes and writes all the numbers required if the task were to happen in a real life scenario, such as calling a medical office, a credit card agency, or another financial institution. The successful completion of the task is determined when the person taking notes and acting as the "company's representative" has gathered all the pertinent information needed to process a call, fulfill a client's request, or deliver a needed service. That person then reports the information he or she has gathered to the whole class. For example, Mrs. Rodriguez called "A to Z financial institution" to ask for a car loan. No one was available at the time so she left her telephone number. Mr. Flores called to report a car accident and gave the time and date of the accident, his policy number, the street address where the accident took place, and the number of people in the car at the time of the accident. Some situations are simple and will require the use of just a few numbers. In contrast, the gathering of numerical information in other situations can be complex, especially where the situation requires mix-matched numbers, such as telephone, social security, addresses, as well as account numbers, and credit card or policy numbers.

Role-plays, followed by the completion of real-life tasks, promote fluency and comfort in the target language and help students automate multifaceted grammar features, which, when used in a specific and actual context, provide the student with the opportunity for authentic use of the target language in scenarios that are real and familiar to the learner, as shown above. Automatization of form occurs naturally, unlike in classroom exercises where form is emphasized and practiced through repetitive exercises that rely on rote memory. The student also could be engaged in written tasks; if one student writes the numbers, the other one provides information requiring numbers. Such tasks contain communicative goals. They force students to interact in the target language, and students do it with a certain amount of ease, because they bring their own knowledge to bear on the task. Such tasks also allow for a clear understanding of meaning.

In my experience at Hartnell College, completion of real-world tasks produces results far beyond those produced with preset dialogues. When students work in pairs, they can expand their use of numbers in interacting by engaging in job-related matters. The unrestrained and near-intuitive use of the foreign sounds represents a strong component of subconscious learning. With subconscious learning bolstering conscious learning, students' nervousness usually disappears and a sense of self-confidence grows.

### A SUCCESS STORY

A representative student's experience outside the classroom exemplifies the sense of achievement and self-confidence the TBI approach delivers. This particular student was faced at work with the need to apply numbers in a situation similar to one performed in class. The student, who worked in the local unemployment office, had been successful in completing the classroom tasks dealing with numbers. Flawless exchanges of dialogues containing numbers had taken place among all classmates. Two days later, a Spanish-speaking man came into the unemployment office and walked up to this student's window. She quickly realized that he spoke no English. So drawing from her experience in the classroom tasks, she asked him his social security number and address. As the person told her the numbers, she repeated them and typed them into her computer. Lo and behold, she found the man's record in her computer. While she shared her story during the following class, one could see her incredible pride and sense of achievement. She had correctly performed a task at work with what days ago was totally unknown sounds and meaningless words to her. This just goes to show that learners really do need opportunities to use the target language for real purpose in order to acquire it in any useful way (Willis, chapter 1 above; Swain 1985; Swain and Lapkin 2001).

### TEACHER AS FACILITATOR

In TBI, the teacher has a special role: he or she is a communication bridge between the student and the meaning he or she needs to understand or express. The teacher first builds the foundation and support of that bridge and then lays the cables, spanning the abutments. From the beginning, the teacher presents the texts, sounds, and codes of the new language and follows up with tasks in which the students extract and rearrange order and meaning. By introducing the elements of the language in a well-planned manner, he or she can concentrate on the students' learning and practice through task-based activities. The constant use of the new language by the students in real life scenarios provides the context for learning. The teacher as facilitator provides the basic information that students need in order to complete tasks successfully; delivers direct instruction when and where necessary before, during, and after task completion; gives guidance to individual groups, as needed; corrects errors; makes suggestions; and in other ways individualizes and supports the learning process.

### THE ROLE OF GRAMMAR: TAGS AND BUILDING BLOCKS

The syllabus for the Hartnell College program was designed based on the concept of "building blocks" and "tagging." Every time the instructor introduces a new text or concept in the target language, a building block is created.[1] The last part of the class is dedicated to performing tasks designed to bring into play the new material Ellis (2003, 17) would call such tasks "focused tasks." This material is reviewed at the beginning of the following class. As new concepts are thereafter introduced, the student adds new "building blocks," which are continuously built and reviewed. Every time a new concept appears, the student reviews previous related building blocks that then "tag" alongside the new ones. Thus, a chain is established, facilitating a steady review of structural features of the target language. Tagging is supported through the use of authentic materials, with students methodically building their understanding of sentence structure in Spanish. Numbers are the initial, postalphabet building block for beginning students after alphabet acquisition. During the first reading of authentic material, the student assimilates basic sentence structure, numbers, and vocabulary. It is the first step in immersion in the target language. The first reading integrates visual and auditory learning. Numbers "tag" along, complementing and expanding on the sound of words. Once pronunciation is mastered sufficiently well, students review numbers in context, in relationship either to the student's work or to every day usage of numbers. Tasks involving numbers in context facilitate the learning of work-related vocabulary. Once numbers are mastered, articles and basic verbs become the second building block to "tag" along, then the verb, *to be*.[2]

Tasks complement the building blocks. As the student continues to tag new concepts to previous ones, tasks, using objects found in the classroom and creating real-life conversations based on personal information such as birthplace, current address, and telephone numbers, result in short conversations like the one below.

*"Soy de Nueva York. Mi dirección es 3472 Calle Principal, Palo Alto, California, 94301. Mi teléfono es 650-369-9138."*

The instructor can add as many tags as he / she wishes, based on specific materials to be reviewed. Examples might be *"mi escritorio es de madera"* and *"son las 6:30pm."* By this point, the student has had contextualized and comprehensive practice with the following building blocks: numbers, gender, basic nouns, and the verb *to be*. One by one, other concepts are added: other verbs, colors, adjectives, and other structural and lexical features.

While completing a focused task, analysis of the grammatical structure of the target language generally occurs at a subconscious level as a result of the tagging process. Tasks can be conducted orally (talking), visually (writing on the board), mechanically (some form of writing), or kinesthetically (moving while doing the task). An example of an authentic task at this level might be to introduce oneself and share personal information. Some products of such tasks have been:

- *"Me llamo Pedro, trabajo en construcción de 7am a 4pm. Soy de Nueva York. Me siento en un escritorio que es de madera, blanco y pequeño. Tengo 5 hijos.* (My name is Peter, I work in construction from 7 A.M. to 4 P.M. I am from New York. I sit at my desk, which is small, white, and made of wood. I have five children.)
- *"Me llamo Margarita, soy enfermera, tengo 28 pacientes. Soy de Chicago, manejo un carro grande y azul. Tengo 2 hijas pequeñas."* (My name is Margaret, I am a nurse; I have 28 patients. I am from Chicago. I drive a big, blue car. I have two small daughters.)

The first paragraph "tags" numbers to personal information. The second paragraph repeats/reviews the new building block and tags to it new concepts of adjectival use and placement, as well as the concept of color. The work is more than just lexical because these adjectives now have to agree with the nouns and the articles that they describe and students have to manipulate singular and plural forms, as well. If the focused task has a specific outcome, for example, introducing oneself to a partner or to several people to see what, if anything, they can find in common, then it is more likely that students will engage fully with the meanings being expressed. The grammar is learned in specific, personal, individualized, and contextualized discourse, not as discrete items in a textbook fill-in or as a translation exercise.

Table 7.2 provides a guide for creating task-based lesson plans, using the "building block" concept. These tasks use authentic and concrete objects. A student can go home and repeat the same task to herself or himself or to a family member.

### ERROR CORRECTION

Even though the instructor may present new material to suit multiple learning styles, adapting the presentation to specific learning variables, and carefully laying building block upon building block, it is natural that students still make mistakes (for reasons why this happens, see Willis, chapter 1, for the concept of interlanguage development). They err in pronunciation, word choice, and structure.

### Pronunciation

When it comes to pronunciation, some students have a harder time getting rid of their "American accent." While other students capture the sounds quite well

TABLE 7.2. **Task Samples Given in Spanish to Put Together "Building Blocks"; Gender and Word Ending of the Nouns Play a Crucial Role**

| Places | Items Found | Size/Height | Color | Gender and Number | Word Ending |
|---|---|---|---|---|---|
| Living room | Table, lamp, sofa, rug, painting | Small, huge, medium, large, big, petite, thick, wide, tall, narrow | Black, white, red | Feminine (La/las) | A (AS) |
| | | | | Masculine (El/los) | O (OS) |
| Bedroom | Bed, closet, night stand, pillow, book | Small, huge, medium, large, big, petite, thick, wide, tall, narrow | Yellow, blue, green | Feminine (La/las) | A (AS) |
| | | | | Masculine (El/los) | O (OS) |
| Kitchen | Stove, jar, blender, juice, spoon | Small, huge, medium, large, big, petite, thick, wide, tall, narrow | Brown, silver, purple | Feminine (La/las) | A (AS) |
| | | | | Masculine (El/los) | O (OS) |
| Office | Desk, pen, telephone, computer, folder | Small, huge, medium, large, big, petite, thick, wide, tall, narrow | Gold, aqua-marine, beige | Feminine (La/las) | A (AS) |
| | | | | Masculine (El/los) | O (OS) |
| Pet store | Fish, snake, lizard, bird | Small, huge, medium, large, big, petite, thick, wide, tall, narrow | Orange, gray, pink | Feminine (La/las) | A (AS) |
| | | | | Masculine (El/los) | O (OS) |

after a few attempts and simple corrections, others simply do not have a very good "ear" for foreign sounds. For those students who experience difficulty pronouncing either the whole word or isolated sounds, the instructor might allow them greater latitude than their counterparts. This is because he or she will have to isolate those few and spend quite some time working with them individually on phonetics, mouth aperture, and tongue position.

### Word Choice and Structure

As the student's vocabulary increases, based on the "building blocks," error correction at different levels needs to be maintained so as to avoid fossilization

(Skehan 1998a). As the course progresses, students with better pronunciation skills and deeper grasp of sentence structure help weaker students. Pronunciation skills and knowledge of vocabulary or sentence structure vary from one student to another. Thus, they can provide much to help each in the area of error correction and increasing lexical and structural accuracy. Just by the mere dint of hearing his colleague using the target language in a specific context, a student can feel empowered, thinking, "If he [my colleague] can do it, I can do it!" The instructor, however, needs to be very careful about correcting the student, where needed, in either pronunciation or structure, yet not overwhelming the student—with correction of small mistakes that don't interfere with comprehension. If error correction happens too often, it can undermine motivation; the student may fail to feel reasonably competent, and, correspondingly, fail to achieve a reasonable level of communicative competence.

### Corrections during Tasks

During the completion of tasks, teachers have several choices in terms of corrections:

1. Individual student errors can be ignored if they do not interfere with understanding.
2. Student errors can be corrected if they interfere with communication.
3. The teacher can stop the class and (re)explain a structural element if the majority of the class is experiencing difficulties that interfere with task completion.
4. Or the teacher can save up things that need correcting until after the task and then go through them (anonymously, making the experience less threatening), perhaps paraphrasing what he or she has heard students use. Fluency and accuracy on the part of the student play a major role in terms of self-confidence; fostering a healthy balance between the two is not only essential for the completion of tasks, it is also important for the development of communicative competence.

## The TBI Foreign Language Programs at the American Global Studies Institute

The American Global Studies Institute (AGSI) was an international educational institution located in Salinas, California, with the mission of providing assistance in developing cutting-edge methodologies in a variety of subject areas to ministries of education and academic institutions worldwide. Until its closure in 1999, it also provided a range of assistance to parents and students in the area of more effective learning. In its foreign language instructional programs (for children and adults), the AGSI used task-based instruction, emphasizing real-life tasks and content. To assist instructors in developing task-based course materials, three templates (sets of sample lessons) were developed: *Content-Based Instruction in Russian*

(Goroshko 1995), *Content-Based Instruction for Spanish* (Macías and Yerokhina 1995), and *Task-Based Instructions for French* (Funke 1995).

These materials were used not only for and by AGSI's own instructors but also in faculty development sessions for teachers at home and abroad. Among these were teachers from the Department of Defense Dependent Schools in Okinawa and Japan, local public school teachers, and teachers in Europe and Eurasia.

The Spanish templates were both content-based and task-based. Materials—magazines and newspapers—were from authentic media sources in countries such as Argentina, Colombia, Mexico, Spain, and Venezuela. The tasks used in these booklets, unlike those described in the previous section, where professionals learned to perform activities that they could be doing at work the very next day, were more pedagogical than authentic in that students would probably not perform them in real-life situations or at work—unless someone happened to go into journalism in television or newspaper work. The tasks were written to engage the student in meaning. Topics included:

- Domestic violence
- Cable television
- Coca and the miners
- The environment
- The economy
- Markets in Oaxaca
- Artistic creation
- Health
- Women in the Parliament
- Poetry

Like the work-related tasks of the Hartnell College program, the AGSI pedagogical tasks focused primarily on meaning for the reasons given earlier in this chapter.

### EXAMPLES OF TASK-BASED INSTRUCTION

The following examples of task-based instruction come from the AGSI sample lessons in Spanish. They were meant to be used as a guide for teachers in preparing similar lessons on these same topics. Figures 7.1 and 7.2 contain two very different, representative lessons. They are meant for varying levels of proficiency, ranging from Intermediate High to Advanced levels of proficiency. They could, however, be adapted for other levels of proficiency.

## Advantages of Task-Based Instruction

There is a real-life validation with TBI. In a bilingual state like California, the advantage for greater learning and comprehension is found not only in the classroom but also in the community at large. Spanish and English sounds can be heard in medical and dental practices, in local stores and small markets, and on television and radio, which serves to reinforce the educational process.

### Sanidad—NUEVOS HALLAZGOS SOBRE EL TABAQUISMO
**La nicotina es casi tan difícil de dejar como la heroína y también esclaviza, según los expertos**

*EL PAIS*
**Nueva York**

La agencia reguladora de los medicamentos en Estados Unidos ha iniciado este mes reunions con expertos para determinar si los cigarillos pueden considerarse drogas adictivas y si el Gobierno tendría que regularlas, según ha publicado *The New York Times*. Porque, de hecho, los expertos, aplicando nuevos criterios, creen que los fumadores son drogodependientes. Algunas de las encuestas que se están manejando reflejan la fuerte capacidad adictiva del tabaco. Un 15% de los que consumen alcohol están *enganchados*. Esta proporción aumenta hasta el 55 % en el caso del tabaco, que es más difícil de dejar que la heroína.

Cuando se le pide a grandes adictos a la cocaína que comparen la necesidad de consumirla con la de fumar cigarrilllos, en torno a un 45% de ellos afirma que la necesidad de fumar es igual o mayor que la de la cocaína. Entre los adictos a la heroína este porcentaje disminuye al 38%, y, cuando se trata de alcohol, más o menos la mitad de los encuestados dice que la urgencia de fumar es como poco tan fuerte como la de beber.

Al fumar no es la nicotina o la adicción lo más perjudicial sino otros compuestos químicos tóxicos que se producen al quemar tabaco. Según Lynn T. Kozlowski, experto en adicción, ésta se puede definir como "el uso repetido de una droga psicoactiva que es difícil de interrumpir". Añadió que puede haber muchas explicaciones para que sea difícil de interrumpir.

Tampoco la nicotina causa o tiene los mismos efectos alucinógenos que la heroína, la cocaína o el alcohol. "Pero si se pasa a otras preguntas como ¿Cuánto cuesta dejarlo?, entonces la nicotina es una droga impresionante", señala Kozlowski.

La definición estándar de la adicción procede de la Asociación Psiquíatrica Americana y la Organización Mundial de la Salud, que enumeran nueve criterios para determinar la adicción, que denominan drogodependencia.

Basándose en ellos, se puede ver que, aunque los cigarillos no producen un efecto tan intenso como la heroína o la cocaína, sí puntúan más en otros factores. Cuando se hace la suma de ellos, el consenso es que la nicotina es altamente adictiva.

Expertos en psicología de las compañías de tabaco niegan que la nicotina sea adictiva. Si se aplican criterios tan generales, dijo uno de ellos, "no se puede distinguir el que fuma crack del que bebe café, el que esnifa pegamento del que hace *jogging* , la heroína de las zanahorias o la cocina de las cocacolas".

FIGURE 7.1. **Nuevos hallazgos sobre el tabaquismo**
*Source*: This article first appeared in El País in 1994 and is reprinted by permission.

*Example 1.*

These pretasks and listening and reading comprehension questions are teacher led. Teacher asks these questions to several students, so there is a communication, listening, and comparison situation. The questions will be asked in Spanish. Level: Intermediate to Advanced.

*Pretask Brainstorm:*

1. What do you think of cigarettes?
2. Do you believe nicotine is addictive?
3. How dangerous are cigarettes and why?
4. What is an addictive substance?
5. Make a list of all the addictive substances that you know.
6. Do you believe nicotine is less addictive than heroine or cocaine?

*Listening Comprehension:*

"Nuevos hallazgos sobre el tabaquismo": This is a newspaper article that can be read as a news broadcast either live or on prerecorded tape.

1. Listen to the information and answer the following questions. Pay close attention to the percentages given.
   a. What is the percentage of people who drink alcohol and are hooked on tobacco smoking?
   b. Among heroine users, what is the percentage of people who compare the need to consume heroine with the need to smoke cigarettes?
   c. Does nicotine produce a hallucinogenic effect? Which drugs do?
2. Write a one-paragraph summary of this article.

*Reading Comprehension:*

1. What is the most harmful thing when you smoke?
2. How does Mr. Lynn T. Kozlowski, an expert on addiction, define addiction?
3. What are the psychologist-experts from the tobacco companies saying about the addictive properties of nicotine?
4. If you apply a general criterion to define addiction, what are the examples a psychologist from the tobacco company might use to distinguish addictions?

*Homework:*

Write an essay on:

1. Do you consider cigarettes addictive or not? Do you think the federal government should regulate cigarettes?
2. Should smokers be considered individuals with a drug dependency?

### *Trabajador Agrícola*

Un Día Más

Cuando el sol aún no brilla su luz,
Sales al campo con la esperanza de trabajar.
Tus ojos reflejan el cansancio que tu cuerpo siente.
Pero sólo el porvenir de tu familia traes en tu mente.
Ni la lluvia, ni el frío, ni el calor que quema tu piel,
Harán que tú te dejes vencer.
Brindemos este día en tu honor
Porque sin ti, estas tierras llenas de cultivos no tendrían valor.

En honor a ti,
Trabajador agrícola
Con respeto

**Alejandra Toledo**

FIGURE 7.2. **Trabajador agrícola**
*Source:* This poem first appeared in *El Sol* in 1994 and is reprinted by permission.

*Example 2: Poetry*

These pretasks and listening and reading comprehension questions are teacher led. Teacher asks these questions to several students, so there is a communication, listening, and comparison situation. The questions will be asked in Spanish. Level: Intermediate to Advanced.

*Prelistening/Prereading:*

1. If you like poetry, which are your favorite poets?
2. Have you ever tried to write poetry?
3. Why does poetry differ from prose?
4. When reading a poem, what attributes of poetry do you like most?
5. Do you have any favorite themes?

*Listening Comprehension:*

Reading aloud by instructor: "Trabajador Agricola"

1. Whom does the author honor?
2. What phrase tells about the person's motivation for working?
3. How does the farm worker feel?

*Reading Comprehension:*

1. Do you think the author has been a farm worker in the past? Why?
2. Explain the last phrase: "Porque sin ti, estas tierras llenas de cultivo no tendrían valor."
3. What does this phrase mean: "Cuando el sol aún no brilla su luz"?

*Tasks:*

- Write two things this poem makes you think about or feel.
- Compare these things with those written by other learners.
- What is your favorite line? Tell your partner why.
- Write two to four sentences, as close as you can in a poetic manner, about a place, a person, an object, or a theme you like very much.

---

### DEEPER LEARNING

The goals of the instructional program at AGSI and Hartnell College were to graduate students with increased communicative competence. Some courses were for beginners, while others were for advanced students with extensive knowledge of the target language. Task-based instruction aided the process by immersing the students in meaning and context. Reading, writing, speaking, and exchanging information in the target language within a context allowed the students to express their own meaning and ideas. Students were encouraged and supported from the beginning with authentic books or materials created specifically for the task-based exercises. Tasks related to household activities, work situations, or social interactions encouraged learning by requiring the understanding of meaning for accomplishing real-life activities. Consequently, the language forms conveying those meanings were absorbed in a deeper fashion, rather than resulting in a superficial grasp of the language. As colleagues not only in foreign language education but in a wide range of subject matter fields have learned, authentic tasks speed up real learning (Phlegar and Hurley 1999).

### IMMEDIATE APPLICABILITY

Task-based instruction proved to be an effective methodology at AGSI, Hartnell College, and in private tutoring classes for medical professionals. TBI enhanced students' ability to transfer language learned in the classroom to the outside world. Students would go to work and put into practice the concepts or new material learned. Opportunities for this appeared daily, whereby vocabulary, as well as grammar, could be used in context of their real work. Some success stories shared by the students included, at a beginning level, a welfare administrator (described above) and a bank teller, who were able to process applicants due to the knowledge of numbers given within a context. At a more advanced level, a medical assistant was able to ask a new patient about his basic symptoms and specific details about the pain being experienced. As Shleppegrell (1987, 3) noted about adult language learners, "Adult learners need materials designed to present structures and vocabulary that will be of immediate use to them, in a context which reflects the situations and functions they will encounter when using the new language. Materials and activities that do not incorporate real life experiences will succeed with few older learners."

### SELF-DETERMINATION OF SUCCESS

Assessment of task completion and of assimilation of Spanish took place at the end of every class. No proficiency test was given. However, the completion of the task gave the instructor the needed evaluation. The way students expressed the material orally in casual communication exchange within a specific task was the ultimate evaluation. The student needed to be understood by his or her partner, who in turn would ask other questions to be answered based on the "building blocks" and "tagging" done up to that point. Students were asked to review previous vocabulary and grammatical concepts by applying them to a context, not through formulaic exercises. Information exchange in small groups and/or with the whole class provided the ideal venue for grammar and vocabulary reinforcement. Some groups had specific medical needs. For these, tasks that addressed parts of the body, pains, and symptoms were designed. In other cases, expressions related to a specific industry, particularly work-specific statements and interactions, were taught through authentic materials from the workplace, as well as by materials created by the instructor based on the type of work that needed to be accomplished by the professional. At the end of every class, students had to demonstrate their ability to accomplish work requirements using Spanish. After all the preparatory and task-based learning activities, students nearly always found these performance-based activities to be relatively easy and enjoyable. In this way, they were able to gauge their own level of success in language learning.

### STUDENT SATISFACTION

Student evaluations at the end of the course were notably high. The students' sense of accomplishment was heightened by the success of their interactions among themselves in the classroom, as well as the following day in the workplace. The instructor felt accountable for student progress, constantly measuring it against classroom and workplace standards and adjusting the instruction to specific student strengths and weaknesses. This, too, likely bolstered the high ratings that students gave the course in formal evaluations.

## Resources

In using TBI most effectively, teachers can select from materials purchased and adapted from commercial books or created by the teacher or native speakers. There is room for immense creativity in classrooms where the Spanish language is taught due to the multicultural elements found in all Spanish-speaking communities, both locally and internationally.

### AVAILABILITY AND ACQUISITION OF MATERIALS

Materials used in the classroom were primarily authentic ones. Given the language —Spanish—books were readily available for any of the topics within a unit: alphabet, adjectives, colors, and the like. Some of these were children's books that can be used both in Spanish as a second language classes or in heritage learning programs in elementary schools. Other books were located that specialized in themes that contained needed vocabulary, that is, fruits, vegetables, farm objects, at the hospital, in the garden, at the zoo. Occasionally, materials came from textbooks; most were created by the author, a native speaker. Authentic materials included books from the library, purchased at bookstores (many of which in the Salinas area cater to the Spanish-speaking population), discovered at garage sales (again, thanks to the large heritage population of the area), magazines, newspapers, and video or audiotapes for children or adults.

I found task-based activities are enjoyable to prepare. They allow the teacher to target specific goals for individual students and to prepare activities that help students to process and understand Spanish in a holistic manner and in context. All materials are geared to aid the learning of grammatical structure and to increase vocabulary as the student performs tasks. The effectiveness of TBI does depend, to a great extent, on the instructor's capacity to develop such a syllabus and implement it in the classroom.

### TEXTBOOKS

Although the tasks themselves, authentic materials, and much supplementation had to be provided by the teacher due to the lack of task-based textbooks in

Spanish,[3] textbooks were helpful at times in providing specific examples or lists of vocabulary or in presenting grammatical rules. For students with analytic, deductive, or visual learning styles, textbooks can be useful. For teachers who do not want to choose between one or another textbook (as can be the case when a course is fully task-based), a variety of textbooks can be placed on reserve in the library.

## Conclusion

If the AGSI and Hartnell College LSP courses are any example, students taught through TBI exhibit a stronger foundation for understanding of the target language and acquire language skills more quickly. The foundation created in this type of learning outweighs the logic-based and linear learning exhibited in activities associated with form-based training. In TBI, learning occurs on a conscious and unconscious level simultaneously. Meaning is interwoven into students' everyday activities. Schemata develop concurrently in many different ways and in many different structures. While task-based instruction is more suitable if used with authentic material, it is not necessary to abandon the use of textbooks. The engagement of the student in constant improvement of oral and writing skills pushes communicative competence. The opportunity to use the language outside the classroom in actual and important situations helps the student to learn the target language not in a linear way but in a complex spiral. Meaning becomes the core of study, and as vocabulary increases, the instructor can introduce ever more explicit vocabulary for specific tasks to accelerate the learning process. Compared with other methods in use, TBI, in my experience, provides students, who are professionals and are learning Spanish, with a superior grasp of the language.

## Notes

1. These building blocks are similar to what Shekhtman (1990; Shekhtman et al. 2002) calls "islands": pieces of discourse that are fully internalized, available for use without thinking, and useful as models that are easily and quickly modified to specific contexts in which the speaker finds himself.
2. The verbs *ser* and *estar* and their differences are introduced. In Spanish, both of these verbs are equivalent to *to be* in English. The main difference is that *estar* conveys the concept of a temporary state of being.
3. While some Spanish textbooks claim to be task-based, none of them are based exclusively on authentic materials and tasks have been created for use by students who were studying in a foreign language classroom and not living in a second language environment, as is the case of any student of Spanish in Salinas, given the availability there of Spanish television, radio, newspapers, videos, and music, along with establishments of all sorts that are either bilingual or monolingual Spanish.

# 8

## BRIDGING THE GAP BETWEEN THE SCIENCES AND HUMANITIES: FRENCH FOR ENGINEERS AND OTHER TECHNICAL PROFESSIONS

Wayne Richard Hager and Mary Ann
Lyman-Hager

EDITORS' NOTE: This chapter discusses the content and origins of an innovative "capstone" course in French language and culture, focused on the advanced proficiency level (American Council on Teaching Foreign Languages, or ACTFL, scale) and intended to prepare American engineering students for internships with companies in heavily industrialized Northern France. The cooperating institutions in the international exchange are the Pennsylvania State University's School of Engineering Technology and Commonwealth Engineering (SETCE) in Central Pennsylvania and the Institut Universitaire de Technologie (IUT) of the University of Artois, located in Béthune, a city of about 50,000 located near Lille.

The binational partnership was created in the early 1990s in order to internationalize engineering curricula at each institution. This was to be accomplished through a series of planned activities using videoconferencing technologies, joint internationally focused industrial problem-solving tasks, and other undergraduate educational internationally focused exchanges. Since the mid-1990s, the culminating experience for each cohort of engineering students has been the international industrial internship. The object of this chapter is to describe the capstone course created three years ago to better prepare American engineering students for this internship and work experience in French industries. In outlining the course for tasked-based learning experiences—and the underlying binational institutional frameworks that support the model—the authors hope that others contemplating international professional internship programs might build upon these experiences and avoid pitfalls sometimes encountered in such international arrangements.

### The Penn State–IUT Partnership

Penn State's engineering program's primary mission is to prepare graduates to enter industry and to enter graduate engineering education programs.[1] The University of Artois engineering school (the IUT) is a small technology-focused undergraduate institute whose mission is to train its graduates for engineering technician positions and middle-echelon managers in the field of technology. This partnership has evolved steadily over a ten-year period and has involved a variety of disciplines, expanding from engineering to include foreign languages, popular American or French culture, and educational technology. The internationalized engineering curricula in both of the institutional partners placed strong emphasis on practical, applied, business-oriented engineering programs: likewise, the language and culture "capstone" course designed for these students headed for the in-country internship needed to reflect a similarly pragmatic approach. A well-developed systems approach in both institutions to internationalizing the curriculum preceded the course and facilitated its development. This approach consisted of multilayered, "scaffolded"[2] learning experiences, intrinsic features of the intensive capstone course and of the preceding courses (see appendix A to this chapter).

The primary partnership first included only faculty and a few select students. This binational collaboration also included the American-based part of the exchange—the French engineering students who were placed in Central Pennsylvanian industries and the native French instructors who prepared them for American internships, but these are outside the scope of this chapter. The activities of the partnership now include faculty exchanges, student exchanges, short-term student industrial placements, joint conferences, seminars, classroom videoconferences, industrial tours, joint class team-based projects, a cultural awareness seminar for American students offered prior to departure, and the intensive two-week capstone course described in this chapter.

## The Need for a Capstone Course in Language and Culture

The specific task-based language and culture course was first constructed in response to differing expectations of the American students and the French industrial companies hosting the American students. Prior to the creation of the in-situ course, interns arrived in France just shortly before their internships began in mid-May. They arrived with limited knowledge of the special region of the Pays du Nord and Pas de Calais and little appreciation for this region's pivotal role in French history. Students' linguistic abilities varied greatly, from Intermediate Mid to Advanced High on the ACTFL scale (see the appendix to this volume). Their motivation to succeed in their French industrial internships was high but the realities of the subsequent placement dampened their enthusiasm, even though they had been given some class time sessions with the French-speaking English as a Second Language (ESL) teachers at the IUT. Participants felt that there was not sufficient time to target personalized communicative needs; nor were they able to establish a personal rapport with the region, the culture, the people, and the language.

The capstone course was designed to meet the immediate needs of those embarking on the final stage of the program, their French internship. Initially, some in the partnership viewed this course as the "icing on the cake"—a nonessential component in the rich, multilayered process of curricular internationalization. However, it has proven to be the very experience that has permitted the American students to engage much more successfully with the French international business and industrial culture and to increase their desire to become lifelong learners of the language. The American and French university-based partners met to propose the creation of the just-in-time in-situ course in language and culture, building upon the in-country Penn State cross-cultural communication course (see the course description in appendix A to this chapter). Another adjustment in the program was to match the industrial placement with the students' area of training and expertise more closely.

Two American professors were assigned to the task of creating a course for Americans that might bridge the gap between the theory of cross-cultural understanding and the practice of applying this to practical, task-based, in-country, and "real life" situations.[3] The American instructors collaborated heavily with their French counterparts—local French nationals who were English language and engineering instructors at the IUT and who had also been involved in this binational project since the early 1990s.[4] The instructors used student-centered, task-based, on-site learning experiences that they constructed shortly after their arrival in France, using authentic materials gathered on location, with the assistance of faculty and staff from the IUT. Very few models can be found in the literature for organizing such intensive language- and culture-focused capstone courses designed for young, working professionals-in-training. The instructors relied on the past seven years of experiences working within the binational collaboration for international engineering and French language education. They realized that an intensive course of two weeks' duration could not remedy all of the possible linguistic and cultural gaps in student interns' French language or cultural repertoires. It would, however, respond to students' expressed wishes—diagnosing and addressing their most pressing communicative and cultural needs—so that the following six-week internships might be of maximum benefit and lasting impact. The first intensive course was taught in May–June 2001, and the second in May–June 2002.

One instructor developed a deep understanding of the linguistic and cultural expressions of the region; the other understood the culture of engineering education and the issues involved in industrial placements. The instructors planned activities and excursions to engage students in firsthand experiences with both the "c" (everyday culture) and the "C" (high culture: history, art, etc.) of the region. They designed embedded tasks at various locations in the region, which they thought would lead students to an appreciation for the Pays du Nord, its people, and its unique culture. The instructors believed that such an appreciation would lead to more successful internship experiences. The challenge was to accomplish this in a two-week intensive course.

### CURRICULUM DESIGN: TASK-BASED, JUST-IN-TIME, AND EXPERIENTIAL

Designing the course involved overcoming institutional and inherent discipline-related challenges. The instructors of the course come from very different disciplines (engineering and French), with rarely overlapping expectations for curriculum design and content. The engineering instructor advocated pragmatic approaches to language learning (i.e., lists of technical terms, or verb conjugation charts). The French instructor argued that lists or charts were of use only as reference materials. She preferred to engage students in guided practice, simulations, and role-plays, followed by task-based activities, noting that student interns would not be able to use the lists and charts in face-to-face, on-the-job encounters. She wanted students to use generalized language strategies, such as circumlocution or asking for clarification. Nonetheless, she acknowledged that engineering interns would need access to a highly technical vocabulary. To accomplish both objectives, the instructors tied technical vocabulary to the simulations and role-plays that the students would practice during the capstone course. In so doing, student interns were making the new technical terms memorable and, hopefully, retrievable when encountered in an on-the-job situation.

## The Capstone Language and Culture Course

In this section, we examine the importance of precourse diagnosis of participants' current functioning in the language. In addition, their motivation and on-the-job tasks were factored into a "just-in-time" approach to curriculum design.

### DIAGNOSIS AND ASSESSMENT

Experiences of the two instructors in observing previous cohorts of American interns reinforced the importance of a diagnostic phase in course construction. Only after the instructors had diagnosed the students' level of functioning in the French language, the students' personal interests, and their existing cultural knowledge could they tailor the basic two-week course to match needs and expectations.

Because of the limited time available, the instructors had to adjust very quickly to student needs and expectations, balancing these with realistic course goals for the short period before the internships began. The instructors arrived as the engineering interns began obligatory preclass industry tours. They joined the interns on the industry tours, not only to observe the factories or industries where students would be placed, but also to observe how the interns interacted with their peers, with French speakers, and with the factory representatives[5] who were teaching on exchange programs with the IUT.

After the tour, the two instructors met the Penn State interns who would be their students for the next twelve days. By virtue of observation, extemporaneous speech "probes" in French, and overt student expression of communicative breakdown and misunderstanding of the system of French engineering environments, the instructors were able to preliminarily assess the linguistic functioning level of the interns and their knowledge of culture. More specifically, by asking pertinent questions about the work conditions, factory operational procedures, etc., that the interns had observed on the industry tours, the instructors were able to discern what sociocultural gaps might be present that could impede functioning in those particular environments, even in spite of strong linguistic abilities.

The next full-day session was focused on a fine-tuned diagnosis of needs and current abilities. The instructors asked, for example: "Expliquez-nous qui vous êtes et d'où vous venez" (Explain to us who you are and where you come from). This open-ended question yielded a wealth of data, all of which was recorded digitally on digital video camera after a small rehearsal to reduce anxiety, so that students would appreciate their baseline level of functioning after the course. Next, instructors explained that they would design tasks that students themselves identified as critical, following concentric circles from the areas directly around them (in their immediate sphere of influence) and their expressed needs, then spiraling outward toward the community, the region, and the country. They were given their only textbook, a blank notebook similar to those that French students use in their university studies, in which they were instructed to keep a diary of their language learning and discovery of the region. They were also given glue, tape, and scissors.

### STUDENT-DETERMINED TASKS: SURVIVAL NEEDS

The instructors asked students to describe their immediate survival needs. Their list included such mundane tasks as doing laundry, finding out about transportation, conducting communication via telephone, fax, and e-mail, purchasing toiletries, buying food, investigating leisure activities, and traveling to Paris (only an hour away via bullet train). The instructors had accumulated an extensive library of second language learning materials at the IUT. These, however, were of limited use in constructing a highly individualized syllabus, one designed to focus on these very basic needs which, from year to year, were likely to have changed as rapidly as the underlying supporting technologies have changed. More useful were the flyers about events, the tourist brochures in French from the Syndicat d'Initiative (tourist office) located in downtown Béthune, timetables for trains, and the like—that is, authentic documents from the culture.

Instructors and students rarely stayed for long in the classroom assigned by the University of Artois. Instead, students traveled to various locations in the city and the region in the instructors' minivan, by train, or by bus. En route in the van they rehearsed the language they had practiced in the classroom, adding variations (sometimes hilarious), and anticipating responses. The initial planned interactions involved survival topics, and students discovered vocabulary and linguistic structures in order to conduct personal business, that is, to ask for laundry detergent, to determine how to buy and use French postage stamps, as well as to calculate and request change.

For example, in this first phase of the course, after a brief preparation for the task of purchasing essential personal items, students were literally dropped in the parking lot of the *supermarché*, each with a task to complete and to report on. The instructors stayed in the background while students conducted their business in the *supermarché*. Once back in the van, students debriefed on what expressions or language they remembered to use what language or knowledge they needed but didn't have, how they asked for what they intended to purchase, what they heard people say in response to their inquiries, and how this worked. They analyzed what went right (and wrong), and were encouraged to write essential information and personal observations in the once-bare class notebook. Without dwelling on mistakes, instructors and classmates offered each other practical, positive solutions, both linguistic and pragmatic, to deal with unfamiliar situations. This strategy of preparation, rehearsal, practice in real life, and reflection via discussion and written observation was applied to all of the immediate situations for which students had expressed a need. Next, the concentric circles of students' in-country experiences were considered as the instructors designed the intensive curriculum.

### EXPLORING THE REGION OF ARTOIS: CULTURAL TASKS

Beyond the immediate "survival" concerns of interns, instructors had previously encountered the need for cultural knowledge in the workplace. Students also envisioned having little time for tourism and exploration of the region once their internship began. Instructors planned for both simulated and direct social and cultural encounters involving exploration of the region. These activities were conducted in a similar task-focused manner as those designed around taking care of survival needs. Pairs of students were given road maps, Michelin guides and/or Routard guidebooks, as well as glossy tourist information brochures to the region. To help students narrow their choices, instructors created a small list of important natural and historical sites about which students were assigned to gather information from authentic sources. They were to choose the best possible sites to visit, given the constraints of distance, time, and budgets. Their reading assignments for the evenings required them to prepare arguments in favor of one site or another, in order to persuade their peers to their point of view regarding sites to visit or activities to do together.

The goal was to move in ever-larger concentric circles, beginning with "self," the university, the city, the region, then the North of France (see figure 8.1). In pairs, students learned to "read" a *Guide Michelin*[6] or *Guide Routard*,[7] make suggestions for a proposed road itinerary, and/or make train reservations, according to the routing map. Individuals or small groups summarized the reasons for their choices, and the larger group selected the locations they would visit. Tasks were selected and guided practice activities created to prepare students for the actual experiences they would encounter, based on their choices for travel and tasks related to that travel. For example, one recent intern cohort had decided, by mutual consent and after some debate, to visit the nearby city of Lille and had expressed interest in taking the train.

The group of students that proposed this alternative had gathered train schedules from Béthune to Lille prior to the class and presented them to the class. Just before leaving for the train station to purchase tickets, students were prompted to rehearse the language they might need to use at the station. They anticipated how the transaction might occur and continued rehearsing variations of their roles and responses as they traveled to the train station. When they were depos-

FIGURE 8.1. **Concentric Circles of In-Country Interns' Experiences**

ited at the train station, they each negotiated travel arrangements and ticket purchases. Upon return to the classroom, the next day, they recalled the language they had used and had heard others using. The physical artifacts of that visit (the train schedule and notes they made about effective linguistic interactions) were recorded in their journals.

The travel time in the van was used profitably to practice language, to observe the countryside and the distinctive regional architecture of the Artois, to read and decipher road signs, and to interpret the intended meaning of billboards and other advertisements. Students also listened to popular music and radio en route to the regional locations they were to visit. Instructors had brought a few audio CDs with them and had budgeted for the purchase of several new ones that were more to the students' liking and free choice. Students selected some of the French popular music that would be played in the van, and made negotiated and informed decisions about which CDs to purchase for the group, primarily by asking for recommendations from French IUT students living in the dorms where they also lodged. In order to select the CDs, they also needed to understand and interpret the lyrics, and they often sang along with them as the van traveled to the next location for their task-based activity.

### THE COURSE'S THIRD CYCLE: TASK-BASED ACTIVITIES FOR THE WORKPLACE

As students gained familiarity with language and popular culture, they became more confident in approaching the next step in their course: interacting effectively as professional interns in a workplace environment. As the time for their internship grew nearer, American engineering students begin to predict the types of professional and job-related interactions they might be required to engage in and to look consciously for the language they would need. Issues of the workplace came sharply into focus, as instructors continued the task-based instruction (TBI) approach. The students had been acquiring language in concentric circles from self and personal needs to, finally, the factories and industrial settings where they would work for the next six weeks. They realized fully that their notions of proper business behavior and attire might be challenged. They wondered what French managers and coworkers would expect of them and how they would clarify these expectations. They envisioned seeking venues of public transportation in order to arrive on time for the job, missing the bus or train, and ultimately finding alternative routes. They even considered how they might request French coworkers to include them in ride sharing. In other words, they were reflecting on experiencing the culture first hand, from the vantage point of the "outsider" functioning as a "semi-insider." They knew that they were to observe and adjust behaviors accordingly: the Penn State–based cross-cultural awareness seminars had prepared them for this.

In this phase, students needed to practice their job-related tasks with French speakers who could provide feedback in nonthreatening, yet authentic situations. They interviewed with French personnel in the IUT's office of international placements and with the IUT professors assigned to the partnership. They sought pertinent information from IUT-based partners about the rules of the workplace and asked for specific clues on French business behaviors, such as arrival times and work ethic. Without the engineering interns' intrinsic motivation to live and work in France and to have a successful experience there, the course would not have been successful. Feedback from the "graduates" of the intensive course has been overwhelmingly positive, and cohorts from both years communicate warmly and frequently with the instructors via email and phone calls. They offer to give guest lectures to the incoming freshmen involved in the freshman seminar and cross-cultural course at Penn State.

### ANALYSIS OF THE METHOD FROM AN INSTRUCTIONAL POINT OF VIEW

Next, the methodology of the course will be summarized in terms drawn from the second language acquisition field. This analysis situates the course within the discipline and illustrates the synergy of theory and practice. For all task-based activities, the strategy of preparation, rehearsal, practice in real life, and reflection via discussion and written observation was applied. Students sometimes ranked themselves on how well they accomplished their communicative tasks, and they asked others in the group (and the instructors) for feedback. They were, in second language acquisition researchers' terms, engaging in *metacognitive strategies* (reflecting on their own cognitive processes as they acquired language skills and cultural information). They also used strategies of *language rehearsal* (preparing to use the language by predicting communicative needs and situations and practicing the language they anticipated they would need) and *repair* (correction of incorrect patterns or behaviors of L2 communication acquired and overt substitution of corrected ones). They were actively involved in *negotiation of meaning* (querying native speakers to ascertain that they have communicated intended meaning) and noticing the differences between their speech characterized as *interlanguage* (that L2 speech which increasingly attempts to approximate L1 speech) and those of native speakers. They were experiencing *interaction enhancement* within the overall framework of TBI. They were being assessed by peers and were also assessing themselves according to *task-based language assessment* criteria (for more information on task-based assessment, see Passos de Oliveira, chapter 12, this volume).

In summary, the in-situ course followed a student-centered approach, with indirect faculty guidance in making choices and observing and sometimes instigating change. The methods used involved role-plays and actual tasks, using appropriate language, for student-generated scenarios. Content included the following:

- Issues of daily life:
  —Washing clothes, buying groceries, going out
  —Communicating with the United States and within France
  —Banking and getting money in France
  —Using public transportation: trains, buses, etc.
- Issues of culture (with a big "C" and a small "c"):
  —Understanding the history and culture of various regions of France
  —Appreciating the fine cuisine and wines of the country
  —Recognizing regional dialects and customs
  —Comparing the Artois (Nord/Pas de Calais) with other areas
  —Mining traditions/regional industry
  —Politics
  —Geography and climate
  —Cuisine and regional products
  —Architecture and artistic expressions
  —The Great War (World War I) and its impact on Artois
  —Daily customs
- Issues of workplace
  —Greetings and leave takings
  —Employers and employees relationships
  —Management styles, workplace hours and habits
  —Safety measures on the job
  —Casual versus formal business behavior and dress
  —Transportation to and from the job

## Sequence of Instruction at Penn State, Leading to the Capstone Course and the Industrial Internship

The integrated systems approach begun the engineers' freshman year and continuing each semester created the backdrop for assuring the success of the in-country capstone course. The task-based engineering education curriculum, encouraging group work in international teams to solve real-life industrial problems, set the stage for a successful in-country TBI course and the following industrial internship.

Reliance on long-term trusting relationships with international partners allows instructors to develop authentic materials just-in-time and to partner with native speakers in constructing the course. Sustaining the complex IUT–Penn State program involves a strong commitment of partners over time. As former IUT director Jacques Lesenne once said, this is essentially a people-to-people endeavor, and we are in this for the long term.

Many paths in the Penn State engineering curriculum can lead to an international industrial internship in northern France. Only students who have completed the cross-cultural seminar (see appendix A to this chapter) can apply for the internship. In close consultation with French companies who sponsor the internships, personnel from the IUT International Office place American students according to their areas of expertise and the collaborating companies' needs. The IUT International office also consults with American colleagues in the Engineering program at Penn State who have been involved with the American students through the experiences listed below. Many of these engineering students will have had the "internationalized" design course, which involves blended French and American student teams engaging in practical, industrial-related, problem-solving tasks, using videoconferencing and desktop video to communicate and propose solutions.[8] In the case of the latter, the winning binational teams are offered paid trips to France (and the United States), to meet their fellow French team members in person and to visit the company that paid for their trips.[9] Other students enrolled in the design course were allowed to accompany the winning team on an in-country visit to businesses and industries in Northern France, sponsored by the IUT and the Chambre de Commerce de Béthune. The Penn State International Cooperative Exchange Office also sends personnel to coordinate the students' visit. This has proven invaluable in establishing firm collaborative links between staff members at both institutions and helps to build a sustainable infrastructure for the international partnership.

A few students who apply for the French industrial internships are concurrently pursuing the dual degree program, which, unfortunately, has had only modest success since its inception in 1992. For selection to the internship in France, extensive screening for skills in the French language and for personal factors (general emotional stability/flexibility/adaptability/integrative motivation) has proven invaluable in forestalling difficulties. Of the two screening areas, the latter (personal factors, etc.) has proven more critical than the former (French language skills). A solid preparation for the internship at Penn State has also proven to be important in addressing cross-cultural issues and in preparing interns to understand their French counterparts. Table 8.1 lists the paths that students might take to prepare for the internship and for the pre-internship capstone language and culture course.

A description of the task-based activities in the preceding engineering course offerings and the successful in-country intern program might likewise encourage foreign language departments to reach out to other professional disciplines to create dual-degree programs involving languages and professional studies. For those existing programs, the discussion of the task-based activities using ad-

TABLE 8.1. **Experiences that PSU Engineering Students Are Offered Prior to the Internship**

| Year | Semester One | Semester Two |
|------|--------------|--------------|
| Freshman | First-Year Seminar[a] | First-Year Seminar[a] / Topics in Design |
| Sophomore | Preparation for study abroad[a] | In situ course / internship first year |
| Junior | Topics in Design (contest) | In situ course / internship first year |
| Senior+ | Dual degree in French and Engineering/ in-situ course / internship first year | |

[a]See appendix B for further information.

vanced communication technologies[10] might propose new ideas for recruiting engineering or other professional students to international programs and for preparing students for these international experiences. A summary of the programs developed in the partnership that both preceded and followed the in situ capstone course is outlined in table 8.1.

## Overcoming Institutional and Discipline-Related Constraints and Challenges

In spite of administrative pressures to "internationalize the curriculum" currently felt in U.S. universities, there are many institutional barriers that effectively prohibit this at most institutions. Engineering students in the United States are often unable to add language courses or other electives to their existing curriculum or plan of study. The prerequisites for entry into engineering fields and the program's requirements for graduation leave little discretionary room for language courses. A major challenge for program planners in international education for the professions is to find innovative ways to permit students to take courses in language and culture without much delay in getting an engineering (or other professional) degree.[11] Only recently has the Accreditation Board for Engineering and Technology, the accrediting agency for engineering programs in the United States, acknowledged the importance of international experience in undergraduate engineering education. The recently adopted accreditation criteria for engineering programs by the Accreditation Board for Engineering and Technology,[12] which are based upon outcomes and assessment, require engineering programs to demonstrate that their graduates have "the broad education necessary to understand the impact of engineering solutions in a global and societal context." This provides an excellent opportunity for language and culture to be infused into the engineering curricula, especially if it can be accomplished without significantly increasing the credits required to attain an undergraduate degree.

University foreign language instructors generally possess an in-depth knowledge of the structure and literature of the language. Their teaching experiences involve sharing that linguistic and literary knowledge, and they have little incentive or occasion to learn technical vocabulary or the language of professional disciplines. Foreign language teachers have expressed the feeling that, with increased pressures of internationalizing professional schools, their knowledge is being categorized as irrelevant and that they are being relegated to a service function in the academy. At most institutions of higher education, undergraduate language enrollments in the more commonly taught languages have fallen, perhaps putting more and more pressure on language professionals to retool or risk becoming irrelevant.[13] Professional schools often hire their own language instructional personnel, mostly nontenure track, creating a parallel system to the traditional language departments.

To attract more Penn State students to the program, and eventually to the possibility of pursuing a dual major in French and Engineering, international programs officers may consider more active recruitment activities in high schools, touting opportunities for study abroad, dual degrees, international internships, and other international experiences. Entering freshmen should be able to complete an online questionnaire regarding their desires to study abroad and to build on prior foreign language study as part of freshmen orientation. Finally, more language faculty should become involved in the kind of "just-in time-learning," as well as task-based approaches that are common in engineering and the sciences. This will lead to more relevant, innovative approaches to language teaching.

### Conclusion: Globalization and Internationalizing the Engineering Curriculum

To the casual observer traveling in France, the predominance of multinational corporations is visually overwhelming. The same is true in American society. Chrysler, once a Detroit name brand, is now Daimler-Chrysler, with branches on many continents. Toyota parts are made in Mexico and the United States, and cars are assembled in various international spots. The concept of "buy American" has become almost meaningless.

Jean-Marie Guéhenno, in *The End of the Nation-State* (1995), points to the blurring of national boundaries and the accompanying mobility and loss of "center" and belonging. While Guéhenno appears to deplore the internationalization of the economy on certain fundamental levels, he also points to the irrefutable necessity for individuals to adjust to the demands of a global society. He suggests that there is no turning back and that adaptive strategies encouraging collaboration and the humanization of an increasingly technology-driven society are imperative. With the growth of this "international" economy, it is becoming increasingly important for students in professional schools to have an international experience, including intensive exposure to foreign languages and their cultures, in their academic curricula. In an interdependent setting, such exchanges are vital, particularly if they have real meaning for the participants—and if they resemble the kinds of international activities that interns are likely to encounter when they have completed their education and are working in internationally based engineering positions. Task-based learning experiences incorporated into the curriculum and involving international colleagues in collaborative problem solving are vital to fostering the kind of knowledge needed in a truly global economy.

## Appendix A: A First-Year Seminar Course

This has been offered as a one-credit course for freshman engineering, science, and technology students during their first or second semester. The purpose of this seminar is to (1) familiarize students with globalization and the importance of being prepared to enter a workforce that is increasing becoming global; (2) encourage students to explore various international educational opportunities, that is, study abroad, internships, and courses, and build a curricular plan that allows the inclusion of that opportunity; and (3) introduce students to testing instruments and activities that can better prepare them for an international experience. The course syllabus is shown in table 8.2.

## Appendix B: Seminar on Preparation for International Exchange

This is a one-credit seminar for engineering students who are preparing for an international exchange opportunity. Initial offerings of this seminar have focused on Western Europe (France, Germany, and more recently Spain), since those countries have represented the bulk of opportunities available to our Penn State engineering students. Students in the seminar include freshman that are going to Europe for industrial tours and students who will be working in-country as part of an internship or cooperative education experience.

It should also be noted that opportunities exist for engineering and other students in many other countries through individual engineering departmental or broader international university programs and initiatives. However, we are unaware of any other efforts at any level to prepare students through an academic course for their international exchange.

The purpose of this seminar is to (1) familiarize students with globalization and the importance of being prepared to enter a workforce that is increasingly becoming global, (2) introduce students to testing instruments and assist them in developing activities that can better prepare them for an international experience, and (3) expose them to the European culture (France, Germany, and Spain) and in particular to the work environment in European business and industry.

TABLE 8.2. **Elements of the Course Syllabus**

| Item | Objective |
|------|-----------|
| Introduction to engineering, science, and technology careers and curricula | Ensure that the students understand the curriculum they have chosen to pursue. |
| Career opportunities and the globalization of industry and the workforce | Expose students to the increasing globalization of industry and the workforce and to the advantages and disadvantages of this movement. |
| International academic opportunities | Have students explore the international opportunities offered by the university, college, and department and gain an understanding of those opportunities. |
| Building an international opportunity into your academic program | Assist students in planning an individualized curriculum for their major that allows them to incorporate their desired international experience(s) into their academic plan. |
| Self-awareness and preparation | Lead the students through individualized self-awareness tests—i.e., Cross-Cultural Awareness Inventory, Global Awareness Profile—and assist them in establishing a program to strengthen their individual areas of weakness. |

Few of our entering Penn State engineering students have experience of international travel and many have come from small towns with little ethnic diversity. Even students from the larger cities of Philadelphia, Pittsburgh, and Harrisburg, in general, lack exposure to international culture, even to the exclusion of having a meal in an ethnic restaurant different from their own cultural background. While this may seem unusual, the authors, who have more than thirty years of experience in higher education, believe that the vast majority of our students in any academic discipline generally lack exposure to different cultures and are ill prepared to study or work in an international environment.

This seminar is an initial attempt to address some of these concerns and observations. Table 8.3 summarizes course content and objectives.

As a result of our experiences, the strongest focus of the course has been the self-awareness testing and the subsequent identification of activities that can assist the individual in addressing these weaknesses. Once weaknesses are individually identified by the Global Awareness Profile and more importantly by the Cross-Cultural Awareness Inventory, students are assisted in establishing a set of activities that they can accomplish before their initiation of their international opportunity. Normally these activities need to be accomplished within the semester prior to their international experience. The students are required to maintain a

TABLE 8.3. **Content of the Capstone Course**

| Topic | Objective |
|---|---|
| Globalization of industry and in particular engineering | Expose students to the increasing globalization of industry and the workforce with emphasis on the advantages and disadvantages of this movement. |
| Self-awareness and preparation for international experience | Lead the students through individualized self-awareness tests—i.e., Cross-Cultural Awareness Inventory (CCAI), Global Awareness Profile (GAP)—and assist them in establishing a program to strengthen their individual areas of weakness. |
| Cultural experiences | Introduce to the students some cultural aspects of the country and in particular unique things that they might experience in the work environment. |
| Travel and safety | Prepare students for the travel environment, including information regarding passports, travel, safety, contacting home, etc. |

journal identifying the activities they wish to accomplish and their experience following the activity.

Anecdotal evidence from the journals clearly demonstrates the value of this course. Some students experience a dinner at an ethnic restaurant for the first time; some students choose to attend a religious service with a roommate or friend of a different religion; some students even spend a weekend at the home of a roommate or friend with a different ethnic background. While any one of these activities may appear to be insignificant, our experience has demonstrated that any expansion of the student's awareness of international cultural is beneficial.

## Appendix C: Task-Based Projects of the Penn State Undergraduate Curriculum (Samples)

### 1997–98 PROJECT

The students were tasked with the design and prototyping of a mechanism to aid in the inspection of 35-inch televsion screens. The work required by the operator would be less than or equivalent to the amount of work required to inspect a 27-inch screen.

### 1998–99 PROJECT

The objective was to design a system for organizing size appropriate containers that are used to store sheet metal as the sheet metal is lifted or pulled by forklifts. Designing one or more new containers is allowed. This project came from a mid-sized French company in Béthune, France.

### 1999–2000 PROJECT

This year's project consisted of designing a housing for fiber-optic cables. As part of this project, students used rapid-prototype technology to make models of their designs. This project came from Corning Technology.

### 2000–01 PROJECT 1 (OF TWO PROJECTS)

The objective was to design a rack to collect parts for a domestic fowl pan feeder as they come out of the machine and store them until they can be used in the next phase of production. This project came from the PIL Company, part of the Lubing International Group.

### 2001–02 PROJECT

The objective was to design an effective method to apply flock onto the surface of a side pocket that fits under the dashboard of a car, taking into account the comfort and health of the workers as well. The project came from Cellusuede Products, Inc. (USA), and Faurecia (France).

### 2002–03 PROJECT

The objective was to design and prototype the next-generation human-powered system for set-up and tear-down of a folding trailer (a.k.a. "pop-up camper") that does not rely on any external power source other than manual power. The project came from Coleman. (Adapted from Alliance by Design 2002.)

## Notes

The authors wish to especially acknowledge the contributions of Christine Lally, as well as those of partnership colleagues Richard Devon, Sohail Anwar, Jacques LeSenne, Jean-Claude Andriqc, Sylvie Fossiez, Jean-Francois Pauwels, Marc Evrard, Dominique Saintive, and many others at Penn State and the IUT–University of Artois.

1. Penn State is ranked in the top twenty undergraduate engineering institutions with 8,000 students enrolled in the College of Engineering, which has several international agreements with French higher education institutions, including with the Grande Ecoles. At first blush, this profile does not match well with our IUT partner, and, as a result, some may question this partnership. Experience has taught us that the partnership is beneficial for a variety of reasons, which are elaborated in this article.
2. Scaffolding refers to the teacher providing external support, such as modeling a targeted learning strategy or task, in order to control elements of the task that are beyond students' current capability, gradually shifting increasing responsibility to students (Gibbons 2002; Hammond 2001; Vygotsky 1978).
3. Both instructors had been involved with the Penn State–IUT partnership from the beginning and had participated in the specialized international seminars listed in appendix C. The Penn State engineering professor had team-taught the cross-cultural seminar at Penn State and had experience as a Fulbright scholar in a

French-speaking country and specialized language learning courses but no experience in task-based language learning or second language acquisition theory.

4. Both instructors needed to become open to the possibility that they may not have all of the specific lexicon and task-based situations needed by engineering interns. They learned to think outside of their disciplines and acquire in-depth knowledge of another field. The building of trust and collaboration between the French and American teacher teams over the previous seven years made it more likely that when the American teachers arrived at the IUT, they would have considerable help from their French colleagues in assembling sources of technical terms, engineering syllabi, and other materials. Further, French colleagues had given guest lectures, had offered to accompany the American engineering students on specialized field trips, and had offered to assume the role of on-site mentors at the end of the course after the two instructors had returned to the United States.

5. A small group of local individuals participated in the industry tour group, composed of around twenty American engineering students, IUT engineering faculty, international program staff, local businesspeople, and other international engineering faculty.

6. The *Guide Michelin* series ranks sites in France in terms of historical or national importance. The descriptions, maps, and narrative prose are thick with historical references and are considered somewhat difficult for nonnative students to read. This provided very good material for students to learn how to extract important details from "dense" textual information in French.

7. The Routard guides are written with the native speaker accustomed to traveling in mind as an audience. As such, they are even more difficult than the Michelin guidebooks.

8. Foreign language faculty judged the design projects and listened to the videoconferencing sessions, which contributed to their appreciation of the technical aspects involved in engineering design.

9. An example of a winning industrial-based solution includes redesigning assembly line procedures for making large-screen televisions, given their greater size, weight, and bulk.

10. Early on, faculty from Penn State and the University of North Carolina–Charlotte planned symposia on Green Engineering, Total Quality Management, Technology and Distance Education, and Instructional Design.

11. At the time the partnership began, the importance of knowing a foreign language and interacting with colleagues from another country was not widely accepted. A dual degree in Engineering and French (also in Engineering and German) was created at Penn State in 1992, paving the way for the international internships.

12. Criteria for Accrediting Engineering Programs, Section I.3.h, http://www.abet.org/.

13. Recent Modern Language Association enrollment data point to significant decreases in French and German nationwide.

# Part III

## Internet Tasks and Programs

# 9

# TASK-BASED INSTRUCTION IN ONLINE LEARNING

Natalia Antokhin, Abdelfattah
Boussalhi, Kuei-Lan Chen, Pamela
Combacau, and Steve Koppany

EDITORS' NOTE: This chapter presents the use of tasks for foreign language acquisition online in the form of learning objects. These are units of instructional materials that can be used by independent learners, assigned by teachers as homework, or even used in the classroom or multimedia laboratory session. The project to develop these learning objects, LangNet, was initially undertaken by the Defense Language Institute and the National Foreign Language Center, with funding from the federal government. Later, LangNet at DLI evolved into a project called GLOSS. In this chapter, the GLOSS developers report on their project. The languages they have prepared materials for are Arabic, Chinese, Korean, Russian, and Spanish. The proficiency levels covered, on the ACTFL scale, are Novice through Superior, or on the ILR scale, 0–3. The challenges unique to developing materials for online use are discussed and solutions found.

Implementing a task-based approach in a digital foreign language (FL) learning environment presents special challenges. Online learning materials are typically characterized as falling into one of two categories: (1) one-way or "broadcast" mode presentations; or (2) interactive learning units, including lessons, modules, and the like (Mayadas 2001). After nearly three decades of evolution in the field of FL Computer-Assisted Study (CAS), there is now general agreement that digitized language programs of the latter variety are usually more effective. Just what constitutes task-based interaction in online programs is still the subject of much debate.

In terms of instructional systems design, the debate centers around two key sets of questions. First, what are the appropriate levels of interaction for accomplishing the objectives of the program or course? What is the highest level of interaction one can hope to implement online?

Second, what are some meaningful tasks at these levels? In designing interactive lessons, modules, and courses, which of these tasks are worth extensive coding/programming? Can or should the online environment ever try to duplicate conventional interactive settings?

It is in the context of these questions that we discuss aspects of designing, developing, and delivering online materials of two sorts: (1) reading comprehension Learning Objects (LOs) for the Global Language Online Support System (GLOSS, formerly known as DLI LangNet),[1] and (2) skills-integrated multimodular courses to help basic program graduates of the Defense Language Institute (DLI) sustain and enhance their proficiency.[2] A Learning Object is defined as an independent unit of instruction, designed to address specific student needs and weaknesses. Currently, DLI developers are building LOs, consisting of five to six activities each, in several languages that focus on deficiencies in the user's reading comprehension. Typically, an LO covers 45 minutes to one hour of instruction.

## Instructional Setting, Target Population

The DLI, headquartered in Monterey, California, is the largest language school in the United States and perhaps in the world. It is a postsecondary institution with federal degree granting authority, accredited by the Western Association of Schools and Colleges. The Institute provides resident and nonresident (continuing) education for Department of Defense and other selected government personnel. Annually, the school graduates about 3,600 students in a total of 63 languages, 22 of which are taught at the Monterey campus[3] and 41 on contract at DLI's satellite location in Washington, D.C.

Students enrolled in courses ranging from 26 weeks (e.g., Spanish) to 63 weeks (e.g., Korean) in duration are expected to achieve a general proficiency level of 2 in listening comprehension, 2 in reading comprehension, and 1+ in speaking on the government's Interagency Language Roundtable (ILR) scale of 0 to 5 (see the glossary and the appendix to this volume);[4] these levels correspond to Intermediate High (1+) and Advanced (2) on the scale developed by the American Council on Teaching Foreign Languages (see the appendix to this volume). Much of the online material development and delivery effort discussed below is aimed at safeguarding the government's investment in this training by providing meaningful and effective ways for linguists to sustain and enhance their hard-earned proficiency.

## General Instructional Design

To ensure that digitized materials produced at DLI incorporate task-based design principles, developers have paid close attention to a number of important instructional-design-related considerations. Key among them have been (1) levels of interaction, (2) the role of technology, and (3) diagnostic assessment.

### LEVELS OF INTERACTION

Roblyer and Ekhaml (2000, 2–3) have devised an interactivity evaluation system consisting of four dimensions: (1) building social rapport; (2) fostering user participation; (3) using technology; and (4) making an impact on learners. By adding a 5-step scale, from "no interactivity" to "high interactivity" within each of these dimensions, they created a matrix that provides a practical framework for a comparative mapping of online materials. Accordingly, in terms of social rapport building, an activity may rank anywhere between "no attempts to encourage personal knowledge of participants" to schemes that offer "several planned or spontaneous opportunities for sharing ideas, opinions, and beliefs in pairs or in small groups." On the "participation" continuum, activities and programs at one end of the continuum may be limited to having "no requirements for interaction with a teacher or fellow students." On the other end of the continuum are materials containing tasks that "require students to work together to analyze and/or solve problems in pairs or small groups and/or with outside experts. . . ."

Army regulations and GLOSS specifications (DLIFLC and NFLC 2002) have provided additional guidelines for interactive task design and technical implementation.[5] At the low end of the ILR proficiency scale, the latter lists LOs that are essentially static, scrollable Web-based documents, compared with ones at the high end, which are fully interactive and multimedia supported.

## THE TECHNOLOGY FACTOR IN ONLINE TASK DESIGN

The DLI online development team consists exclusively of teachers and teacher programmers, that is, experienced FL educators, some of whom also have strong programming skills. Consequently, team members have never really needed convincing that it is the instructional purpose of the online program that should govern the technology, not the other way around. The challenge has been to reflect on their classroom practices and decide which of these should be replicated, adapted, and fully programmed for self-study and which should be handled through other more open-ended means and/or alternate delivery options. In the process of making these decisions, team members have had to reconcile effectiveness with practicality without compromising creativity. This has required finding the middle ground between allowing the technology tail to wag the methodology dog and setting out to prove to the world "at any cost" that there is no difference between the real classroom and virtual learning environments when it comes, for example, to feedback and answer judging. Complicating matters is the inescapable reality that the digital environment of "zeros and ones" best lends itself to activity types with black or white outcomes, which means that it more readily facilitates testing schemes than real task-based activities.

From the student-centered online developer's perspective, activities may be divided into four categories (table 9.1):

1. Task-based activities, with a large variety of possible outcomes and individually tailored feedback. Typically, these involve some kind of problem solving at the analysis, synthesis, and evaluation levels of Bloom's (1956) Taxonomy of Educational Objectives.[6] Activities in this category may require extensive programming.
2. Task-based activities with a controlled number of possible outcomes and individually tailored feedback. These still require analysis and synthesis but, with parameters to channel responses, programming may be less complicated.

TABLE 9.1. **Sample Chinese LO Design from GLOSS**

| | |
|---|---|
| Pre-Reading Activity | Predict the content of the article using limited information |
| Task 1 | Comprehend and interpret the meaning of idioms in context so that learners can infer from their understanding of the contextual information the likely meanings of the idioms. With properly designed multiple choice items, additional hints can be embedded to help the learners make correct inferences. If the learners make incorrect selections, feedback, hints, and cultural notes provide further information and detailed explanation or other examples to help learners comprehend the idioms. For example, in order to explain the idiom 卷土　来 , the following example is used: 四年前奥运会女花式溜冰国家代表关颖珊小姐，不幸赛前失马。今年她又卷土　来，可惜，不幸又经　了一次失败。 (*Four years ago, Michelle Kwan represented the United States at the Olympics in the figure skating event. Unfortunately, she lost in the competition. This year, she came back to compete in the same event, but experienced yet another failure.*) |
| Task 2 | Identify the correct usages of idioms using multiple-choice content questions. Content questions provide learners an opportunity to refine their comprehension of idioms within a specific context. In the case of wrong choices, the learners are guided with feedback or further information. |
| Task 3 | Summarize the content of the text by paragraph and then summarize the whole text. At this stage, competence in using idioms is stable and previously learned idioms are melded into the content. |
| Wrap-up Activity | Read and comprehend a short story that includes all the idioms in the text as a final assessment or extended study. |
| * | In addition, a vocabulary list is provided for each LO. Cultural notes are provided to facilitate better understanding of the Chinese culture. |

3. Test-oriented activities with a large variety of possible outcomes, and individually tailored feedback. Although these activities are usually limited to checking memorized information, comprehension, and the ability to apply information gathered, the unpredictability of responses makes individually tailored feedback a complex challenge for programmers.

4. Test-oriented activities with clear right or wrong outcomes: The user clicks and gets immediate feedback. These activities are almost always

limited to comprehension-level processing. Programming such schemes presents very little challenge.

As will be shown later in this chapter, developers of full online courses at the DLI have been able to leverage the growing variety of synchronous and asynchronous means of student-to-student and student-to-teacher communication available today to ensure an overall task-based focus.

### ROLE OF DIAGNOSTIC ASSESSMENT

One of the challenges developers and teachers of online FL materials face is calibrating the language ability of their students. Although they may have identical proficiency test scores, users of remedial and enhancement materials are typically very disparate in terms of their individual strengths and weaknesses. "One-size-fits-all" online programs have proved to be particularly ineffective in meeting the needs of such users.

To remedy this problem, DLI has implemented a formative process for mapping individual strengths and weaknesses. Prior to enrollment, participants in DLI's online programs are administered a three-skill face-to-face diagnostic assessment interview conducted by two native speakers. The diagnostic specialists use carefully selected and rated authentic materials to establish the working proficiency level of each candidate in listening and reading comprehension and to identify areas language learners need to work on in order to improve their proficiency. The speaking profile of candidates is established by means of a protocol that could best be described as a formative Oral Proficiency Interview (OPI).[7] Teachers of the online courses use the data thus collected to tailor the non-programmed asynchronous and synchronous portions of the course to the individual needs of the participants.

At its current stage of development, the diagnostic assessment tool included in GLOSS is a collection of carefully targeted "can-do" questions organized by level and functional objective, which users are asked to answer according to their own understanding of their ability. The hope is to eventually replace this self-assessment tool with a computer-adaptive task-based instrument.

## Task-Based Instruction in Online Learning

The basic premise for including task-based activities as part of the GLOSS LOs is essentially the same as for incorporating task-based activities in the classroom. When learners are involved in a meaningful and interesting activity that requires the use of the foreign/second language, their motivation is increased, their language processing capacities are challenged and enhanced, and a more effective interlanguage is developed. Doughty (2001), Long and Norris (2000), and Robinson (2001) contend that task-based instruction can remedy some of the linguistic inaccuracy that often accompanies the use of purely communicative methods while simultaneously mitigating deficiencies in fluency of learners who were taught through an emphasis on linguistic forms. For that reason, it seemed logical to make interactive, task-based activities the focus of LO instructional design.

It has been argued, especially by Krashen (1982), that reading is a valuable source for language acquisition. He maintains that the text should be generally comprehensible and the topic should be interesting to the learner, something "that he would read in his first language" (Krashen 1982, 164). Educational research has expanded on this issue and has offered information important for our project. Several different categories of interest have been defined:

1. individual or personal interest, which means preferences on the part of a particular reader for certain topics (Schiefele 1992);
2. situational interest, which is generated by situational factors, including text-based situational interest, generally defined as interest that is elicited by a text through topics or ideas that are of universal appeal (Hidi and Anderson 1992); and
3. reading purpose—as a form of situational interest (Knutson 1998). Schraw and Dennison (1994), examining in their study the effect on interest and recall of reading with a specific goal, found that focusing readers' attention on selected text information increases what they call purpose-driven interest and that text segments that are relevant to a reader's purpose are recalled better. The factor of interest is reflected in the selection of a broad range and variety of topics for our project, topics that would appeal to the personal interests of our customers, as well as address issues relevant to their current jobs. The factor of purpose is central for creating task-based LOs: the learner is presented with the main focus of the LO in the LO Overview (e.g., the overview tells the learner that it will help him/her to "recognize lexical, structural and discourse-related tools and techniques authors of editorial articles use to counter supported arguments"). The learner is also given the specific purpose of each activity in the Activity description, such as "this activity will teach how to skim for the main idea(s) in a limited amount of time" or "it will help you to summarize an opinion piece written as a rebuttal with well supported arguments and details."

Two other important issues of recent studies—the importance of focal attention and its facilitative role in language learning and the relationship between meaning and form when the learner processes a new language input—were considered while preparing task-based LOs. One of the significant outcomes of Van Patten's (1990, 1994) studies for developers of task-based activities is the idea of primacy of meaning over form when learners process a new language sample. Examining learners' input processing, he demonstrated that when learners encounter unknown language, their attentional resources are limited, resulting in attention to form only if it is necessary for the recovery of meaning. That was an important factor for LO developers to consider for sequencing tasks in such a way that learners first familiarized themselves with the main issues of the text and then were presented with tasks that require more attention to specific language features.

Carr and Curren (1994), examining the research on the subject of focal attention on formal language features, pointed to the facilitative role of such attention in the processing of new language. Researchers (Long and Crookes 1992; Schraw and Dennison 1994) argued for the benefits of working with text for the purpose of drawing learners' attention to formal features. They emphasized that form could become a focus of learners' attention, even if it is not crucial for meaning, and that it is possible to channel attentional resources to important aspects of form by helping learners to notice these forms (Schmidt 1990, 1994; Skehan 1996a). These findings were helpful to the LO developers for identifying language features that needed learners' special attention. The challenge for LO developers, as for any language task designers, has been to take into consideration the above-mentioned factors and to create task demands that would effectively control the learner's attention and direct it to relevant aspects of meaning and form in the reading material. Some LO tasks were directly derived from the context of the text and were crucial for its comprehension, while others were more language specific and contributed to the ability to understand a text's style, tone, underlying message, and so on. For successful fulfillment of these higher end tasks (such as to identify an author's intention, to detect the idea "between the lines," or determine the tone of the author of the text), learners needed some more thorough knowledge of certain formal language features. At the same time, these tasks helped to ensure learners' attention to these features (lexical items, structure, or discourse features). In task-based LOs, language-specific information was presented to learners through multilayered feedback. In addition, learners were offered cultural and sociolinguistic information through pop-up windows, notes, and a "teacher" button.

## Selection of Reading Texts

In selecting texts, language material developers need a framework of selection criteria that are compatible with the objectives of the learning material at hand. The framework that delineates the selection process of source texts in learning objects is based on language proficiency notions and standards. One of the implications of proficiency-oriented content development is the use of real-world samples of language use.

### ROLE AND USE OF AUTHENTIC TEXTS

While one cannot completely dismiss the value of contrived texts, the use of authentic texts remains an integral part of creating meaningful tasks. Authentic texts present learners with real-life challenges that a well-meaning and resourceful material writer may not think of. Authentic texts offer developers infinite possibilities for content exploration. The difficulty for lesson developers comes when we try to match an authentic text with a specific level of textual difficulty.

### Interagency Language Roundtable

The Interagency Language Roundtable skill level descriptions (ILR), mentioned above and provided in full in the first part of the book's appendix, not only serve as a language proficiency assessment instrument but also lie at the core of text selection criteria for all DLI projects. The ILR scale includes descriptions of the types of texts that readers and listeners are expected to handle at each level of foreign language proficiency. For example, at ILR Level 2, readers should be able to locate and understand the main ideas and details in authentic factual material, and listeners should be able to understand factual content delivered at a normal native rate.

### Text Typologies

Child (1987) provides a further classification of text types on the basis of their communicative intent. He identifies what he terms four modes of texts. The purpose of *orientation* mode texts is to orient addresses to places and events. Their textual difficulty corresponds to ILR Level 1. *Instructive* mode texts convey factual information (without any significant commentary) and correspond to ILR level 2. *Evaluative* mode texts, on the other hand, contain argumentation of views and analysis of situations. They correspond to ILR Level 3. *Projective* mode is reserved for texts that are highly individualized and present innovative approaches to the topics addressed. They correspond to ILR Level 4. Child does not address Level 5.

The ILR guidelines and Child's text types are not without critics. Allen and others (1988), and Lee and Musumeci (1988) conducted studies in which they concluded that the ILR guidelines and Child's text types did not accurately predict learners' performance in tests. Edwards (1996) contended that these investigations had serious design flaws. Specifically, the investigators did not use a sufficient number of samples at each level nor did they use the complete ILR level descriptions.

As a government standard, the ILR has been in existence for nearly fifty years and has gained the reputation of measuring accurately enough the kinds of performance that are required of government workers. As such, the ILR scale is the only viable standard developed to date for use at the DLI.

For selecting reading texts, Child's typology provides a link to the original purpose behind the text. A report of a news event, for example, will generally fit the requirements of the Level 2 ILR description as well as Child's instructive mode definition (of conveying information). But this is only the beginning of text selection.

#### CAPACITY FOR DIDACTICIZATION

Writers of authentic texts, native speakers writing to native speakers in a target-language setting, do not concern themselves with writing a pure and consistent piece of discourse that would fit some curriculum or testing standard; they write to fulfill a real-life function, such as to inform, to share an opinion, or to respond to one. Therefore, successful text selection is a careful balancing act of standards and the pragmatics of the learning situations at hand. Successful text selection, if measured by the extent to which it accomplishes the desired learning goal, is relative to the consideration given to the multilayers of the dynamic factors involved.

Not every text that can be rated as Level 3 on the ILR scale is worth presenting to a learner. Some Level 3 articles are more interesting than others; what is interesting for one population of learners may not be so for another population.

There are also language-specific particulars to consider when selecting texts for didacticization. A learner of Arabic, for example, may want to learn about the Arab world as a whole. This means that text selection should cover as many Arab countries as possible. Alternatively, the learner may want to focus on one particular country. The balancing is not always a matter of focusing the selection process on one outcome or on one geographic area but on making numerous decisions on what to use and what to omit from the syllabus or lessons to be included in an online program. For well-rounded proficiency in a foreign language, utilizing interesting texts only may not be enough. Some exposure to less exotic topics, such as law and sciences, may be needed for students with specific job requirements.

Since GLOSS's overarching goal is general proficiency maintenance and enhancement, the text selection process covers as many subject areas as each language or culture, level, text type, and nature of publication allow. Certain subject areas are naturally more closely linked to a range of text difficulty. Announcements of social events, for example, tend to be delivered in basic language forms (ILR Level 1 / orientational mode). On the other hand, advocacy of an opinion on a social issue is most likely to be delivered in more complex and sophisticated language forms (starting at ILR Level 3 / evaluative mode). The standards that we use are simply tools that help us organize the multitude of choices that each language offers. The benefit to a learner is what ultimately determines the final selection. A text, for example, may have interesting content, but it may be so atypical that it is not likely to be encountered often.

We select all of our reading materials from copyrighted, original foreign language publications,[8] in both printed and Web-delivered forms. Many of the Web sources we use are electronic versions of paper publications and have, therefore, fewer limitations than Web-only materials have.

## DIDACTICIZING TEXTS: ACCOMPANYING ACTIVITIES

The selected texts usually lend themselves to certain types of tasks and activities, but they are not limited to these (see chapter 1, this volume, for a presentation of task typologies). The instructional design of LOs depends on many factors, but the choice of Level 3 general reading proficiency objective(s) (e.g., recognizing patterns of organization of texts, reading for critical appraisal, understanding conceptual meaning, and drawing inferences or conclusions) serves as its principle organizing design principle. This choice, in turn, determines the primary learning task that the learner should accomplish while completing the LO, which is often, but not always, defined in terms of functional objectives. The following are examples of learning tasks / functional objectives in LOs:

- Read an evaluative text to determine the author's hypothesis and to find supporting evidence in the text.

- Read an evaluative text to determine the interrelationship of a complex set of facts.
- Read a text to find implications.

The text chosen for the development of an LO is also analyzed to determine the challenges to be exploited among the components of communicative competence, that is, lexical, structural, discourse, and sociolinguistic competence (Canale and Swain 1980). Only those challenges that would hinder or help the learner in accomplishing the learning task are selected as language features to be addressed in the LO. The primary learning task is then divided into smaller reading tasks and activities that provide the learner with opportunities to use a variety of reading skills (skimming, scanning, extracting salient points for summarization, interpreting a text by using information external to it, understanding implicit information, and so forth) and to focus on specific lexical, structural, and discourse features of the text.

### COMPOSING THE LEARNING OBJECT

Each LO is a sequence of task-based activities composed of the following:

1. A prereading task that serves as an "advanced organizer";
2. Three enabling tasks that promote skill using and focusing on specific language forms; and
3. A wrap-up activity that consolidates what the learner has learned.

The primary goal for an LO designer is to develop logically connected sequences of activities that allow the learner to move from task to task of different types with degrees of complexity, gradually moving toward tasks that require increasingly more sophisticated use of reading skills. The range and the variety of skills employed by the learner in accomplishing activities are intended implicitly or explicitly to facilitate focusing the learner's attention on important features of the text. During the final activity, the principal objective of the LO directly comes into play, since the fulfillment of this task depends on how well the learner synthesizes his/her learning experiences in working on the LO.

Many LOs contain simulations—real-world scenarios or contexts that are presented to the learner before or during the prereading activity. Establishing a context makes LOs more motivating to a learner and gives some guidance on what can be expected in the accompanying activities. Since it is difficult to predict a context appropriate to all learners, a generic context is sometimes used.[9] Alternatively, learners may supply their own context, imagining themselves in a personal or business situation where the LO text and the tasks attached to it would be relevant to them.

Prereading activities do not have to be highly sophisticated since they serve to ease the processing of material and engage learners with the knowledge domain of the LO that becomes available as the basis for subsequent dealing with the task (Foster and Skehan 1996; Skehan and Foster 1997). Prereading activities serve as advanced organizers to introduce the topic and to activate schemata and all associations connected with the reading topic. The skills and techniques involved in this stage are simple: The learner is asked to make decisions concerning the text (its usefulness for the primary objective and specific tasks, general content issues, possibilities for exploration, and the like), based on pictures, titles, captions, the first paragraph, and similar features. These activities start the process of developing the skills to solve progressively more difficult problems that involve higher-order thinking skills, such as analysis, synthesis and evaluation (Bloom 1956), and require the use of higher level reading skills (e.g., understanding the conceptual meaning of the text, interpreting a text by using information external to it, transcoding information from text format to diagrammatic display, and other such activities).

After the primary objective is presented in the introductory context and the learner has completed the pretask activity, he or she is led through a series of activities that support the overall instructional purpose of the LO: drawing conclusions, identifying the author's point of view, understanding intentions and ideas "between the lines," and the like. A wrap-up activity enables the learner to consolidate gains and to review important points of the LOs.

The activities within the LO lead the learners to the point, represented by the wrap-up activity, at which they have developed the ability to do the kinds of tasks normally related to the objective of the LO. For example, the learner is able to summarize the main points of the text in the wrap-up activity because that activity is based on the previous task-based activities, such as analyzing the text to infer the main and supporting ideas, identifying idioms to decipher the author's attitude, or recognizing the rhetorical organization or linguistic devices to clarify the organization of the text. These tasks facilitate the development of reading skills: skimming, scanning, referencing, recognizing indicators in discourse, understanding relations between the parts of the text through lexical and grammatical cohesion devices, and so forth.

Here is an illustration. For the article about new developments in Russian business, two general reading proficiency objectives were identified: *critical appraisal of the text* as the main objective and *recognizing patterns of organization of the text*, as a subobjective. The learner was provided with a context: *The company you work for is about to undertake a new project in Russia as a joint venture with a major Russian company. However, since a new Russian president was elected a year ago, the situation in the Russian business world has been changing. Your boss has asked you to search the media and give him information on the relationship between the Russian government and Russian entrepreneurs.* While accomplishing the tasks, the learner is given an opportunity to identify the main idea and supporting ideas and to practice skimming, scanning, and referencing. He is shown how different literary devices (columns, dashes, conjunctions, particles, quotation marks) make the text clear and concise and help the author to express certain emotional overtones. The article also serves as an example of typical text organization for argumentative types of Russian articles. The last task returns the learner to the context of the LO:

> You need to write a list of the most important points of the article that would be helpful to your boss in making decisions on future interactions

with Russian big business. He also wants you to give him suggestions on possible future developments in Russian business.

The task requires the learner to summarize the most important points of the text from a specific perspective, as well as to go beyond it by critically evaluating the text and providing some predictions concerning future possible outcomes.

Conceptually, the tasks discussed above are not different from those used in the classroom. On the one hand, the design and format of these activities, which include such techniques as matching, numbering, reconstructing, reordering, filling out a table, cloze exercises, multiple choice, true/false, and guided questions, are similar to classroom activities. On the other hand, the fact that these are computerized activities affects how the learner interacts with the LO. One difference attributed to the medium is obvious: the learner must possess basic computer skills to be able to conduct operations like highlighting, dragging and dropping, or copying and pasting. The other difference is not so obvious perhaps but is much more significant. The fact that learners usually work alone without a teacher or a partner and that LOs are self-contained units, which in most cases are not linked to other LOs, makes it imperative to ensure that learners who have to manage their own learning receive considerable guidance. Since this guidance is provided via instructions, feedback, hints, and help buttons, LOs presuppose strong interactive involvement on the part of the learner.

## Providing Feedback

Depending upon the task, the feedback provided in LOs may vary. Such operations as highlighting and drag and drop can provide immediate feedback by displaying various colors or rejecting misplaced items. These are used in lower-order activities that may involve the learner in finding an appropriate equivalent in English, the best paraphrase in the foreign language, or the most suitable synonym or antonym, based on the context (examples). They also work with multiple-choice exercises, when simple feedback indicating correct and incorrect answers (usually answering such questions as Who? What? Where? When? and How?) is sufficient for the learner to figure out what he or she missed. Multiple-choice questions work well also with more complicated content questions. These, along with reading tasks, often require a higher level of language processing from learners, and learners may need more guidance and help in completing them than they do with other kinds of exercises. Such tasks as matching the main points of the text with corresponding paragraphs that explicate and elaborate these points, reordering pieces of texts according to the logic of the story, rearranging disconnected paragraphs to reflect the author's sequence of argumentation, or predicting the consequences of the actions described in the text by making a coherent text out of disconnected statements are examples of tasks that sometimes require additional guidance. Here immediate feedback, for example, providing correct responses for incorrect answers, prevents the learner from taking an active role in focusing on appropriate information and making informed choices. In order to allow the learner to reflect on why the answer is incorrect, he or she is provided with hints, clarification, focusing questions, and comments that guide him to discover the answer himself. Depending on the difficulty of the task, different levels of feedback may be provided. In some cases, a link back to the key paragraph, text segment, or word is sufficient. In other cases, hints may be provided to activate a learner's thinking before he or she actually answers the question or reconstructs the text. Another, more focused hint and/or feedback may follow if the answer or the action of the learner was incorrect. This multiple feedback allows the learner to notice and recognize the problem, and it facilitates its resolution and ultimately helps him to become an autonomous, self-sufficient language learner. Multiple layers of feedback allow learners with both lower and higher levels of proficiency to work efficiently with the LOs.

### FOCUS ON FORM: GRAMMAR AND DISCOURSE

Addressing formal features of the language (grammar structures and lexicon) is an important part of LOs. There are several approaches to this issue. Prabhu dismisses the need to focus on form, arguing that learners will subconsciously incorporate the formal code of the language into their interlanguage while performing the task (Prabhu 1987). Other applied linguists and theoreticians consider a very brief switch, a short "time out" to focus on form, useful when the learner's successful fulfillment of an otherwise meaning-focused activity is hindered (Long and Robinson 1998); their position is bolstered by work on fossilization that indicates that lack of focus on form can produce interlanguage and productive language that is incorrect and ultimately nearly noneradicable (Higgs and Clifford 1982). Still others argue that linguistic focus in the form of grammatical consciousness-raising activities should be incorporated into task-based instructional design (Nunan 1989a; Skehan 1996a; Willis, chapter 1, this volume). Since addressing linguistic competencies is an important part of instructional goals of LOs, formal features do need to be addressed, and we, like Nunan, Skehan, and Willis, have incorporated these into the GLOSS design.

In developing LOs for GLOSS, aspects of grammar and discourse are addressed as they emerge from the functional dictates of the reading materials on which these LOs are based. These aspects attempt to answer questions about the manner through which an author achieves a particular function, the language forms he uses to achieve his goal, the group of language forms from which he makes his choices, the change of meaning that would have taken place if another choice had been made, and other contexts for which the same use would have been appropriate. Hymes (1977) considered such choices integral to a speaker's communicative competence.

The formal organizational principles behind the development (and generation) of LOs have to do with (1) the level of the text, (2) the linguistic competence addressed (currently LOs address lexical, structural, and discourse competence), and (3) Language-Specific Features, which deal with language issues specific to a given language (and not necessarily to languages in general) in each of the competencies. The objectives of the Language-Specific Features are themselves tied to their textual usages and are not locked into any perceived sequence of features.

Here is a sample of a Language-Specific Feature of Chinese (for students needing to work with ILR Level 3 materials):

> Recognize the purpose of rhetorical devices and identify correctly the relationship of complexities of thought that appear in a variety of prose on unfamiliar subjects that may include opinions, hypothesis, and analysis.

At ILR Level 3, it is even more critical to address aspects of grammar in the light of their discourse functions. Being familiar with one language form is important, but experiencing how it works as a building block in the composition of the text puts the learner in a much better position to understand the text in a manner that approximates the author's intention. A student of Arabic who becomes familiar with how certain patterns (of words) are derived from basic roots and understands what those patterns mean also needs to understand how they are used (context and purpose). One of the patterns, for example, indicates the performer of a verb, but the actual purposes for which it is used are numerous, among which is to function as a discourse connector, facilitating the transition from one idea to another.

The principal objective of each LO is to provide the learner with opportunities to interact with authentic texts in ways that are comparable to those of a native reader. A text corresponding to ILR Level 3 has a message, stated or otherwise. An LO includes activities that prompt the learner to explore that message, and perhaps react to it. It is at this point that Language-Specific Features enter the picture. In a real-life situation, a native reader does not need to reflect on the mechanisms employed to communicate the message. The mechanisms are part of his or her proficiency. For a learner of Chinese as a foreign language, for example, this process may need to be reconstructed. Incorporating activities that deal with these mechanisms into an LO not only serves to raise awareness of the mechanisms themselves, but also directly improves understanding more about the message and more of it, especially when texts are those that present and argue issues. The subtleties are often part of the message. Use of a discourse device may be all that is needed to suggest a particular stance on an issue.

Although discourse is listed as a separate competence (in the generation of LOs), all language forms are presented in their actual discourse types. Following up on the example above, the relationship between verb forms and some derivational patterns in Arabic is explored in "factual and abstract authentic texts of general interest," such as in daily newspaper columns. In one of the texts that we have used in an LO—dealing with the relationship between developed and developing countries—the relationship between verb forms and some derivational patterns to a large extent deploys the author's arguments.

At Level 3, discourse is an essential piece of the reading process. We have found that many of the challenges that such texts present to the reader are related to discourse, while some are linguistic in nature and others a consequence of the cultural schemata of texts. In all the languages for which we are currently developing LOs, argumentation of ideas, elaboration of opinion, or explication of an issue is usually accompanied by complexity in language forms. Figuring out how multiple clause embeddings interconnect is a major step toward enabling the learner to follow the message of the text. Equally important, but more difficult to design activities for, are all the cultural and transactional elements that hold the reading text together.

One of the challenges is that these elements are "external" to the text. For an ILR Level 2 (or Advanced on the ACTFL scale) learner wishing to read higher-level texts, these elements are not visible. So, if they cannot be located anywhere in the text, how is one going to find out about them? How can we develop reading activities that allow the learner to explore these seemingly unobservable constituents? Some activities have taken the form of prereading information and exercises, in which the learner's attention is directed toward key background concepts or issues that the learner is encouraged to explore.

Another difficulty in developing and designing reading activities for a stand-alone online medium is matching the complexity of a reading activity with available electronic manipulation means (e.g., dragging, matching, checking, drop-menu, highlighting), although there is always the possibility of designing activities that allow the learner to respond freely. An example of this would be to draw the learner's attention to a particular problematic area in the text and ask him to write his response in a provided blank field. The feedback is provided in a "compare" pop-up window.

## VOCABULARY AND DISCOURSE

At Level 3, vocabulary and grammar do not exist in a vacuum. They are always tied together to form abstract meaning and express evaluative concepts. Their meanings and connotations depend on the context in which they appear. Thus, learning the meanings of words and idioms is most effective through the association of proper context.

How to help learners build up their vocabulary in an effective way and learn the correct usages of vocabulary is the first step in task-based foreign language teaching. Puns, common colloquial expressions, adverbial adjuncts, connotative meaning, common idiomatic expressions, and abstract words are all included in lexical competence. Within the domain of structural competence, Language-Specific Features are tied to the textual usages of the foreign language, reflecting the inseparability in many, if not most, languages of the structural and discourse components of communicative competence. For example, idiomatic expression in Arabic and Russian is categorized as lexical competence, while in Chinese it is categorized as discourse competence because of its unification in form and abundant cultural origin in meaning. This is because most Chinese idioms are composed of four characters that contain historical or cultural information. Such idioms are highly dependent on cultural and sociolinguistic knowledge for correct interpretation; it is, therefore, necessary for learners to make inferences from the discourse in which the idioms appear in order to correctly grasp the meaning of both them and the whole text. Therefore, learning idioms in Chinese cannot be separated from developing discourse competence. A Chinese LO dealing with idioms may be laid out as shown in table 9.1.

In the Language Feature requirements of the GLOSS's LOs, Level 2+/3 lexical competence depends on Language-Specific Features that vary among languages because of the variation in nature (form, format, locus of meaning) of the communicative components of each language. Thus, in Arabic, lexical competence for Level 2+/3 includes lexical association between verbs/verbal nouns and objects, the connotative meaning of common words, and common idiomatic expression. In Russian, lexical competence for Level 2+/3 includes abstract nouns and idioms. In Chinese, lexical competence for Level 2+/3 includes puns, colloquial expressions, and adverbial adjuncts.

To expand on this concept, Chinese can serve as an illustration. In the Chinese LOs, learners may learn to (1) comprehend puns with their double meaning or intentionally disguised meanings in culturally specific contexts, (2) interpret common colloquial expressions correctly by making good use of clues embedded in the context, and (3) distinguish the tone of adverbial adjuncts indicating anger, disappointment, satire, in order to comprehend accurately the emotional state of the native speaker in the written text.

One of the challenges for learners in reading a Level 2+/3 reading text in any language is that they can usually find some expressions they have difficulty comprehending. As in the case with grammar (see previous section), the relevant information that would allow them to interpret the lexical expressions through strategies such as inducing from context cannot be found in the text. What, then, can learners be expected to do? What reading activities will enable the learner to explore lexical constituents that are not obvious or readily observable? In such cases, we have often planted the seed for the learner by providing prereading activities that draw attention to key background concepts or issues associated with the significant expressions.

Another difficulty in developing reading activities for a stand-alone online medium is matching the complexity of a reading activity with available electronic manipulation means (e.g., dragging, matching, checking, drop-menu, highlighting), although there is always the possibility of designing activities that allow the learner to respond freely. Without interaction with their instructor, when learners make an incorrect assumption or encounter difficulties, there is no easy way to provide instant feedback.

Some of the tasks that were used to explore language forms include identification, comparison, rearrangement, evaluation, categorization, and application.

Good activities should help learners recall lexical phrases and their functional uses naturally from the situational meaning of the context associated with lexical phrases. Repeated practice is one such activity. According to Porto, instructional order is different from acquisition order. Adjusting the order of instruction to correspond to that of acquisition should facilitate the process of learning (Porto 2001).

## Task-Based Activities in Online Courses: An Arabic Example

In June 2002, a Hybrid Course was tested in the School of Continuing Education at the Defense Language Institute. The Arabic online course (accessible on Lingnet)[10] consisted of two components: videoconferencing sessions and an online section relying on the computer as a tutor, with a focus on skill development.

The online course adopted a thematic approach that consisted of five themes: Culture, Society, Military, Geography, and Politics. The choice of the themes was dictated by the client's interest (i.e., by the agency that sent the students to DLI). Video clips and audio clips from television and radio comprised the essence of each theme. The source of reading texts was newspaper articles. Although the course was designed for Level 1+ and 2 users, the developers included comics from magazines, video clips of songs, and proverbs, which are considered to be at a higher level. In addition to the ways in which these genres added appeal, they also provided a significant challenge for sociolinguistic competence.

Additionally, the course incorporated links to radio stations, search engines, newspapers, and dictionary Web sites in the target language. These features were provided to encourage the user to navigate and seek materials of personal interest. This way, the user feels free to choose without having to follow a pattern or perform a task.

The interface design depended upon clear navigational tools that integrated simple elements in the presentation. The designers intended to avoid any source of confusion that might distract the learner from the main task. Further, the instrctions that accompanied each activity were carefully written to indicate to the learner how to navigate the system. In writing instructions, the designers attempted to apply the recommendations of Plass (1998):

1. Select the instructional activity that supports cognitive processes of the competence or skill to be developed.
2. Select the attributes of the feature.
3. Select the design feature.

The design of activities was determined by the instructional methods and competencies to be developed. Functionality and design features were implemented afterward. The designers incorporated the principles of Universal Design (Story, Mueller, and Mace 1998) into a Foreign Language Learning environment.

### LEARNER FEEDBACK

In their evaluation of the course, the learners praised the design, which they found to be "clear and appealing." The variety of Web site links was also mentioned as a positive facet by students in their end-of-course questionnaires. In fact, none of them used the backup CD; ostensibly the CD did not give users access to all the potential links.

The users have appreciated the thematic approach because each theme presented the same linguistic features several times in different manners. The developers' use of video captions—listening sequences in addition to reading texts—enhances the user's contact with the topic and the target language.

### FIVE CHALLENGES

Experience in conducting the Hybrid Course also indicated a number of challenges to be overcome in developing interactive, communicative, learner-centered online courses. These included the following:

- handling a dispersed "classroom,"
- interaction without a classroom,
- strategic development,
- non-Roman alphabets and non-alphabetic writing systems, and
- evaluating open-ended responses.

### Challenge 1: Handling a Dispersed "Classroom"

The videoconferencing component of the course enabled the teacher to include simulations and to approximate traditional communications. However, the learners were located at three different sites, which added another challenge to the degree of interaction in exchanging information. Checking understanding was restricted by the quality of reception that differed from site to site. This situation precipitated a greater need for improvisation. Also, it required the teacher to be more flexible in setting time constraints on activities in order to allow equal opportunity for all learners at all sites. Nevertheless, learners and teachers interacted successfully.

### Challenge 2: Interaction without a Classroom

In the case of Web delivery, the real challenge lies in designing communicative activities without the classroom setting and its direct interaction between learners and teachers. The designers of the online course deliberated on the possibilities of creating opportunities for interaction. The commonly used means to achieve this objective are e-mail and online bulletin boards, which are included to provide space for synchronous and asynchronous communication. However, immediate feedback cannot be provided in this way. The first approach was to have the learners submit their production and have a teacher evaluate it and respond to them through e-mail. The goal of the course was to provide a tutorial independent of teachers and test-mode responses. Thus, the initial approach had to be disregarded, whereas including feedback became necessary to help learners monitor their progress and the appropriateness of their actions.

### Challenge 3: Strategic Development

Another goal of the course was to use computer technology to support strategic development (i.e., expanding the use of learning, reading, and other strategies used by students and helping them to select the appropriate ones for specific kinds of tasks). Interactive activities such as multiple-choice and drag-and-drop are expected in this environment, and were used. At the same time, the activities varied in their degree of difficulty, from simple and brief to more complex and demanding. The learner is challenged on a vocabulary, syntax, or discourse level. During reading or listening, the learners interact with the text, monitor their comprehension, reread confusing parts, and evaluate and receive feedback. They are engaged in semantic mapping, summarizing, choosing options, and testing their comprehension. Some activities are based upon the assumption that reading and writing share key cognitive mechanisms and are considered to be collaborative events (Carson 1996). Therefore, writing as a form of feedback is emphasized. The tutoring feedback is given mainly in English, which indirectly provides a successive contrastive analysis of both languages and, according to Schwienhorst (1997), aids in the development of metalinguistic awareness. However, the ongoing feedback on performance is mainly designed to support student engagement and to provide external confirmation of the learner's sense of accomplishment and guidance while working.

### Challenge 4: Non-Roman Alphabets and Non-Alphabetic Writing Systems

It was a real challenge to provide the learner with an on-screen keyboard for "writing" in languages such as Arabic, but the technical challenge was overcome by the programmers. Yet, the problem was more complex than simply providing a tool to use in typing in foreign languages. The lack of competence of learners in typing in Arabic became an impediment to the completion of the task.

The developers subsequently focused on using client-side, on-screen interactivity—JavaScript being preferred because it can take advantage of forms. Form elements allow the learner to submit various responses that can be easily evaluated and, in turn, the appropriate feedback can be provided. Since the server is not involved in this operation, the process is much faster—everything happens on the learner's computer. Moreover, JavaScript allows certain flexibility in programming that is exploited by having teachers with programming skills of differing levels work on the same project. Teachers with limited experience in programming can, in a relatively short time, produce interactive pages, while more experienced programmers can develop more complex applications. Along with JavaScript, Dynamic HTML, and Style Sheets, a small segment was programmed using Perl.

### Challenge 5: Evaluating Open-Ended Responses

Another factor that hindered writing, in general, was the desire of learners to have their production evaluated. Through their classroom experience, most learners have developed an expectation of feedback that specifically targets their responses. Artificial intelligence, at this stage, is not capable of fully replacing the teacher in providing this kind of individualized feedback. Therefore, learners have to rely on the standard feedback built into the system. As a result, they have appreciated the e-mail and bulletin boards that did offer individually tailored contacts.

## Conclusion

No respectable academic institution would chance being caught today without at least a fledgling e-learning or distributive learning program in its arsenal of enrollment options. Indeed, in discipline after discipline, colleges and universities have been making rapid progress in providing students with learning options that are comparable in terms of quality and effectiveness with those one would expect to find in conventional settings. It is safe to say, however, that given the complexity of the challenges discussed above, in the field of second language acquisition much remains to be done to provide students with true task-based learning experiences online.

In the past few years, developers and programmers of Web-deliverable materials at the DLI have been working hard to leverage their wealth of experience in proficiency-oriented teaching, diagnostic assessment, authentic text selection, and activity design against the objective limitations of the digital environment. Their aim has been not to supplant the teacher, but rather to augment their role by exploiting the technology in ways that are cost-effective, yet task-driven and student-centered. The personalized and targeted LOs and multimodal online courses developed to date at the Institute have shown great promise, but the full implementation of task-based principles, involving both reception and production skills, will require continuous experimentation and further advances in such areas as broadband delivery, true speech recognition, artificial intelligence, and virtual reality simulation.

## Appendix A

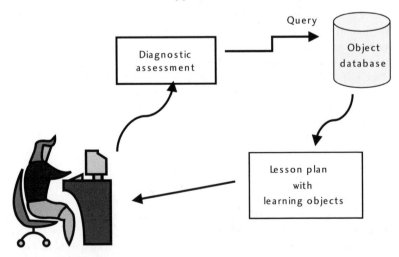

FIGURE 9.1. **GLOSS—Learner's view**

# Appendix B

FIGURE 9.2. **A Sample Page from Arabic Online Course**

# Appendix C

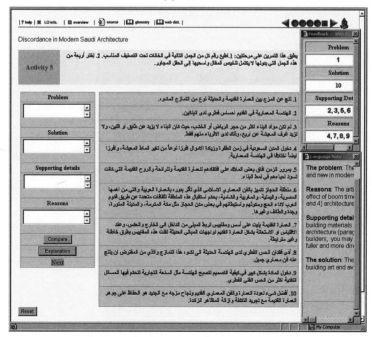

FIGURE 9.3. **A Sample Arabic Activity from GLOSS**

# Appendix D

FIGURE 9.4. **A Sample Chinese Activity from GLOSS**

# Appendix E

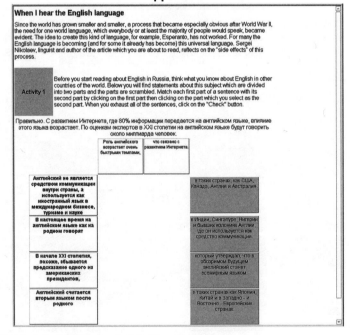

FIGURE 9.5. **A Sample Russian Activity from GLOSS**

## Notes

1. GLOSS is an integrated online language learning support system designed to provide users with a personalized roadmap toward proficiency enhancement. It is a collaborative effort that has involved DLI, the Foreign Service Institute (FSI), the National Foreign Language Center (NFLC), and other partners. The project was launched in March 2001, with government funding. Currently, it may be accessed at http://www.lingnet.org.

2. Language training at the DLI is both intensive and expensive. After graduating from one of DLI's basic programs with a minimum score of L2 in reading, L2 in listening, and L1+ in speaking (see the appendix to this volume for a description of these levels), military linguists typically end up in assignments that require specific and often limited use of their hard-earned skills. This often results in a degradation of proficiency. In order to protect the services' investment in language training, DLI provides extensive support to its graduates through a wide array of distance learning services and technologies.

3. See Leaver and Kaplan (chapter 2, this volume) for a description of task-based programs taught in classrooms at the DLI.

4. From here on, when we refer to levels, such as Level 1, Level 2, etc., in this paper, we are referring to ILR levels.

5. Training and Doctrine Command (TRADOC) Pamphlet 350-70, chapter 2, section III, establishes four categories of interaction in digital programs, ranging from "low simulation presentations" of minimal interaction to "real-time simulation" in which "every possible subtask is analyzed and presented with full-screen interaction, similar to the approach used in aircraft simulator technology."

6. On Bloom's taxonomy, responses that require knowledge, comprehension, and application are considered lower-order thinking skills, requiring simple cognitive functioning and limited, if any, critical thinking. Higher order thinking skills (analysis, synthesis, and evaluation), on the other hand, require complex cognitive functioning and increasingly critical thinking, which usually results in longer term learning, deep processing, and greater transferability (Bloom 1956; Brown, Collins, and Duguid 1989).

7. The OPI is a task-based proficiency test of unrehearsed language. It is administered by trained testers in accordance with a carefully laid out protocol that includes a warm-up, probes, level checks, and a wrap-up. The aim of the interview is to determine the working proficiency level of the candidate.

8. We obtain copyright permissions by corresponding with the source publications through either regular mail or e-mail. The success rate varies. Some publications reply promptly; others never reply at all. In our correspondence to publications we explain the non-profit and educational nature of our work.

9. Here is an example: You need to develop outlines for your supervisor's presentation in the foreign country; this text may provide you with the necessary information.

10. Lingnet is a Bulletin Board Service (BBS) and resource center, created and maintained by the DLI for the purpose of providing military and other government linguists with a convenient hub of discussion forums, and links to materials in over 80 languages (http://www.lingnet.org). It is not to be confused with GLOSS, which is a portal of interactive LOs, designed to address diagnosed individual learning needs.

# 10

## WEBHEAD COMMUNITIES: WRITING TASKS INTERLEAVED WITH SYNCHRONOUS ONLINE COMMUNICATION AND WEB PAGE DEVELOPMENT

Vance Stevens

EDITORS' NOTE: In this chapter, Vance Stevens continues the discussion of learning beyond the classroom walls, thanks to Internet technology. He describes groups of voluntary participants in writing tasks; the community that has evolved he calls Webheads. The kinds of learning that take place are highly unpredictable, the kinds of interactions quite stochastic, and the amount of freedom for self-directed learning quite high. The tasks take place outside of the classroom, are very much "real" in the sense that individuals have real-life reasons for accomplishing them, and are not graded or reviewed in any traditional manner. Nevertheless, high-quality learning does appear to take place, with participants improving their written language skills. Further, much motivation is built to continue e-learning (learning in an electronic environment).

*Webheads* is an umbrella term for an online community of language learners and teachers that has developed in two distinct directions. The first, *Writing for Webheads* (http://sites.hsprofessional.com/vstevens/files/efi/webheads.htm), started in 1998 as a synchronous reincarnation of an e-mail-based online writing course. Meeting in text- and *avatar*-based chat areas, a community of students and teachers gradually formed online.[1] The community was based at a Web site that served not only as a platform for displaying corrected student writings but as a focal point for community members to get to know each other's faces, voices, and stories. Although much of the interaction is done in writing (hence, Writing for Webheads), a community of practice has formed where improvement in writing has always been a secondary goal of the course, if indeed this could be called a course in any traditional sense. Rather, community members seem to be motivated primarily to interact for interpersonal reasons. In so doing, they learn as much as they can about the synchronous online multimedia computer-mediated communication (CMC) tools that make this possible and enhance the experience, with development in writing being a secondary focus of the program.

The community has also attracted interest within the wider community of educators who use technology in language learning, seeding the formation of a second group, *Webheads in Action* (http://www.vancestevens.com/papers/evonline2002/ webheads.htm, or http://www.webheads.info/), a community that started life early in 2002 as an online workshop program in community building using CMC tools. So why this growing interest in online community building? Proponents of participation in such communities feel that they encourage scaffolding among members. Bonk and Cunningham (1998) felt that learning is best accomplished when learners are able to construct knowledge from elements that they have internalized in a meaningful fashion and in a highly social environment where learners interact and learn from others in their immediate surroundings. More recently, there has been increased interest among educators using CMC in how these principles mediate the formation and functioning of communities of practice, a construct articulated particularly well by Wenger (1998) (see Snyder, n.d., for a simplified overview of how communities of practice aid professional development). Essentially, communities of practice are groups of people who meet to discuss a topic (or *domain*) of such interest to community members that they are strongly motivated to enhance their understanding of the topic through frequent interaction in order to further their work or interest in the field to which the topic pertains. Thus, it comes as no surprise that CMC tools should promote the development of communities of practice over distances.

To achieve their aims, the two flourishing Webheads groups have explored and successfully exploited the potential of a great variety of free Internet text, voice, and video CMC tools. Members' skills in utilizing these Web-based tools have been developed through direct interaction. We feel that the Webheads projects model the benefits to e-learning of adopting a pedagogical stance that is much more flexible and interactive than teacher-directed models, which are being widely supplanted in any event in both physical and virtual classroom environments. Given that there is a trend toward learner-centered, constructivist approaches to learning, it is convenient and more than coincidental that the greater empowerment that personal computing has brought us all should be a strong factor in this development, especially the ability of computers to facilitate exploration and communication in any target language.

## Writing for Webheads

The Webheads group was a natural product of constructivist approaches to learning facilitated by wider connectivity, making it possible for like-minded people to come together in worldwide distributed communities of practice. What follows is a consideration of how these ingredients translate through Webheads into pedagogy.

### WRITING TASKS FOR PURPOSEFUL INTERACTION

How do our CMC tools facilitate task-based approaches to writing? According to the report of the Curriculum Development Council of Hong Kong (1999, 47) every learning task should include the following features, which the subsequent paragraph elucidates:

- A task should have a purpose. It involves learners in using language for the kinds of purposes that are described in the Learning Targets and Objectives.
- A task should have a context from which the purpose for using language emerges.
- A task should involve learners in a mode of thinking and doing.
- The purposeful activity in which learners engage while carrying out a task should lead toward a product.
- A task should require the learners to draw upon their framework of knowledge and skills.

The Writing for Webheads course engages learners in purposeful tasks. Its targets and objectives are geared toward developing proficiency in English by getting a heterogeneous group of language learners communicating at a distance with other group members. Although Writing for Webheads is composed of a unique target group of students (non-fee-paying, highly heterogeneous, self-motivated) in a distinct setting (completely online, tasks spontaneously undertaken, students not evaluated), elements of the model can be applied to curricula in contexts in which there are other specific targets. In our case, much of the language used revolves around the vagaries of online communication (exchange of URLs, logistics of broadcasting Web cams, adjusting microphones, developing Web pages, etc.). Clearly, such language emerges from within a purposeful context, where all involved (learners and teachers) have to constantly invent novel ways to use the available tools and then give directions and explain processes to one another. Thus, all participants draw upon their respective frameworks of prior knowledge and skills (with skills so distributed that students often help teachers over technical hurdles, as well as visa versa). Our successes are often documented in Web pages, which facilitate the production of further products in the form of student writings and chat logs.

### TECHNOLOGY AND E-LEARNING

It is important to clarify that technology does not drive the process. Technology is a vehicle through which the most viable pedagogical principles can be delivered so as to optimize their impact and success. Therefore, it is of utmost importance that the pedagogical models underlying e-learning courses be compatible with the uses envisaged for the technology. In the case of language learning, technology not only serves to provide a framework for discourse but also leads students to a limitless source of relevant, authentic, and communicative target language by putting information and interactants literally at the learner's fingertips and then helps the learners take meaningful advantage of these language resources.

## Support for Webhead Communities

The Webheads projects have developed through the efforts of numerous individuals, online support sites, and teachers. Let us look briefly at each in turn.

### ONLINE LEARNING SUPPORT SITES

Three entities have provided supportive frameworks in which Webheads have operated. All have, in one way or another, had roles in funneling newcomers into our programs and contributing to the robust and varied nature of our community.

Study dot Com, or English for Internet (http://www.study.com), offers free courses for language learners, which are taught by founder David Winet and qualified instructors volunteering to teach online. Features include an always-busy Chatterbox voice chat room and a prominent link on its Web page to Writing for Webheads. Tapped In (http://www.tappedin.org) is a well-funded, virtual space dedicated to educators that hosts regular weekly synchronous Webheads meetings and promotes them on its periodical announcements and e-mail lists. Finally, TESOL, the largest international professional organization for teachers of English, has often hosted Webheads presentations at its annual conferences, as well as special events such as Webheads in Action participation in annual EVOnline[2] sessions.

### TEACHERS AND STUDENTS

Webheads thrives and is managed through the interest of a growing community of teachers and students who find they benefit intrinsically from involvement with each other. To maintain its appeal to as wide a range of users as possible, Webheads relies entirely on free software and free Web sites. There has never been any institutional backing for the Webheads projects other than that available to individual community members. No funding for these communities has ever been requested or granted (except in the form of occasional offers of beta-test software), nor is there any budget whatsoever. No fees have ever been charged students nor is any expenditure required from them other than access to a computer and the Internet.

To maintain broad appeal, the Webheads communities have utilized freely available CMC tools, and incidental expenses (cost of internet and Web hosting, often free) have been borne by the individuals involved as part of normal expenses for professional development and continuing education. All concerned must feel that return on investment is high, as many have remained actively involved in these communities (from as long ago as 1998).

## The Evolution of the Webheads

Webheads have shown themselves over time to be capable of maintaining high levels of professionalism and sophistication through community support without the need for fees or funding. It is instructive to examine the early development of these communities in order that others can initiate their own successful grassroots programs.

### HOW WEBHEADS GOT STARTED

The Webheads projects reach back to 1996 when I started to conduct an online e-mail writing and grammar course: English for Internet. Students who signed up for the course received my directives by e-mail. I encouraged them to write to each other, but they exchanged e-mails mainly with me, the teacher, and almost never with each other. Once I had sent around "assignments" motivation dropped. "Work" (e.g., home*work*) was not what they had bargained for, and the word *assignment* carried connotations of obligation. They were far more interested in exploring options on the Internet in hopes they might have fun using it constructively.

The course was not entirely without merit, however, and one of my students voluntarily prepared a Web page for it. Now, this was fun! Just collaborating on the project was enjoyable, and the activities we came up with were interactive and graphically attractive. I was so impressed with the potential of Web documents to serve as a class focal point that I quickly learned HTML myself, registered with a free Web host, and started to put up pages to anchor all my online materials. I went on to set up Web pages to both introduce the students to each other and publish their writing, changing the name of the course to English for Webheads. Meanwhile, I was dabbling in synchronous communication tools and when I began work at a language institute in Abu Dhabi with a fast Internet connection accessible through its LAN, I was able to "hang out" in these chatrooms and meet others interested in online learning, as both students and teachers.

Then, in late 1998, I restructured the course yet again so that participation in the course and distribution of e-mails could be managed through eGroups, a free *listserv*.[3] In order to do this, I had to close down English for Webheads (where I was forced to maintain class rolls and manage distribution lists for class e-mails myself) and resurrect it under the name Writing for Webheads (where eGroups kept tabs). I invited all involved to enroll in the new system, and most (around 50 participants) made the changeover.

Self-enrollment (and unenrollment, and a whole host of learner-managed features) was a strong appeal of the move to eGroups, now Yahoo! Groups, not only as a means of relieving the moderator of mundane record-keeping duties, but also in allowing learners to come and go in the community as they pleased. In fact, participation increased and now the low rate of attrition in the Writing for Webheads course (or, more correctly, community) is interpreted as positive feedback by the community's facilitators.

By May 2003, approximately 250 students and teaching peers had enrolled. However, active participation occurs between 10 and 20 percent of the group members, the others (known as "boundary members") hardly ever contribute to our discussions. Many seem to stay on the list because they appreciate what they learn from our list traffic. As one such member put it, she was a silent participant but a "loud" reader. As our popularity increases by word of mouth (or its Internet equivalent) and links to us on other people's Web pages proliferate, we have a constant influx of new members. The new members sometimes simply "lurk" on the sidelines, sometimes join us in a flurry of e-mails and then lapse into boundary member status, and sometimes become active participating members. It is the latter group of newcomers who constantly rejuvenate our communities.

## Development of the Student Community

The student community was slow to develop, but after an initial period where gaining trust became crucial to course success, a threshold was crossed as students gradually sent in photos and shared personal vignettes, and numbers grew steadily. As Writing for Webheads accumulated students and, not insignificantly, their pictures and/or enough writing to reveal personality, its online presence continued to grow in the form of Web pages and in synchronous meetings at the Palace (an early avatar-based chat environment) and in other chat areas each week at Sunday noon Greenwich Mean Time (GMT). The effect was the formation of a community whose members, despite never having met, felt they were getting to know one another, and thus a climate favoring trust and sharing of knowledge through scaffolding was fostered.[4]

## Learning from Communities, Conferences, and Real-World Interaction

The thrust of the Writing for Webheads project has been to help students develop English skills by completing tasks in a communicative exploration of free online CMC tools. Learning takes place through a two-way channel between native and nonnative speakers of English in a flourishing online community, where all concerned experiment with and share their knowledge of the technology, with language development taking place incidentally, on demand, and as a secondary focus of activities.

As this approach to language development gradually proved itself successful (in terms of learner enthusiasm for the program, as evidenced through growth in numbers and almost negligible attrition), it attracted the attention of teaching practitioners, especially when we started to use synchronous voice communication and announced our chats on listservs. Voice chat being a novelty at the time, our events proved quite popular.

We had already been involving our students in live online demonstrations of our use of CMC in language learning at both face-to-face and purely online professional conferences, but at the turn of the century our innovations with voice chatting resulted in our being invited to demonstrate our skill with voice and avatar-enabled chat at several international conferences, including Vancouver, Barcelona, Cyprus, Dubai, California, and Salt Lake City. We also participated in a number of purely online conferences, where our students had the opportunity to interact meaningfully in authentic communication with conference-goers. When the task is to prepare for and participate in an online conference, these purely online venues have proven to be a highly appropriate medium because all participants start out on an equal footing. The old joke (a *New Yorker* cartoon showing a mutt at a computer), "On the Internet, no one knows you're a dog," works well at online conferences, where interactants tend to take each other at face value, and students find to their pleasant surprise that that they can hold their own in real conversations with native speakers who make no effort to patronize them.

## Students and Other Community Members

One reason that "real-world" tasks work well with Webheads is that they are real-world people. That is, it is difficult to conceive of activities that could be contrived (not concerned with real-world tasks) for such a diverse audience, and therefore it seems logical to introduce tasks with intrinsic appeal to individuals in the group. We now take a look at who the Webheads are, and how they interact in such a way that task-based instruction is appropriate to their various learning objectives.

### WRITING FOR WEBHEADS

The students in Writing for Webheads range in age from early teens to septuagenarians, and come from all over the world. The most typical students are looking for ways to augment language skills, either after work or, if they are students, as an adjunct to more formal classes. Some of our "students" are nonnative-English-speaking teachers of English in their own countries, and their proficiency in English varies, with some frequently requesting help from the group on matters of translation or nuance, while others in this category are almost indistinguishable from native speakers. Thus, their distinction blurs with members of a third group of Webheads: native English speakers wishing to learn about CMC tools in order to gain experience of using them with students and then implement them in ways that will foster community development in their own teaching situations.

Teachers and students coexist in symbiotic relationship in Writing for Webheads. The teachers all volunteer, and students sign on without concern for fees. Essentially the teachers gain through firsthand experience with CMC tools while using these to facilitate language learning in a live community of learners online. Students appreciate the opportunity to develop their language skills in conjunction with learning the same computer skills favored by instructors. Table 10.1 shows how teachers and students interact and what they gain from their part in the process.

### WEBHEADS IN ACTION

More recently, teaching professionals have joined our groups in such numbers that student participation has waned as that of teachers predominated. A way of introducing practitioners to methods of promoting community formation in online language learning was needed without diluting the integrity of student participation in the original project.

Webheads in Action, whose students are teaching professionals, began as part of the Electronic Village program of online sessions that have preceded each TESOL conference since 2001. Sessions are offered on any topic that contributes to the field of teaching English to speakers of other languages. They last six to eight weeks, are taught on a volunteer basis, and are open to anyone without fee. I offered to conduct a session on community building online. The plan was to bring the techniques that had worked so well in developing a community of stu-

TABLE 10.1. **Webheads in Action**

| Aspect | Teaching Practitioners | Students |
| --- | --- | --- |
| Motivation | Volunteer | Take advantage of opportunities for free English development in a communicative, supportive environment |
| Skills | Learn how to use CMC tools to teach | Develop language skills according to inclination |
| Tasks | Use CMC tools to facilitate language learning through maintenance of communities online | Learn how to use CMC tools for communicative and personal purposes |
| Outcomes | Teachers learn how to use CMC tools for personal, professional, and pedagogical purposes, and to correct what students write for their Web pages | |

dents and teachers to bear on a community of teaching professionals who would learn not through being "taught" in a lecture environment but by working with a model that was set up to enable them to experiment with the concepts under consideration. Webheads in Action was thus a laboratory for creating communities so construed as to develop into the real thing. Accordingly the community did not disband in March 2002, as did every other session at the end of eight weeks, but continued to function organically until one year later when the experimental community embarked on its second EVOnline session on the topic of a principled inquiry into communities of practice through introspective study of its own development.

### HOW THE TWO GROUPS INTERACT

At the time of this writing the two active groups, Writing for Webheads and Webheads in Action, remain very distinct in aims and in the nature and topics of postings to the respective groups. However, there is much overlap of membership, with many teaching Webheads participating in the student group and some bona fide students participating in the Webheads in Action group.

## Topics and Tasks

The examples below give a sampling of the range of topics broached and illustrate some of the many genres of writing possible when students are given, or better, allowed to invent, purposeful tasks designed to facilitate their language learning.

## TEACHERS COOPERATING ON PROJECTS

Aiden Yeh, a nonnative-English-speaking teaching professional at National Kaohsiung First University of Science and Technology, has utilized Writing for Webheads in several projects. In one, her students listened to a song by Michael Coghlan, an active member of Writing for Webheads and Webheads in Action and an accomplished guitarist and composer, who posts links to his music and accompanying exercises for English as a second language on his Web site. Aiden developed a Web page to set the task. The students were asked to listen to one of Michael's original compositions, "Fear of Being Too Good," and then give their own interpretation of the song. After her students had listened to the music, Aiden invited Michael to meet the class online and discuss the deeper meaning of the song. She followed up, using the transcripts of the conversation with Michael, and posted a Web page recording the event, as well as her students' reactions to the song and their interpretations of it in both text and student-recorded sound files.

Dr. Arif Altun, a nonnative-English-speaking professor with an Ed.D. in CALL from an American university, divides his time between two universities in Turkey, teaching methodology to Turkish EFL students. His class joined a Webheads Sunday noon GMT chat session; this resulted in a follow-up meeting with a class in China headed by yet another nonnative-English-speaking teacher of English in Liuzhou. The two classes later repeated the meeting as remote participants in a presentation that I orchestrated live at a conference in Abu Dhabi (Stevens and Altun 2002).

## WRITERS COOPERATING ON THEMES AND TASKS

Writing for Webheads is a virtual counterpart to classes where students organize the activities and take responsibility for bringing materials to class to carry out projects in an environment rich in scaffolding provided by others. Initially there is no plan of action beyond an agreement to meet online and use English as a medium of discussing a topic or engaging in a loosely directed activity (or a somewhat formally constructed one, as in the case where we meet for conference presentations).

More directed activities have included variations on Webquests; for example, where several NNS students and teachers collaborated on a Web site describing Carnival and how it was celebrated in different parts of the world (see Susanne Nyrop's http://home19.inet.tele.dk/susnyrop/sambaschool.html). Going from the theme of "carnival schools," a group of Webheads discovered they had in common an interest in preparing national dishes and so they collaborated on a "cooking school" where they produced Web pages with pictures showing how they made their dishes and "projected" them (on the browsers of virtual participants) during a joint presentation in Tapped In during one of its Summer Carnival events to showcase progressive uses of that medium (http://home19.inet.tele.dk /susnyrop/cooking/pancakes.html). We have made other imaginative uses of seemingly simple features of Tapped In, such as the ability to create and project text notes. It has become a tradition at Halloween time for Webheads to hold a fancy dress party, where we "design" elaborate costumes by describing them on these "notes" and then project them so that others present can imagine what we look like. The result is a collective role-play, with teachers and students acting out roles of fantasy creatures, which students very much enjoy, especially for the cultural insights, which we have supplemented by collectively preparing a Web site on Halloween themes (http://www.homestead.com/prosites-vstevens /files/efi/hallowebhead.htm); also see our chatlogs from two such events: October 28, 2001 (http://www.homestead.com/prosites-vstevens/files/efi/chat2001 /wfw011028.htm), and November 3, 2002 (http://www.homestead.com /prosites-vstevens/files/efi/chat2002/wfw021103.htm).

In a sense, participants in such chats are constantly role-playing through what is known as "emoting;" for example one participant might give another a virtual "hug" (or worse ;-) ):

ChristopherMJ [sleepy] exclaims, "Hi everyone!"

VanceS [^-^] gets bucket of water ready to pour on Chris

ChristopherMJ [sleepy] says, "Hi Ying"

SusanneN hugs Chris and Ying

VanceS [^-^] says, "Hi Chris, Hi Ying"

ChristopherMJ [sleepy] enjoys the feeling of ice water running down his back

Ying [guest] says, "hi"

ChristopherMJ [sleepy] says, "Thanks, Vance, I needed that"

Role-plays can get even more elaborate. In one synchronous chat at the Palace the participants each spontaneously took on roles and put on an impromptu play (Stevens 1999). In this case, it started when one of the participants said she would like to write a play but didn't know how, so we offered to help her conceive one:

VANCE: Another idea is to come to class prepared to take on roles and use the chat logs as a script, or the start of one.

MAGGI: and the teacher is only a monitor or helps to jumpstart things when they stall

VANCE: But we'd have to have a storyline and characters defined.

MICHAEL C: That would be interesting Vance. Kind of develop the play as we go!

FELIX: let's start one now?

MICHAEL C: I'm willing Felix.

VANCE: Well, we could start on a plot now.

MAGGI: who wants to start

The characters were defined as the participants dreamt them up. Here, Ying Lan creates the role of a beautiful doctor named Sam:

YING-LAN: Sam is a doctor.

VANCE: Good start.

YING-LAN: ^she is a beautiful woman too.

MAGGI: What kind of doctor

MICHAEL C: Sam is a woman?

YING-LAN: ^Like thrapist

MAGGI: good . . . a beautiful female doctor

In this way, a set of roles was conceptualized. Then the participants in the chat changed their name designations to assume the roles of the characters they had hypothesized, and made up dialogue as they went along. It was easy for participants to become emotionally involved in their roles and in the impact of other roles on their character. Here is an excerpt from the resulting role-play:

BILL (FBI): Joyce—while you're waiting could you get out the files on all Dr Sam's patients please?

JOYCE: ^Sam, I have already noticed the lawyer, he will be here after one hour. Actually he is in court now.

SAM: those files are the my property dective

BILL (FBI): Did you speak with the dead woman jack?

SAM: and you need a court order to have them

JOYCE: ^But, sir . . . all the files are still in our office.

JACK: Yes, we had a small talk . . .

SAM: dead women can't speak

BILL (FBI): I have a court order. Here it is.

BILL (FBI): Very funny Dr.

JOYCE: ^ I did not bring those file.

SAM: excuse me a second while I read this over

BILL (FBI): Well go and get them would you Joyce.

JOYCE: But what do you want to know?

BILL (FBI): jack—are friends with Jseph?

SAM: Jooyce stay right here

BILL (FBI): I want to know everything Miss JOyce.

JACK: yep.. we used to play tennis together.

BILL (FBI): Dr—you are not being very helpful.

In other instances, the projects can be more personal. For example, one of our original Writing for Webheads students likes to write about her travels and feelings, especially in appreciation for something she has read or heard, such as the songs of Leonard Cohen, the poetry of Shel Silverstein, or the fantasy of the Harry

Potter series, which she was reading in the original before it became popular (see http://sites.hsprofessional.com/vstevens/files/efi/efw_ying.htm). A Webhead from Brazil likes to tell us *about his country*, especially about the beaches and carnival, as well as get help with his studies. His Web pages show the nature and history of his region (and he was the *first Webhead to broadcast video* to the rest of the group) (see http://sites.hsprofessional.com/vstevens/files/efi/efwbahia.htm). Another Webhead sends instant messages when she gets stuck translating documents for her school. In each of these cases the tasks are instigated by the students.

## CMC Tools and Modalities

It can be seen that Webheads are communicative within the group in inventive and imaginative ways. This is quite an accomplishment for a group of people who in most cases have never met one another in person. We turn now to a consideration of the online tools that facilitate interaction.

### SELECTION OF TOOLS

Primarily our materials are our computer-mediated communication (CMC) tools. These tools comprise text, graphics, voice, and video-based chat clients,[5] which are often nominated by participants in the community. New CMC tools are not always discovered by the instructors, who are also participants, but often by the students. These tools are selected according to suitability to the purpose. For example, participants often enjoy using voice and video for communication, but there are times when text chat seems more appropriate to the purpose at hand. For example, there may be people in the chat who have no sound capability, so the group will opt for text chat mode. At other times, groups of voice chatters and those broadcasting Web cams will form breakout groups and find it hard to pay attention to the text chat. Higher than usual demands are placed on participants who fiddle with managing chats in multiple modes, which one of our participants characterized as "chaos navigation" (though once she started to get the hang of it, she changed that to "intuitive chaos navigation"). All of these modes of CMC interaction, whether challenging or phatic, contribute to the cohesion of the community of users that comprises the Webheads projects.

This brings us to the question of what CMC tools best lend themselves to distance language practice and formation and cohesion of communities of practice. Here are four considerations in selection of such tools (see appendix A to this chapter for a fuller description of specific tools used):

1. Cost: appropriate to the means of the institution. In an implementation such as Webheads, where there is no funding and the appeal to participants is to as broad a spectrum of users as possible, these tools must be free (to members of the community); that is, simply downloadable by anyone in the community with an Internet connection.

2. Ease of use: easy installation, no complicated registration, intuitive interface.
3. Multicasting capability: in order to engage groups of people, the ideal CMC tools need to broadcast one-to-many. Text chat easily meets this test, but the choices for multicasting voice and video (for free!) are limited.
4. Cross-platform adaptability: run on Mac *and* PC.

There is no need to look for an all-in-one CMC tool. Several communications tools can usually be run simultaneously over slow Internet connections on common denominator computers (although users can normally have only one sound and one video device running from the same computer at any given time). Thus CMC enthusiasts should be able to select from a choice of clients according to suitability to perform a given task. Webheads, for example, favor Tapped In for text chat, but Tapped In does not have multimedia capabilities. Therefore, we text-chat in Tapped In while using *other* CMC tools to effect our voice and Web cam sessions. There is no one tool that meets all our needs at all times, so we choose the tool that meets the occasion as one would select an arrow from a quiver to dispatch the target at hand.

## Cooperation Worldwide

When starting out with CMC the first hurdle is to find a remote partner to experiment with. Once you begin to interact with a community, partners appear out of the virtual woodwork. For example, suppose I install a Web cam and want to see if it works. One good way to find out is to go online and check my buddy lists to find someone else who is online at the same time I am. I use several programs that tell me when other users of those programs are online; for example, ICQ, MSN Messenger, and Yahoo! Messenger. Chances are there will be someone online that I can ask if he or she can see my Web cam. Most people in my virtual community will take a few minutes to help each other with online troubleshooting of this nature. Thus, the community serves not only to inform, but also to assist with experimentation.

One teacher in China, Yaodong Chen (Stevens 2002b), has often asked me to help him surmount a technological hurdle, join him at an interesting Internet site, or speak with his students or colleagues for whom he is demonstrating techniques with CMC tools. In one such instance, he met some of our students at the Military Language Institute in Abu Dhabi online. In another, we engineered a meeting between students in his class and one in Turkey. That encounter presaged a reunion of the two classes before a live audience at the Teacher to Teacher 2001 conference in Abu Dhabi (Stevens and Altun 2002).

On another occasion, this same teacher contacted me for help in answering riddles in English. It turned out he was at a MOO,[6] called Grassroots (http://www.enabling.org/grassroots/). One characteristic of MOOs is that they can have "bots"[7] to interact with real people who visit the MOO. Yaodong had found a bot at Grassroots that asks riddles and handles attempts at answering them. This teacher was doing these with his students who were getting language practice not only with comprehending and attempting to answer the riddles, but through interaction with native English speakers in the "greater" online environment who were available at the time to help them understand the riddles and their possible answers. And this teacher was making use of the native speakers in his online community to successfully compensate for his own shortcomings in the language he was teaching, thus overcoming a common problem often faced by nonnative speaker teachers of foreign languages. This kind of interaction is an almost daily occurrence among Webheads community members who might find each other online and ask for various kinds of help.

## MODALITIES, TASKS, AND MODERATOR ROLES

In a classroom or *blended* learning environment,[8] an implementation such as Webheads would have a face-to-face component, but because Webheads is a purely online phenomenon, it has no classrooms but uses instead virtual spaces on the Internet. In these spaces, Writing for Webheads bases its interactions with students around three modalities. These are (1) e-mail funneled through our Ya-hoo! Groups listserv, (2) Web pages for publishing introductions and writing "as-signments," and (3) synchronous multimedia chats. In this section, we will see what tasks are distributed throughout these modalities.

### E-mail via Yahoo! Groups Listserv

The Yahoo! Groups for Writing for Webheads not only distributes e-mail but also allows individual members to self-regulate whether they want to receive this mail by choosing to remain on the list or not. It also provides other useful features such as allowing members to determine how e-mail from the group is delivered to them (choices are receive messages individually, in digest form, on none at all in case Web access is sufficient). However they prefer to receive e-mail, members are also able to read Webheads e-mail and post replies directly from any Internet-connected computer anywhere in the world. Besides archiving all Webheads list traffic at its Web site, Yahoo! Groups also provides convenient (and generous) upload and access to Files and Photos areas on each group's Web site, also accessible from (in theory) any Internet connection anywhere in the world. All these features are available for free to anyone who wishes to start a group on Yahoo! Groups.

Webheads make use of all these features, especially the e-mail list facility. Most writing in Webheads is geared toward developing fluency, and e-mail is a good vehicle for this. Webheads are encouraged to post on any topic they like, and the list can attract over 100 messages in a given month. The list moderator takes some of the messages (introductions and those that address threads under discussion), corrects them, and posts them to Web pages. Students are encour-aged to compare their e-mail with what they see posted at the site. We do have some evidence that this is done: one student writes, for example, "About other e-mails that you sent to me I print all of them and I study, compare, and under-lined your corrections" (Stevens 2002a). Other than offering corrections when asked, posting corrected e-mails to Web pages is the extent of attention paid to accuracy by Writing for Webheads. Some of the tasks associated with this modality are

- sending and managing e-mail;
- joining a listserv (such as *efiwebheads*);
- creating, configuring, and managing participation in a learner management system (LMS), for example, starting a group on Yahoo! Groups and accumulating participants through a call of some kind; and
- uploading digital photos to an LMS space.

### Web Pages for Publishing Introductions and Writing "Assignments"

Although training and assistance have been offered, most of the Webheads Web pages have been created and posted by the main Webheads instructor. The content of the students' pages derives from the students and is harvested as follows: Once students find us on the Internet and subscribe to our Yahoo! group, they might eventually be invited or take it upon themselves to send an introduction message to the group. This introduction will be made into a Web page linked from the Student Page where all Writing for Webheads students are listed (see http://sites.hsprofessional.com/vstevens/files/efi/students.htm). If a student supplies a picture, it will be put on the Web page in near-original form, with a thumbnail version on the Student page and in the gallery of all available student portraits on the *main portal page*. Then a message is sent to the list indicating how everyone can meet the new student at the new URL. Often this is the first time that these students will have had any kind of a Web presence and they are usually pleased and impressed to see their writing made so widely accessible.

The portals for all the Webheads projects follow a formula that we believe enhances community building. The ingredients in this formula are all items that project pictures and personalities of community members in an effort to introduce participants in the community to one another. To accomplish this, the group portals each have a main page with a description of the group and a gallery of thumbnail pictures of everyone who has sent a photo. With more than fifty such portraits on each portal page at present, the portal becomes a tableau of our community. When the pictures are clicked on, details of community members are revealed. Through this network of pages, visitors to the site can get to know the person behind the face.

As members address various topics, their writings are collected onto pages devoted to each topic. Each message as it appears on the page is illustrated with thumbnail portraits (where available) linking back to the student's page, so that visitors to the site can read a message or essay, click on the adjacent portrait, and read about the person who has written that piece. The Student's Page can serve as a portfolio for a student's work and link to other pieces the student has written. As many such pages accumulate over the years, an interesting gazette is developed that effectively records and contributes to the culture of the community. Some of the tasks associated with this modality are

- writing on various topics and genres;
- creating Web pages;
- taking digital photos and manipulating them (cropping them, resizing them, making thumbnail versions);
- recording digital audio and/or video, compressing it, and posting it to Web pages;
- putting students and teachers in communication with one another through as many senses as can be conveyed via Web pages posted on the Internet; and
- building Web pages explaining how the tools are used and exploited (e.g., Webheads in Action has a syllabus [http://www.geocities.com/vance_stevens/papers/evonline2002/syllabus.htm] to explain CMC and applying this to language learning; and Writing for Webheads has tutorials [http://sites.hsprofessional.com/vstevens/files/efi/tutorials/tutorlist.htm]).

## Synchronous Multimedia Chats

Chatting online is the third modality on which Webheads bases its interactions with students and other participants in the community. In addition to numerous other virtual venues, Webheads have met every Sunday noon GMT synchronously online in one place or another since late 1998. Most of these chats have been logged and placed on the Internet with graphics showing screen shots of our interactions and pictures of people in the chats (http://sites.hsprofessional.com/vstevens/files/efi/chatlogs.htm).

The base for our chats has varied over the years. At first, we used ICQ to find each other online. ICQ was unique in the late twentieth century for being one of the first chat clients to tell you when other people you wanted to meet had actually logged on to the Internet—essential knowledge when consummating group meetings online. We used ICQ to chat with each other and to even engage in multiuser conferences, though its multiple windows, one for each user, were not ideal for following such conversations.

Meanwhile, we had discovered the Palace, one of the most enjoyable text-chat clients we have encountered. The Palace was rich with features conducive to language learning. It allowed us to make our own avatars with our photos or graphics of fanciful objects. The avatars displayed cartoon bubbles when speaking, so it was easy to distinguish who had said what, and meanwhile a chat log was generated so that learners could recoup what they couldn't follow in the chat itself. From the log we could copy URLs we showed each other and paste them to our browsers. We started logging our chats at our Web site in an effort to share the experience with members in our community vicariously, and to give those who were there a record that they could use to study what had been said and thus improve their English.

A significant portion of the discourse generated in the Palace was about using features of the Palace, explaining to newcomers how to make their speech bubble stay on screen, for example, and, thus, it generated a rich matrix of contextualized comprehensible input for students. It was also not at all beyond the capabilities of second language learners to use. We would often encounter students on line in ICQ, invite them to the Palace, find out they had never installed the program, and have them with us in the Palace and using the software within about half an hour (and most of that was download time).

Meanwhile we were exploring other playgrounds to enhance our chat. We early on experimented with voice-enhanced communications across the Web, sending each other e-mails with Real Media or Pure Voice attachments, sometimes putting the Real Media files up on Web pages. This was at a time when expensive phone calls were considered to be the only option for most people to hear each other's voices from half a world away, so it was a significant breakthrough to have a means of speaking to one another at no cost, and to the students' advantage, be able to attend to pronunciation issues (one of which was learning how to pronounce each other's names). The students often took the lead in this. One student, for example, thought it would help her pronunciation if she could send us compressed sound files of her reading poetry and short stories, and we could give her feedback on her pronunciation in real time using our voice tools during our Sunday chats. It was also a student, this one from Brazil, who broadcast the first video to be seen on Webheads (http://sites.hsprofessional. com/vstevens/files/efi/felix_see.htm), leading others among us to follow in his footsteps once greater availability of bandwidth became possible.

The real-time voice tool that had the biggest impact on our development at the turn of the century was Hear Me. This allowed multiple users to gather in voice chat rooms and not only talk clearly to one another but converse in text chat. Inevitably someone would join the chat who could hear us but had no microphone, so this person would respond in text while others talked. The text feature was also valuable when we wanted to convey certain information such as proper names or URLs, or when there was a breakdown, or breakup, in voice communication. Sometimes several of us would be interacting in combination text and voice when someone would appear online who had no sound capabilities. Rather than break off and regroup elsewhere, this person would be invited to join us, and then the chat might proceed in silent text for some time, so as to include the newcomer.

What is the purpose of these chats and what would be their counterpart in traditional education, usually conducted face to face? Classes in brick and mortar institutes meet regularly for class business, and transactions in class assume some degree of formality in order to enhance the efficiency of time spent there. After class, classmates might retire to a more social venue and talk about whatever they like. Though this is not seen as part of the class, any college freshman understands that this is a valued aspect of life at college. Thus, in Webheads, chatting is carried out in after-class mode. The moderators quickly learned that there was really no place for moderators in these chat sessions. If there was ever any attempt to set *regular* topics for the chats, this was abandoned early in our interactions together, since any attempt to keep participants on topic was invariably met with asides on the weather and greetings and interruptions from people coming and going (this applies to a *long* term course of interaction; perhaps not for a course of limited duration).

It has become clear that the modalities of e-mail and Web sites are the places in our online environment where business is conducted, not, as one might extrapolate through false analogy to face-to-face learning in a bricks-and-mortar institute, the chat rooms. Chat venues create good opportunities for people to come together to expound briefly on central themes, and in fact these might be discussed *out of interest*, and this is important, *not* because a moderator has made any sustained effort to keep people's noses to the grindstone. It has become clear over the years that people value these chats for social reasons, the same way villagers might gather regularly in pubs or tea houses, not to conduct business but to socialize. But there might be some business conducted in these gatherings, and in fact the socialization is critical to the way business is conducted when it comes time for that. So in the same way that a village sustains its community spirit around its after-hours meeting places, Webheads has sustained its community spirit in large part by virtue of its weekly chats. Furthermore, the fact that people regularly turn up by the dozens week after week and year after year for these chats lends credence to the assertion that they do so due to their enjoyably interactive nature; it is hard to imagine that they would remain so loyally committed to events more like business meetings run week after week.

Another draw of these online meetings is their exploratory nature. Webheads are generally eager and willing to experiment with each other's new discoveries. Willingness is important; Webheads do not respond "not now" when asked out of the blue in an instant message suddenly appearing on one's computer screen in the middle of the work day if they can stop what they are doing to help the interlocutor test a Web cam or see if PowerPoint slides can be made to launch remotely on the former's computer. This kind of thing happens at any time when Webheads leave their instant messengers up and running,[9] but of course during the regular Sunday chat times, when so many Webheads are online at the same time, the urge to experiment can lead to challenging dimensions in multitasking. Some of the tasks associated with this modality are

- registering, installing, and using *instant messenger* software;
- establishing Internet connections from remote locations including home, school, and cybercafes;
- exploring a variety of virtual worlds, and creating and manipulating objects in those worlds;
- engaging in creative role-plays online;
- saving and exploiting chat logs;
- using synchronous voice communications online in communicative ways that enhance language acquisition;
- conducting phatic and communicative activities utilizing the broadcasting of Web cams; and

- communicating with community members while managing voice and video Webcasting with multiple participants, such as conducting online tours, engaging in online training, or participating in conferences online.

## Evaluation

There have been a few efforts to evaluate Webheads through qualitative methods (see http://www.homestead.com/prosites-vstevens/files/efi/reports.htm for a listing of many such reports). Stevens and Coghlan (2001a, 2001b, 2001c) did a study in which students in Writing for Webheads were asked what was important to them about the class, and from responses a questionnaire was drawn up and commented on by many of the students. The most interesting offshoot of this limited study was that it started an introspective dialogue between students and practitioners in the group; the latter were forced to explain and defend *their methods* against the more traditional views of the students. This airing of views was a healthy outcome for a community trying to reconcile its focus on communication and socialization with lack of assignments of grammar and reading exercises for the students (http://sites.hsprofessional.com/vstevens/files/efi/ methods.htm).

There is, however, a wealth of anecdotal evidence on how individual Webheads are responding to the learning environment created on their behalf. Coghlan (2000) cites a remark made by one of our original Webheads students from Taiwan: "We could find a lot of English grammar books in bookstores, libraries and other Web sites. But only the Webheads teachers give us a response fast. That's our Webheads' wonderful treasure. I can not find such a good precious pearl in the world as Webheads."

More comments from Writing for Webheads students have been collected at Stevens (2002a). For example: "I've been connecting on the Internet since last year and it was one of the best things that ever happened to me because as I don't have any English native speakers living down here, it was difficult for me to correct my accent, mistakes and the like. But now I have lots of help. The classes at The Palace have been an important source of information for me. They have good teachers: Vance, Margaret, Vera, Michael, Claudia, and Begum to name but a few" (Felix, Bahia, Brazil, March 1999).

We have also had interaction with passersby to our Web pages. Bicknell (1998), in one of the first reports ever done on Webheads, found "the public nature of their discussions and the work on their Web pages/sites is the ultimate evaluation as the other students . . . and any Internet user who happens on their site . . . are free to comment on the English content of the pages." The Webheads in Action group too has accumulated a collection of testimonials, which can be found on the Webheads in Action portal page (Stevens 2003). Some examples:

"You have all contributed to my personal development as examples of 'can do, will do' people. I am amazed at your skills, energy and dynamism and impressed by your talents and output" (posted to the evonline2002_webheads Yahoo! Groups list, February 2003).

"We are so lucky to be part of Webheads, this resourceful and sharing group of human beings who have introduced us to the wonderful world of e-learning" (posted to EVOnline moderator training Yahoo! Groups list, November 2002).

"This CoP [community of practice] has been one of the best professional development opportunities of my entire career—thank you all for being so supportive and eager to work together!" (posted to the evonline2002_webheads Yahoo! Groups list, March 29, 2003).

Additionally, this group recorded some longer essays on what the experience has meant to them professionally at the end of the EVOnline 2002 eight-week sessions (see http://www.geocities.com/vance_stevens/papers/evonline2002/week8.htm#reflections).

In early 2003, the group hosted a second EVOnline session whose purpose was to study itself as an example of a distributed community of practice. In the course of this session and subsequent colloquium, several Webheads in Action members evaluated how participation in the community had informed their teaching practices. Some documents to emerge from this introspection are Teresa Almeida d'Eça's comprehensive listing of the many Webheads sites all over the Web (http://www.malhatlantica.pt/teresadeca/webheads/wia-index.htm), and Arlyn Freed's database approach at getting to grips with all the output and organizing it in a searchable Web page (http://www.eslhome.com/cop2003/db.htm). During the sessions themselves Dafne Gonzales organized a weeklong session on "How participation in a community of practice informs and influences the participants' personal teaching practices" and documented her work at a Web page with links to testimonials prepared by her comoderators (http://dygonza.esmartweb.com/evonline2003/week5/w5p1.htm). One of the most intriguing outcomes from that session was Buthaina Al Othman's impressive Web page documenting her capabilities before and after joining Webheads in Action (http://www.geocities.com/esl_efl_ku/). The transformation is apparent and clearly illustrated from the relatively flat pages before the influence and the JavaScript and frames effects of the more recent pages. These pages also link to a list of things Buthaina learned from Webheads in Action (http://geocities.com/esl_efl_ku/thingsilearned_wia.htm).

I was once asked after a conference presentation how we handled evaluation in the Writing for Webheads group. I realized the question was about how we judged the students, but I answered that we judge ourselves highly on the fact that after several years we are still going strong with increases in student numbers, many participants having stayed with the community since the very beginning. Although there is no testing or formal evaluation in the Webheads projects, we receive constant and mostly unsolicited positive feedback in terms of growth in and enthusiasm for our endeavors.

## Conclusion and Recommendations

In this chapter I have tried to explain the many facets of the Webheads projects in the context of current trends in the facilitation of language learning through constructivist and task-based approaches. In so doing I am hoping to provide a model that others might use to achieve similar implementations in their own learning contexts. For example, we show in our model how students might practice and improve fluency through chat, e-mail, and postings of extemporaneous compositions to Web pages. In your situation you might want to include other genres, or build in mechanisms for greater feedback or evaluation.

It is important to realize that application of such a model to one's own context will depend on many factors. For example, do you meet your students primarily face-to-face or, like in the Webheads projects, almost entirely online? Or are you working in a blended environment where you see your students but are developing components for them to interact online? What performance objectives are set for your students and how do you evaluate them? Do you have enough flexibility in your situation that you can engage in exploratory learning, or can you write rubrics that will accommodate learning within constructivist frameworks? Your specific application of the principles explored in this chapter will depend on your answers to these questions.

The main message from the Webheads projects is that e-learning environments can and should be set up to lower the affective filter and promote the formation of a sense of community among members of those environments. Techniques for accomplishing this online include the sharing of still and moving images, and voices as well as text messages that give participants in a community an indication of who they are and what values and aspirations they share. It is the contention of this chapter that tasks directed at sharing such information can be powerful catalysts for language learning. Certainly these contribute to the willingness and motivation of learners to want to communicate with each other, thus giving them a reason for wanting to use the language under study that can be lacking in learning environments where attention to community has not been well developed.

The Webheads experience has shown that our model can be applied successfully in language learning and teacher training in predominantly online, or distributed, communities of practice. It seems reasonable to assume that there are countless other situations to which the tenets of our project might be applied.

## Appendix A: Chat Clients Useful in CMC (as of Early 2003)

The following are CMC tools we have used and their limitations:

### SOFTWARE MENTIONED AND WHERE TO GET IT

Blackboard–Blackboard, Inc., http://www.blackboard.com (license required)
Chatterbox voice chat client, Talking Communities Online,
   http://www.talkingcommunities-online.com/Client.html (license required)
ICQ–ICQ.com, web.icq.com (free)
iVisit–iVisit, http://www.ivisit.com (free)
MSN Messenger–MSN, http://messenger.msn.com (free)

Netmeeting–Microsoft, http://www.microsoft.com/windows/netmeeting/
   (free)
PalTalk–PalTalk.com, http://www.paltalk.com/
Wimba, http://www.wimba.com (license required for threaded voice and
   voice chat software; voice e-mail still free as of early 2003)
Yahoo! Messenger, http://messenger.yahoo.com/messenger/download/in-
   dex.html

### FIVE FACTORS TO CONSIDER

### 1. Cost

Wimba is a great product and has working relations with Longman, IBM, and
Blackboard, but users must purchase the ability to create threaded voice boards.
Webheads are currently helping to beta-test a Wimba product called Voice Direct. Another fairly robust voice chat client allowing the creation of voice chat
rooms to accommodate numerous users is Chatterbox, but again, it's not free
(however, Chatterbox can be tried out online, for free, at StudyCom English for
Internet; http://www.study.com).

### 2. Ease of Use

Most of the free CMC tools are fairly easy to use (with the possible exception of
iVisit—not intuitive how to use it).

### 3. Multicasting Capability

*Do not support multiple conference users:* Some free chat clients, in their freely downloadable form, are strictly one-to-one. This is the case (in early 2003) with MSN
Messenger's voice enhanced chat, and Netmeeting (which is especially easy to
use when conveniently launched from an MSN Messenger session). Netmeeting
is an excellent CMC tool, with a useful whiteboard in addition to robust voice
and video broadcast capabilities. The whiteboard enables users, for example, to
draw or paste an image onto the whiteboard of one computer and have it appear
on the whiteboard of the remote computer (very handy). Server software to enable Netmeeting multicasting is available but, unfortunately, not for free.

*Allow multicasting:* There are at least three free chat clients that will enable
voice and video multicasts. PalTalk will allow one voice speaker at a time to communicate in conference with multiple listeners, and these conference participants
can select up to four available Web cams to view at any one time. Yahoo! Messenger does even better than that, allowing voice users to meet en masse and speak
in duplex in conference mode, with voice quality and users allowed seemingly
limited only by bandwidth available. Yahoo! also allows broadcast and reception
of multiple Web cams, again limited only by system resources available to the
computer. Mac users can broadcast and receive video, though it seems that they
can't access Yahoo! Messenger voice (as of this writing, but this appears likely to
change).

### 4. Cross-Platform Adaptability

Enter iVisit, a cross-platform Mac and PC chat client that allows free creation of chat rooms and the ability to get multiple Web cams and voice users therein. However, in practice, I have found the downside to be that the interface is not intuitive (how *do* you create a chatroom?), voice can be erratic or not function at all, and the video display is inferior to Yahoo!'s. However, if the community contains both Mac and PC users, and if there is a need for voice and video enabled chat, iVisit is currently the only choice.

### 5. Ability to Fit into an Eclectic Approach to Usage of CMC Tools

*The best in text chat:* All the above clients are text-enabled, and this is important when sound is not clear, or when someone wants to copy and paste a URL that the others in the conference can click on. Most will also allow you to save your chats (though not Yahoo! Messenger conference chat). The best free text chat client, is Tapped In (http://www.tappedin.org), the portal for a community of educators who can join for free, keep and decorate offices, have chat transcripts mailed to them, join in online community activities, have avatars, project URLs on remote computers, and avail themselves of other features ranging from the amusing to truly utilitarian.

*The preferred choices for an eclectic approach to implementation of CMC in language learning:* The ideal CMC environment available today is an amalgam of all that is useful. My own choice for multimedia CMC on a PC is to meet in Tapped In and then open a multiple-user voice chat conference in Yahoo! Messenger and share video windows with those who have Web cams. If Mac users are present, iVisit might be the best bet, but look for Yahoo! to do more in the near future to accommodate Mac users.

## Notes

1. An avatar is a digital representative of a participant in an online environment. An avatar can be an icon of some kind (a flat graphic representation of the participant) or an animated object.
2. EVOnline is the Electronic Village associated with TESOL.
3. A listserv is a mailing list that can be subscribed to in such a way that members can send e-mail messages to one another simply by addressing the "list."
4. As of May 2003, there are approximately 350 Webheads involved in Writing for Webheads and Webheads in Action. There are about 110 participants only in Webheads in Action, about 220 solely in Writing for Webheads, and perhaps 20 involved in both groups. Given current trends, these numbers are likely to increase in the near term.
5. Chat client is an interface through which participants in a chat connect with one another, e.g., Yahoo! Messenger.
6. A MOO is a MUD Object Oriented; object-oriented means it has graphics objects. MUD is a multiuser dungeon, from the game Dungeons and Dragons, a virtual

navigable maze. A MUD supports multiple players connecting from remote locations to the same virtual maze space. A MUD is usually text-based.

7. A *bot* is short for *robot*. It is an automated process that is programmed to interact with a user in such a way that the user perceives intelligence in what is, in fact, mechanically algorithmic.

8. Blended refers to learning environments where a curriculum has both online and face-to-face components (as opposed to purely one or the other).

9. An instant messenger (sometimes called instant messager) is a kind of chat client that registers a user's "buddies" in such a way that they can "see" each other whenever they log on to the Internet (and on to that particular chat client).

# 11

## USING WEB TECHNOLOGY TO PROMOTE WRITING, ANALYTICAL THINKING, AND CREATIVE EXPRESSION IN GERMAN

### Franziska Lys

EDITORS' NOTE: In this chapter, Franziska Lys describes a Northwestern University advanced German course in writing, based on interviews with German speakers in the community. The course involves learning to use technology to develop a Web project but in a very different way than in the Webheads project described in the previous chapter. At Northwestern, the students are part of a traditional course but elements of community-based learning, peer review, and self-directed learning are added to the advanced course in composition. Results have been Web pages (some available to the general public) that tell life stories of a collection of interesting people, written in German by students, and appearing online in a form that has been reviewed for accuracy of content and linguistic structure.

### Writing across the Curriculum in Undergraduate Courses

One of the goals of Northwestern University, as stated in the undergraduate catalogue, is to provide students with an excellent education by emphasizing effective communication and by fostering "the ability to think analytically and write and speak clearly and persuasively" (Northwestern University 2001, 1). However, after a cursory look at various course descriptions across the curriculum, I realized that quite a few courses either did not have a writing component as part of the course or only listed "final paper" as part of student evaluation but were not very specific about the process of arriving at this final paper. A more detailed study of course descriptions presented to a group of instructors during a meeting in the fall quarter 1997 at the Searle Center for Teaching Excellence at Northwestern University revealed that only 14 percent of the 200-level and 300-level courses (second- and third-year) surveyed and only 34 percent of the 400-level courses (fourth-year) surveyed had a significant writing component as part of the teaching, learning, and evaluation process.[1] In an effort to increase the amount of writing required of students, each instructor was asked to develop new ideas for courses in his or her respective fields that would stress writing across the undergraduate curriculum. The ensuing discussion focused on writing as a tool for self-expression being a critical skill for all students; students would need nurturing and constant practice to develop language for presenting their thoughts effectively.

228

## Writing in Language Courses in General

Nurturing and constant practice to advance students' writing skills is even more crucial when one writes in a foreign language. The struggle for linguistic accuracy adds to the complexity of expressing one's thoughts succinctly and often affects the logical argumentation and flow of written work. Roebuck (2001, 208) writes:

> The task of writing in a second language poses a number of cognitive difficulties to the learner. Whereas in the communicative classroom learners are encouraged to speak freely in spite of errors, the task of writing on paper . . . imposes a more rigid standard of accuracy and precision. Moreover, the foreign instrument is often so unwieldy or difficult to manage that few college level learners can use it with the same automaticity that they enjoy in their first language.

During the first two years of language instruction, learners are exposed to a variety of very short writing exercises intended to practice language in a controlled environment. Learners can do these successfully even with a limited knowledge of vocabulary and grammar. Further, linguistic mistakes are downplayed in favor of semantic accuracy and corrections focus on getting the message across or the task accomplished. Successfully communicating the main idea is the primary goal. This attitude often changes when students move to upper-level courses. Instructors appear impatient with students' skills and expect them to be fluent once they are beyond second year. They complain that students cannot write clearly and that their essays are riddled with mistakes. Such observations, of course, do not take into account what can be reasonably accomplished during the few hours students are exposed to a foreign language in lower-level classes. Met (2001; reported in Schulz 2002, 286) explains: "useable language proficiency cannot be obtained in only two years of . . . language instruction." Additional reasons why students are sometimes unsuccessful in upper-level classes is that (1) assignments often do not fit their linguistic abilities and (2) there is not enough time in the span of the course for intensive work or for instructors to provide guidance and feedback on student papers. Students research and develop their assignments in isolation outside of class with no opportunities to discuss their ideas with other members of the learning community. They hand in "a good first draft" that becomes the basis for a final grade in the course. This first draft, if it finds its way back to the student, is then discarded, not only wasting the instructor's grading efforts but robbing students of valuable learning opportunities. The sole emphasis, quite often, is on the finished product rather than on the process of arriving at this product.

## Writing across the German Curriculum at Northwestern University

Designing a coherent curriculum that allows for vertical articulation across four years of instruction in language, literature, and culture is difficult at best. Many instructors have their own way of teaching and strong feelings about the content of their courses and are not necessarily open to a more structured curriculum. Yet, it is the only way we can assure that our students are exposed to materials that reinforce and build on content and language skills acquired in lower-level classes. I agree with Schulz (2002, 288), who writes: "high quality language instruction . . . needs lengthy, articulated sequences to bring worthwhile and lasting results."

The curriculum in the German department at Northwestern University, at first glance, is a more traditional curriculum, as described in Weber (2000). What makes it different is the attempt to articulate some of the language tasks across all four years of instruction to ensure continuity across classes without discouraging instructors' individuality. Here is an example: learners will interview a German mystery guest in the first year of language instruction asking personal questions such as his or her name, birthday, and likes and dislikes. The German guest interview is repeated in the second year of language instruction with more complex questions through which learners gather information from the guest on a cultural topic such as sport, schooling, or free-time activities of young people. In the third year, students interview a guest speaker or listen to a guest lecture about a cultural topic and then research and prepare a Web page based on the information. The topic explored in 2003 was German architecture in Chicago.[2] These three tasks prepare the learner for the more advanced project done in the fourth year of language instruction in which students are asked to prepare a Web project about the life of a German speaker they interview.

### FIRST- AND SECOND-YEAR LANGUAGE COURSES

In our first- and second-year language courses we strive to teach a balanced program in which we practice all four language skills (reading, writing, speaking, and listening) through various culture-based activities. Both levels meet four times a week (fifty minutes each) over three quarters. We have eighty to one hundred students in each level.

In our first-year language classes, we stress productive skills. Many student assignments are task-based, modeled after the concept of real-life rehearsals to real-life tasks (Jennings and Doyle 1996, reported in chapter 1, this volume), to practice situations students might encounter. For example, students write fictitious postcards to each other and the teacher, compose and send letters to companies and firms asking for specific information, write questions for a mystery guest interview, put together a European breakfast, keep a daily journal, and write and perform a short skit.

Our second-year language classes follow a similar teaching philosophy with lots of opportunities to practice all four skills. Since we want the classroom portion of the course to be as communicative as possible, we review grammar outside of class through an online grammar program that provides immediate feedback to students. The grammar is thematically based, which means each chapter has a cultural/thematic focus. Students also work with an interactive CD-ROM program, containing short documentary vignettes that highlight the lives of people in a former East German town. The cultural focus of the material allows each instructor to develop and practice interactive activities similar to the ones developed for first year. For example, students meet a Trabi-owner and his car in one of the video vignettes. In class, students are then asked to compose an advertisement with the intent to sell the Trabi by listing its appealing features. Subsequently, each student tries to sell his Trabi to another student by negotiating price. Finally, all students write a letter to a German friend about the trip they are going to take with their new car.

### THIRD- AND FOURTH-YEAR LANGUAGE COURSES

Our language courses for third- and fourth-year students are carefully designed to teach language skills that reinforce each other and are applicable to other course work and later careers. We offer intermediate and advanced composition and conversation classes, an intermediate class on current events (reading news periodicals), and an intermediate and two advanced business German language classes. The assignments in these classes vary, depending on the content of the class. Overall, writing assignments tend to be shorter (one to two pages) and of a more practical, task-oriented nature, such as writing letters (letters of complaints, job applications), composing resumes and vitas, requesting information, and similar compositions.

We also offer third- and fourth-year culture and literature courses that are taught in German. While most of them have a writing component to assess students' performance, they follow a traditional teaching approach with lectures and discussions, a midterm and a final exam or a final term paper.[3]

## A New Writing Course for German Majors and Minors

Students majoring or minoring in German are required to take the advanced conversation class and the intermediate and advanced composition classes, among other language and literature courses. The focus in intermediate and advanced composition classes had traditionally been on reviewing grammar concepts, practiced through grammar exercises. To shift the emphasis toward an approach that would emphasize the development of individual students' writing competence, the German department redesigned both composition classes. In the intermediate class today, grammar is treated as one component in the process of developing writing, and the syllabus contains many activities geared toward the improvement of writing at various levels and contexts with an emphasis on practicing genres. Since writing takes time and students need ample practice to move to a more advanced level, we generally offer two intermediate writing classes with different material, and students are encouraged to take both before moving to the higher-level writing class. During each quarter, students write approximately five compositions, each dealing with a different topic and writing style. In the first quarter, students work with portrait descriptions, description of places, narrative texts, and reports. In the second quarter, students work with film critiques, advertisements, controversial issues, and approaches to literary works. Each topic occupies about two weeks, during which relevant vocabulary, grammar, and short writing exercises leading to the final composition are covered. The types of activities vary with the different topics chosen. Students may do writing tasks such as journal entries, news groups, and e-mail exchanges, or they may combine writing and speaking in role-play tasks such as Siskel and Ebert's television show in which they critique current films or conduct a skit performance in which they advertise a product. Even in classes where conversation or writing is the focal point, all activities include other language skills.

In order to distinguish the advanced-level writing class from the intermediate composition class, we were searching for a writing assignment that would not repeat but expand and build on the previous experience. We wanted to emphasize the process of writing, including revising over an extended period of time, and give students an incentive to work on a longer piece of writing on a topic of their choice.

### GOALS FOR THE ADVANCED WRITING COURSE

In choosing the content for the advanced composition course and designing appropriate writing tasks, we had several goals in mind. Overall, we were looking for a course that would advance students' writing skills, tap their analytical thinking skills through research activities, and encourage successive revisions and a more creative approach. In order to achieve these goals, we set certain guidelines:

- The topic or topics for the writing projects would be chosen by students themselves to ensure that it was something they really wanted to write about. The only restriction was that it had to be a topic that would require a fair amount of independent research over an extended period of time.
- The format of the writing project had to inspire students to continue writing and had to encourage revisions of first, second, and possibly third drafts by teaching students to view their writing as an organic whole with a definite structure.
- The project should encourage students to write for a broader audience. At any point during the quarter, students would be encouraged to share their writing with other members of the class and with the broader community: evaluating, criticizing, and presenting ideas to an audience were part of the strategy to learn from each other.
- The presentation of the material should foster the creativity in students by giving them a chance to incorporate more than text.

In planning for the class it became clear that technology would play a major role as many of the goals were more easily achievable by incorporating technology. For example, online spell-checkers and online dictionaries are readily accessible tools to help in writing and revising. Font variations, size, and color can add interesting differences and highlight important parts. Illustrations—digital pictures and photographs—can enhance comprehension. The Internet can encourage students to research difficult or unknown concepts and allow them to link the original text with explanations on other Web pages. And finally, posting the project on the Internet has various advantages for the instructor. First, it is an effective way for students to share their work with other students, teachers, and mentors outside of class. Second, the creation of student pages can be a rewarding experience as "students communicate, connect, and build community using the language and the technology for personal enjoyment and enrichment" (McGee 2001, 536). Third, because of the public aspect of presenting Web pages on the Internet, we hoped that students would be more willing to work through several drafts. Kubota (1999) points out in her article on word-processing and Web-based projects that in her experience publishing Web pages requires a greater number of drafts than the conventional submission of essays. This is similar to the rationale behind the Report stage in J. Willis's (1996b) task-based framework—the more public writing is, the more students will want it to be accurate and well organized and so the more drafts they are willing to do.

## A Task-Based Writing Project for an Advanced Grammar and Composition Class: Project Description

The name of the project is Geschichten die das Leben schrieb (stories written by life or life stories). We had assigned this project for the first time as an experiment in the winter quarter 1997–98.[4] Since it was so successful, we have continued to assign the project annually for the past five years in the advanced composition class.

For this project, students are asked to find a German-speaking person on campus or in the community with an interesting life story to tell. They then interview the person at least once a week for eight weeks, carefully preparing questions and taking notes. Students write up the information by dividing it into linked chapters (about seven to eight chapters, one to two pages each), creating an illustrated book of the person's story in German. This illustrated book is written, designed, and published as a Web project. For the Web pages, students experiment with color, font size, and text layout. They also link each part of the project so that a reader can easily navigate the pages. In addition, they incorporate navigational elements, such as links to sites on the Internet that highlight the history of the main character. They may also add image files such as scanned photographs and digital stills.

Initially, the most difficult part for students is finding an appropriate topic or person to write about. We start by brainstorming in class: each group is asked to write down places in the community where one could find German speakers, including people with Swiss or Austrian nationality and even students who have studied abroad. Then students are asked to do some research at home and bring their ideas to class. Specific tasks include:

1. Consult the phone book for businesses with German-sounding names (a German bakery, restaurant, or pub) and follow up with a phone call.

2. Ask your parents, other relatives, acquaintances, or friends for suggestions.
3. Call the local library.
4. Think about your own high school or visit the local high school to find a German instructor.
5. Contact local homes for the elderly and ask for German-speaking residents.
6. Walk around with open eyes and ears.[5]

During the next class hour, students are given a chance to read previous projects to come up with an additional list of topics.[6] Topics of previous projects have included the following:

- A 100-year-old German living in a local nursing home tells about his journey from Germany to South America and to the New World.
- A German artist explains her paintings and what it means to be an artist in America.
- A German professor retells his experience as a young boy in Hungary during World War II.
- An opera singer talks about her work experience in an opera house in Germany.
- A student visits a local German café and describes its audience.
- A group of students describe their study abroad experience in Germany.
- The owner of a German restaurant tells her story as a female entrepreneur.
- A young man recounts his experience growing up in former East Germany.

These examples also serve as good illustrations for new students of what a Web project might look like. The importance of providing a model for the production of student Web pages has also been pointed out in McGee (2001, 542). She advocates that instructors provide students with an instructor-created student page so that students can see what they are to produce. The approach here takes it a step further in that students learn from other student projects. Viewing and discussing finished projects also gives the instructor a chance to clarify the elements he or she expects to see in each project: a title page (index page) with a title, the name of the author linked to the biography page of the author, and a list of the chapters linked to each chapter page.

## The Syllabus: Combining Writing and Technology

One of the difficulties in teaching a course that requires students to design Web pages is that you cannot expect them to have the necessary technological skills. Although most students nowadays are using the Internet and e-mail daily, few of them know how to transfer files using an ftp program or have used an HTML editor before.[7] Since this is a course in teaching German writing and reviewing grammar points, only a minimal amount of class time can be devoted to learning the technology, thus requiring a careful balance between teaching the subject and teaching the necessary technological skills.

The class lasts ten weeks (one quarter). We meet three times a week for fifty minutes, a total of thirty sessions. The basic technology for writing and illustrating a Web page is taught in six sessions, in German. In each technology session, we spend half an hour learning a new aspect of technology. The rest of the session is then devoted to individual work on the project. The topics for each technology session are arranged in the following way:

Session 1: File transfer (ftp) to the class server (Microsoft Word documents, HTML documents, and image file documents)

Session 2: Basic Web design: text and color (HTML software Dreamweaver)

Session 3: Digital image files: still camera and image processing (Photoshop)

Session 4: Advanced Web design: formatting text, tables, linking to pictures (HTML software Dreamweaver)

Session 5: Introduction to scanning and image processing (Photoshop)

Session 6: The Internet: evaluating and linking to existing Web pages

All other class sessions are devoted to improving writing: grammar problems, including lexical and syntactic difficulties, are reviewed and inconsistencies associated with logical structure, clarity, and organization of ideas are discussed. Students have various backgrounds, so we do not follow a set grammar syllabus but topics unfold, based on the mistakes students make in their writings. In this way, students review what is needed at the time. After reading and commenting on the first drafts of each chapter, I prepare a worksheet that contains a selection of problems encountered in these first drafts. In class, we then work through these problems together, suggesting solutions for grammar and lexical mistakes to which students can refer when they rewrite their first draft. In these classes, the focus is mostly on form to help learners achieve greater levels of accuracy (Lightbown and Spada 1999; Lightbown 2000).

## A RIGOROUS WRITING SCHEDULE

One of the goals of the course is that learners practice how to express themselves succinctly by working out successive drafts. Therefore, the schedule for the writing assignments is very rigorous: students turn in one new chapter every week while revising the chapter or chapters of the previous weeks. Students interview their partner once a week. For the interview, they prepare a set of questions. (These questions are not turned in but students can ask for guidance.) During the interview, students take notes. Based on these notes, they write the chapter, which is collected by the instructor. Major corrections are worked out in class (peer-editing; see Roebuck 2001) and students write their first revision as home-work (self-editing; see Roebuck 2001). The instructor reads each revision and makes additional suggestions. The chapter is posted online when the students think it is ready but no later than one week after evaluation and return of the initial draft. Students are encouraged to share their posted chapters with their interview partner to verify content and facts. Sometimes, chapters get organized differently, based on feedback and discussions. I will read and comment on as many rewrites as the student wants to hand in. Overall, the writing schedule and the technology schedule are broken up into manageable steps and tied to a time line that presents a series of connected tasks to help students pace their work. This is important to ensure that students progress steadily and have enough time for each revision.[8] The building blocks and timeline for the writing and technology assignments are presented in table 11.1.

TABLE 11.1. **Writing and Technology Assignments**

| *Writing* | *Technology* |
| --- | --- |
| *Week 1* | *Week 1* |
| Brainstorm about possible topics. | |
| *Week 2* | *Week 2* |
| Find interview partner and conduct initial interview. Report to class. Write short biography about yourself, hand-in. | Introduction to server technology. Learn how to ftp various files (word document, HTML document, image file document). |
| *Week 3* | *Week 3* |
| Write first chapter, hand in. Revise and post biography. | Introduction to HTML and Dreamweaver. Design title page document and biography document. Link the two documents. Post documents on server. |
| *Week 4* | *Week 4* |
| Write second chapter, hand in. Revise and post chapter 1. | Introduction to the digital camera: take picture of another student for the biography and post-process image file in Photoshop. |
| *Week 5* | *Week 5* |
| Write third chapter, hand in. Revise and post chapter 2. | Introduction to page design in Dreamweaver: background and text colors, fonts, and tables. Link image to text. |
| *Week 6* | *Week 6* |
| Write fourth chapter, hand in. Revise and post chapter 3. Share project with another student. Revise text and design based on discussion. | Introduction to scanning: scan picture, post-process in Photoshop and link to text. |

| *Writing* | *Technology* |
|---|---|
| *Week 7* | *Week 7* |
| Write fifth chapter, hand in. Revise and post chapter 4. | Introduction to the Web. Search for, find, and evaluate relevant background Web pages. Create links to other Web sites. |
| *Week 8* | *Week 8* |
| Write sixth chapter, hand in. Revise and post chapter 5. Share project with another student and revise text and design. | |
| *Week 9* | *Week 9* |
| Write final chapter, hand in. Revise and post chapter 6. Discuss project with instructor. Instructor makes final corrections and gives suggestions. | |
| *Week 10* | *Week 10* |
| Make final revisions and post project by middle of the week. Present your project to the whole class during presentation day. | |

### USING A WORD PROCESSOR AND ONLINE RESOURCES

Students use word processors for all initial writing tasks since this facilitates revisions (Pelletier 1992). In addition, we ask students to use online resources frequently as resource guides for their writing since there is a wealth of information available.

Most students are familiar with at least some online resources and we usually start the class by gathering their suggestions for important and helpful URLs. We then spend some time looking at the links available for German from the Web page http://de.dir.yahoo.com/Nachschlagen/. Each student checks one entry in a dictionary, in a thesaurus, and in an encyclopedia. The results are discussed in class with special emphasis on what are useful sites and why. Invariably, students choose http://dict.leo.org[9] as their most favored site as it is fairly easy to use and contains many useful entries. Indeed, this site not only lists various translation options but it also lists idiomatic expressions and orthographically similar words.[10] The site also links to grammatical information, which includes, for example, inflection and plural forms for nouns and most tense forms with verb entries (including present and past participles). The grammatical information is found on the canoo-net Web site, http://www.canoo.net/index.html, a comprehensive Web site, listing spelling, inflection, word formation, and the morphology of many German words. The word formation is useful for students as they can easily increase their vocabulary by looking up entries. The grammatical information is helpful for instructors as most grammar explanations have good examples that can be used together with advanced students. Of course, students also work with the dictionary and the thesaurus in Microsoft Word since they are required to use the electronic spell-check for all of their chapters.

## Choosing Software and Hardware

Choosing software and hardware for such an assignment can be difficult. Before we made the final choice we considered what was available in the teaching lab and for use outside of class and the instructor's knowledge of hardware and software.

Northwestern University is quite fortunate with regard to technology. The whole campus is networked: this includes the library, computer classrooms, smart classrooms (equipped for multimedia), faculty offices, and student dorms. For language teaching, we have several smart classrooms available in the building where languages are taught. The Multi Media Learning Center has two, well-equipped computer classrooms, both of which function as public computer labs outside of class hours. The class regularly meets in a smart classroom; this allows us to view any of the projects during class hours for comparisons and discussions. The classroom computer lab is reserved one hour a week for seven weeks to work through the computer assignments and to share the developing Web sites. All students are expected to do homework on their own computer or in the public computer labs.[11] Many are hooked up to the campus network from their dorm rooms.

For this particular project, we need to have access to several distinct software packages:

- word-processing software to write and spell-check the various drafts of each project chapter;
- software for file transfer to the server to make all files accessible from various sites on campus;
- HTML software to develop and build Web pages; and
- image-processing software to post-process images from the digital camera or scanned images.

We chose software based on availability and support in the teaching lab, in the public computer labs, and on student computers: Microsoft Word for word processing, Fetch (an easy-to-use, full-featured ftp client) for file transfer for the Mac and Absolute FTP (an easy-to-use ftp client with a simple, Explorer-like interface) for the PC, Dreamweaver to develop Web pages (which circumvents the need to learn html programming code), and Photoshop for image processing.[12] Since the teaching lab houses Macintosh computers and students own Windows machines, we had to make sure that the selected software packages were available cross-platform.

## A Designated Server

The question of where (on which server) the Web projects would be stored and served from was a tricky one to solve for us. Students potentially can work on their projects from different locations (i.e., teaching lab, public computer labs, or their personal computer in their dorm rooms), and they need convenient access to their files. In the first year, we asked students to use their personal server space called Pubweb for their projects.[13] This turned out to be a difficult solution because the instructor did not have access to students' Web pages and server space, and sharing of material and communication about the material became cumbersome. We have in the meantime purchased a departmental server, which is accessible to the students and the instructor alike. This allows the instructor to make small changes and corrections immediately (other than corrections in the writing portion of the project for which students themselves are responsible). The instructor may adjust a table, link a picture, or improve the layout of a Web page if the student has difficulty with the technology. It eliminates frustration on the student side and ensures that the projects meet a minimum standard.

One of the most difficult areas in teaching students to build their own Web site has been the transfer of files. Although we spend time in each course discussing appropriate file names and appropriate suffixes for each file transfer (.doc for Word documents, .html for Dreamweaver documents, and .jpg for image files), transfer protocols are difficult to remember and students are not used to labeling files correctly. Access to the server allows the instructor to transfer or post project pages if for some reason the ftp transfer does not work from the student computer or the student is not sure how to go about it.

To assure uniformity in the Web address and to make sure that all students link their files and images appropriately, we prepare a folder on the server for each student with the same internal structure as seen in figure 11.1. The initial folder is labeled with the student's last name. We ask students to keep similar files together: In the main folder, we save all .html files; the Bilder (picture) folder contains all .jpg images; and the Text (text) folder contains all Microsoft Word documents including the revisions.

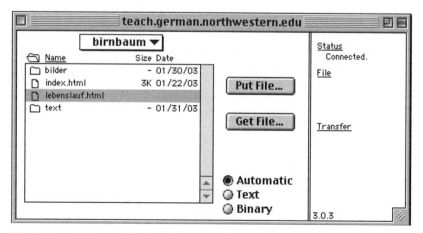

FIGURE 11.1. **Folders and File Structure on the Class Server**

### TEACHING BASIC FUNCTIONS ONLY

Even though a substantial portion of this chapter deals with the setup and teaching of the technology (a difficult part for many instructors), it is important to stress that this is not a class in learning how to produce the perfect Web page. The development of content, the writing task, occupies much of the class time. This is also mirrored in the fact that we teach students only the basic features of the software they are using. Both Dreamweaver and Photoshop are professional software packages, and it can take hours of instruction before one understands all of the available tools. Students receive step-by-step instruction in the following basic areas:

### The Digital Camera

We bring the digital still camera, which is housed in the Multi Media Center and can be checked out, to class and point out basic features. Students then get to take each other's pictures so that they have handled the camera at least once. During class, we download the pictures from the camera and distribute them to appropriate folders on the server.

### PHOTOSHOP

We postprocess each image file in Photoshop, checking the size of the picture, adjusting the contrast and the sharpness, cropping it if necessary, and saving it in an appropriate format. The picture is then used for the student's biography in the Web project.

### Scanning of Image Files

Scanning is demonstrated in one of the latter technology sessions for students who have pictures they want to scan. If there is a student familiar with the scanning software, he or she will give tutoring lessons to individual students freeing up the instructor to help with Web design questions and grammar or stylistic questions.

### Illustrating a Web Page

We instruct students in the use of various fonts and font sizes, font colors, and background colors. We look at sample pages prepared by the instructor or by students and discuss what would be good color combinations so that the pages are easy to read. In a later session, we discuss the organization of text and pictures on a page (how much text should be on a page to avoid excessive scrolling) and introduce the concept of tables to format the text. And finally, we teach students to link from the title page (the index page) to other project pages and to other sites on the Internet to give readers more information and the project more depth.

### LEARNING FROM EACH OTHER

The project, Geschichten die das Leben schrieb, is a unique way of approaching learning as students take sole responsibility for topic and content development of their Web project. For many, it is the first time they are asked to go out into the community, find a German speaker with an interesting story, and convince him or her to be part of their project. What is equally important is the fact that students are encouraged to work collaboratively with others.

## The Role of Mentors

Many of the interviewees become mentors to the students. In addition to the weekly interview sessions, students are asked to share their writings with their interview partner to make sure that factual information is correct and that interviewees have some control over the way their life story is presented. More than once, the mentor–mentee relationship has afforded students learning experiences that would be hard to replicate in a conventional classroom. Some interview partners share their family albums liberally with the students and allow them to scan pictures for their report. On one occasion, a student brought his interview partner, an elderly woman who had never heard of the Internet, to the library regularly so that she could see the project unfold online. Students also have permission to do the interview over the phone if the story is compelling and if traveling to a particular location is too costly or time-consuming. One student wrote about a family who emigrated from Germany to Fredericksburg, Texas. The phone interviews went really well. However, in order to experience the current life of her interviewee, the student was invited and subsequently traveled to Fredericksburg over the weekend to meet the family and to see firsthand how the family was living.

Sometimes, the research for the projects resembles history lessons; students can decide what to research or learn on their own. One student developed a Web project about an East Prussian who was driven from his homeland by the Soviet Army at the end of World War II. He researched the man's childhood in his homeland, his expulsion at the end of the war, his capture by the Russians, his work on a Russian collective farm, and his eventual escape to the West. Another student developed a project about a German living in Chicago in a senior home. She researched his journey from Germany to South America to the United States. Her interviewee was born on February 11, 1898 (he was 102 years old at the time of the interviews!) in a small village close to Berlin with the name of Hoch Jeser. The student researched the name in the library but could not find the location on any map. After following up many leads, the student finally found a librarian in the main library in Warsaw who found out that Hoch Jeser today was called Jeziory Wysokie and had become Polish territory after World War II. He prepared and e-mailed several digitized maps for the student's Web project that showed the location of Hoch Jeser before and after World War II.

## Collaboration among Students

In a regular writing class students work alone on their assignments with minimal input from others. Collaboration and student and instructor feedback are difficult to achieve. Yet, review and revisions of their own work and that of other students are important steps in the learning process. As Roebuck (2001, 210) puts it: "They give the author the opportunity to read his or her composition as a reader (and not as the writer) to determine where and how it can be improved."

The introduction of technology in this class has made it feasible for students and instructors to share their work and use each other's work as models on a regular basis. Students read each other's projects on the Internet, and they give advice on content, as well as on layout and ease of navigation. The class homepage has convenient links to the students' index pages, and at the beginning of each week, we briefly glance at each project and discuss the progress each student has made. This is also a very good way to pressure students a little to work on their assignments regularly as they do not want to be the one in the class with nothing to show. Sharing material over the Internet gives ideas on what else could be done in terms of writing content and developing the design. McGee (2001, 540) writes: "By posting their work on the Web, students can have an enhanced experience of both *process* and *content* when they see each others' work. . . . Posting student projects online also encourages students to learn content from each other." Sharing and revising has been one of the most valuable experiences for this project.

### PROJECT EVALUATION

Evaluating and grading such a project can be challenging for the instructor and daunting for students. Students often ask how and by whom their writing will be evaluated and how much it will matter if their technological skills are not good or if they do not have an artistic sense. Students are informed early on about ongoing evaluations in class, about the final evaluation, and about the criteria used for assessing each project.

### Student and Instructor Evaluation

In order to give students several chances to improve their projects, we have two types of evaluation in class. The informal evaluations are intended to help students progress and give them suggestions for project improvement. This happens spontaneously during project time as students are encouraged to walk around and look at other Web pages. In weeks six and eight, we pair students and give them time to evaluate and discuss their Web projects in more detail. In week nine, the instructor meets with each student separately to make final corrections and give final feedback on each project.

During the formal evaluation part, students receive letter grades for their writings and for their Web projects. The first draft of each chapter is evaluated during the quarter by the instructor according to content (50 percent) and according to grammar and complexity of language (50 percent). At the end of the quarter, students have seven chapter grades. These grades count toward homework assessment.

Each finished project is evaluated at the end of the quarter. In this phase, there are two evaluations; one by the instructor and one by a student in the class. Both evaluations are taken into account when a final grade is assigned.

## Evaluation Criteria

Not all students are similarly gifted with technology, and it can be frustrating if a student thinks his or her project is not as flashy as others' and therefore might not get a good grade. Similarly, some students may feel as long as they can dazzle with the technology, the content is not that important. Toward the end of the quarter, we spend some time discussing how the project will be evaluated. The final evaluation considers five areas: (1) content, (2) organization and presentation of material, (3) topic research, (4) vocabulary and expressions, and (5) grammar.

- In the category *content*, the semantic quality of the writing is assessed. How interesting is the reading? Does it flow? Does it hang together? Is there enough information? Does the reader have a sense of what the writer tried to say? Is there a story to be told?
- In the category *organization and presentation of material*, we look at the organizational structure of the writing and at the illustrations. Are there six or seven distinct chapters? Do the titles reflect the chapter content? Is everything linked appropriately? Are there navigational features that make it easy to move around in the project? Did the student use color and fonts appropriately? Are there illustrations to help the reader understand?
- In the category *research*, we look for the following: Did the students make an appropriate attempt to research places that were mentioned in the text, historical dates, historical facts, and famous names? Are there appropriate links to external Web pages that give the project depth and let the reader investigate and branch out to additional topics?
- The category *vocabulary and expressions* addresses the question of language choice such as vocabulary and the use of idiomatic phrases. In general, the writing should have an adequate amount of sophisticated vocabulary and expressions (beyond what you would see in the writing of an intermediate or second-year student).
- The category *grammar* assesses grammatical accuracy. Since students had a chance to revise each chapter several times, the grammar should be almost flawless at this point. We also take into consideration whether the chapters contain features of advanced writing such as extended modifiers, subordinating clause constructions, and appropriate tense forms including subjunctives. Since students are reporting what has been said in an interview, we expect to see direct quotes and indirect quotes from the interviews with appropriate tense forms and punctuation marks.

Table 11.2 contains the evaluation sheet used for the evaluation of each project. Usually, there are two graders per project, the instructor and one student from the class.

TABLE 11.2. **Web Site Evaluation**

Web site title:

Name of Web site author:

Name of person evaluating the project:

*1. Content (up to 10 points)*
Boring, put me to sleep (0 points) to very interesting, could not stop reading (10 points)
1   2   3   4   5   6   7   8   9   10

*2. Organization and Illustration (up to 10 points)*
Not well organized, no artistic flair, no illustrations (0 points) to very well organized, artistically well developed, well illustrated (10 points)
1   2   3   4   5   6   7   8   9   10

*3. Research (up to 10 points)*
Uninteresting, I did not learn anything new (0 points) to very interesting, I learned a lot of new facts (10 points)
1   2   3   4   5   6   7   8   9   10

*4. Language: Vocabulary and Expressions (up to 10 points)*
A native speaker would have serious problems understanding (0 points) to perfect descriptions, a native speaker would understand everything (10 points)
1   2   3   4   5   6   7   8   9   10

*5. Grammar Accuracy (up to 10 points)*
Still many major errors in spelling and grammar (0 points) to impeccable, almost no mistakes  (10 points)
1   2   3   4   5   6   7   8   9   10

TOTAL POINTS: _____

*Overall Evaluation*
Describe in a short paragraph what you think about this project. What are its strengths? What could the student have done better? What was your reaction as a reader?

_____

_____

_____


## Project Appraisal in Terms of Task-Based Instruction

The project Geschichten die das Leben schrieb fits squarely into the framework of task-based instruction. The pedagogical goals of the project encompass the three basic assumptions underlying task-based instruction outlined in chapter 1 (this volume) and restated here in abbreviated form.

*Assumption 1.* Learners need opportunities to use the target language in real situations to learn it (Swain 1985; Swain and Lapkin 2001). When students meet with their interview partner to gather information for each chapter, they use the target language in real situations: They ask questions in German, listen to the information, make notes in German, and ask follow-up questions to fill in gaps.

When students learn how to put together a Web page from their instructor by experimenting with fonts, colors, posting of pictures and linking of documents, the instructor and the students use the target language in a real-life situation.[14]

*Assumption 2*. The learning of language form occurs when language learners focus on meaning (Prabhu 1982, quoted in Brumfit 1984). Students write each chapter, based on the notes and anchored in what they remember from the conversation. Each chapter takes shape by focusing on presenting content in an appropriate form: when writing, students carefully select words and string them together to give meaning and depth.

*Assumption 3*. Language learning does not proceed in a linear additive fashion but is a gradual and complex process (Long 1985a; Lightbown 2000). Multiple revisions allow students to work out their problems in grammar and syntax gradually, when focus on form is needed and at the level it is needed. This is a continuing process, in which students work to discover the most effective way for communicating their ideas and thoughts.

The project Geschichten die das Leben schrieb is a true task, according to the definitions offered in chapter 1. In fact, Skehan's definition (1998a, 95)—"an activity in which meaning is primary; there is some sort of relationship to comparable real world activities; task completion has some priority; and the assessment of the task is in terms of outcome"—fits well. There is another characteristic exemplified by this project that is often associated with task-based instruction, namely, integration of skills. Even though the project focuses on writing, it allows for other skills to be used to arrive at the final result: oral production and listening during the interview, writing to present information, and reading to assess and advance one's own and other students' projects.

The project Geschichten die das Leben schrieb can be categorized further by using the four either-or distinctions described in chapter 1 (this volume).

1. The project is an open task. The content and design of the final product vary quite widely, and the project contributes to the growth of students' confidence and competence.

2. The project is a reciprocal or two-way task. It involves interactions between the interview partner and the learner on the one hand, and between the students and the instructor on the other. All involved can ask for information or clarification.

3. The project is a real-world target task. The task of interviewing people and asking for information is a type of activity that students may encounter regularly in the real world. However, at the beginning of the ten-week session, we prepare students through pedagogical tasks in the classroom (such as explaining the project in German to another student, writing a vita, asking another student for personal information about family members, etc), which specifically help students with the real-world task of interviewing.

4. The project encompasses both unfocused and focused tasks. One part of the task—interviewing people and gathering information—is unfocused in the linguistic sense. Students are not given specific phrases or

samples of language to use in their interview portion but use any language available to them. Revising the chapters in class in small groups becomes, in Willis's words, "a consciousness-raising activity, where the focus is on examining samples of language to explore particular features of it in order to encourage comprehension and correct use" (chapter 1, this volume).

What makes the project Geschichten die das Leben schrieb particularly interesting pedagogically is that it is composed of cycles that reinforce and build on each other. Each task cycle includes various subtasks as outlined in Willis's "components of a task-based framework" (presented in chapter 1, appendix B). There is the "pretask phase," which includes planning the topic for each interview session and writing down questions. Included in each task cycle is the "task phase," where students gather information during the interview, and the "planning phase" and "reporting phase," where students work on presenting the information in written form. The "language focus" phase actually has two components: (1) during class time, instructors and students analyze and practice linguistic problems encountered in each composition (the work sheets and grammar focus sheets prepared by the instructor) and (2) at home, each student analyzes and makes corrections to his or her own composition based on the instructor's comments and the work done in class. This phase, with its focus on language form, is intended for the learners to achieve greater levels of accuracy. Since interview partners quite often get involved beyond the interviewing phase, there is an additional stage in this cycle—a "verification phase" in which the interview partner checks the information online for linguistic accuracy and content.

Over the course of the quarter, there are six to seven similar cycles that allow for repetition of the various tasks. Indeed, as chapters unfold, students' compositions are more interesting, more focused, and linguistically more accurate.

### Evaluation and Conclusion

We are currently offering this class for the fifth time and plan to continue teaching it in a similar fashion as the task-oriented nature of the project has allowed us to incorporate all of the pedagogical goals described above, incorporating student choice of topic, revisions of successive drafts, writing for a broader audience, and encouraging creativity.

The class structure with its emphasis on learning from others by sharing and evaluating has for the most part only been possible through the use of technology. The introduction of Web technology in a language class can be of concern for the students as well as for the instructor. Generally, few students come with prior knowledge about writing Web pages. However, experience has shown that most of the students acquire the necessary skills to handle the basic technology quite easily and quickly.

The biggest problems usually are found in the following areas: the posting of pages on a server; the linking of documents and images; the transfer of files between Macintosh and PCs; and overuse of colors and patterns, which we discuss in class. The easiest means for instructor assistance with technical problems has been a departmental server, which allows the instructor access to the students' files: broken links or corrupted files can easily be fixed by the instructor. Extra office hours in the computer lab are offered during the last two weeks of class to those with special problems or needs.

Another area of potential problems is the choice of interview partner(s). From time to time, an interview partner cannot meet with the student for a couple of weeks, making it difficult for the student to keep up with the assignments. Conversely, students sometimes choose to write a story about a friend they met during their stay abroad or at the university. Sometimes, younger interview partners have not experienced enough in their life to cover six or seven chapters. In all these cases, the instructor has to work closely with the student to find individual solutions so that the student can complete the project. If an interview partner is not available anymore, I sometimes ask a student to write his or her own impression about the interview partner and the interview. Or, if the interview partner does not have enough to say about his or her life, I suggest that the student ask the interview partner about the future. How do you imagine your life will be in twenty or thirty years? So far, we have been able to complete each project.

We also regularly use a midterm evaluation sheet (see appendix A to this chapter) to make sure that students don't feel overwhelmed and are satisfied with the progress they are making in class. This midterm evaluation allows us to adjust our schedule slightly to offer additional help. The university also distributes a final class evaluation sheet called CTEC, which is a standard form to evaluate each class being taught in terms of content and instruction. The CTEC information is available to students on the Web.

Of course, teaching a course that relies on technology and on outside speakers for content is time consuming and a bit unnerving at times. As a teacher, you need to approach the class with flexibility and an open mind. The structure does not allow you to completely determine the content of each class session at the beginning of the quarter; the writing topics and writing practice unfold, based on what students write. There is no doubt in my mind, however, that introducing the Web project into this writing class instills a sense of reward when students present their finished projects to the class and to their interview partners. In addition, because many of the students in the class are seniors, they often use their project as a showcase for prospective employers.

In general, the resulting projects have been amazing, in my opinion.[15] Students not only produce a large amount of high-quality writing but also show enthusiasm and excitement toward their assignment. As one student put it, "the Internet project was the highlight of the class." It is particularly gratifying to see that students are revising, rereading, adjusting: what seems initially appropriate for a first chapter gets rewritten several times based on how the project unfolds.

Students want to revise their work because the assignments are short enough to finish and to do regular revisions. One student wrote, "I think the idea of interviewing someone and write [sic] one part per week is great. Weekly assignments are much less overwhelming than one big composition." Further, there is constant positive feedback from peers, from the teacher, and from their mentors outside class. Since the projects on the Web are accessible to others to see and read, students take pride in producing the best work they can. They write not just for the instructor; they write for the other members of the class and for an audience outside the university.

The topics the students choose are generally engaging and show a genuine concern for and interest in the life experience of other human beings. They research topics based on these life stories that they would not have been interested in before, simply because it concerns the person they are writing about.

Moreover, the task-based nature of the project teaches students skills that are important beyond the learning of a language: interpersonal skills, organizational skills, perseverance and patience, creativity, and clarity of presentation and expression. There is a general feeling that what students learn is useful beyond learning how to write in German, and, therefore, students are willing to struggle through some of the technology parts. One of the students wrote in the final evaluation: "I loved the Internet project. It's a great way to force us to write in German and it teaches us a valuable skill for the future."

For all these reasons, we intend to continue this approach in German classes at Northwestern. We also recommend it highly to our colleagues who are looking for ways to improve student writing and, at the same time, to motivate students to be more self-directed and interested in learning German language and culture.

### Appendix A: Midterm Evaluation

1. Please comment briefly on the handouts and material for the class. How useful are the writing explanations? The grammar explanations? The exercises?
2. Please comment briefly on the Internet project. What are the best features? What are the most difficult aspects?
3. Please comment briefly on the amount of writing in this class. Is it too much? Just fine? Not enough? Are there enough opportunities for feedback?
4. Tell us about your computer skills. Which areas on the Web project are difficult?
   [ ] composing text in Microsoft Word
   [ ] transferring files to the server with Fetch
   [ ] designing Web pages with Dreamweaver
   [ ] using a digital still camera
   [ ] scanning photographs with a scanner
   [ ] manipulating images in Photoshop

5. Where do you work on your project outside of the weekly class hour?
   [ ] on a friend's computer   [ ] on my own computer   [ ] in a public lab
6. Which computer platform(s) do you use most often outside of class?
   [ ] Macintosh      [ ] Windows
7. How much time a week do you spend on your Internet assignment?
   [ ] 1–2 hours   [ ] 3–4 hours   [ ] more than 5 hours
8. We have covered quite a bit of material in this course so far. Are there any specific problems or areas you would like to cover in detail in the next four weeks?
9. What do you like best about this class? Do you have suggestions for improvements?

## Notes

1. A description of the goals and the mission of the Searle Center for Teaching Excellence at Northwestern University can be found at http://president.scfte .northwestern.edu/.
2. Information on the architecture project, student writing samples, and sample tasks including worksheets are available at http://www.german.northwestern.edu /zeller/.
3. For a more detailed description of these and other courses offered in the German department, including courses for majors and minors, visit http://www.german .northwestern.edu.
4. A brief description of this first course appeared in Computer Enhanced Learning: Vignettes of the Best Practice from America's Most Wired Campuses in 2000.
5. This proved to be a good suggestion. One student reported that while waiting in the checkout line at the local grocery store she overheard the people in front of her—a young couple—speaking German. She immediately started to speak with them in German, explaining the project, and they both agreed to be interview partners.
6. We have taught this course six times so far, once a year from 1997 to 2003. A selection of student projects can be seen at http://www.german.nwu.edu/web-projects /index.html.
7. My class in 2003 had 14 students. Less than 50 percent of the class had used ftp before. Only 2 out of the 14 students had used an HTML editor and have designed a Web page.
8. Roebuck (2001) also used the idea of a building block time line for the Internet projects she assigned to her students to ensure that students stay on task.
9. The site, http://dict.leo.org, was developed by the Department of Informatics at the Technical University in Munich (Technische Universität München).
10. This is particularly helpful for students who have studied abroad and have learned many words through conversations but are not always sure about accurate spelling.
11. The campus infrastructure is quite well developed at Northwestern University. There are currently 972 networked computing workstations in 46 labs or libraries.

About 90 percent of the students own their own computer (from the *Report from the NU Computer Lab Planning Task Force*, January 1999).

12. Microsoft Word and Fetch were available on student computers and in the public and teaching labs, Dreamweaver in the public and teaching labs, and Photoshop only in the teaching lab.

13. Staff, faculty, and students at Northwestern University have a chance to experiment with Web publishing by posting personal pages on the Pubweb server. This server space is provided by the university free of charge. It is not a server intended to host organizational or departmental Web sites, however.

14. Since students in this class are in their fourth year of language instruction, it is possible for the instructor to conduct the technology sessions in German, which adds another layer of meaningful involvement in the target language. Of course, for students with a lower proficiency in German, the technology sessions could easily be taught in English.

15. A selected number of student projects from the last six years can be accessed at http://www.german.northwestern.edu/web-projects.

# Part IV

## Assessment and Teacher Development

# 12

## IMPLEMENTING TASK-BASED ASSESSMENT IN A TEFL ENVIRONMENT

Cláudio Passos de Oliveira

EDITORS' NOTE: In this chapter, Cláudio Passos de Oliveira shares efforts made by his institution, an English-language teaching center in Brazil, to convert from a traditional testing format to a task-based assessment approach in order to parallel changes made in the instructional program from a more traditional approach to a task-based one. In the same way that paradigmatic change has been enacted gradually and incompletely in the instructional approach, paradigmatic change in the testing program has also been gradual and incomplete for a number of reasons, some of which are of a purely testing nature and others of which reflect the link between teaching and testing. Passos de Oliveira explains the progress made, the problems encountered, the solutions adopted, and the compromises made in implementing task-based testing. His insights and experiences—along with those of his colleagues as reported herein—can inform other programs hoping to move a task-based assessment framework.

Adequately assessing learners' performance is always a complex matter for language schools. Tests, grades, and how they relate to classroom practices have to be constantly monitored to make sure they keep being useful tools (rather than burdens), both pedagogically and administratively. Programs that use task-based instruction (TBI) in the classroom ought to require students to show what they have learned via task-based assessment (TBA). However, many, if not most, TBI programs still rely on more traditional forms of testing language competence rather than language performance. As a result, students are taught in one way and tested in another. Lopes in chapter 4 was also aware of this problem and changed exam boards as a result.

This chapter describes a TBA approach developed by and instituted at the Instituto Cultural Brasileiro Norte-Americano (ICBNA) in Porto Alegre, Brazil. It analyzes key factors that emerged during the process of implementation, which we believe should be taken into consideration in the use of task-based elements in assessment in a Teaching of English as a Foreign Language (TEFL) environment. The role of TBI in contemporary Brazilian TEFL practices influenced ICBNA's decisions in many cases; the pedagogical and institutional issues influencing the implementation of TBA are discussed in this chapter. The system chosen by ICBNA can serve as an example of what might be expected of a TBA system in any country and for any foreign language.

## English as a Foreign Language Instruction in Brazil

Following a decades-long (if not centuries-long) grammar-translation approach to teaching foreign languages, two methods consecutively came to the forefront of English as a Foreign Language (EFL) methodology. The earlier of the two methods, presentation–practice–production (PPP), still dominates many Brazilian programs as Lopes describes in chapter 4. TBI, while beginning to supplant PPP, is found far less commonly in Brazilian EFL classrooms. As will be seen, in language schools where the transition from PPP to TBI is taking place (an example being the ICBNA), the gradual shift from one teaching paradigm to the other has created hybrid teaching practices. This mixture has important implications for assessment, as discussed below.

### PRESENTATION, PRACTICE, PRODUCTION

After more than 400 years of classical language teaching, modernity arrived in Brazil in the 1930s with the first discussions about the scientific basis of methods (Almeida Filho 2002). It was only in the late 1970s, however, that CLT was officially introduced in the local teaching scenario. The PPP method, bred in the 1950s as part of the audiolingual approach, has survived the arrival of CLT by mingling with it and is still pervasive in Brazilian TEFL. As Almeida Filho (2002) points out, CLT is often used in Brazil to label neostructural teaching practices.

In the PPP method, the teacher typically follows a prescribed lesson plan, including the following:

1. *Presentation*—the instructor starts by introducing a specific language feature (a grammatical structure or a language function) embedded in a context. This is done through providing examples (sentences, dialogues, text excerpts, audio, video, acting out) and using elicitation techniques (e.g., brainstorming, asking questions, use of realia, assigning a controlled pretask).

2. *Practice*—the instructor describes a situation (individual, pair, or group work) in which students are to practice the emphasized patterns by reading scripted dialogues or sentences aloud to each other, do completion or matching exercises, ask and answer specified questions, or write examples of the patterns being taught. At this stage, the teacher checks student work for accuracy of form.

3. *Production*—the instructor presents students with an activity in which they are expected to use the forms just practiced. This could be a situation for a role-play, a topic for writing, or any task presumably requiring the use of the language patterns learned.

A PPP lesson on buying clothes in a store, for example, could be briefly described as displaying the following steps:

1. The teacher brings pictures of clothing items to class and elicits from students vocabulary and functions related to shopping for clothes (what they like to buy, where, prices, etc.).
2. The teacher goes over the sample dialogue from the textbook, clarifying vocabulary and explaining structures and functions. Students are then asked to practice the dialogue in pairs (i.e., to read aloud script) with different partners. The teacher walks around, giving students feedback on pronunciation and providing further clarification and other individualized assistance.
3. The teacher gives pairs of students strips of paper containing their role (customer, A; or clerk, B) and information about what they have to buy (A) or a table of available clothing items and prices (B). The teacher walks around, helping students in the use of the language provided, as they enact these role-plays.

### TBI

TBI differs from PPP in significant ways. Both the nature of the classroom activities and the framework in which they are presented represent a paradigmatic change for EFL in Brazil. The old paradigm, represented by PPP, was based on structural principles of language acquisition, in which the teacher was the knower, the student more or less tabula rasa, and behavior modification via extensive practice the key to learning. In the new paradigm, represented by TBI, the teacher is a facilitator, the student a doer, and discovery the key to learning. In the latter, spontaneous use of language and genuineness play an important role in students' learning process.

As J. Willis (1996b, 135) points out, PPP has serious limitations: "The irony is that the goal of the final 'P'—free production—is often not achieved. How can production be 'free' if students are required to produce forms which have been specified in advance?" Such limitations have led teachers to adopt an approach that emphasizes free production in a more natural and self-directed way.

### Activity Attributes in TBI

Communication tasks, according to most practitioners, exhibit the following characteristics:

1. Meaning is primary.
2. There is an established, communicative goal.
3. The activity is outcome-based.
4. The task has a real-world relationship (Skehan 1998b, 268).

What this means is:

1. Activities related to the training of specific forms or functions for which a context is artificially created do not belong in a TBI classroom.

2. As Leaver (chapter 2, this volume) points out, a task is an activity that results in a product, that is, it is outcome driven and, therefore, not a language display (for a good example of the latter, see Willis's Spanish learning experience in chapter 1, this volume).

3. The level of success in performing a task should be assessed in terms of how close learners come to the expected outcome on a nonlinguistic basis, not on the basis of the language used in the process (i.e., giving "priority to process over predetermined linguistic content"; Larsen-Freeman 2000, 137).

4. Tasks must, as much as possible, resemble the real world of language use. Activities such as writing a dialogue that requires the inclusion of the present perfect tense are ruled out, as such demands are not normally found outside the boundaries of the language classroom.

Fitting the Skehan conditions for real-world tasks is, for instance, a task performed last semester by my Level 1 students at the ICBNA. After being exposed to language related to giving directions through the textbook, students were invited to devise an instructive tourist leaflet for visitors to Porto Alegre. The written instructions in the leaflet told visitors how to go on foot from one of the main hotels downtown to several nearby attractions. When completed, the leaflet was given to the hotel as a present.

### TBI Framework

J. Willis (1996b, 38) proposed a framework, composed of three distinct phases:

1. Pretask, the introduction to topic and task, through which the teacher prepares the class by exploring the topic, highlighting useful words and phrases, and helping in the understanding of task instructions;

2. Task Cycle, in which groups of students do the task proposed under monitoring (Task Phase), plan a report to the whole class on how they did the task and what they found out (Planning Phase), present it, and compare results with other groups (Report Phase); and

3. Language Focus, in which students examine and discuss specific features of the material used and the work done in the Task Cycle and the teacher conducts a practice session on new words, phrases, and patterns occurring in the data analyzed.

This framework relies on a combination of teacher aid and students' purposeful use of their own linguistic resources for the successful accomplishment of tasks. It also emphasizes the fact that the TBI process proceeds from fluency to accuracy, not the other way around as in PPP. This allows for genuineness in communication and creates real needs for both fluency (getting things done in time, meaningful communication) and accuracy (public reporting, careful language analysis).

As can be seen, in TBI there is a definite shift away from behaviorist beliefs on practice for the sake of practice as the key to learning. This framework is also a means of solving crucial PPP problems such as communication unnaturalness, false mastery, and frustrated expectations as to the language learners "should have used" during class work.

## Contemporary EFL Practices in Brazil

What is frequently seen in EFL in Brazil at the moment is a pedagogic orientation that lies midpoint between more traditional practices, such as PPP, and the more progressive ones associated with TBI. If an EFL language center follows a TBI approach to teaching, the implementation of a TBA system is naturally in order. However, many schools do not espouse approaches that are so clear-cut. A number of programs, for example, incorporate a higher proportion of task-based activities in EFL instruction, mostly in an embedded context, that is, as a component of a syllabus design that promotes the use of tasks in assignments—this would be what Ellis refers to as "task-supported learning"(see Willis, chapter 1). Although language schools vary widely as to the teaching approaches they prefer, many institutions use a mixture of notional-functional and form-based textbooks (or else they devise their own eclectic course materials). Such textbooks provide room for supplemental task-based work such as projects, physical products, student-conducted lessons, and jigsaw problem-solving, among any number of possible creative language tasks. As a consequence, instruction in many language centers typically does not use English as a conduit for learning or doing something new but rather focuses on learning to apply the knowledge of English in various contexts. TBI and other approaches that teach "through communication rather than for it" (Larsen-Freeman 2000, 137) are often not the predominant basis of the pedagogical work carried out in those centers.

The contextual inadequacy of many such activities—devised to be used either in ESL situations or in EFL contexts that differ radically from Brazilian reality—and the need to make classes less artificial (and therefore more motivating) have prompted many local teachers of English to substitute and supplement textbook activities with tasks.

## Instituto Cultural Brasileiro Norte-Americano

The ICBNA is a private nonprofit institution that was founded in 1938 by a group of local intellectuals to serve as a link between the Brazilian and American cultures. Its main activity has always been to pursue high standards in the teaching of English as a foreign language in the community.

### LANGUAGE INSTRUCTION

The ICBNA is a large binational center in Brazil offering English courses to a wide range of ages (eight-year-old children through adults) and proficiency (beginning to advanced) levels, mostly twice a week for classes of one hour and twenty minutes. Courses are divided into forty-eight-hour levels: eight successfully completed levels grant students an intermediate-level certificate, twelve an advanced one, and fourteen or more a certificate with specialization (grammar, translation, business or integrated skills—speaking, listening, reading, and writing). The ICBNA's five schools enroll just over 4,000 students and employ approximately seventy-five teachers, with a typical class size of eight to fourteen students, homogenous in age and proficiency level. Students of different ages follow different programs. Most students are children and teenagers, but there is also a significant adult population.

Decisions on assessment are large-scale ones and consider the perspective of both the student body and the teaching staff. Also, assessment has to, at least as far as children and teenagers are concerned, address the dual purpose of the Institute's language program: (1) help learners become proficient speakers of the English language and (2) provide the means for their passing the Vestibular, a comprehensive university admission paper-and-pencil-based test whose English section focuses on grammar and reading comprehension.

Instruction at the ICBNA is conducted using textbook-based syllabi and guided by pedagogical principles favoring learner-centeredness and communication. As institutional guidelines, one can naturally expect oscillation in the extent to which teaching staff members actually follow those principles fully in their classroom practice. Nonetheless, a reasonable example of a typical English class at the ICBNA can be illustrated by the lesson in table 12.1 (one hour and twenty minutes).

This sample lesson contains both PPP and TBI elements. An example of the former is the Dialogue Practice (6–8) and of the latter the Reading and Writing Task (14–18). The Speaking Task (9–11) is also an example of TBI, nonetheless lacking the real-world relationship mentioned in Skehan's definition (1998b) and described in detail in chapter 1 (this volume). While this lesson, as a whole, does not perfectly fit Willis's TBI framework (1996)—for example, there is no Planning Phase, no actual Report Phase as far as the large group is concerned, although Steps 11 and 17 do involve reporting as students hear or read what other groups have said or written and the language focus is less structured—it does introduce some pedagogical tasks for students to work on.

As can be seen from the above, language instruction at the ICBNA takes a hybrid format. How to assess the results of such hybrid instruction can be very complicated. Any tool to do so must take into consideration the instructional practices of the school, the textbook-based syllabus, as well as expectations for transfer of language skills to situations and events outside the classroom.

#### HISTORICAL FORMS OF ASSESSMENT

Offering EFL courses since 1943, the ICBNA has gone through various stages in its teaching practices and consequently in the ways students are assessed. In general, assessment at the Institute was summative in nature from the 1940s to the 1970s, in tune with the grammar translation methodology of the time. It tested structure, vocabulary, and reading comprehension through end-of-term written exams. Nonetheless, compositions produced during the term were already considered part of grades. By the end of the 1970s, when speaking had grown in importance as

TABLE 12.1. **Sample Lesson**

*Review and Homework*

1. Teacher greets class and conducts a quick review of the content dealt with in the previous class.

2. Teacher checks homework orally with students.

*Listening Tasks*

3. Teacher elicits information from students (using realia, games, flashcards, etc.), aiming at the listening activity (in the textbook) that is to come.

4. Teacher sets a pretask (questions, gap-filling exercise, tick the words you hear, etc.) for the listening.

5. Tape is played a number of times as more challenging comprehension tasks are presented to learners. Learners get both teacher and peer feedback (pair work) during the process.

*Dialogue Practice*

6. Teacher reads aloud follow-up dialogue in the textbook (intended for pair work) and drills it with students.

7. Learners are then asked to practice it in pairs.

8. Teacher walks around providing learners with feedback on pronunciation.

*Speaking Task*

9. Learners are given a handout with an oral information-gap task based on the information dealt with so far, in which they have to talk to several peers and gather information.

10. Teacher monitors learners' work to help out and to try to minimize the use of Portuguese.

11. Learners are called on to share some of the data collected with the rest of the class.

*Grammar Focus*

12. Teacher explains some of the grammar in the unit and asks them to do a written exercise (in the textbook) on that, either individually or in pairs.

13. Teacher corrects exercise orally.

*Reading and Writing Task*

14. Teacher brainstorms following topic on the board, eliciting information from learners.

15. Teacher gives learners strips of paper with parts of an authentic reading excerpt related to the topic of the book unit and asks them to, in groups, put the pieces together.

16. Learners are then asked to devise comprehension questions about the reading to be assigned to other groups. Teacher monitors learners' work to help out and to try to minimize the use of Portuguese.

17. Groups get the questions devised by the other groups and answer them. Questions are then returned to the groups that initially devised them for correction.

18. Teacher visits groups to check their corrections.

*Homework Assignment*

19. Teacher assigns a piece of writing related to the work done in class.

a learning goal (audiolingualism), oral tests started being used. Together with that came the evaluation of commitment to the course, which strengthened the role of formative assessment in the system. By the beginning of the 1980s, the emphasis on oral skills had led to the introduction of listening comprehension as an assessment item. Since the mid-1980s, the dominance of communicative language teaching and its focus on process caused it to become a more balanced system: summative and formative criteria were evenly used. Prior to the introduction of TBA, assessment at the ICBNA had been based on the following criteria:

1. Participation. Grades included the quantity and quality of a student's classroom participation. Subitems scored included (a) students' willingness to interact in English; (b) their willingness to overcome learning challenges (e.g., attendance at remedial classes, use of learning facilities in the school); (c) their diligence in completing homework; (d) their attitude toward peers, the teacher, and the school; and (e) their assiduity and punctuality. For each subitem, a maximum of four points could be achieved (4, very good; 3, good; 2, fair; 1, weak), which was calculated as the arithmetical average of students' self-assessment on that sub-item and the teacher's assessment of it. In all, 20 points were possible. Students were assessed twice during each term: at midterm and at the end of the term.

2. Oral. Students were observed by the teacher during the course and assessed based on (a) how often they used English in class, (b) their fluency, (c) their level of listening comprehension, (d) their accuracy, and (e) their pronunciation and intonation. As in the Participation grade, a maximum of four points was achievable in each of the subitems, determined by the instructors' perception of students' performance in class. In all, 20 points were possible.

3. Quizzes and midterms. These were paper-and-pencil tests that checked functions, knowledge of structure, and vocabulary and were administered to students after each couple of textbook units. The tests were graded by the teacher, contained questions that had right and wrong answers, and carried a maximum of 20 possible points.

4. Compositions. Written assignments (either done in class or assigned as homework) handed in by students and scored by the teacher added a maximum of 10 points to students' overall score, based on the structural accuracy of the compositions.

5. Final examination. A comprehensive test of all units was administered. This test contained four sections: (a) listening comprehension, (b) grammar and language functions, (c) vocabulary, and (d) reading comprehension. The final exam was worth thirty points and was scored on the basis of right and wrong answers.

A total of seventy points was required for promotion to the next level of study.

As can be observed, the ICBNA evaluation was a mixture of formative and summative criteria, where process-oriented teacher long-term observation and learner production (Participation, Oral Test, and Compositions) were combined with product-oriented assessment (Quizzes/Midterms, Final Exam) on a fifty-fifty basis. The two salient features of this system were paper-and-pencil tests to rate learning product and informal performance measures to rate learning process. A balance of both approaches to assessment was therefore already a concern before the implementation of TBA and has continued to be since. The evaluation system did not have good tools for reliably assessing oral production, as the rating criteria did not specify what was "very good" or "fair"; it also presented heavily grammar-based criteria for the assessment of learners' written production.

## The New Assessment System

The new system was devised to increase the time given to the testing of speaking and writing skills (language production) and also to give a better balance between formative and summative assessment. Opting for a fully process-based assessment system such as portfolios, i.e., running away from what can be pictured as an "image of an examination room, a test paper with questions, desperate scribbling against the clock" (McNamara 2000, 3), was not considered practical as a first step. In addition to such factors as local educational culture, the ICBNA's administrative needs, and teaching staff beliefs about language assessment, there is something about summative testing that has kept it alive. It does not have simply to do with resistance to paradigm changes. A fully formative assessment system may fail to achieve the level of commitment needed on the part of both young and adult learners. Summative tests seem to help students to take things more seriously. They also motivate people to pursue goals. Above all, summative tests must be both useful to the learning process and nontraumatic. Brown (1994) lists seven ways in which testing can aid learning: (1) increase learner motivation as milestones of progress, (2) spur learners to set goals for themselves, (3) aid retention of information through feedback, (4) provide a sense of periodic closure, (5) encourage learner self evaluation on progress, (6) promote learner autonomy by pointing out areas of weakness to be worked on, and (7) serve as a means to evaluate teaching effectiveness. Even though summative tests are seldom described as highly pleasant experiences, their results are regarded by many as concrete evidence of their progress. The belief at the ICBNA was that, when combined with process-based assessment elements, they could render a more balanced picture of students' communicative abilities.

Brown (1994) presents four principles that we have kept in mind when devising tests. These are:

1. advance preparation;
2. face validity;
3. authenticity; and
4. washback.

According to this set of principles, giving students advance preparation is essential to successful testing. Specifically, students must be prepared in the subject matter to be tested and well informed about test procedures themselves. At the

ICBNA, teachers explain the assessment system to students in detail at the beginning of every term, so that newcomers are fully aware of its format (and the others are constantly reminded). Lesson plans include review classes prior to tests, where students can clarify their doubts on test contents and natural pretest anxiety can be minimized.

Face validity means that the exam tests what it is supposed to test, which is critical to a successful testing program. The ICBNA's testing policy strongly advocates no unpleasant surprises. During the implementation of the new system, when coordinators missed the point in devising suitable assessment items, the reaction from both teachers and students was quite strong. Even though unpleasant, it at least demonstrated that local testing culture advocated and expected face validity.

In testing reception and production skills, authenticity of the language used on the test is important. By authenticity, Brown means that the language in the test is natural and contextualized. The speaking and writing tasks in the new assessment system at the ICBNA were conceived as an attempt to escape from the pervasive artificiality typically present both in the language test items and in the language production required by them. By better contextualizing oral and written tasks it was hoped that the quality and quantity of language production by students during tests would improve.

The "washback" effect is especially relevant for the implementation of changes for it can help fine-tune teaching to correspond to modifications in assessment. In introducing changes at the ICBNA, administrators also hoped for a washback effect on one specific area of difficulty: reliance on their native language (L1). EFL schools in Brazil, as in many other locations, face a major challenge in overcoming the overuse of Portuguese by students in the classroom. Unlike multinational ESL classes in English-speaking countries, all learners in Brazilian foreign language classes are native speakers of Portuguese who are too easily tempted by the comparative ease of communicating with their peers in their mother tongue. So, getting young learners (not that the same would not hold true for adults at times) to speak a reasonable amount of English during class time can be difficult, especially when most of them are classmates in regular school as well, hang out together, and always have lots to catch up with (in addition to the fact that Brazilians learn from early ages to consider socializing a prime factor in their lives). Bearing this problem in mind, assessment changes at the ICBNA aimed at providing the teaching staff with another tool—the requirement to use English to accomplish a task—to try to change local culture and ingrained student habits. Use of English in the classroom should now directly lead to higher test scores.

In conjunction with this, it was decided that assessment would place heavier emphasis on production. The outcome of the institution's dual purpose (preparation for university entrance exams and development of communication) was the reality that many advanced students being granted certificates were good paper-and-pencil test takers but did not necessarily become fluent speakers and writers of English. The general feeling was that the language produced by students, both oral and written, was below institutional expectation. The decision then was to place greater pressure on our Portuguese "chatterboxes" to produce English in the classroom.

The new system—based on achievement of curriculum goals and primarily focused on direct production skills (speaking and writing)—was devised during in-service sessions with coordinators and the teaching staff. The sessions consisted of workshops on assessment, in which teachers read material on the topic, discussed it, and presented ideas for the new system. In addition, pilot oral tests were recorded on audio and video tape and scored during standardizing sessions with teachers. Likewise, sample compositions were collectively analyzed and scored. Standardizing did not, however, cover all courses in the ICBNA due to time constraints.

The system had two distinct phases, each covering one-half of the level's content. Both phases had the same format and the same assessment criteria. Phase 2, however, was assigned double weight, so that learners who did not do well in Phase 1 could have a second chance. Likewise, learners who did very well in Phase 1 had to maintain their grades during Phase 2. After Phase 1, all parents received a comprehensive grade report to be signed and returned. This improved parent-teacher communication, which helped solve learning difficulties in a timely fashion. As each ICBNA unit contained about one thousand students, control over cases that needed pedagogical support became more effective.

## PROCEDURES: CRITERIA AND WEIGHTING

The assessment criteria chosen were created based on the previous system (never throw the baby out with the bathwater!) and contained the following elements:

1. **Participation.** Same items as before, however, now the possible points total is 10. Graded twice during each level, once each phase.
2. **Daily Oral Grade.** Same as the previous Oral section: students are observed by the teacher and assessed based on certain criteria. Those criteria were, however, slightly changed and include (1) pronunciation, (2) listening comprehension, (3) vocabulary, (4) structure, and (5) fluency. A total of 20 points are possible.
3. **Compositions.** Written assignments (as both homework and class work) handed in by students and scored, with a maximum of 10 points, based on an analytic rating scale with the following domains: (1) focus, (2) organization, (3) sentence formation, (4) vocabulary, and (5) conventions.
4. **Structure Test.** A paper-and-pencil test covering language functions and grammar, mostly using multiple choice, sentence completion, and short answers. Worth 20 points.
5. **Reading and Writing Test.** A writing task based on a reading, scored with the analytic rating scale used to assess students' compositions. Worth 20 points.
6. **Oral Test.** An oral task performed as pair work and scored by the teacher with the aid of an analytic rating scale, based on the following

domains: (1) pronunciation, (2) listening comprehension, (3) vocabulary, (4) structure, and (5) fluency. Worth 20 points.

A grade of seventy points was retained as the minimum score for promotion.

In comparison with the previous system, the weight given to the Participation Grade, where students assessed themselves on behavior considered important for their development, was lowered. In principle, that is a drawback as it diminishes student participation in the evaluation of their work, which ignores the value of learner commitment. Such decision was taken because of the numerical requirement to increase the weight of the testing of speaking and writing components.

Both formative items (Daily Oral Grade and Compositions) were kept as part of the system. As Brown (1994, 375) points out, "Our success as teachers is greatly dependent on this constant informal assessment for it tells us how well learners are progressing toward goals and what the next step in the learning process might be." The two summative components in the new test help the teacher monitor his or her students' development.

The decision to retain the Structure Test (previously represented by Quizzes, Midterms, and most of the Final Exam) was predicated on the need to focus on the particular details of grammar, vocabulary, and functions presented in the curriculum, thus helping students prepare for the traditional paper-and pencil tests they take at school and to enroll in a university (Vestibular). Nevertheless, as such tests were devised in a decontextualized fashion, they suffer from the validity limitations associated with their format. As Perkins (1998) emphasizes, research has shown that knowledge on how to handle selected response test items, rather than on the content being checked, may often be the determinant factor in getting multiple-choice questions right.

Of special interest are the task-based Oral Test and Reading and Writing Test, in Phases 1 and 2, which are scored with analytic rating scales (see part one of the book's Appendix). In the former, students are asked to perform, in pairs, oral tasks performed during the course, and in the latter, to produce a piece of writing based on a reading passage. A typical task for the Reading and Writing Test would be to read an e-mail sent by a friend taking a course abroad and reply to it. The Reading and Writing Test was taken together with the Structure Test, requiring about 40 minutes. The Oral Test had more stringent time constraints, as it was meant to be taken in pairs, so tasks were devised to take no longer than 10 minutes—some groups had fourteen students and all of them were supposed to be tested on the same day. Four 1.33-hour meetings for formal testing were considered by the Institute's coordinator staff to be a reasonable maximum. Typically, in the Oral Test students are given two different sets of role-play instructions, such as buying certain clothing items in a store, in which one student plays the role of a customer and the other a clerk. The clerk does not know in advance what the client wants and, likewise, the client does not know what the store has available.

## FEEDBACK

Both teachers' and students' feedback were collected during the implementation of the new system. In the case of the former, the information was gathered through a form in which teachers wrote evaluative comments (since a broad survey of negative and positive aspects of the system was wanted, no specific questions were posed) after Phase1 and Phase 2. In the case of the latter, data was collected through administering, shortly after Phase 1, the semester institutional class survey, which includes, besides specific items about classes, room for general comments.

The information collected was analyzed during coordination meetings, in which adjustments in some test items were made. In the Oral Test, for instance, some tasks were considered by teachers and/or students to be too long, somewhat artificial (form-based or too scripted), or off-target in terms of curriculum objectives. Regarding the Reading and Writing Test, there were cases of texts chosen to serve as a lead to writing that were felt not to be working in the intended way, and therefore new ones had to be substituted. Examples of difficulties included: Students did not have to read the text to do the written assignment, that is, there was a poor link between the text and the task; the text was too difficult, that is, required schemata that students did not have; or the text was confusing, that is, not well written.

As expected in major changes, even though the overall format of the new system was welcomed by the majority of the teaching staff and student body, it presented problems that needed adjustment. This need has not disappeared. As mentioned in the beginning of this chapter, constant monitoring is one of the elements that make such systems useful assessment tools.

## THE ICBNA TASK-BASED ASSESSMENT SYSTEM

As seen, the ICBNA assessment system was not designed on a purely methodological basis. Many factors influenced the choice of format. These ranged from instructional content and method to staff beliefs, local educational context, student behavior, curriculum needs, and time limitations. Pedagogically speaking, the assessment system resembles the mixed ICBNA instructional context, displaying both similarities and dissimilarities with a typical TBA system.

Bachman and Palmer (1996) provide a useful framework for analyzing the fundamental characteristics of language tasks used in testing. Tables 12.2 through 12.6 below use this framework to compare the characteristics expected in ideal TBA conditions and the characteristics of the assessment criteria used by the ICBNA. Sample test items are shown in appendix B to this chapter to help illustrate the descriptions provided. Following each table is a discussion of what elements in the ICBNA's new assessment system are task-based and what are not, together with the mentioning of some issues brought about by the new system.

Table 12.2 shows no difference between the conditions expected for a typical TBA situation and the ICBNA system in setting. As no problems were noticed

TABLE 12.2. **Characteristics of the Setting**

| The physical circumstances under which testing takes place | | | |
|---|---|---|---|
| *TBA* | *ST* | *RWT* | *OT* |

1. *Physical Characteristics:* Location, noise level, temperature, humidity, seating conditions, lighting, familiarity with materials and equipment

| | | | |
|---|---|---|---|
| Similar in all aspects to the conditions met during instruction. | Administered in the same class-room where students have classes. Paper-and-pencil format familiar to students. | Administered in the same class-room where students have classes. Paper-and-pencil format familiar to students. | Administered in the same class-room where students have classes. Test format based on pair work, frequently performed during the course. |

2. *Participants:* Status and relationship to test takers of people involved in the task

| | | | |
|---|---|---|---|
| Involves only the teacher and the students, whose relations have already been established. | Involves only students and the teacher. | Involves only students and the teacher. | Involves only students and the teacher. |

3. *Time of Task:* The time of the day when the task is administered

| | | | |
|---|---|---|---|
| Same time students normally perform their tasks in class. | Same time students normally perform their tasks in class. | Same time students normally perform their tasks in class. | Same time students normally perform their tasks in class. |

*Note:* TBA = Task-Based Assessment; ST = Structure Test; RWT = Reading and Writing Test; OT = Oral Test.

during implementation in this regard, it is likely to be true that a familiar setting is a positive element in language assessment, helping diminish learners' anxiety level.

As can be seen in table 12.3, Instructions in the ICBNA system differ significantly from typical TBA. They are mostly test-oriented, that is, the role of the instructor, both in the Structure Test (ST) and the Reading and Writing Test (RWT), is one of simply going over what is written in the test. There is no pretask moment where students are tuned into what is to come. This is bound to have a negative impact on students taught through TBI as the conditions met during instruction are cut short during testing. Time constraints are a problem here, as ideal contextualizing conditions for each task would demand too much time. A possible resolution might be to split such tests in several parts and give the parts throughout the term thus allowing for preparation for each of them. In the Oral Test (OT), there is more flexibility in regard to teacher assistance before and dur-

TABLE 12.3. **Characteristics of the Test Rubric**

| *Test structure and scoring procedures* | | | |
|---|---|---|---|
| *TBA* | *ST* | *RWT* | *OT* |

1. *Instructions:* How test takers are informed about procedures.

| | | | |
|---|---|---|---|
| Introduction of topic and task, with the activation of related words and phrases. Guidance during the completion of the task. | Instructor goes over test to clarify possible doubts on what is to be done. | Instructor goes over test to clarify possible doubts on what is to be done. | Instructor explains task in detail and may help out during the task to avoid silence or to clarify misunderstandings. |

2. *Structure:* How the parts of the test are put together.

| | | | |
|---|---|---|---|
| Steps defined based on the sequences used in the work performed in class (pretask, task cycle, and optional language focus). | Sequence of various paper-and-pencil exercise types related to the syllabus both in content and in order. | A reading passage serving as lead or model for the subsequent writing task proposed. | Instructions followed by (a) syllabus-related speaking task(s) performed by students. |

3. *Time Allotment:* The time allotted for individual test tasks.

| | | | |
|---|---|---|---|
| Depending on the task, but on a power (as opposed to speed) test basis. | First forty minutes of an eighty-minute class. Exceeding this time means having less time for the RWT part. | Last forty minutes of an eighty-minute class. More time available if less than forty minutes were spent in the ST part. | About ten minutes. More time available if group is small. |

4. *Scoring Method:* Specification of how numbers will be assigned to test takers' performance.

| | | | |
|---|---|---|---|
| Use of a criterion-referenced ability-based analytic rating scale with theoretical constructs pertaining to the language abilities needed to perform task cycles successfully (grammatical, textual, functional, sociolinguistic, and metalinguistic). | Based solely on grammatical and lexical accuracy. | Use of criterion-referenced ability-based analytic rating scale. Constructs are *focus, organization, sentence formation, vocabulary,* and *conventions.* | Use of criterion-referenced ability-based analytic rating scale. Constructs are *pronunciation, comprehension, vocabulary, structure,* and *fluency.* |

*Note:* TBA = Task-Based Assessment; ST = Structure Test; RWT = Reading and Writing Test; OT = Oral Test.

TABLE 12.4. **Characteristics of the Input**

*Features of the linguistic material present in the test, to be processed by test takers and to which they have to respond.*

| TBA | ST | RWT | OT |
|---|---|---|---|
| 1. *Format:* The way the input is presented in the test. | | | |
| Input consists of aural / visual material (linguistic or not), in the target language, in extended discourse, with the use of prompts, at class-like speed, printed or reproduced electronically. | Input consists of printed test items (single words, phrases, sentences) in the target language. | Input consists of a written prompt in the target language. | Input consists of visual material (linguistic or not), in the target language, in sentences or in extended discourse, with the use of either items or prompts, at class-like speed, in printed form. |
| 2. *Language:* The nature of the language used in the test. | | | |
| Input includes, in varying degrees, language knowledge at the organizational (grammatical and textual) and pragmatic (functional and sociolinguistic) levels and of topic knowledge (personal, academic, cultural, and technical, depending on the syllabus). | Input includes language knowledge at the organizational (grammatical) and pragmatic (functional) levels and of some topical knowledge (lexical level). | Input includes language knowledge at the organizational (textual) and pragmatic (sociolinguistic) levels and of topical knowledge (prompt-related). | Input includes language knowledge at the organizational level (textual) and pragmatic level (functional and sociolinguistic) and of topic knowledge (item or prompt-related). |

*Note:* TBA = Task-Based Assessment; ST = Structure Test; RWT = Reading and Writing Test; OT = Oral Test.

ing the assessment process, but still there is the absence of a proper warm-up. Finding an ideal solution here is harder, as oral tests work better without an audience, thus requiring teacher assistance on an individual or small-group basis. For large schools like the ICBNA, this may not be feasible, but it should remain an objective, as replicating classroom conditions could make students more comfortable, optimizing their performance.

The Structure of the ICBNA tests reflects attributes of a TBA system, that is, it follows sequences normally found in classroom practices. The sequences are nevertheless different, as TBI is not the only method used at the ICBNA. The ST re-

TABLE 12.5. **Characteristics of the Expected Response**

| *The language use we expect to elicit with the task proposed* | | | |
|---|---|---|---|
| *TBA* | *ST* | *RWT* | *OT* |

**1. *Format:* The way the response is produced.**

| TBA | ST | RWT | OT |
|---|---|---|---|
| Expected response consists of oral/written output in the target language, either itemized or in extended discourse, at the average speed for the proficiency level of the student. | Expected response consists of recognition of grammatical correctness and lexical appropriateness or of itemized written production at the average speed for the proficiency level of the student. | Expected response consists of extended discourse produced in writing at the average speed for the proficiency level of the student. | Expected response consists of extended discourse produced orally at the average speed for the proficiency level of the student. |

**2. *Type of Response:* The kind of production.**

| TBA | ST | RWT | OT |
|---|---|---|---|
| Extended production response. | Selected (multiple-choice, matching) and limited (cloze, short completion) production response. | Extended production response. | Extended production response. |

**3. *Degree of Speed:* The amount of time the test taker has to produce the response**

| TBA | ST | RWT | OT |
|---|---|---|---|
| Relatively untimed (power testing). | Relatively untimed (power testing). | Relatively untimed (power testing). | Relatively untimed (power testing). |

*Note:* TBA = Task-Based Assessment; ST = Structure Test; RWT = Reading and Writing Test; OT = Oral Test.

sembles paper-and-pencil exercises typically done in class or as homework, the same being true for the RWT. The OT resembles a PPP activity without the second P (practice), so it is a better match for TBA as students are invited to use their own language resources to accomplish the task. As mentioned earlier, oral tasks that were too straight-jacketed in terms of form or functions were rejected by teachers and students.

In terms of Time Allotment, the ICBNA system is in tune with TBA for all tests are power tests, that is, devised to give students the time they need. The time for the OT is quite short, but so are the proposed tasks. However, the time limitation of the OT means the content taught can only be sampled, which can lead to questions about its validity. No ideal solution for this problem has been found so far, but it is partially minimized by the formative component of the system (Daily Oral Grade).

TABLE 12.6. **Relationship between Input and Response**

| | | How input and response relate to each other | | |
|---|---|---|---|---|
| *TBA* | *ST* | *RWT* | *OT* | |

1. *Reactivity:* The extent to which the input or the response directly affects subsequent input and responses.

| | | | | |
|---|---|---|---|---|
| Relationship is reciprocal, i.e., responses and input are expected to affect each other constantly. | Relationship is nonreciprocal. | Relationship is nonreciprocal. | Relationship is reciprocal. | |

2. *Scope of Relationship:* The amount or range of input that must be processed for the response.

| | | | | |
|---|---|---|---|---|
| Broad scope, i.e., much input is to be processed to respond. | Narrow scope, i.e., a limited amount of input is to be processed. | Broad scope. | Broad scope | |

3. *Directness of Relationship:* The extent to which the response depends on the information in the input.

| | | | | |
|---|---|---|---|---|
| Relationship is both direct and indirect, as student's own topical and contextual knowledge combines with information in the input. | Relationship is direct, because responses will depend mostly on input. | Relationship is both direct and indirect. | Relationship is both direct and indirect. | |

*Note:* TBA = Task-Based Assessment; ST = Structure Test; RWT = Reading and Writing Test; OT = Oral Test.

The Scoring Method also presents similarities between the systems. Apart from the ST, which is corrected on a right/wrong basis, both the RWT and the OT use criterion-referenced ability-based analytic rating scales, which are suitable for TBA as they represent a both flexible and accurate tool to be used for various types of tasks. Different kinds of domain are, nonetheless, covered in the RWT and in the OT. The former includes both grammatical and textual abilities, whereas the latter is heavily grammatical. Ideally, any assessment system, be it TBA or not, should not only cover organizational aspects of language use, but also pragmatic ones. In the case of the ICBNA, pragmatics was left aside because of the subtleties involved, which were seen as not standardized enough in instruction and difficult to be measured reliably by the nonnative teaching staff. A good option here may be the devising of a specific rating scale for the formative Daily Oral Grade, with criteria more similar in nature to those used in the RWT. The formative aspect of this grade would probably also allow for more comprehensive and process-based assessment of the constructs targeted. Observing a dozen students interacting together is, nevertheless, always a limitation for the formative part of the ICBNA system.

Table 12.4 shows that the Format used in the ICBNA tests does not bear elements that would make it very different from formats in a TBA situation. Listening comprehension is, however, limited to teacher-student and student-student interaction in the OT, being taken care of by the formative Daily Oral Grade. ICBNA's textbook-based syllabus includes plenty of CD-ROM or audio activities but, as mentioned earlier, leaving both reading and listening comprehension out of the summative part of the system was not a pedagogical decision, but rather a choice to focus on production skills made on the basis of time constraints and a technical limitation—the difficulty in obtaining good listening excerpts matching the syllabus of the courses. Ideally, all skills should be tested with both the summative and the formative assessment tools, thus improving the balance between them.

As far as the nature of the Language in the input is concerned, the presence of extended discourse, an ideal condition for TBA, varies considerably among the tests used at the ICBNA. The input in the ST is particularly poor in this regard, being generally limited to the sentence level, whereas the RWT and the OT make use of more elaborate prompts. The ST was devised in a decontextualized fashion because of the difficulty involved in creating content from form, an unnatural starting point that frequently wields artificial results (many textbooks suffer from this illness). Bearing in mind this difficulty and the dual purpose of the ICBNA instruction, the struggle did not seem worthwhile, so a simpler format was deliberately chosen. Nonetheless, decontextualized language does represent impoverishment of the input in the test. Eliminating the ST is certainly an option. This (via washback from the remainder of the test) would certainly help positively change views on language learning on the part of both teachers and students. Problems with parents are to be expected, though, as they are usually not fully aware of the rationale behind the process and tend to hold more traditional views on testing.

In table 12.5 the description of the Format and Type of Response of both the RWT and the OT fits a TBA context: neither of them limits learner production to specific language forms. However, if we compare the RWT to the OT, we will realize that the former matches TBA better. Items on the latter reflect oral practices routinely performed in class, which many times follow a PPP format. It was perceived at times that students were concerned about what would be the "right response" for some of the oral tasks—that is, the rehearsed language item—rather than focused on how to carry out the interaction in a more natural format.

The ST is where, once more, the main difference between typical TBA and the ICBNA system resides: it is bound to recognition of grammatical correctness and to selected production responses. Again, ST could be eliminated from the system where possible. Another option would be to make it part of formative assessment, in the form of short classroom assignments not worth many points: a way of smoothly moving away from traditional beliefs on language acquisition.

In terms of Degree of Speed (defined as work completion in a specific time limit), all ICBNA tests work on a power (as opposed to timed) basis, the same as would be expected of a TBA system. This is an important aspect for TBA tests: there is no point in pressing learners for time—which causes anxiety and harms performance—unless they have a specific need to be trained (and therefore tested) on a timed basis.

Table 12.6 shows the relationship between input and response in a TBA situation would be expected to be, as far as Reactivity is concerned, reciprocal, i.e., input and response would constantly influence each other as in real interaction. In such reciprocity-based tests, students would be invited to interact and be given scores from an analytic rating scale. The format chosen by the ICBNA does not allow for reciprocity in either the ST or the RWT, but does so for the OT. The ICBNA system is, therefore, more static than an ideal TBA situation would be. Whereas the ST may be intrinsically static, in the case of the RWT a potentially good but time-consuming solution might be a task in which students interact in writing during the test (either by exchanging sheets of paper or in a virtual chatroom).

The Scope of Relationship in the ICBNA system is generally broad, as would be the case for TBA, the exception being the ST. This has to do with the belief in the interdependent nature of language interaction espoused by TBI, which is partially adopted by ICBNA instruction. The same holds for the Directness of the Relationship between input and response, as the ST is the only situation in which learners' own topical and contextual knowledge would count little. The dynamism of the OT is, however, where the interdependence is most accentuated.


## Conclusion

We began this chapter by stating that assessing learners' performance is a complex matter, in which several key elements had to be in tune for success. To illustrate that, the case of the implementation of TBA in the ICBNA was described. As mentioned throughout the discussion, among the key factors to be taken into consideration when TBA is implemented in a TEFL environment are the following:

1. the relationship between different classroom practices and their consequences for assessment;
2. the history of how learners have been tested (gradual change counters resistance);
3. involvement of the teaching staff and student body;
4. the connection to the broader local educational context; and
5. monitoring and adjusting.

We fine-tuned our analysis by using the Bachman and Palmer (1996) framework to better investigate the characteristics of the new ICBNA assessment system and how they relate to what would be expected of a typical TBA system. The comparative description presented showed several pedagogical and institutional points of interest, among which were

1. time constraints;
2. the usefulness of analytic rating scales;
3. the importance of the balance between formative and summative assessment;
4. the limiting implications of focus choices such as the one made by the ICBNA (production skills);
5. the importance of contextualization and the possible pedagogical draw-backs caused by form/function binds; and
6. the influence of more traditional teaching practices on the interaction taking place in TBA format.

The successful implementation of a TBA system in an EFL environment will logically depend on the level of TBI present in instruction, but it will also be affected by the many other factors (institutional, social, etc.) mentioned above. The educational and administrative practices of any language school will always need to be responsive to the demands of the local community, creating an intricate reality in which any assessment system will have to fit. I hope the ICBNA case has been illustrative of the dynamism of such relationships and the real-life challenges they pose, offering some insights on how to make reasonable choices.

## Appendix A

### ANALYTIC RATING SCALES

**Oral Test**

The objective of the oral test is to assess students' performance in a task related to the syllabus of the course, that is, it is meant to test achievement of curriculum objectives. The following items are taken into consideration by the tester:

*Table A: Levels 1 through 6*

1. *Pronunciation:* Student is intelligible when performing the task and accurate at articulating the sounds of English (table 12.7).
2. *Comprehension:* Student demonstrates understanding by being able to reply adequately to what is said (table 12.8).
3. *Vocabulary:* Student produces the vocabulary needed to accomplish the task (table 12.9).
4. *Structure:* Student's speech shows control of word order (subject-verb-object, adjective-noun sequences, etc.) and agreement (plurals, verb conjugation, etc.) (table 12.10).
5. *Fluency:* Student's speech flows smoothly (table 12.11).

TABLE 12.7. **Analytic Rating Scale: Pronunciation**

4  Mispronunciation occasionally occurs but intelligibility is always maintained.

3  Mispronunciation is recurrent and causes occasional problems as to intelligibility.

2  Mispronunciation is recurrent, and frequently interferes with tester's understanding of student's speech.

1  Mispronunciation is constant, and seriously interferes with tester's understanding of student's speech.

TABLE 12.8. **Analytic Rating Scale: Comprehension**

4  Understands nearly everything said by tester and replies appropriately, with little need for adjustments or repetition on the part of the tester.

3  Understands fairly well and usually replies appropriately, needing some repetition and/or adjustment on the part of the tester.

2  Understands very little and needs constant adjustments and repetitions on the part of the tester to reply adequately.

1  Understands very little; needs constant adjustments and repetitions on the part of the tester, but fails to reply adequately.

TABLE 12.9. **Analytic Rating Scale: Vocabulary**

4  Produces the vocabulary required to carry out the task successfully.

3  Sometimes lacks the right words, but manages to accomplish the task reasonably well.

2  Lacks many of the right words, but manages to accomplish the task.

1  Lacks most of the vocabulary required, which seriously harms his/her performance in the task.

TABLE 12.10. **Analytic Rating Scale: Structure**

4  Speech shows very few problems with word order and agreement.

3  Speech shows few problems with word order and agreement.

2  Speech shows several problems with word order and agreement.

1  Speech shows constant problems with word order and agreement.

TABLE 12.11. **Analytic Rating Scale: Fluency**

4  Student hardly ever halts or hesitates.

3  Student is occasionally hesitant, but manages to accomplish the task.

2  Student frequently halts and hesitates, compromising the accomplishment of the task.

1  Student halts and hesitates, seriously compromising the accomplishment of the task.

*Table B: Levels 7 through 10*

1. *Pronunciation:* Student is intelligible when performing the task and accurate at articulating the sounds of English (table 12.12).
2. *Comprehension:* Student demonstrates understanding by being able to reply adequately to what is said (table 12.13).
3. *Vocabulary:* Student produces the vocabulary needed to accomplish the task (table 12.14).
4. *Structure:* Student's speech shows control of word order (subject-verb-object, adjective-noun sequences, etc.) and agreement (plurals, verb conjugation, etc.) (table 12.15).
5. *Fluency:* Student's speech flows smoothly (table 12.16).

**TABLE 12.12. Analytic Rating Scale: Pronunciation**

4  Mispronunciation rarely occurs and intelligibility is always maintained.

3  Mispronunciation occasionally occurs but intelligibility is always maintained.

2  Mispronunciation is recurrent, and it causes occasional problems as to intelligibility.

1  Mispronunciation is constant, and it frequently interferes with tester's understanding of student's speech.

**TABLE 12.13. Analytic Rating Scale: Comprehension**

4  Understands everything said by tester and replies appropriately, with no need for adjustments or repetition on the part of the tester.

3  Understands nearly everything said by tester and replies appropriately, with little need for adjustments or repetition on the part of the tester.

2  Understands fairly well and usually replies appropriately, needing some repetition and/or adjustment on the part of the tester.

1  Understands very little and needs constant adjustments and repetitions on the part of the tester to reply adequately.

**TABLE 12.14. Analytic Rating Scale: Vocabulary**

4  Shows excellent vocabulary range to carry out the task successfully.

3  Produces the vocabulary required to carry out the task successfully.

2  Sometimes lacks the right words, but manages to accomplish the task reasonably well.

1  Lacks many of the right words, but manages to accomplish the task.

**TABLE 12.15. Analytic Rating Scale: Structure**

4  Speech shows very few, if any, noticeable problems with complex structures.

3  Speech shows few problems with complex structures.

2  Speech shows several problems with complex structures.

1  Speech shows a lot of problems both with basic and complex structures.

### Reading and Writing Test

The objective of the Reading and Writing Test is to assess students' performance in a task related to the syllabus of the course, that is, it is meant to test achievement of curriculum objectives. The following items will be taken into consideration by the tester:

*Table C: Levels 1 through 10*

1. *Focus:* how clearly the text presents and maintains a main idea (table 12.17).
2. *Organization:* how logical and well-supported the sequencing of points is (introduction—development—conclusion) (table 12.18).
3. *Sentence formation:* how well structured and complete the sentences are (table 12.19).
4. *Vocabulary:* how appropriate and accurate word choice is and forms are (table 12.20).
5. *Conventions:* how accurately words are spelled and sentences punctuated (table 12.21).

**TABLE 12.16. Analytic Rating Scale: Fluency**

4   Student's halts and hesitations are typical of a fluent nonnative speaker.

3   Student sometimes halts or hesitates due to language limitations.

2   Student is considerably hesitant, but manages to accomplish the task.

1   Student frequently halts and hesitates, compromising the accomplishment of the task.

**TABLE 12.17. Analytic Rating Scale: Focus**

4   Text not only presents and maintains topic clearly but also enhances it.

3   Text addresses and maintains topic competently.

2   Text addresses suggested topic but includes some off-topic information.

1   Text does not have a clear main topic or is off topic.

**TABLE 12.18. Analytic Rating Scale: Organization**

4   Text is very well sequenced and shows smooth transitions. Ideas are effectively supported.

3   Text is well sequenced and shows appropriate transitions. Ideas are sufficiently supported.

2   Text is fairly sequenced and shows some transitions. Ideas are not sufficiently supported.

1   Text shows poor or no sequencing and mostly lacks transitions. Ideas are weakly supported.

TABLE 12.19. **Analytic Rating Scale: Sentence Formation**

4  With very few exceptions, syntax is accurate and sentences are complete.

3  Syntax is usually accurate and sentences are generally complete.

2  Syntax is somewhat faulty and some sentences are not complete.

1  Syntax is faulty and most sentences are not complete.

TABLE 12.20. **Analytic Rating Scale: Vocabulary**

4  Word choice is precise and word forms are accurate.

3  Word choice is appropriate and word forms are mostly accurate.

2  Word choice is often inappropriate and word forms are frequently inaccurate.

1  Word choice is mostly faulty and word forms are usually flawed.

TABLE 12.21. **Analytic Rating Scale: Conventions**

4  With very few exceptions, spelling and punctuation conventions are respected.

3  Spelling and punctuation conventions are usually respected.

2  Spelling and punctuation conventions are faulty.

1  Basic spelling and punctuation mistakes are recurrent.

## Appendix B

### SAMPLE TEST ITEMS

### Oral Test

*Level 2*

Situation I: Ask your partner what he/she can do (table 12.22).

Situation II: Ask your partner about his/her plans (table 12.23).

Situation III: Tell your partner about two things you have to do every day and two things you do not have to do.

TABLE 12.22. **Prompt for Situation 1**

| | | |
|---|---|---|
| *sports* | *cooking* | *musical instruments* |

TABLE 12.23. **Prompt for Situation 2**

| | |
|---|---|
| *plans for tomorrow* | *plans for next weekend* |

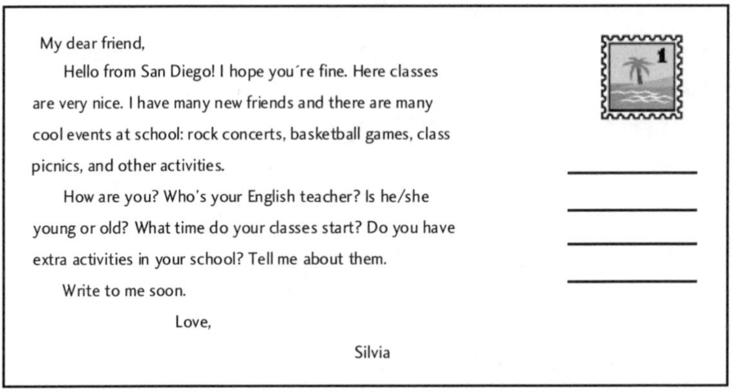

My dear friend,

    Hello from San Diego! I hope you´re fine. Here classes
are very nice. I have many new friends and there are many
cool events at school: rock concerts, basketball games, class
picnics, and other activities.

    How are you? Who's your English teacher? Is he/she
young or old? What time do your classes start? Do you have
extra activities in your school? Tell me about them.

    Write to me soon.

        Love,

            Silvia

FIGURE 12.1. **Model Postcard**

*Level 7*

You are an exchange student in the United States. You have just arrived and you
are supposed to talk about yourself. Talk about . . .

- your city,
- your school,
- your family,
- your eating habits,
- what you usually do with your friends, and
- your likes (movies, music, sports, etc.).

**Reading and Writing Test**

*Level 2*

Write a postcard to Silvia (figures 12.1 and 12.2). Answer her questions with complete sentences.

FIGURE 12.2. **Blank Postcard**

TABLE 12.24. **Model Text**

### Technology

Some people think that technology is a new idea. But technology has been around for a long time.

Long before we had electricity or telephones or factory machines, we had technology. Technology means that we use our knowledge and our skills to make something. Then we use the thing we have made to help us do other things we need to do. Tools are certainly part of technology. We also need to know, however, how to use those tools. If we did not have the knowledge that enables us to use the tools, those tools would be useless. Knowledge is just as important to technology as are tools.

New technologies often bring changes to our world. For example, Johann Gutenberg invented the printing press in 1445. When this happened, many more people could afford to buy books. More and more people were able to learn to read. Before that time, all books had to be copied by hand and thus were very expensive. There were very few books and even fewer people who could read them.

If we use a new technology well, it can bring us benefits. If we misuse a technology, we can end up in trouble.

*Level 6*

As you have just read, technology can bring with it advantages and some disadvantages (table 12.24).

Think about the present. What has technology brought to the world? Write a paragraph talking about modern technology using the ideas from the text above (table 12.25).

Revise your text after finishing it. Do not forget to check spelling, punctuation, capitalization and verb tenses.

TABLE 12.25. **Prompt for Writing**

| Technology: The Printing Press | |
|---|---|
| *Advantages* | *Disadvantages* |
| Allowed more people to buy and read books. | For those who did the printing, the original printing presses were slow (it took a long time to typeset and print even a single page) and dirty (the printers got their hands covered in printer's ink). |

## Acknowledgment

I would like to express my gratitude to all members of the ICBNA's teaching team, who are in many ways all coauthors of this chapter. The ICBNA would like to thank the U.S. Department of State for the grant that made in-service sessions with teachers financially feasible. These sessions were crucial to the successful implementation of the new system.

# 13

## IT'S ALL IN THE TEAM: APPROACHES TO TEACHER DEVELOPMENT IN A CONTENT-BASED, TASK-BASED EFL PROGRAM

Kathryn Cozonac

EDITOR'S NOTE: In this chapter, Kathryn Cozonac, American Language Center (Chisinau, Moldova) looks at task-based instruction from the viewpoint of a program administrator and selects one aspect that all administrators must manage: faculty development. The program that she describes has taken place annually for the past eight years. Since the faculty are summer hires, most of whom are marginally, if at all, familiar with task-based instruction, intensive faculty development activities must precede the summer programs each year. Cozonac outlines the teacher development schema used that consists of three parts: teacher education, cooperative planning, and class observation. She then examines what happened one year when, due to prior experience of the teachers in task-based instruction, the first part was omitted.

The one factor that can single-handedly bring the success or failure of any educational program is the team of instructors. Their qualifications, level of motivation, experience, energy, and teamwork can, in the end, determine whether or not program goals are met, to what extent students are motivated, and how effectively the overall educational program operates. A team of highly motivated and qualified instructors can bring about the success of even a weak program design; likewise, a team of neglected or disillusioned instructors can undermine a strong program from day one.

After twenty years of teaching high school French, Mrs. Johnson burned out. Her school was recognized as one of the best academically in the district, not to mention that for three consecutive years students from her department had been state champions in the annual state-wide French honors contest. But after twenty years of teaching French day in and day out to largely unmotivated students and dealing with faculty meetings, including verbal abuse that characterized them, Mrs. Johnson was ready for a break. She packed her bags for a week-long vacation. When the substitute arrived at Mrs. Johnson's high school French class, she found a simple handwritten note on the teacher's desk, "Sorry, the dog ate my lesson plans."

Lack of motivation, lack of innovation, and a nonsupportive environment can drive any educator to the edge of their senses, as they did Mrs. Johnson with her French class. Innovation itself and encouragement to pursue developments in the field give educators the professional encouragement they thrive on, as well as promote professional relationships built on mutual respect.

Once educators are adequately motivated and supported, attention is rightly turned to classroom practices and the theory behind those practices, which again is a source of motivation and innovation for instructors. A major factor in the equation of teacher performance and teacher development is methodology. Every instructor, whether novice or veteran, teaches in accordance with some methodology or a mixture of methodologies, regardless of whether or not he or she can articulate the premises and practices associated with it. Either consciously or unconsciously, each teacher has a methodology that derives either from theory turned into practice or from practice learned and described by theory. One reason for a book such as this is to encourage instructors to think deeply about their theory and their practice within the classroom and determine if the two coincide. What follows in this chapter is an account of class designs by four different instructors, each professing to use the same content-based, task-based methodology within the same program—the same goals, benchmarks, and the like—but realized by different practices in the classroom. The program is the U.S. State Department–sponsored Junior Faculty Development Program (JFDP) English as a Foreign Language (EFL) course, a thirty-day intensive program to train junior faculty in communicative and academic English before they spend an academic year at a designated American university. This chapter gives an overview of the program (stressing the specific needs of the participants) and the framework of task-based instruction (TBI) within the program, including two models that, due in one instance to lack of training and in another to a difference in interpretation, created puzzle pieces that did not fit into the jigsaw. It is these models of TBI that can serve as examples of teacher development object lessons.

## Junior Faculty Development Program

Each year, the American Councils for International Education (ACIE) runs the Junior Faculty Development Program (JFDP), in which a number of junior faculty (fellows) from universities in Eurasia are sent to America for one academic year. While in America they will attend courses in their field, work under a senior faculty member, and participate in academic life, including conferences and seminars. The goal is to bring modern teaching practices in their field to their home country and home university. Upon return, fellows are expected to attend alumni events, give presentations on the new methods they learned, and participate in faculty development activities to advance their home universities.

Of course, to succeed in this, the fellows need a level of communicative English that facilitates academic participation in their specialization at American universities. From the group of selected fellows, the thirty with the lowest TOEFL scores are sent to Moldova (located between Romania and Ukraine) for one month of intensive English study.[1] For those chosen, further participation in JFDP becomes conditional upon successful completion of the EFL program.

## The American Language Center in Moldova and JFDP EFL

Located in Chisinau, Moldova, the American Language Center (ALC) runs the session as an intensive month of English immersion. Since 1996, the ALC has been the leading language school within Moldova in its adherence to content-based and task-based instruction (CBI-TBI). All instructors for the course are selected specifically for the degree to which they will contribute to the program goals.

Interestingly, during the time of the USSR, Moldova was a top vacation spot for Soviet citizens. Its location in the southern part of the Soviet Union provided the best weather without leaving the country. With rolling hills, beautiful countryside, excellent wines and food, and a warmer climate than the rest of the country, Moldova was a favorite destination.

Given Moldova's reputation, it is natural that when the JFDP fellows arrive, they expect a month-long vacation. Participants come from the Western newly independent states (Russia, Ukraine, and Moldova), the Caucasus region (Georgia, Armenia, Azerbaijan), and Central Asia (Kyrgyzstan, Kazakhstan, Uzbekistan, and Turkmenistan).[2] Some of them have never left their country, and many have never spent an extended amount of time with people from another region. Just as Americans have jokes about people from certain states, the former Soviet Union has jokes about people from different regions and republics. By bringing them all together for four weeks, and doing so in what they expect to be a vacationer's paradise, from the first day they are challenged much more than they anticipate as their expectations are changed one after another.

The thirty days together in an English-speaking academic environment breaks down territorial walls and any existing hostilities until what is created resembles more closely a tapestry rather than a haphazard mixture of C-4 and dynamite. The diversity of the fellows contributes to the overall scheme of the program, as their first languages are very different. While they all speak Russian (as a second or third language, if not first), there is a hesitation to use Russian for communication when Russian is considered a "loaded" language. Also, speaking only in English quickly becomes an issue of pride and somewhat of a contest among the fellows—who can rise to the challenge?

The thirty participating fellows are housed in dormitory-style rooms, with their classrooms in the same facility's conference rooms. Meals, social outings, and informal gatherings encourage instructors to join the fellows for conversation and a time of relaxation. The program is considered intensive in two senses: (1) it is a concentrated time-frame for learning, and (2) it is a demanding program of complete immersion in an English-speaking environment. While this task places heavy demands on the fellows, it is equally daunting for instructors, considering the fact that their "time off" is typically spent with the fellows.

## The JFDP Model for CBI

There are two ways to assess the model used for this English program. The first is at the macro level of overall program design and objectives, including syllabi, and the second is at the micro level of actual classroom practice and lesson plans. Since 1999, when the program first came to the American Language Center in Moldova, there have been minor changes and alterations each year to ensure that the program continues to run smoothly and benefit from developments in the field of foreign language teaching. The discussions in this chapter are based on the summer 2002 program.

### PROGRAM DESIGN AND OBJECTIVES

At the macro level, there are a number of elements in the JFDP EFL program, including the simulated English-speaking environment, cultural excursions, and academic requirements, that work to create a real purpose for language use and provide a natural context for language study (see discussion of task aims by Willis, chapter 1, this volume).

### English-Speaking Environment

Fellows, instructors, and one administrator are all housed in a dormitory-styled hotel. Upon arrival in Moldova, fellows are asked to sign a pledge that they will speak only in the target language (English) for the duration of the program. Meals are taken together in the hotel's cafeteria, during which instructors and administrators join the fellows, actually sharing meals together. Progress is seen even before academic study begins (typically fellows arrive two days before classes begin), as the fellows already become comfortable with the target language simply through using it in the preprogram orientation phase. All necessities are handled in English—finding a phone, getting directions to the store, explaining special dietary needs, etc. This specifically teaches strategic skills for coping with ambiguities, such skills being precisely what allows fellows to continue learning outside of the classroom.

### Cultural Excursions

While the majority of the tasks during the JFDP EFL program are of a formal nature, informal gatherings are just as important. For instance, the program provides two or three cultural excursions in which participants, instructors, and administrators go together to some of Moldova's treasures, such as wine cellars and historical sites. These cultural outings provide valuable practice for informal gatherings the fellows will attend in America. And again, fellows are encouraged to use their strategic skills to cope with uncertainties and learn to understand from context. These different types of trips appeal to different learners and help provide each participant with a learning task that can be optimally effective for him or her.

### Academic Coursework

While all of these are integral parts of the program, what is typically regarded as the "meat" of the EFL program is the academic coursework. Participants attend four classes each day, Monday through Friday: Cultural Geography, Academic Writing, Pop Culture and Campus life, and Changing Paradigms in American History. The standards required for successful completion of each course depend largely on agreement between the instructor and the program coordinator. They can include anything from a successful culmination project, a written test, or a paper submitted, to a pass/fail grade based on class participation. It varies widely from class to class but is ideally designed to be objective and impartial, and appeal to a variety of learning styles. Table 13.1 gives an example of the syllabus outline from the Cultural Geography course.

In addition to courses, all fellows must fulfill two further academic requirements. The first of these is a brief presentation at a capstone conference at the close of the program. Presentations typically fall into three groupings: home regions (participants' home country, village, university, etc.); field of study (outlining one aspect of the fellow's field of expertise); or teaching methodology (explanations of various theories and practices within the classroom in a fellow's field). Fellows are further required to submit a written portfolio at the end of the program, including a brief research paper, an abstract for an academic paper, a résumé, and a cover letter. Therefore, when the participants finish the program, they leave with a ready portfolio of items they will be able to use at their universi-

TABLE 13.1. **Cultural Geography Syllabus Outline**

| | |
|---|---|
| Lesson 1 | Overview of geographic regions |
| Lesson 2 | Country of immigrants: What is an American |
| Lesson 3 | Country of immigrants: Asian Americans |
| Lesson 4 | Country of immigrants: Mosaic versus melting pot |
| Lesson 5 | Regional dialects with *On the Road with Charles Kuralt* video |
| Lesson 6 | Regional dialects with *O Brother Where Art Thou* video |
| Lesson 7 | More regional dialects |
| Lessons 8–9 | Microdialects (Creole/Cajun/Gullah/Munjeon/Appalachia) |
| Lessons 10–12 | Native Americans / Myths |
| Lessons 13–14 | Ebonics |
| Lessons 15–16 | Perceptions of home |

*Note:* This syllabus is designed to give students an introduction to the breadth of varieties that make the United States unique. It also underscores issues related to ethnicity, variations in American English, regionalism, and the effect those issues have on value systems. In the scope of the program there is no room for overview courses such as Survey of American History, but important cultural factors deriving from historical background are covered by other means with greater academic depth.

The academic writing course covers topics such as classical argument, research methods, paragraph and sentence structure, and writing an academic abstract. Because the Soviet educational system was virtually void of any mention of writing skills or writing practice, this course fills a greatly felt need for these scholars and university faculty.

Both courses—Pop Culture and Campus Life, and Paradigm Changes in American History—imbue students with an overview of the cultural fabric in the North American shared consciousness, including how history shaped the United States, and generally known factors of campus life (the campus newspaper, student life center, and recognized figures such as Andy Warhol, Charlie Brown, and Jimmy Stewart).

ties in America and the experience of giving an academic presentation to their peers in English.

### TBI IN THE CLASSROOM

Task-based instruction is based on the notion that "real language learning is most likely to occur when the context of that learning is not only typical, but real, when the learners are not merely acting out roles, but trying to use their new language to fulfill genuine communicative purposes" (Eskey 1997, 136). Thus far, we have seen that the JFDP EFL program aims to fill this need at the macro level. At the micro level, within each classroom each day, the aim is no less ambitious. The conditions necessary for language learning can be divided into essential and desirable. The essential conditions are exposure, use, and motivation. The desirable condition is instruction in the language (Willis, chapter 1, this volume).

The program design immediately meets the needs of the essential conditions. Exposure and use come simply from living in an English-speaking hotel and participating in English-speaking cultural excursions. Instruction in the language itself, the desirable but not necessary condition, is met through giving fellows a book of English grammar with explanations and exercises. Those who wish to study grammar may do so, and instructors are ready to help when the need arises. Thus, simply from participating in the program, the fellows gain all the essential requirements for language acquisition.

In the classroom these are stressed even more. Within each class, instructors are expected to provide exposure (time of lecture, reading, or other presentation of new information); use (time of student interaction based on the new information); and motivation (reason for students to participate—this ranges from direct motivation such as a grading system, to indirect motivation such as level of interest in and usefulness of the given task).

In order to create appropriate tasks for the classroom, instructors were encouraged to follow a TBI framework in which the task itself is preceded by a pretask (or introduction to the topic) and can then be followed by a language focus if the instructor deems necessary. This language focus reinforces the form, after discussion of the meaning, in accordance with Nunan's (1989a) definition of task as an activity in which meaning is the principal focus rather than form. An example of such an approach is given in table 13.2, which is taken from the Cultural Geography course.

In this lesson, the instructor gives students a verbal introduction to the theme and the task, and as early as the introduction elicits participation from students about the theme. Then the students carry out the task, ending it by reporting their results to the class. Following this, language related to creation is reinforced, and the theme is developed through a reading on the topic. After the reading, students are encouraged to compare and contrast information not only from the reading but also from their own knowledge base (including misassumptions and myths). The lesson ends as they link creation myths and their Native American tribes to geographical locations, looking for potential explanations for similarities.

TABLE 13.2. **Plan for Lesson 10, Cultural Geography**

*Theme:* Creation myths in Native American traditions

*Objective:* To gain exposure to creation myths and think critically about our own ideas of creation.

**Lesson Plan**

| | |
|---|---|
| 5 | Introduce creation myths—define and give examples, then elicit from students examples they can think of of creation myths |
| **25** | **With students in pairs, have them invent a creation myth** |
| | **Allow pairs to share their creation myths with the class** |

*Reading: Native American creation myths*

| | |
|---|---|
| 10 | Have pairs verify if their creation myth is similar to any of those they just read about. What similarities can they find between different myths? |
| 11 | With creation myths handy, give students a map of where Native American tribes were centered. Can students find geographical reasons for correlations between myths? |

Therefore, each lesson plan, ideally, is an effort to combine exposure, use, and motivation, through a task framework, using pretask, task, and, when necessary, language focus. By so doing, instructors reinforce the idea that language is communicative, they create a real purpose for language learning, and they provide a natural context for language study.

After being a part of classes such as this, participating in all the activities, and successfully completing the specifically academic portion of the JFDP EFL program, fellows are qualified and prepared to spend one academic year in America.

## Teacher Development

The instructors for the JFDP EFL program are mainly Americans, recruited specifically for this program. The typical background of the instructors is (1) master's degree in a related field (foreign language teaching, English as a foreign language, linguistics, or a field in education or English), (2) extensive experience teaching English to speakers of other languages, (3) familiarity with content- and task-based instruction or exposure to the principles and practices of the methodology, (4) knowledge of at least one foreign language, and (5) experience living or working in another country. The most heavily weighted of these are the teaching experience and experience abroad. While familiarity with the methodology is preferable, it is not required, as the ALC conducts effective teacher training in content-based and task-based methodologies on site in Moldova.

The ALC teacher development schema is threefold. The first part is a preprogram, top-down teacher training session. The second part is bilateral, mutual accountability meetings during the preprogram week of lesson planning.

The final part of teacher development is class observation conducted by program administrators. Each section builds upon the others, and the cycle itself is a continual process—training, collaboration, observation, then back to the start with further training, etc. In the following pages, we will examine each of these to see what conclusions can be made as to the effectiveness of this schema.

### TRAINING SEMINAR

Before discussing the first part of the teacher development schema, which is referred to here as a teacher training session, it will be necessary to defend my choice of terminology. As stated by Larsen-Freeman (1983), Britten (1985), Richards (1987), and Lange (1990), and noted in Peterson (1997, 161–62), there is an inherent difference between teacher preparation as defined as teacher training or as teacher education. Specifically, the difference is between "the type of program that *trains* teachers to perform in a specific type of situation whereas the other *educates* teachers to be effective in any situation they encounter" (Peterson 1997, 162). According to this distinction, our training seminar was more of an educating seminar. However, due to conventions of speech, to the nature of English as a second language in Moldova, while nonetheless acknowledging the sometimes pejorative associations of the word *training* by American teachers, within Moldova the ALC invited instructors to a "training seminar." In keeping with the terminology that was used at the time, this paper will continue with the wording, but not without noting that what is implied therein is education for all situations rather than training to give a programmed response.

The first year the JFDP EFL program was implemented in Moldova, the training session for instructors was prepared and conducted by an American consultant, Betty Lou Leaver, for three categories of instructors: JFDP EFL instructors, ALC English teachers, and a number of invited guests from the EFL community in Moldova. As a respected authority in the field of foreign language teaching, and especially in methodologies of CBI and TBI, Leaver was the perfect person to design the training program. It focused on learning styles (taking material from her book, *Teaching the Whole Class* [Leaver 1998], and grounding it with even more examples and practical application) and how learning styles affect the success of other classroom practices. The session was a five-day intensive seminar that consisted of lectures, collaborative learning, and "hands-on" sessions of creating classroom activities, designing syllabi, and altering preexistent lesson plans to include TBI.

The training session took place at the ALC, commencing two weeks prior to the start of the JFDP EFL program. That is, JFDP EFL instructors came to Moldova two weeks before the start of their program to benefit from this week-long training session. While the variety of session participants granted a broad exchange of knowledge and experience, the focus here is on the JFDP EFL instructors and how they profited from the training. Topics included in the training were as follows:

- history and development of methodologies (focusing on the progressive element underlining the changes in classroom practices);

- content- and task-based methodologies: from theory to practice;
- teaching the whole class: differences in personality archetypes and learning styles;
- syllabus design and lesson planning; and
- error correction (as influenced by learning styles).

Interestingly, the seminar was planned to mirror the practices of task-based instruction. Each new piece of information was presented in a well-defined task framework. The pretask phase was a presentation of material or new information. The tasks themselves split the participants into small groups and allowed time for active practice with the newly presented material. For example, after a presentation on lesson plan design with a focus on appealing to different learning styles, groups were given content (magazines, newspapers, articles, etc.) and asked to use a selection of the materials to design a single lesson that would appeal to a variety of learning styles. Each group then presented their lesson plan to the remaining groups and engaged each other in constructive criticism, helping to refine the lesson plans developed.

After five days of such training, participants had a firm grounding in theory, which was enhanced by their experience in a task-based classroom. They had participated in a model that was theoretically sound and fully realized in practice. Additionally, the task assignments of the week gave each participant something unique they had created and were able to take with them to their own classrooms to put into practice.

Feedback from the training was all positive. Theory, practice, and tangible results—both given to them and created by them in the sessions—equipped the participants with the tools necessary to adapt their current and future classrooms. In many cases, what was most important was the material they created in the sessions. As Leaver granted participants the opportunity to create, individually or in groups, classroom activities, lesson plans, and syllabus outlines, each participant left with actual materials to use in class; in addition to materials distributed, they had in hand actual activities and classroom tools they had worked out on their own based on their own contexts. They had presented each of these to the group and been given feedback on them by other teachers and by Leaver herself.

For the JFDP instructors, this was their introduction to their job over the next month, it was their on-the-job training. They were expected to actively participate, clarify anything they did not understand, and absorb virtually all the material. By the time they finished the seminar, they were expected to create lesson plans similar to those discussed in class, from scratch, and for a month's worth of daily classes.

In subsequent years, when Leaver was unavailable or budgeting did not allow for a repetition of this training seminar, local EFL professionals were invited to conduct a seminar based on Leaver's seminar program. For instance, in the summer of 2001, Anne Jackson, who had previously worked with Leaver on a number of projects, participated in multiple seminars, and was overall well versed in the methodology and necessary training, conducted the seminar using a mixture of lectures, videos of Leaver's presentations, and hands-on activities to develop materials.

### MUTUAL ACCOUNTABILITY

To ensure that the JFDP instructors were able to carry out their courses with a focus on communicative proficiency, cooperative meetings are scheduled during their lesson planning week. This week falls directly after the training session and ends with the start of the JFDP EFL program. Thus, the instructors' schedule in Moldova contains three phrases: (1) teacher development seminar (week 1); (2) collaborative lesson planning (week 2); (3) instruction of the JFDP EFL program (weeks 3–6).

During the lesson planning week, instructors work individually to prepare for their courses. They first create a syllabus for their course (reviewed by the course coordinator for adherence to program goals and compatibility with other program syllabi), then a lesson plan skeleton for the first week of classes, and by the end of the planning week have daily lesson plans firmly drawn up for the first week of classes. During this time of planning, there is daily time for teachers (sometimes with the course coordinator) to meet as a group, share their work, compare ideas, and cooperatively deal with questions, problems, and so on.

It is during this time that instructors are expected to keep each other accountable, look over each other's lesson plans, taking care not to duplicate or challenge material among courses and to ensure that each instructor is clear about the task and the methodology—and that the principles and practices of the methodology are actually reflected in the lesson plans. By working together, with the assistance of the course coordinator (who is effectively the academic supervisor), the goal is that any misunderstanding of TBI, misunderstanding of tasks, or failure to incorporate all learning styles into the lesson plans will be caught and remedied before the fellows arrive.

Typically, the atmosphere is not one of "big brother is watching," but rather all instructors come with their lesson plans and syllabi and armed with questions and concerns. Each instructor, with full respect for the others, brings up issues of group concern and questions about appropriateness of materials, lack of specific materials, or other topics related to their course, and which they think the group can either answer and help with, or benefit from discussion.

### CLASSROOM OBSERVATION

Like anything else, there is room for error, and not only error in terms of methodology. Instructors, even seasoned instructors, do things in their classes of which they are unaware. These may take the form of overly stern body language or giving students unequal attention. Interpersonal and intragroup dynamics can also play a role in teaching success (Ehrman and Dornyei 1998). Therefore, the third stage of teacher development is class observation, typically conducted by the program director.[3] The program director sometimes visits entire class sessions of each instructor and of each group of students; occasionally there are brief visits to classes.

These two types of observations serve different purposes. A brief visit to a class gives the director an idea of the instructor's body language, rapport with students, style of teaching, learner- or teacher-centered methods, and a basic vignette of the instructor's specific classroom practices. Attending an entire class provides all of the above benefits, as well as a great deal of information about timing, overall lesson plan design, incorporation of learning styles into the lesson, and complete follow-through with a task or series of tasks. During class observation, specifically for an entire class, and equipped with the lesson plan and handouts, the director uses a worksheet like the one in table 13.3 to assess all these issues.

After completing class observations for each instructor, the program director is able to gain an overall feel for what the fellows are doing in their courses, the effectiveness of the program, and wider issues that need to be dealt with in teacher development. This schema, with all three aspects put together, creates an efficient way of ensuring high-quality classroom instruction.

### COPING WITH CORRECTION

Preprogram training, collaborative planning, and class observation are three methods of ensuring adherence to program goals. However, what happens when there are problems? How does a program administrator get the desired results out of these methods of professional development and teacher training? From a management point of view, correcting policies and practices can be a daunting task. What follows are a few brief points on confronting instructors about deficiencies in their classroom practices.

TABLE 13.3. **Class Observation Worksheet for Administrators**

Instructor _____ Date _____ Class _____

Lesson Theme / Title _____

Objectives_____

| | | | | | Suits Learning Styles | | | | |
| Activity | Planned Time | Actual Time | Place in Task Framework | How It Meets Objectives | Auditory | Motor | Visual | Oral | Notes |
|---|---|---|---|---|---|---|---|---|---|
| | | | | | | | | | |
| | | | | | | | | | |
| | | | | | | | | | |
| | | | | | | | | | |
| | | | | | | | | | |
| | | | | | | | | | |
| | | | | | | | | | |

Overall style: ☐ learner centered ☐ teacher centered

Body language: ☐ facilitated goals ☐ hindered goals

Error correction: ☐ appropriate ☐ insufficient ☐ overly zealous

☐ varied ☐ static

Note: The top and first two columns can be filled in by the instructor prior to the start of class.

First of all, a greased wheel is less likely to squeak. In other words, instructors who are sufficiently encouraged and given positive feedback are more likely to respond positively to constructive criticism than those who lack encouraging feedback. If the focus begins with the positive aspects, then criticizes constructively (that is, suggesting ways to improve), and ends with a kind word, motivation increases and the will to improve grows stronger.

Likewise, while personality, professionalism outside of the classroom, and other subjective issues may cause problems within the classroom—or even among coworkers—only performance issues are fair game for administrative intervention. If subjective issues do not cause on-the-job performance problems, there is no reason for an administrator to get involved. However, when performance problems do occur, regardless of any subjective issues that may be the driving force behind them, issues are always handled at the performance level only.

Finally, all confrontations, corrections, and disciplinary measures are of a highly confidential nature. Criticism and confrontations are best done behind closed doors, and always with a degree of sensitivity and delicacy. What an administrator sees as a minor piece of constructive criticism may be seen as a severe attack by an instructor. Further, the situation is less likely to be inflamed when privacy is respected and reputation is guarded. Counselings are positive, with the focus on progress, learning, and development.

Human resource issues can be the trickiest part of program administration. When a large number of students, teachers, and administrators are working toward the same goal, it is almost inevitable that problems will arise. The key to dealing with these is a healthy combination of mutual respect with a high level of professionalism and patient understanding.

## Case Study: JFDP EFL 2002

The following case study is employed to give a tangible example of how teachers' backgrounds, training, and classroom styles have affected the delivery of their courses and the overall success of the aforementioned program. With an adequate system of teacher development, such as that described below, many of the issues that arose in this case could have been prevented. Though the success of the program was not marred by these issues, the lessons learned about teacher development could have brought the program to an even higher level.

### CBI-TBI VARIATION AND TEACHER BACKGROUNDS

The teacher development schema consists of three distinct parts: (1) teacher education, (2) cooperative planning, and (3) class observation. When these three work together and cycle back on one another to create a healthy program of development, the result is a group of faculty fully prepared to handle task-based programs, with all of the accompanying pressures and complexities.

However, the summer JFDP program of 2002 was somewhat of an anomaly in this area. Two of the instructors had been at Leaver's seminar in previous years, another instructor had given presentations based on Leaver's work, and the fourth instructor, while not present at these training seminars, had two years' experience teaching with the methodology. Due to the instructors' backgrounds, the program administrators decided that the teacher training seminar would not be necessary. All instructors seemed to be well versed in the methodology, and any discrepancies could be dealt with at faculty meetings during the program and through class observations.

In the week of teacher lesson planning, the course coordinator began to notice that the instructors had a wide degree of variance in their interpretations of TBI. This was not an alarming fact, as personal background and experience will necessarily cause differences in practice even when working with the same theory. Just as learning styles affect the way a student responds to stimuli in the classroom, there is a similar effect on the way an instructor's learning style affects the way he or she presents material. Variations are not to be shunned; rather, they add depth to a given curriculum. Therefore, as the instructors planned their courses with somewhat different foci in terms of classroom practices and activities, the variation between courses and instructors gave the administration no cause for concern.

For any program, successful implementation can be measured with a type of target. The bull's-eye, or center of the target, is the goal. The concentric circles surrounding the bull's-eye represent acceptable variation, to a point. As the JFDP EFL program was implemented and classes were observed, the variance in interpretation revealed two courses that were acceptably close to the bull's-eye, and two that were operating somewhere on opposite outskirts of the target, yet still within the reasonable range.

In describing the variance between realizations of the methodology, a framework of task components will be helpful. The three components of a task can be defined as (1) goals, (2) input, and (3) activities (Nunan 1989a). When these three components work together, they balance each other and meet the needs of a communicative task-based classroom. Yet, input and activities, when lacking a clearly defined goal, have no direction and the effort is lost, suspended somewhere in the arena of "busy work." A lack of input deprives students of needed exposure to language, as well as the deductive instruction some learners require. When activities are missing, the applicability of the task disappears as the classroom loses its communicative nature.

In the 2002 JFDP EFL course, two of the four classes had a reasonable balance of these components. However, in the Pop Culture and Campus Life course, there was an over-reliance on class participation. The teacher was, in the majority of classes, an observer while the students gave presentations, speeches, and other performance-based tasks. According this rubric, the course was heavy on activities, but lacked input and goals.

On the other side, the Paradigm Changes in American History course turned out to be nearly a lecture series, during which information was periodically elicited from the class, but more often the instructor's classroom practices only dimly reflected student-centered, student-empowered, communicative methodology. This course had an overabundance of goals and input but lacked the amount of activities that would have given target-centered balance.

Whereas other teachers had all participated in training seminars, this instructor had missed out on the very important teacher education module of the teacher development program. Her prior experience was, in fact, with content-based instruction, rather than task-based instruction, yet without a firm grounding in the theory behind content-based instruction. And, if taken only for the literal meaning of the words with the theory behind them placed aside, her JFDP course was content-based in the sense that it taught the content of American history through the target language. Unfortunately, the only component of the task framework was input. The actual task itself was largely missing (see figure 13.1).

For the instructor of the course on pop culture (the previous example), the problem was of a different nature. She had participated in the training seminar in the past (one year earlier) under the direction of Anne Jackson. She was familiar with the methodology, but a year had passed without using it, and her memory was somewhat selective. The same happens to all of us. When one is distanced from a particular body of knowledge, that knowledge sinks into the back recesses of the brain. The longer the period of time one is away from the field, the farther away it sinks, until, when an attempt is made to retrieve it, it comes back in chunks—some parts still fully intact, other parts lost somewhere in the gray matter. As this instructor planned her course, she fully remembered the importance of student-centered activities. What was left out was input, introduction to tasks, and exposure to authentic materials.

It was the course observation that revealed these two departures from the target goal of the program, at which point the course administrators took to "rehabilitating" the syllabi and lesson plans. An attempt was made over the remaining duration of the program to supplement the instructors' current field knowledge with focused materials in methodological theory and practice, to re-implement

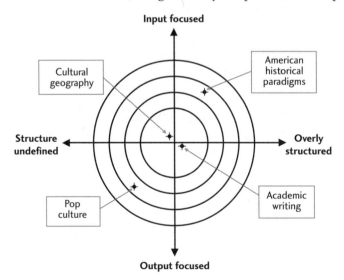

FIGURE 13.1. **Target Goal for JFDP Courses**

collaborative staff and faculty meetings with the goal of restoring adherence to the program's design, and to vary the type of course observations under different conditions (different times of day, teachers with different groups of students, brief class visits, etc.). While the improvements made over the following two weeks were minor in terms of a return to program goals, the team of instructors benefited from career development in the form of education to be implemented in future courses. It was a learning experience for all involved, as the issue itself underlined the necessity of proper instruction in methodology from the start, as well as continual review and reinforcement of theory and practices learned.

### RESULTS FROM JFDP EFL 2002

Of the four courses, two were at the center of program goals, while two others lay near the perimeter. Perhaps it was because these two off-center courses were set on opposite sides of the scale that they balanced each other. In one class, the students received little input; in the other, they were given more input than necessary. In the first, they did only activities; in the second, they participated in relatively few activities. In their interpretation of the methodology, the two instructors were virtually opposites, but as such, they had an equalizing effect on each other. In exit testing of the fellows, results showed no less improvement in the fellows' acquisition of English than they had in previous years. Fellows' evaluations of their courses showed that they appreciated the foci of each of the courses, individually, and as a comprehensive curriculum. They noticed a difference in classroom activities among the various instructors, but they took it as different backgrounds interpreting the methodology differently, which they understood would happen at their host universities in America.

Following the fellows' later success in achieving their ultimate goal—active participation in their specializations in American universities—the fellows who participated in the JFDP EFL program performed much better than their JFDP colleagues (those with higher TOEFL scores who were not placed in the EFL course), especially at the early stages of their placement. The JFDP EFL fellows knew what to expect—out of the program itself, out of being in an English-speaking community, out of American culture, and out of American university faculty. The results were overwhelmingly positive. The fellows were beneficiaries of a program that provided what they needed—an opportunity to take part in an academic program in English, given various classroom settings, and an empowering, communicative environment to bolster their English proficiency.

## Conclusions

Teacher development starts with teacher education. In the summer of 2002, the instructors whose courses did not correlate exactly to the TBI framework had, in one case, selectively remembered the framework as given years before in the teacher education/development seminars, and in another case, missed out completely on teacher education. While the collaborative sessions during the week of lesson planning gave the teachers an opportunity to compare and contrast their lessons, drawing experience and expertise from one another, the sessions focused primarily on what each instructor individually did not fully comprehend regarding the methodology; unfortunately, instructors were unable to anticipate what problems might occur, and, further, they were unaware of the scope of the model and, thereby, unaware of how their own interpretations departed from the goal.

Classroom observations are meant not to overhaul current situations in the classroom but to enhance them. While these are a powerful way of working alongside teachers to improve classroom practices, without the other aspects of teacher development, classroom observation is insufficient. Instructors do not operate on an island, and the community of colleagues they work with provides a prime opportunity to adjust classroom practices based on cumulative experience.

In the JFDP EFL 2002 program, the lack of teacher education left room for wide interpretations of the methodology. The other components of teacher development are, of course, constructive and valuable, but without the first component of education/training, which we might think of as *input*—as there would be input in a task framework—the effectiveness of the entire teacher development framework is compromised. The three should work together, mutually supporting one another to obtain the most effective results from teacher development.

## Notes

1. The Test of English as a Foreign Language (TOEFL) is an achievement test, based on knowledge of vocabulary and grammar presented in limited context.
2. This includes all of the republics of the former Soviet Union except Belarus and Tajikistan.
3. Class observations were included for feedback to both instructors and students. It should be noted, however, that classroom observations can serve another purpose entirely when instructors observe their peers' classes. This is usually a part of teacher education or certification programs, but it is not as often emphasized at the professional level. It can be highly valuable, especially when teachers are working with a methodology, subject matter, or level of students they are not accustomed to. It provides new ideas and also gives insight that administrators may miss, since their focus is usually on a specific agenda (observation worksheet, standards rubric, etc.).

# Glossary of
# Multicontinent Terms

NOTE: This is not intended to be an exhaustive list of TESOL terminology (for this, see Ellis 2003, 339–53) but to provide support for readers worldwide in countries where the use of these terms may differ from those used in this book—in which authors, regardless of location, have agreed to use U.S. definition of terms (because of location of the publisher) to provide for consistency within the pages of this book.

**ACTFL.** Abbreviation for American Council on Teaching Foreign Languages. See the appendix.

**ALM.** Abbreviation for *audiolingual method*. For definition, see *audiolingual approach*.

**audiolingual approach.** An approach to teaching based on the theories of behaviorism and introduced by Lado (1964). In the United States, the series of textbooks that used an audiolingual approach were considered to represent the *audiolingual method* (ALM).

**audiolingual method.** See *audiolingual approach*.

**CLT.** See *communicative language teaching*.

**communicative competence.** The ability to negotiate meaning, interact in the foreign language in functional and successful ways, and comprehend and use language in context for unilateral and multilateral purposes (Hymes 1972).

**communicative language teaching.** Teaching that is oriented to the development of communicative competence. The term, CLT, is more common in Europe and Latin America and in ESL/EFL than in US FLED, which tends to prefer the term "communicative approaches."

**comprehensible input.** This generally refers to the spoken form of the target language that learners can understand sufficiently to grasp the general meaning but without necessarily being familiar with all the words, phrases, or structures. A term coined by Krashen (1985).

**conversion course.** See *cross-training course*.

**cross-training course.** A course that teaches an additional language in the same family to students already proficient in one language (e.g., at the DLI, Russian students were cross-trained in Serbian). Also called a *conversion course* (Corin 1997).

**EFL.** The abbreviation for English as a foreign language, that is, the teaching of English for learners who do not live in an environment in which English is one of the local official languages. It is also sometimes used for short-term courses in an English-speaking country for students coming to stay on a temporary basis (e.g., summer courses) but not live.

**ESL.** The abbreviation for the teaching of English as a second language, that is, in an environment in which English is spoken natively by a large proportion of the local residents.

**faculty development.** In the United States, this term is used to mean the teaching of teachers in any environment. This can include initial schooling, in-service workshops, or continuing education, among a variety of possibilities. In Europe, this term is only rarely used. See *teacher training*.

**FLED.** An acronym, commonly used in the United States, for foreign language education.

**form.** Usually refers to grammatical form, as in a focus-on-form approach (Doughty and Williams 1998). Long (1996) makes the distinction between *focus on form* in general, where learners are concerned with grammatical accuracy in the context of a communicative activity, and *focus on forms*, which involves explicit grammar teaching, focusing on specified forms.

**four-handed teaching.** This is a particular form of team-teaching in which two teachers are in the classroom and work with the whole class or subgroups of students in multiple ways (Goroshko and Slutsky 1999).

**functions.** Language functions highlight the purposes or roles to which items of language can be put; these range from specific speech acts like requesting, agreeing, apologizing in social communication to broader purposes in both written and spoken text, like comparing and contrasting, appraising, and anecdote telling.

**ILR.** See *interagency language roundtable*.

**Input Hypothesis.** Krashen (1985) believes that, when learners are exposed to language that they can mostly understand but which still contains forms that they do not know, they will, in time, acquire such new forms naturally from the input they hear and read.

**Interaction Hypothesis.** A term proposed by Long (1989) to refer to the belief that when learners interact with other speakers of the target language and have a communication problem, the resultant process of negotiating meaning is likely to lead to the acquisition of new language forms.

**Interagency Language Roundtable.** The Interagency Language Roundtable is composed of representatives from each of the U.S. government agencies that teach or employ users of foreign languages. The ILR has met in Washington, D.C., on a monthly basis for more than forty years. As a body, it seeks to make uniform the rating of language proficiency, share teaching practices, and otherwise economize through collaboration. (See also ILR Proficiency Descriptions in the appendix.)

**interlanguage.** A system of rules for the foreign language developed by an individual student in the process of language acquisition. The amount of variance from the actual linguistic system of the foreign language depends upon the individual student and the level of proficiency (Selinker 1972).

**notional-functional syllabus.** A syllabus itemized in terms of categories of meanings (both notional and functional), with the emphasis on communicative purposes (Wilkins 1976). Grammar is not ignored but is generally taught in the contexts of the realizations of the functions and notions.

**notions.** A syllabus strand based on notions would include categories of meaning such as duration of time, points in time, location, possibility, certainty, quantity, size, and so on. A notional syllabus often goes hand in hand with a functional syllabus.

**outcomes-based education (OBE).** This sets out specific performance objectives for learners to attain by the end of their program. Learners are assessed on their performance in specified tasks. Outcomes for each field of learning will differ, and standards are set for each level. See Braskamp and Braskamp (1997).

**Output Hypothesis.** Swain (1985) believes that in addition to the Input Hypothesis, learners need to have opportunities themselves to speak and write in communicative situations in order to acquire the target language. "Pushed output" is when the learners perceive a need to be accurate and precise in their communication.

**PPP.** See *presentation–practice–production*.

**presentation–practice–production.** A teaching cycle in widespread use primarily in European and Latin American ESL and EFL programs for the explicit teaching of grammatical structures and realizations of functions and notions. It consists of three phases: (1) presentation (in which the new language item is illustrated and explained), (2) practice (an opportunity to drill or otherwise practice the new item in controlled situations), and (3) production (in which learners are encouraged to use the new language in free communication, for example, in a specific task or spontaneous role-play).

**prochievement test.** A test that is partially achievement and partially proficiency-oriented. Typically, such a test might include authentic materials that students have not seen before on topics that they have studied.

**SLA.** An acronym used to refer to Second Language Acquisition.

**SLAR.** An acronym that is sometimes used in the United States to denote SLA Research.

**task-based instruction (TBI).** In the United States, this term is used in free variation with task-based learning and in some educational contexts is the preferred variant (Canale 1983.)

**task-based learning (TBL).** In Europe, and other countries, this term is preferred to TBI. For example, Prabhu (1987) and Ellis (2003) use the terms *task-based learning* and *task-based teaching,* depending on whether the focus is on the learning or the teaching. Note that the term TBLT stands for task-based language teaching.

**teacher development.** In Europe, this term is used in the same way that *teacher self-development* is used in the United States.

**teacher self-development.** In the United States, this term is used to refer to teachers' efforts to improve their own knowledge and skills, usually with little assistance from a professor or other kind of faculty developer.

**teacher training.** See *faculty development*. In Europe, this term is used in the same way as "faculty development" is in the United States. It generally refers to sessions or courses led by a trainer, as opposed to *teacher development*, where teachers work or study on their own in or groups (but with little direct intervention from a trainer or an instructor) to reflect on and improve the way they teach and thus to raise their professional standards. In the United States, the term *teacher training* is usually avoided because it can be considered condescending.

# Appendix: Multiscale
## Proficiency Descriptors

This appendix contains descriptions of the levels contained in the two language proficiency scales referred to by the various chapter authors. More information can be found from the organizations that have promulgated these scales, the Interagency Language Roundtable (ILR), whose scale is mainly applied to U.S. government personnel, and the American Council on Teaching Foreign Languages (ACTFL), whose scale is principally used in schools and postsecondary educational institutions.

## I. Test Bands for the ILR Proficiency Scale

*Note:* This is a summary taken from the ILR Web site, http://www.govtilr.org.

### LISTENING COMPREHENSION DESCRIPTIONS

**Listening 0 (No Proficiency)**

No practical understanding of the spoken language. Understanding is limited to occasional isolated words with essentially no ability to comprehend communication.

**Listening 0+ (Memorized Proficiency)**

Sufficient comprehension to understand a number of memorized utterances in areas of immediate needs. Can understand only with difficulty even persons such as teachers who are used to speaking with nonnative speakers. Can understand best those statements where context strongly supports the utterance's meaning.

**Listening 1 (Elementary Proficiency)**

Sufficient comprehension to understand utterances about basic survival needs and minimum courtesy and travel requirements. In areas of immediate need or on very familiar topics, can understand simple questions and answers, simple statements, and very simple face-to-face conversations in a standard dialect. Understands main ideas.

**Listening 1+ (Elementary Proficiency, Plus)**

Sufficient comprehension to understand short conversations about all survival needs and limited social demands but limited vocabulary range necessitates repetition. Understands common time forms and most question forms, some word order patterns, but miscommunication still occurs with more complex patterns.

### Listening 2 (Limited Working Proficiency)

Sufficient comprehension to understand conversations on routine social de-mands and limited job requirements, also face-to-face speech in a standard dia-lect, delivered at a normal rate with some repetition and rewording, by a native speaker not used to dealing with foreigners, about everyday topics, common per-sonal and family news, well-known current events, and routine office matters through descriptions and narration about current, past, and future events; can fol-low essential points of discussion or speech at an elementary level on topics in his/her special professional field.

### Listening 2+ (Limited Working Proficiency, Plus)

Sufficient comprehension to understand most routine social demands and most conversations on work requirements as well as some discussions on concrete top-ics related to particular interests and special fields of competence. Often shows re-markable ability and ease of understanding, but under tension or pressure may break down. Normally understands general vocabulary.

### Listening 3 (General Professional Proficiency)

Able to understand the essentials of all speech in a standard dialect, including technical discussions within a special field. Has effective understanding of face-to-face speech, delivered with normal clarity and speed in a standard dialect, on general topics and areas of special interest; understands hypothesizing and supported opinions. Can follow accurately the essentials of conversations be-tween educated native speakers, reasonably clear telephone calls, radio broad-casts, news stories similar to wire service reports, oral reports, some oral technical reports, and public addresses on nontechnical subjects; including all forms of standard speech concerning a special professional field.

### Listening 3+ (General Professional Proficiency, Plus)

Comprehends most of the content and intent of a variety of forms and styles of speech pertinent to professional needs, general topics and social conversation, to-gether with many sociolinguistic and cultural references. However, may miss some subtleties and nuances.

### Listening 4 (Advanced Professional Proficiency)

Able to understand all forms and styles of speech pertinent to professional needs, even with extensive and precise vocabulary, subtleties, and nuances, in all stan-dard dialects on any subject relevant to professional needs, including social con-versations; all intelligible broadcasts and telephone calls; and many kinds of technical discussions and discourse. Understands language specifically tailored (including persuasion, representation, counseling, and negotiating) to different audiences, and the essentials of speech in some nonstandard dialects.

### Listening 4+ (Advanced Professional Proficiency, Plus)

Increased ability to understand extremely difficult and abstract speech including all forms and styles of speech pertinent to social and professional needs. Increased ability to comprehend native speakers using extreme nonstandard dialects and slang, and speech in unfavorable conditions. Strong sensitivity to sociolinguistic and cultural references. Accuracy is close to that of the well-educated native listener but still not equivalent.

### Listening 5 (Functionally Native Proficiency)

Comprehension equivalent to that of the well-educated native listener. Able to understand fully all forms and styles of speech intelligible to the well-educated native listener, including a number of regional and illiterate dialects, highly colloquial speech, extremely difficult and abstract speech, and speech, distorted by marked interference from other noise. Able to understand how natives think as they create discourse.

### READING COMPREHENSION DESCRIPTIONS

### Reading 0+ (Memorized Proficiency)

Can recognize all the letters in the printed version of an alphabetic system and high-frequency elements of a syllabary or a character system. Able to read some or all of the following: numbers, isolated words and phrases, personal and place names, street signs, office and shop designations.

### Reading 1 (Elementary Proficiency)

Sufficient comprehension to read very simple connected written material in a form equivalent to usual printing or typescript. Can read either representations of familiar formulaic verbal exchanges or simple language containing only the highest frequency structural patterns and vocabulary. Can identify general subject matter in some authentic texts.

### Reading 1+ (Elementary Proficiency, Plus)

Sufficient comprehension to understand simple discourse in printed form for informative social purposes. Can read material such as announcements of public events, simple prose containing biographical information or narration of events, and straightforward newspaper headlines. Can guess at unfamiliar vocabulary if highly contextualized, but with difficulty in unfamiliar contexts.

### Reading 2 (Limited Working Proficiency)

Sufficient comprehension to read simple, authentic written material in a form equivalent to usual printing or typescript on subjects within a familiar context. Able to read with some misunderstandings straightforward, familiar, factual material, but in general insufficiently experienced with the language to draw inferences directly from the linguistic aspects of the text. Can locate and understand the main ideas and details in material written for the general reader.

### Reading 2+ (Limited Working Proficiency, Plus)

Sufficient comprehension to understand most factual material in nontechnical prose as well as some discussions on concrete topics related to special professional interests. Is markedly more proficient at reading materials on a familiar topic. Is able to use linguistic context and real-world knowledge to make sensible guesses about unfamiliar material.

### Reading 3 (General Professional Proficiency)

Able to read within a normal range of speed and with almost complete comprehension a variety of authentic prose material on unfamiliar subjects. Reading ability is not dependent on subject matter knowledge, although some cultural knowledge may be outside his/her general experience. Almost always able to interpret material correctly, relate ideas, and "read between the lines."

### Reading 3+ (General Professional Proficiency, Plus)

Can comprehend a variety of styles and forms pertinent to professional needs. Able to comprehend many sociolinguistic and cultural references. Able to read with facility, understand, and appreciate contemporary expository, technical, or literary texts that do not rely heavily on slang and unusual idioms.

### Reading 4 (Advanced Professional Proficiency)

Able to read fluently and accurately all styles and forms of the language pertinent to professional needs, can relate inferences in the text to real-world knowledge and understand almost all sociolinguistic and cultural references. Able to "read beyond the lines" (i.e., to understand the full ramifications of texts as they are situated in the wider cultural, political, or social environment). Can follow unpredictable turns of thoughts readily in, for example, editorials, conjectural, and literary texts in any subject matter area directed to the general reader.

### Reading 4+ (Advanced Professional Proficiency, Plus)

Near native ability to read and understand extremely difficult or abstract prose, a very wide variety of vocabulary, idioms, colloquialisms, and slang. Strong sensitivity to sociolinguistic and cultural references. Little difficulty in reading less than fully legible handwriting. Accuracy is close to that of the well-educated native reader, but not equivalent.

### Reading 5 (Functionally Native Proficiency)

Reading proficiency is functionally equivalent to that of the well-educated native reader. Can read extremely difficult and abstract prose, for example, general legal and technical as well as highly colloquial writings. Accuracy of comprehension is equivalent to that of a well-educated native reader.

Multiscale Proficiency Descriptors

### SPEAKING PROFICIENCY DESCRIPTIONS

### Speaking 0 (No Proficiency)

Unable to function in the spoken language.

### Speaking 0+ (Memorized Proficiency)

Able to satisfy immediate needs using rehearsed utterances. Shows little real autonomy of expression, flexibility, or spontaneity.

### Speaking 1 (Elementary Proficiency)

Able to satisfy minimum courtesy requirements and maintain very simple face-to-face conversations on familiar topics. The native speaker must strain and employ real-world knowledge to understand even simple statements/questions from this individual.

### Speaking 1+ (Elementary Proficiency, Plus)

Can initiate and maintain predictable face-to-face conversations and satisfy limited social demands. The speaker at this level may hesitate and may have to change subjects due to lack of language resources. Speech largely consists of a series of short, discrete utterances.

### Speaking 2 (Limited Working Proficiency)

Able to satisfy routine social demands and limited work requirements. Can handle with confidence, but not with facility, most normal, high-frequency social conversational situations including extensive but casual conversations about current events, as well as work, family, and autobiographical information.

### Speaking 2+ (Limited Working Proficiency, Plus)

Able to satisfy most work requirements with language usage that is often, but not always, acceptable and effective. Shows considerable ability to communicate effectively on topics relating to particular interests and special fields of competence. Native speakers often perceive the individual's speech to contain awkward or inaccurate phrasing of ideas, mistaken time, space, and person references, or to be in some way inappropriate, if not strictly incorrect.

### Speaking 3 (General Professional Proficiency)

Able to speak the language with sufficient structural accuracy and vocabulary to participate effectively in most formal and informal conversations on practical, social, and professional topics of shared knowledge and/or international convention. Discourse is cohesive. Errors virtually never interfere with understanding. Speaks readily and fills pauses suitably. Pronunciation may be obviously foreign.

### Speaking 3+ (General Professional Proficiency, Plus)

Is often able to use the language to satisfy professional needs in a wide range of sophisticated and demanding tasks. Despite obvious strengths, may exhibit some hesitancy, uncertainty, effort, or errors that limit range of language-use tasks that can be reliably performed.

### Speaking 4 (Advanced Professional Proficiency)

Speaks effortlessly and smoothly and is able to use the language with a high degree of effectiveness, reliability, and precision for all representational purposes within the range of personal and professional experience and scope of responsibilities. Can serve as an informal interpreter in a range of unpredictable circumstances. However, would not be mistaken for a native speaker.

### Speaking 4+ (Advanced Professional Proficiency, Plus)

Speaking proficiency is usually equivalent to that of a well-educated, highly articulate native speaker. Language ability does not impede the performance of any language-use task. However, may not be perceived as culturally native.

### Speaking 5 (Functionally Native Proficiency)

Speaking proficiency is functionally equivalent to that of a highly articulate well-educated native speaker and reflects the cultural standards of the country where the language is natively spoken. Pronunciation is typically consistent with that of well-educated native speakers of a nonstigmatized dialect.

### WRITING PROFICIENCY DESCRIPTIONS

### Writing 0 (No Proficiency)

No functional writing ability.

### Writing 0+ (Memorized Proficiency)

Writes using memorized material and set expressions. Can produce symbols in an alphabetic or syllabic writing system or fifty of the most common characters and write simple lists of common items. Spelling and even representation of symbols (letters, syllables, characters) may be incorrect.

### Writing 1 (Elementary Proficiency)

Has sufficient control of the writing system to meet limited practical needs. Can create by writing statements and questions on very familiar topics. Writing vocabulary is inadequate to express anything but elementary needs.

### Writing 1+ (Elementary Proficiency, Plus)

Sufficient control of writing system to meet most survival needs and limited social demands. Generally cannot use basic cohesive elements of discourse to advantage. Writing, though faulty, is comprehensible to native speakers used to dealing with foreigners.

## Writing 2 (Limited Working Proficiency)

Able to write routine social correspondence and prepare documentary materials required for most limited work requirements. Can write simply about a very limited number of current events or daily situations. Uses a limited number of cohesive devices. Writing is understandable to a native reader not used to reading the writing of foreigners.

## Writing 2+ (Limited Working Proficiency, Plus)

Shows ability to write with some precision about most common topics and those relating to particular interests and special fields of competence. Often shows surprising fluency and ease of expression, but under time constraints and pressure language may be inaccurate and/or incomprehensible. Style is obviously foreign.

## Writing 3 (General Professional Proficiency)

Able to use the language effectively in most formal and informal written exchanges on practical, social, and professional topics. Control of structure, spelling, and general vocabulary is adequate to convey his/her message accurately, but style may be obviously foreign. Errors virtually never interfere with comprehension and rarely disturb the native reader.

## Writing 3+ (General Professional Proficiency, Plus)

Able to write the language in a few prose styles pertinent to professional/educational needs. Not always able to tailor language to suit audience. Organization may suffer due to lack of variety in organizational patterns or in variety of cohesive devices.

## Writing 4 (Advanced Professional Proficiency)

Able to write the language precisely and accurately in a variety of prose styles pertinent to professional / educational needs. Consistently able to tailor language to suit audience, to express subtleties and nuances. Uses a wide variety of organizational patterns and cohesive devices such as ellipsis and parallelisms, and subordinates in a number of ways. Writing adequate to express all his/her experiences.

## Writing 4+ (Advanced Professional Proficiency, Plus)

As above. May also have some ability to edit but not in the full range of styles. Has some flexibility within a style and shows some evidence of a use of stylistic devices.

## Writing 5 (Functionally Native Proficiency)

Has writing proficiency equal to that of a well-educated native, employing a very wide range of stylistic devices. In addition to being clear, explicit, and informative, the writing and the ideas are also imaginative.

## II. The ACTFL Proficiency Scale Levels

The descriptions below are provided with permission of the American Council on the Teaching of Foreign Languages (ACTFL). Revised ACTFL Proficiency Guidelines currently exist for Speaking (Revised 1999) and Writing (Revised 2001). The original (1986) ACTFL Proficiency Guidelines for Reading and Listening are currently under revision. The speaking guidelines, referred to by chapter authors, are below. *Note*: Each level is divided into low, mid, and high. *Source*: ACTFL Web site (http://www.actfl.org), where the writing guidelines can be found.

### SUPERIOR LEVEL

Superior-level speakers are characterized by the ability to participate fully and effectively in conversations in formal and informal settings on topics related to practical needs and areas of professional and/or scholarly interest; provide a structured argument to explain and defend opinions and develop effective hypotheses within extended discourse; discuss topics concretely and abstractly; deal with a linguistically unfamiliar situation; maintain a high degree of linguistic accuracy; and satisfy the linguistic demands of professional/scholarly life.

### ADVANCED LEVEL

Advanced-level speakers are characterized by the ability to participate actively in conversations in most informal and some formal settings on topics of personal and public interest; narrate and describe in major frames of time with good control of aspect; deal effectively with unanticipated complications through a variety of communicative devices; sustain communication by using, with suitable accuracy and confidence, connected discourse of paragraph length and substance; and satisfy the demands of work/school situations.

### INTERMEDIATE LEVEL

Intermediate-level speakers are characterized by the ability to participate in simple, direct conversations on generally predictable topics related to daily activities and personal environment; create with the language and create personal meaning to sympathetic interlocutors by combining language elements in discrete sentences and strings of sentences; obtain and give information by asking and answering questions; sustain and bring to a close a number of basic, uncomplicated communicative exchanges, often in a reactive mode; and satisfy simple personal needs and social demands to survive in the target language culture.

### NOVICE LEVEL

Novice-level speakers are characterized by the ability to respond to simple questions on the most common features of daily life; convey minimal meaning to interlocutors experienced in dealing with foreigners by using isolated words, lists of words, memorized phrases, and some personalized recombinations of words and phrases; and satisfy a very limited number of immediate needs.

# References and
# Bibliography

ACTFL (American Council on Teaching Foreign Languages). 1999a. *Proficiency guidelines*. Hastings-on-Hudson, N.Y.: ACTFL.

———. 1999b. *Standards for foreign language learning in the 21st century*. N.p.: Allen Press, Inc.

Al Othman, B. 2003a. *How participation in a CoP informs and influences personal teaching*. www.geocities.com/esl_efl_ku/.

———. 2003b. *Why am I still here? Things I learned from WIA*. www.geocities.com /esl_efl_ku/thingsilearned_wia.htm.

Allen, E., E. Bernhardt, M. Berry, and M. Demel. 1988. Comprehension and text genre: An analysis of secondary school foreign language readers. *Modern Language Journal* 72: 163–72.

Alliance by Design. 2002. www.ecsel.psu.edu/alliance/projects.html#edg98.

Almeida d'Eça, T. 2003. *Index of "Webheads in Action" web pages and related sites*. www.malhatlantica.pt/teresadeca/webheads/wia-index.htm.

Almeida Filho, J. C. P. 2002. *Ontem e hoje no ensino de línguas no Brasil*. Unpublished manuscript.

Alosh, M. Mahdi. 1984. Implications of the use of Modern Standard Arabic in the Arabic adaptation of "Sesame Street." Unpublished master's degree thesis, Ohio University, Athens.

———. 1987. Perception and acquisition of pharyngealized fricatives by American learners of Arabic and implications for teaching Arabic phonology. Ph.D. diss., Ohio State University.

———. 1989. *Ahlan wa Sahlan, Part I, Teacher's manual*. Columbus: Ohio State Foreign Language Publications.

———. 1989–91. *Ahlan wa Sahlan, Parts I-III*. Columbus: Columbus: Ohio State Foreign Language Publications.

———. 1991. Arabic diglossia and its impact on teaching Arabic as a foreign language. In *ACTFL review of foreign language education: International perspectives on foreign language teaching*, ed. G. Ervin. Yonkers, N.Y.: American Council on Teaching Foreign Languages.

———. 1992a. Designing a proficiency-oriented syllabus for Modern Standard Arabic as a foreign language. In *The Arabic Language in America*, ed. A. Rouchdy. Detroit: Wayne State University Press.

———. 1992b. *Intermediate Arabic, Parts 1 and 2*. Columbus: Ohio State Foreign Language Publications.

———. 1996. *Modern Arabic reader*. Columbus: Ohio State Foreign Language Publications.

———. 1997. *Learner, text and context: An Arabic perspective*. Columbus: National Foreign Language Resource Center.

———. 1999. *Arabic selections*. Columbus: Ohio State Foreign Language Publications.

————. 2000a. *Ahlan wa Sahlan: Functional Modern Standard Arabic.* New Haven, Conn.: Yale University Press.

————. 2000b. *Ahlan wa Sahlan: Teacher's handbook.* New Haven, Conn.: Yale University Press.

————. 2000c. *Arabic composition.* Columbus: Ohio State Foreign Language Publications.

Austin, J. L. 1962. *How to do things with words.* London: Oxford University Press.

Aytan, L. 1994. Why do Orta 1 students have problems studying science through the medium of English at the Özel Izmir Amerikan Lisesi? M.S. in teaching English for special programs diss., Aston University, U.K.

Bachman L. F. 1990. *Fundamental considerations in language testing.* Oxford: Oxford University Press.

Bachman, Lyle F., and A. S. Palmer. 1996. *Language testing in practice.* Oxford: Oxford University Press.

Bicknell, J. 1998. *CMC case study.* www.homestead.com/prosites-vstevens/files/efi/bicknell.html.

Bloom, Benjamin S. 1956. *Taxonomy of educational objectives: Handbook 1, Cognitive domain.* New York: McKay.

Bloomfield, L. 1942. *Outline guide for the practical study of foreign languages.* Baltimore: Linguistic Society of America.

Bolinger, D. 1975. Meaning and memory. *Forum Linguisticum* 1: 2–14.

Bonk, C., and D. Cunningham. 1998. Searching for learner-centered, constructivist, and sociocultural components of collaborative educational learning tools. In *Electronic Collaborators: Learner-centered technologies for literacy, apprenticeship, and discourse,* ed. C. Bonk and K. King. Mahwah, N.J.: Lawrence Erlbaum Associates.

Bowen, T. 2002. Task based learning. *Onestop Magazine.* www.onestopenglish.com/News/Magazine/Archive/taskbased.htm

Braskamp, L. A., and D. Braskamp. 1997. The pendulum swing of standards and evidence. *CHEA Chronicle* (July): 8.

Brecht, Richard D., and William P. Rivers. 2000. *Language and national security in the 21st century.* Washington, D.C.: Kendall Hunt and National Foreign Language Center.

Breen, M. P., and Christopher N. Candlin. 1980. The essentials of a communicative curriculum for language teaching. *Applied Linguistics* 1, no. 2: 89–112.

Britten, D. 1985. Teacher training in ELT: Part 1. *Language teaching* 18: 112–28.

Brown, H. Douglas. 1994. *Teaching by principles: An interactive approach to language pedagogy.* Upper Saddle River, N.J.: Prentice Hall Regents.

Brown, James S., A. Collins, and P. Duguid. 1989. Situated cognition and the culture of learning. *Educational Researcher* 18, no. 1: 32–42.

Brumfit, C. J. 1984. *Communicative methodology in language teaching.* Cambridge: Cambridge University Press.

Bygate, Martin. 1987. *Speaking.* Oxford: Oxford University Press.

————. 2001. Effects of task repetition on the structure and control of oral language. In *Researching pedagogic tasks: Second language learning, teaching and testing.* Harlow, U.K.: Longman Pearson Education.

California Foreign Language Project. 1993. *The classroom oral competency interview (COCI).* Stanford, Calif.: Stanford University Press.

————. 1996. *The classroom writing competency assessment (CWCA).* Stanford, Calif.: Stanford University Press.

California State University. 1989. *Student outcomes assessment in the California State University: Report of the California State University Advisory Committee on Student Outcomes Assessment.* Long Beach: California State University Office of the Chancellor.

Canale, Michael. 1983. Personal communication with Betty Lou Leaver, March.

Canale, Michael, and Merrill Swain. 1980. Theoretical bases of communicative approaches to second language teaching and testing. *Applied Linguistics* 1, no. 1: 1–47.

Candlin, Christopher N. 2001. Afterword: Taking the curriculum to task. In *Researching pedagogic task: Second language learning, teaching, and testing*, ed. Martin Bygate, Peter Skehan, and Merrill Swain. Harlow, U.K.: Longman Pearson Education.

Carr, T., and T. Curren. 1994. Cognitive factors in learning about structured sequences: Application to Syntax. *Studies in Second Language Acquisition* 16, no. 20: 5–30.

Carroll, J. B. 1975. *The teaching of French as a foreign language in eight different countries.* New York: John Wiley and Sons.

Carson, J. G. 1996. Cognitive perspectives on reading/writing relationships. Paper presented at the 1996 Groupe d'Etudes et de Recherches en Anglais de Specialité conference, Aix-en-Provence, France.

Carter, R. 2001. Vocabulary. In *The Cambridge guide to teaching English to speakers of other languages*, ed. R. Carter and David Nunan. Cambridge: Cambridge University Press.

Child, J. 1987. Language proficiency levels and the typology of texts. In *Defining and developing proficiency: Guidelines, implementations, and concepts*, ed. Heidi Byrnes and Michael Canale. New York: NTC / Contemporary Publishing.

Chomsky, Noam. 1959. Review of *Verbal Behaviour* by B. F. Skinner. *Language* 35: 26–58.

Coghlan, M. 2000. An online learning community: The students' perspective. www.chariot.net.au/~michaelc/TCC2000.htm.

Corder, S. P. 1981. *Error analysis and interlanguage.* Oxford: Oxford University Press.

———. 1967. The significance of learners' errors. *International Review of Applied Linguistics* 5: 161–170. Reprinted in S. P. Corder, *Error analysis and interlanguage* (Oxford: Oxford University Press, 1981).

Corin, Andrew. 1997. A course to convert Czech proficiency to proficiency in Serbian and Croatian. In *Content-based instruction in foreign language education: Models and methods*, ed. Stephen B. Stryker and Betty Lou Leaver. Washington, D.C.: Georgetown University Press.

Cox, D. 2005. Can we predict language items for open tasks? In *Teachers exploring tasks in English language teaching*, ed. C. Edwards and Jane Willis. Basingstoke, U.K.: Palgrave Macmillan.

Crocetti, María Maritno. 2003. Teaching and testing. Paper presented at Paths to Advanced Proficiency conference, Yale University, New Haven, Conn.

Crookes, Graham, and Susan Gass, eds. 1993a. *Tasks and language learning: Integrating theory and practice.* Clevedon, U.K.: Multilingual Matters.

———. 1993b. *Tasks in a pedagogical context: Integrating theory and practice.* Clevedon, U.K.: Multilingual Matters.

Cunningham, P., and S. Moor. 1996–99. *Cutting edge.* Reading, Mass.: Addison Wesley Longman.

Curriculum Development Council of Hong Kong. 1999. Task based learning. Revised CDC secondary English language syllabus (draft). www.cdc.org.hk/english/taskbase.html.

Davis, Robert L. 1997. Group work is not busy work: Maximizing success of group work in the L2 classroom. *Foreign Language Annals* 30, no. 2: 265–79.

Defense Language Institute. 1999. *Interagency Language Roundtable skill level descriptors.* www.dli.army.mil.

Dinou, L. N.d. A new approach to course design: Task based learning. *TESOL Greece Newsletter.* www.tesolgreece.com/dinou01.html.

Djapoura, A. 2005. The effects of pre-task planning time on task performance. In *Teachers exploring tasks in English language teaching,* ed. C. Edwards and Jane Willis. Basingstoke, U.K.: Palgrave Macmillan.

Doughty, Catherine. 2001. Cognitive underpinnings of focus on form. In *Cognition and second language instruction,* ed. P. Robinson. Cambridge: Cambridge University Press.

Doughty, Catherine D., and E. Varela. 1998. Communicative focus on form. In *Focus on form in classroom second language acquisition,* ed. Catherine Doughty and Jessica Williams. Cambridge: Cambridge University Press.

Doughty, Catherine D., and Jessica Williams, eds. 1998. *Focus on form in classroom second language acquisition.* Cambridge: Cambridge University Press.

Duff, P. 1986. Another look at interlanguage talk: Taking task to task. In *Talking to learn: Conversation in second language acquisition,* ed. R. Day. Rowley, Mass.: Newbury House.

———. 1993. Tasks and interlanguage performance: A second language acquisition research perspective. In *Tasks in language learning: Integrating theory and practice,* ed. Graham Crookes and Susan Gass. Clevedon, U.K.: Multilingual Matters.

Dulay, H., and M. Burt. 1973. Should we teach children syntax? *Language Learning* 23: 245–58.

———. 1974. You can't learn without goofing. In *Error analysis,* ed. Jack C. Richards. London: Longman.

Duri, Jane. 1992. Content-based instruction: Keeping DLI on the cutting edge. *The Globe* 5: 4–5.

Edwards, A. 1996. Reading proficiency assessment and the ILR/ACTFL Text typology: A reevaluation. *Modern Language Journal* 80, no. 3: 350–61.

Edwards, Corony, and Jane Willis, eds. 2005. *Teachers exploring tasks in English language teaching.* Basingstoke, U.K.: Palgrave Macmillan.

Ehrman, Madeline E. 2001. Bringing learning strategies to the learner: The FSI Language Learning Consultation Service. In *Language in our time: Bilingual education and Official English, Ebonics and Standard English, immigration and the Unz Initiative,* ed. James E. Alatis and J. Tan. Washington, D.C.: Georgetown University Press.

———. 2002. Understanding the student at the superior-distinguished threshold. In *Developing professional-level language proficiency,* ed. Betty Lou Leaver and Boris Shekhtman. Cambridge: Cambridge University Press.

Ehrman, Madeline E., and Zoltan Dornyei. 1998. *Interpersonal dynamics in second language acquisition instruction: The visible and invisible classroom.* Thousand Oaks, Calif.: Sage Publications.

Ellis, N. 1997. Vocabulary acquisition: Word structure, collocation, word class and meaning. In *Vocabulary: Description, Acquisition and Pedagogy,* ed. N. Schmitt and M. McCarthy. Cambridge: Cambridge University Press.

Ellis, Rod. 1985. *Understanding second language acquisition.* Oxford: Oxford University Press.

———. 1994. *The study of second language acquisition.* Oxford: Oxford University Press.

———. 2002. The place of grammar instruction in the second/foreign language curriculum. In *New perspectives on grammar teaching in second language classrooms*, ed. E. Hinkel and S. Fotos. Mahwah, N.J.: Lawrence Erlbaum Associates.

———. 2003. *Task-based language learning and teaching.* Oxford: Oxford University Press.

Ervin, Gerard. 1988. Purposeful practice with the four-by-six card: Quick, convenient, and communicative. *Foreign Language Annals* 21, no. 4: 337–39.

Eskey, D. E. 1997. Syllabus design in content-based instruction. In *The content-based classroom: Perspectives on integrating language and content*, ed. Marguerite Ann Snow and Donna M. Brinton. New York: Longman.

Essig, W. 2005. Story-telling: Effects of planning, repetition and context. In *Teachers exploring tasks in English language teaching*, ed. C. Edwards and Jane Willis. Basingstoke, U.K.: Palgrave Macmillan.

Estaire, S., and J. Zanon. 1994. *Planning classwork: A task-based approach.* Oxford: Heinemann.

Ferguson, Charles A. 1959. Diglossia. *Word* 15: 325–40.

Foster, P., and Peter Skehan. 1996. The influence of planning on performance in task-based learning. *Studies in Second Language Acquisition* 18, no. 3: 299–324.

Freed, A. 2003. *Webheads in Action (WiA): Database of 2002 discussion topics with Llinks to Yahoo group messages, ancillary materials, and artifacts.* www.eslhome.com /cop2003/db.htm.

Funke, Renata. 1995. *Task-based instruction for French: Nine sample lessons.* Salinas, Calif.: AGSI Press.

Gallagher, C. N.d. *Lev Semyonovich Vygotsky (1896–1934): Biography, theory, time line, bibliography.* http://fates.cns.muskingum.edu/~psych/psycweb/history/vygotsky .htm.

García Márquez, Gabriel. 1996. *Noticia de un crimen.* Bogotá: Grupo editorial Noma.

Garrett, Nina. 1991. Theoretical and pedagogical problems of separating "grammar" from "communication." In *Foreign language acquisition research and the classroom*, ed. Barbara F. Freed. Lexington, Mass.: D. C. Heath.

Gass, S. M. 2003. Input and interaction. In *The handbook of second language acquisition*, ed. C. Doughty and M. H. Long. Malden, Mass.: Blackwell.

Gass, S., and E. Varonis. 1994. Input, interaction, and second language production. *Studies in Second Language Acquisition* 16: 283–302.

Gibbons, P. 2002. *Scaffolding language: Scaffolding learning.* Portsmouth, U.K.: Heinemann.

Gonzales, D. 2003. Webheads in EVOnline 2003, week 5. http://dygonza.esmartweb .com/evonline2003/week5/w5p1.htm.

Goodison, R. A. C. 1987. *Language training and language use—The uncertain connection.* Arlington, Va.: U.S. Foreign Service Institute.

Goroshko, Natalia. 1995. *Content-based instruction in Russian: Ten sample lessons.* Salinas, Calif.: AGSI Press.

Goroskho, Natalia, and Leonid Slutsky. 1999. Four-handed instruction. In *Twelve years of dialogue on teaching Russian*, ed. Betty Lou Leaver. Washington, D.C.: ACTR/ACCELS Publications.

Grice, H. P. 1975. Logic and conversation. In *Syntax and semantics III: Speech acts*, ed. P. Cole and J. L. Morgan. New York: Academic Press.

Guéhenno, Jean-Marie. 1995. *The end of the nation-state.* Trans. Victoria Elliot. Minneapolis: University of Minnesota Press.

Halliday, M. A. K. 1973. *Explorations in the functions of language.* London: Edward Arnold.

————. 1975. *Learning how to mean.* London: Edward Arnold.

Hammond, Jennifer, ed. 2001. Scaffolding: teaching and learning in language and literacy education. Newtown, Australia: Primary English Teaching Association.

Hancock, Charles R., and C. Edward Scebold. 2000. Defining moments in foreign and second language education during the last half of the twentieth century. In *Reflecting on the past to shape the future,* ed. Diane W. Birchbickler and Robert M. Terry. Lincoln, Ill.: National Textbook Co.

Harley, B., and Merrill Swain. 1984. The interlanguage of immersion students and its implications for second language teaching. In *Interlanguage,* ed. A. Davies, C. Criper, and A. Howatt. Edinburgh: Edinburgh University Press.

Harlow, Linda. 1998. Teaching language as communication. A lecture given at the Combined Graduate Teaching Assistants Training Course at Ohio State University, Columbus.

Hidi, S., and V. Anderson. 1992. Situational interest and its impact on reading and expository writing. In *The role of interest in learning and development,* ed. K. A. Renninger, S. Hidi, and A. Krapp. Hillsdale, N.J.: Lawrence Erlbaum.

Higgs, T. V., and R. T. Clifford. 1982. The push toward communication. In *Curriculum, competence, and the foreign language teacher,* ed. T. V. Higgs. Lincolnwood, Ill.: National Textbook Co.

Howatt, A. P. R. 1984. *A history of English language teaching.* Oxford: Oxford University Press.

Hunston, S., and G. Francis. 2000. *Pattern grammar: A corpus-driven approach to the lexical grammar of English.* Philadelphia: John Benjamins.

Hunston, S., G. Francis, and E. Manning. 1997. Grammar and vocabulary: Showing the connections. *ELT Journal* 51, no. 3: 208–16.

Hymes, Del. 1972. On communicative competence. In *Sociolinguistics,* ed. J. B. Pride and J. Holmes. Harmondsworth, U.K.: Penguin Books.

————. 1977. *Foundations in sociolinguistics: An ethnographic approach.* London: Tavistock.

Jennings, K., and T. Doyle. 1996. Curriculum innovation, team-work and the management of change. In *Challenge and change in language teaching,* ed. J. Willis and D. Willis. Oxford: Heinemann Macmillan.

Johnson, K. 1982. *Communicative syllabus design and methodology.* Oxford: Pergamon.

Johnston, C. 2005. Fighting fossilization: Language at different stages in the task cycle. In *Teachers exploring tasks in English language teaching,* ed. C. Edwards and Jane Willis. Basingstoke, U.K.: Palgrave Macmillan.

Kearsley, G. 2002. *Constructivist theory (J. Bruner). Explorations in learning and instruction: The theory into practice database.* http://tip.psychology.org/bruner.html.

Kirkgoz, Y. 1993. A conceptual framework for a proposed academic reading syllabus based on the computerised analysis of economic texts. Master's in teaching English for special purposes diss., Aston University, U.K.

Knowles, Malcolm. 1990. *The adult learner.* Houston: Gulf.

Knutson, Elizabeth M. 1998. *Reading with a purpose: Communicative reading tasks for the foreign language classroom.* Washington, D.C.: ERIC Digest Clearinghouse on Languages and Linguistics.

Krashen, Stephen. 1982. *Principles and practice in second language acquisition*. Oxford: Pergamon.

———. 1985. *The Input Hypothesis*. London: Longman.

Krashen, Stephen, and Tracy Terrell. 1983. *The natural approach*. Oxford: Pergamon and Alemany Press.

Kubota, R. 1999. Word processing and www projects in a college Japanese language class. *Foreign Language Annals* 32, no. 2: 205–18.

Kuhn-Osius, K. E. 2001. Professionalizing: Foreign languages, the working world, and the standards. In *Beyond the boundaries: Changing contexts in language learning*, ed. Roberta Z. Lavine. New York: McGraw Hill.

Labov, William. 1972a. *Language in the inner city*. Philadelphia: University of Pennsylvania Press.

———. 1972b. *Languages across cultures*. Ann Arbor: University of Michigan Press.

Lado, R. 1957a. *Linguistics*. Oxford: Pergamon.

———. 1957b. *Linguistics across cultures*. Ann Arbor: University of Michigan Press.

———. 1964. *Language teaching: A scientific approach*. New York: McGraw Hill.

Lakoff, G., and M. Johnson. 1980. *Metaphors we live by*. Chicago: University of Chicago Press.

Lange, Dale L. 1990. A blueprint for a teacher development program. In *Second language teacher education*, ed. J. C. Richards and D. Nunan. Cambridge: Cambridge University Press.

Larsen-Freeman, Diane. 1983. Training teachers or educating a teacher. In *Applied linguistics and the preparation of second language teachers: Toward a rationale*, ed. Jack C. Richards and David Nunan. Washington, D.C.: Georgetown University Press.

———. 2000. *Techniques and principles in language teaching*. Oxford: Oxford University Press.

Lazar, G. 1993. *Literature and language teaching*. Cambridge: Cambridge University Press.

Leaver, Betty Lou. 1997. Content-based instruction in a basic Russian program. In *Content-based instruction in foreign language education: Models and methods*, ed. Stephen B. Stryker and Betty Lou Leaver. Washington, D.C.: Georgetown University Press.

———. 1998. *Teaching the whole class*. Dubuque, Iowa: Kendall Hunt.

Leaver, Betty Lou, and Sabine Atwell. 2002. Preliminary qualitative findings from a study of the processes leading to the Advanced Professional Proficiency level (ILR4). In *Developing professional-level language proficiency*, ed. Betty Lou Leaver and Boris Shekhtman. Cambridge: Cambridge University Press.

Leaver, Betty Lou, and Paula M. Bilstein. 2000. Content, language, and task in content-based programs. In *Languages across the curriculum: Interdisciplinary structures and internationalized education*, ed. Regina-Maria Kecht and Katharina von Hammerstein. Columbus: Ohio State University Press.

Leaver, Betty Lou, and Boris Shekhtman. 2002. Principles and practices of teaching superior-level language proficiency: Not more of the same. In *Developing professional-level language proficiency*, ed. Betty Lou Leaver and Boris Shekhtman. Cambridge: Cambridge University Press.

Leaver, Betty Lou, and Stephen Stryker. 1989. Content-based instruction for foreign-language classrooms. *Foreign Language Annals* 22, no. 3: 269–75.

Leaver, Echo. 1999. Making the most of memory. In *Passport to the World: Learning to communicate in a foreign language*, ed. Betty Lou Leaver, Inna Dubinsky, and Melina Champine. San Diego: LARC Press.

Lee, J., and Diane Musumeci. 1988. On hierarchies of reading skills and text types. *Modern Language Journal* 72: 173–87.

Leedham, M. 2005. Exam-oriented tasks: transcripts, turn-taking and back-chanelling. In *Teachers exploring tasks in English language teaching*, ed. C. Edwards and Jane Willis. Basingstoke, U.K.: Palgrave Macmillan.

Legutke, M., and Thomas. 1991. *Process and experience in the language classroom.* Harlow, U.K.: Longman.

Lightbown, P. M. 1985. Great expectations: Second language acquisition research and classroom teaching. *Applied Linguistics* 6, no. 2: 173–89.

———. 2000. Classroom second language acquisition research and second language teaching. *Applied Linguistics* 21, no. 4: 431–62.

Lightbown, P., and N. Spada. 1999. *How languages are learned*, rev. ed. Oxford: Oxford University Press.

Littlewood, William. 1981. *Communicative language teaching: An introduction.* Cambridge: Cambridge University Press.

Liskin-Gasparro, Judith E. 1982. *ETS oral proficiency testing manual.* Princeton, N.J.: Educational Testing Service.

Long, Michael. 1976. Inside the black box. *Language Learning* 30, no. 1: 1–42.

———. 1983. Does second language instruction make a difference? *TESOL Quarterly* 17: 359–82.

———. 1985a. Input and second language acquisition theory. In *Input in second language acquisition*, ed. Susan Gass and C. Madden. Rowley, Mass.: Newbury House.

———. 1985b. A role for instruction in second language acquisition: Task-based language teaching. In *Modelling and assessing second language acquisition*, ed. by K. Hyltenstam and M. Pienemann. Clevedon, U.K.: Multilingual Matters.

———. 1989. Task, group and task-group interactions. *University of Hawaii Working Papers in ESL* 8: 1–26.

———. 1991. Focus on form: A design feature in language teaching methodology. In *Foreign language research in cross-cultural perspectives*, ed. K. de Bot, D. Coste, R. Ginsberg, and C. Kramsch. Amsterdam: John Benjamin.

———. 1996. The role of the linguistic environment in second language acquisition. In *Handbook of second language acquisition*, ed. W. Richie and T. Bhatia. San Diego: Academic Press.

———. 1999. Workshop handout on task-based instruction (unpublished photocopy distributed at ELT Conference, British Council, Bogotá).

Long, Michael H., and Graham Crookes. 1992. Three approaches to task-based syllabus design. *TESOL Quarterly* 26, no. 1: 27–56.

Long, Michael. H., and J. M. Norris. 2000. Task-based teaching and assessment. In *Encyclopedia of language teaching*, ed. M. Byram. London: Routledge.

Long, Michael H., and P. Porter. 1985. Groupwork, interlanguage talk and second language acquisition. *TESOL Quarterly* 19, no. 2: 207–27.

Long, Michael H., and Peter Robinson. 1998. Focus on form: Theory, research, and practice. In *Focus on form*, ed. C. Doughty and J. Williams. Cambridge: Cambridge University Press.

Lorenzini, E., and C. Ferman. 1988. *Estrategias discursivas.* Buenos Aires: Editorial Club de Estudio.

Lynch, Tony, and Joan MacLean. 2001. "A case of exercising": Effects of immediate task repetition on learners' performance. In *Researching pedagogical tasks: Second lan-*

guage learning, teaching and testing, ed. Martin Bygate, Peter Skehan, and Merrill M. Swain. Harlow, U.K.: Longman Pearson.

Lys, Franziska. 2000. Using technology to increase writing. In *Computer enhanced learning: Vignettes of the best practice from America's most wired campuses*, ed. David G. Brown. Bolton, Mass.: Anker Publishing Co.

Macías, Clemencia, and Bella Yerokhina. 1995. *Content-based instruction for Spanish: Eight sample lessons*. Salinas, Calif.: AGSI Press.

Mackey, A. 1999. Input, interaction, and second language development: An empirical study of question formation in ESL. *Studies in Second Language Acquisition* 21: 557–87.

Magnan, Sally S. 1991. Just do it: Directing TAs towards task-based and process-oriented testing. In *Assessing foreign language proficiency of undergraduates: Issues in language program direction*, ed. R. V. Teschner. Boston: Heinle and Heinle.

Maly, Eugene. 1993. Task-based instruction from the teacher's perspective. *Dialogue on Language Instruction* 9, no. 1: 37–48.

Martín Vivaldi, G. 1993. Géneros periodísticos. Madrid: Editorial Paraninfo.

Masso, A. 1999. *Diario de un cibernauta*, España. http://cibernauta.eldiariomontanes.es.

Mayadas, Frank. 2001. Testimony to the Kerrey Commission on Web-Based Education. *ALN* 5, no. 1.

McGee, L. G. 2001. Building community and posting projects: Creating "student pages" in web-based and web-enhanced courses. *Foreign Language Annals* 34, no. 6: 534–49.

McNamara, T. 2000. *Language testing*. Oxford: Oxford University Press.

Meara, P. 1995. The dimension of lexical competence. In *Performance and competence in second language acquisition*, ed. G. Brown, K. Malmkjaar, and K. Williams. Cambridge: Cambridge University Press

Met, Myriam. 2001. Changing contexts in early language learning. In *Beyond the boundaries: Changing contexts in language learning*, ed. Roberta Z. Lavine. New York: McGraw Hill.

Montgomery, C., and M. Eisenstein.1985. Reality revisited: An experimental communicative course in ESL. *TESOL Quarterly* 19, no. 2: 317–34.

Moser, Jason. 2005. Using language-focused learning journals on a task-based course. In *Teachers exploring tasks in English language teaching*, ed. Corony Edwards and Jane Willis. Basingstoke, U.K.: Palgrave Macmillan.

Muranoi, Hitoshi. 2000. Focus on form through interaction enhancement: Integrating formal instruction into a communicative task in EFL classrooms. *Language Learning* 50, no 4: 617–74.

Nation, I. S. P. 2001. *Learning vocabulary in another language*. Cambridge: Cambridge University Press.

Nation, I. S. P., and P. Meara. 2002. Vocabulary. In *An introduction to applied linguistics*, ed. N. Schmitt. London: Arnold; and New York: Oxford University Press.

Nicholas, H. P., P. Lightbown, and N. Spada. 2001. Recases as feedback to language learners. *Language Learning* 51: 719–58.

Norris, John M. 2002. Interpretations, intended uses and designs in task-based language assessment. *Language Testing* 19, no. 4: 337–47.

Norris, J. M., J. D. Brown, T. Hudson, and J. Yoshioka. 1998. *Designing second language performance assessments*. Manoa: Second Language Teaching and Curriculum Center, University of Hawaii at Manoa.

Northwestern University. 2001. *Northwestern undergraduate catalog 2001–03*. Evanston, Ill.: Northwestern University.

Nunan, David. 1989a. *Designing tasks for the communicative classroom*. Cambridge: Cambridge University Press.

———. 1989b. *Syllabus design*. Cambridge: Cambridge University Press.

———. 1993. Task-based syllabus design: Selecting, grading, and sequencing tasks. In *Tasks in a pedagogical context: Integrating theory and practice*, ed. Graham Crookes and Susan Gass. Clevedon, U.K.: Multilingual Matters.

Ozdeniz, D. 1996. Introducing innovations into your teaching. In *Challenge and change in language teaching*, ed. J. Willis and D. Willis. Oxford: Heinemann ELT.

Paulston, C. 1974. Linguistic and communicative competence. *TESOL Quarterly* 8: 347–62.

Pawley, A., and F. Syder. 1983. Two puzzles for linguistic theory: Nativelike selection and nativelike fluency. In *Language and communication*, ed. Jack Richards and Richard Schmidt. New York: Longman.

Pelletier, P. 1992. Word processing as a support to the writing process. *International Journal of Instructional Media* 19, no. 3: 249–57.

Perkins, K. 1998. Assessing reading. *Annual Review of Applied Linguistics* 18: 208–18.

Peterson, Pat Wilcox. 1997. Knowledge, skills, and attitudes in teacher preparation for content-based instruction. In *The content-based classroom: Perspectives on integrating language and content*, ed. Marguerite Ann Snow and Donna M. Brinton. New York: Longman.

Phlegar, Janet M., and Nancy Hurley. 1999. Designing job-embedded professional learning: The authentic task approach. Stoneham, Mass.: Learning Innovations.

Pica, T. 1994. Research on negotiation: What does it reveal about second language learning conditions, processes and outcomes? *Language Learning* 44: 493–527.

Pica, T., R. Kanagy, and J. Folodun. 1993. Choosing and using communication tasks for second language instruction. In *Tasks in language learning: Integrating theory and practice*, ed. Graham Crookes and Susan Gass. Clevedon, U.K.: Multilingual Matters.

Pienemann, M. 1988. *Language processing and second language development: Processability theory*. Philadelphia: John Benjamins.

Pike, Kenneth L. 1959. Language as particle, wave and field. *Texas Quarterly* 2, no. 2: 37–54.

Pinter, A. 2005. Task repetition with ten year old children. In *Teachers exploring tasks in English language teaching*, ed. C. Edwards and Jane Willis. Basingstoke, U.K.: Palgrave Macmillan.

Plass, J. 1998. Design and evaluation of the user interface of foreign language multimedia software: A cognitive approach. *Language Learning & Technology* 2, no. 1: 35–45.

Porter, P. 1986. How learners talk to each other: Input and interaction in task-centered discussions. In *Talking to learn: Conversation in second language acquisition*, ed. R. Day. Rowley, Mass.: Newbury House.

Porto, M. 2001. Second language acquisition (SLA) research implications for language teachers. *Applied Language Learning* 12: 45–54.

Poupore, Glen. 2005. Quality interaction and types of negotiation in problem-solving and jigsaw tasks. In *Teachers exploring tasks in English language teaching*, ed. Corony Edwards and Jane Willis. Basingstoke, U.K.: Palgrave Macmillan.

Prabhu, N. S. 1982. The communicational teaching project, South India (photocopy, British Council, Madras).

————. 1987. *Second language pedagogy*. Oxford: Oxford University Press.

Reading aloud: Are students *ever* too old? 2003. *Educators' World*. www
.educationworld.com/a_curr/curr081.shtml.

Ribe, Ramon. 1997. Tramas creativas y aprendizaje de lenguas: Prototipos de tareas de
tercera generacion. Barcelona: Publicacions de la Universitat de Barcelona.

Richards, J. C. 1987. The dilemma of teacher education in TESOL. *TESOL Quarterly* 21,
no. 2: 209–26.

Richards, J., J. Platt, and H. Weber. 1985. *Longman dictionary of applied linguistics*. London: Longman.

Rivers, William P. 2001. Autonomy at all costs: An ethnography of metacognitive
self-assessment and self-management among experienced language learners. *Modern Language Journal* 85, no. 2: 279–91.

Robinson, P. 2001. Task complexity, cognitive resources, and syllabus design. In *Cognition and second language instruction*, ed. P. Robinson. Cambridge: Cambridge University Press.

Roblyer, M. D., and Letcicia Ekhaml. 2000. Assessing interactivity in distance learning
courses. Presentation at the 2nd Distance Learning Managers' Conference, Gar-
dens, Georgia.

Roebuck, R. F. 2001. Teaching composition in the college level foreign language class:
Insights and activities. *Foreign Language Annals* 34, no. 3: 206–15.

Ryder, M. 2002. *Constructivism (University of Colorado at Denver, School of Education*.
http://carbon.cudenver.edu/~mryder/itc_data/constructivism.html.

Saito, Y., E. Horwitz, and T. Garza. 1999. Foreign language reading anxiety. *Modern
Language Journal* 83, no. 2: 202–18.

Salmon, Gilly. 2000. *E-moderating*. London: Kogan Page.

Samuda, Virginia. 2001. Guiding relationships between form and meaning during task
performance: The role of the teacher. In *Researching pedagogic tasks: Second language
learning, teaching and testing*, ed. Martin Bygate, Peter Skehan, and Merrill Swain.
Harlow, U.K.: Pearson Education.

Sanders, D. 2002. EFI: English language for Internet with Webheads. In *Learning from
the innovators: Internet communication technologies changing business practices (2/3)
ICT's in different cultural contexts*. http://www.imakenews.com/ict1
/e_article000089866.cfm?x=193008,0.

Schiefele, U. 1992. Topic interest and levels of text comprehension. In *The role of interest in learning and development*, ed. K. A. Renninger, S. Hidi, and A. Krapp. Hillsdale,
N.J.: Lawrence Erlbaum.

Schleppergrell, Mary. 1989. *The older language learner*. Washington, D.C.: ERIC Clearinghouse on Languages and Literatures.

Schmidt, Richard. 1990. The role of consciousness in second language learning. *Applied
Linguistics* 11: 17–46.

————. 1994. Deconstructing consciousness: In search of useful definitions for applied
linguistics. *AILA Review* 11: 11–26.

Schraw, G., and R. S. Dennison. 1994. The effect of reader purpose on interest and recall. *Journal of Reading Behavior* 26: 1–17.

Schulz, R. A. 2002. Changing perspectives in foreign language education: Where do
we come from? Where are we going? *Foreign Language Annals* 35, no. 3: 285–92.

Schwienhorst, K. 1997. Modes of interactivity: Internet resources for second language
learning. In *Multimedia-internet-lernsoftware: Fremdsprachenunterricht vor neuen*

*Herausforderungen?* ed D. Kranz, L. Legenhausen, and B. Lüking. Münster: Agenda Verlag.

Selinker, Larry. 1972. Interlanguage. *International Review of Applied Linguistics* 10, no. 3: 209–31.

Shehadeh, A. 1999. Non-native speaker's production of modified comprehensible output and second language learning. *Learning* 49, no. 4: 627–75.

Shekhtman, Boris. 1990. *How to improve your foreign language immediately.* Rockville, Md.: SLTC.

Shekhtman, Boris, Betty Lou Leaver, Ekaterina Kuznetsova, Natalia Lord, and Elena Ovtcharenko. 2002. Developing professional-level oral proficiency. In *Developing professional-level language proficiency,* ed. Betty Lou Leaver and Boris Shekhtman. Cambridge: Cambridge University Press.

Sinclair, J. 1991. *Corpus, concordance and collocation.* Oxford: Oxford University Press.

Skehan, Peter. 1996a. A framework for the implementation of task based instruction. *Applied Linguistics* 17, no. 1: 38–62.

———. 1996b. Second language acquisition and task-based instruction. In *Challenge and change in language teaching,* ed. J. Willis and D. Willis. Oxford: Heinemann.

———. 1998a. *A cognitive approach to language learning.* Oxford: Oxford University Press.

———. 1998b. Task-based instruction. *Annual Review of Applied Linguistics* 18: 268–86.

Skehan, Peter, and P. Foster. 1997. Task type and task processing conditions as influences on foreign language performance. *Language Testing Research* 1, no. 3: 185–211.

Skinner, B. F. 1957 *Verbal behavior.* New York. Appleton-Century-Crofts.

Smallwood, Betty Ansin. 1992. *Children's literature for adult ESL literacy.* ERIC Digest, ED353864.

Snow, Marguerite Ann, Donna M. Brinton, and Marjorie Wesche. 1989. Content-based second language instruction. New York: Newbury House.

Snyder, E. N.d. *CoPs (Communities of practice). tcm.com inc. Training and Development Community Center.* www.tcm.com/trdev/cops.htm.

Staley, Amy. 1997. Reading aloud: Bringing whole language into the writing classroom. *Language Teacher Online* 21, no. 3. http://langue.hyper.chubu.ac.jp/jalt/pub/tlt/97/mar/aloud.html.

Steele, J. 2002. Herding cats: A descriptive case study of a virtual language learning community. Ph.D. diss., Indiana University of Pennsylvania.

Stern, H. H. 1983. *Fundamental concepts of language teaching.* Oxford: Oxford University Press.

Stevens, Vance. 1999. *Chat with students Gosia from Poland, Felix from Bahia, Ying-Lan from Taiwan, and Gao from Brazil; and teachers Michael C, MAD Maggi, and Vance August 15, 1999.* www.homestead.com/prosites-vstevens/files/efi/ch15aug9.htm.

———. 2002a. Here's how to join Writing for Webheads. www.homestead.com/prosites-vstevens/files/efi/join_wfw.htm#testimonials.

———. 2002b. *Meet Yaodong.* http://sites.hsprofessional.com/vstevens/files/efi/yaodong.htm.

———. 2003. *Webheads in action: Communities of practice online.* www.geocities.com/vance_stevens/papers/evonline2002/webheads.htm.

Stevens, Vance, and A. Altun. 2002. The Webheads community of language learners online. In *The process of language learning: An EFL perspective,* ed. Z. Syed. Abu Dhabi: Military Language Institute.

Stevens, Vance, and M. Coghlan. 2001a. *What students feel about Writing for Webheads Part 1: Preliminary reflections.* www.homestead.com/prosites-vstevens/files/efi/testimonials.htm.

———. 2001b. *What students feel about Writing for Webheads Part 2: Rank the questionnaire.* www.homestead.com/prosites-vstevens/files/efi/testimonial2.htm.

———. 2001c. *What students feel about Writing for Webheads Part 3: Open-ended questions.* http://www.homestead.com/prosites-vstevens/files/efi/testimonial3.htm.

Story, M., J. Mueller, and R. Mace. 1998. *The universal design file: Designing for people of all ages and abilities.* Raleigh: North Carolina State University.

Stryker, Stephen B., and Betty Lou Leaver. 1997. Content-based instruction: From theory to practice. In *Content-based instruction in foreign language education: Models and methods,* ed. Stephen B. Stryker and Betty Lou Leaver. Washington, D.C.: Georgetown University Press.

Swain, Merrill. 1985. Communicative competence: Some roles of comprehensible input and output in its development. In *Input in second language acquisition,* ed. Susan Gass and C. Madden. New York: Newbury House.

———. 1988. Manipulating and complementing content teaching to maximise second language learning. *TESL Canada Journal* 6, no. 1: 68–93.

Swain, Merrill, and Sharon Lapkin. 2001. Focus on form through collaborative dialogue: Exploring task effects. In *Researching pedagogic tasks: Second language learning, teaching and testing,* ed. Martin Bygate, Peter Skehan, and Merrill Swain. Harlow, U.K.: Longman Pearson Education.

Tenewicki, I. 1995. *Curso de periodismo.* Buenos Aires: Editorial Troquel.

Terrell, Tracy. 1986. Acquisition in the natural approach: The binding/access framework. *Modern Language Journal* 70, no. 3: 213–27.

Tsui, A. B. M. 2001. Classroom interaction. In *The Cambridge guide to teaching English to speakers of other languages,* ed. R. Carter and David Nunan. Cambridge: Cambridge University Press.

Van Ek, J. 1973. *The threshold level in a European unit/credit system for modern language teaching by adults: System development in adult language learning.* Strasbourg: Council of Europe.

Van Patten, Bill. 1990. Attending to content and form in the input: An experiment in consciousness. *Studies in Second Language Acquisition* 12: 287–301.

———. 1994. Evaluating the role of consciousness in SLA: Terms, linguistic features, and research methodology. *AILA Review* 11:27–36.

Vygotsky, L. S. 1978. *Mind in society: The development of higher psychological processes.* Cambridge, Mass.: Harvard University Press.

Weber, Richard A. 1994. Evaluating the role of consciousness in SLA: Terms, linguistic features, and research methodology. *AILA Review* 11: 27–36.

———. 2000. Re(de)fining the college German curriculum: A program proposal. *Die Unterrichtspraxis / Teaching German* 33, no. 1: 50–61.

Wenger, E. 1998. *Communities of practice: Learning as a social system.* www.co-i-l.com/coil/knowledge-garden/cop/lss.shtml.

Whittington, D., and Campbell, L. N.d. *Task-based learning environments in a virtual university.* http://www7.scu.edu.au/programme/posters/1848/com1848.htm.

Widdowson, H. G. 1983. *Learning purpose and language use.* Oxford. Oxford University Press.

————. 1990. *Aspects of language teaching*. Oxford: Oxford University Press.

Wilkins, David A. 1976. *Notional syllabuses*. London: Oxford University Press.

Williams, M., and R. Burden. 1997. *Psychology for language teachers*. Cambridge: Cambridge University Press.

Willis, D. 1983. The implications of discourse analysis for the teaching of oral communication. Ph.D. diss., Birmingham University.

————. 1990. *The lexical syllabus: A new approach to language teaching*. London: HarperCollins/Cobuild.

————. 1996. Accuracy, fluency and conformity. In *Challenge and change in language teaching*, ed. J. Willis and D. Willis. Oxford: Heinemann Macmillan.

————. 2003. *Rules, patterns, and words: Grammar and lexis in English language teaching*. Cambridge: Cambridge University Press.

Willis, D., and J. Willis. 1996. Consciousness-raising activities in the language classroom. In *Challenge and change in language teaching*, ed. J. Willis and D. Willis. Oxford: Heinemann Macmillan.

Willis, J. 1994. TBI: Is it PPP up-side down? In *The Teacher Trainer*, March. Revised as A flexible framework for task-based learning in *Challenge and change in language teaching*, ed. J. Willis and D. Willis. Oxford: Heinemann Macmillan.

————. 1996a. A flexible framework for task-based learning. In *Challenge and change in language teaching*, ed. J. Willis and D. Willis. Oxford: Heinemann Macmillan.

————. 1996b. *A framework for task-based learning*. Harlow, U.K.: Longman.

————. 1998. Task-based learning: What kind of adventure? *Language Teacher Online*. http://langue.hyper.chubu.ac.jp/jalt/pub/tlt/98/jul/willis.html.

Willis, J., and D. Willis. 1988–89. *The Collins Cobuild English Course*. Levels 1–3. New York: Harper Collins.

————, eds. 1996. *Challenge and change in language teaching*. Oxford: Heinemann ELT.

Yeh, A. 2003. CMC and Webheads: Hand in hand in education without borders. Paper presented at the annual TESOL meeting, Baltimore, March 26. Also available at www.geocities.com/aidenyeh/tesol/CMCandWebheads.htm.

Yule, G., and D. Macdonald. 1990. A direction for contrastive analysis: The comparative study of developmental sequences. *TESOL Quarterly* 16, no. 2: 169–83.

# Contributors

**MAHDI ALOSH** (Ph.D., the Ohio State University) is associate professor of Arabic and applied linguistics and director of the Arabic Language Program at Ohio State University. He is the author of *Learner, Text, and Context: An Arabic Perspective* (Ohio State University Press), as well as several textbooks and numerous articles, book reviews, and book chapters.

**NATALIA ANTOKHIN** (KFN, Moscow State University; M.A., Monterey Institute of International Studies) is associate professor and curriculum development specialist at the Defense Language Institute in Monterey, California. Prior to that, she has held positions at Moscow State University and the Center of Culture and Art, Ministry of Culture of the USSR. She has authored several publications.

**ABDELFATTAH BOUSSALHI** (Ph.D., University of Glasgow) is associate professor at the Defense Language Institute, Foreign Language Center in Monterey, California. He is currently a member of the GLOSS development team. Prior to that, he was a teacher of Arabic and an Oral Proficiency Tester Trainer.

**KUEI-LAN CHEN** (Ph.D., University of Illinois at Champaign-Urbana) is assistant professor, curriculum development specialist, at the Defense Language Institute in Monterey, California.

**PAMELA COMBACAU** is the instructional design chief of the Curriculum Development Division at the Defense Language Institute in Monterey, California. She implements task-based instruction in the design of online materials and oversees six educational technnology specialists developing Web-based language learning components.

**KATHY COZONAC** (M.A. candidate, Gordon-Cornwell Theological Seminary) is the director of the American Language Center in Chisinau, Moldova, where she previously worked as an English teacher and curriculum design specialist. She regularly gives presentations at teacher training sessions throughout Moldova on methodology in practice. Her current research interests are based on sociolinguistics, with a focus on education in multilinguistic societies.

**WAYNE HAGER** (Ph.D., University of Idaho) is professor emeritus at Pennsylvania State University, where he served as professor and head of the School of Engineering Technology and Commonwealth Engineering. He has had two Fulbright Scholarships to French-speaking Mauritius, served as president of the Fulbright Association of Central Pennsylvania, and was a founding faculty member of the dual degree program in Foreign Languages (French and German) and Engineering.

**MARSHA A. KAPLAN** (Ph.D., University of Pennsylvania) is currently serving as senior technical director of the University Affiliated Research Center's oversight board at the Center for Advanced Study of Language. Since 1991, she has been with the U.S. Department of State's Foreign Service Institute, where she is head of Russian and Ukrainian language training. She has presented and published on government language training initiatives.

**STEVE KOPPANY** (M.A., Monterey Institute of International Studies) is associate professor and dean of curriculum development at the Defense Language Institute (DLI) in Monterey California. Prior to this, he worked as a teacher of Hungarian, department chair, faculty developer, video teletraining specialist, faculty development coordinator, academic associate dean for curriculum and faculty development, and associate dean for continuing education over a span of twenty-two years at the DLI. For two years, he also served as Assistant Head of Hungarian Research for RFE/RL, Inc. Language Institute in Munich.

**BETTY LOU LEAVER** (Ph.D., Pushkin Institute, Moscow) is director of the Coalition of Distinguished Language and an international consultant on education, including task-based instruction. She has more than 150 publications in the area of foreign language education.

**JUAREZ LOPES** (B.A., Universidade Católica de Pelotas, Pelotas, Rio Grande do Sul, Brazil) is academic coordinator at British House in Rio Grande, Brazil, where he has worked as a course coordinator, English teacher, and teacher trainer. He has served as a freelancer for Pearson Education, piloting a series of books titled *Cutting Edge: A Practical Approach to TBL*, and reviewed the manuscript for Jane Willis's book, *A Framework for Task-Based Learning*.

**MARY-ANN LYMAN-HAGER** (Ph.D., University of Idaho) is professor of French at San Diego State University and director of the National Language Resource Center. Prior to that, she was associate professor of French and Director of Instructional Technology for the College of Liberal Arts at Pennsylvania State University. She has also served as director of the Five-College Language Resource Center in Amherst, Massachusetts.

**FRANZISKA LYS** (Ph.D., Northwestern University) is associate professor of German at Northwestern University. She has lectured throughout the United States and in Europe on a variety of topics, ranging from the teaching of Swiss culture, the adaptation of authentic videos for the language classroom, to computer-assisted language instruction. She is the coproducer and author of numerous educational documentaries and CD-ROM multimedia software.

**CLEMENCIA MACÍAS** (B.A., University of California, Berkeley; B.A., University of Bogotá) is cofounder of the Latin American component of the San Francisco International Film Festival. She is an interpreter resources manager at Language Line Services and oversees the recruitment and testing of interpreters. She has a background in media and was formerly an editor in bilingual projects for Hampton Brown Publishing.

**CLÁUDIO PASSOS DE OLIVEIRA** (M.A., Universidade Federal do Rio Grande do Sul, Porto Alegre, Brazil) is academic coordinator at the Instituto Cultural Brasileiro-NorteAmericano in Porto Alegre, Brazil, where he has also worked as a course coordinator and English teacher.

**YOSHIKO SAITO-ABBOTT** (Ph.D., the Ohio State University) is director of the Monterey Bay Foreign Language Project and Coordinator of the Japanese Program at California State University, Monterey Bay. She has numerous publications in the area of foreign language education, specifically, technology, affective factors, and reading.

**VANCE STEVENS** (M.A., University of Hawaii) is a computing lecturer at Petroleum Institute in Abu Dhabi, United Arab Emirates. His interests include multimedia computer-mediated communication and the development of communities of practice utilizing Web-based software tools.

**ALICIA MORA VAN ALTENA** (master's equivalent, University of San Juan, Argentina) is a senior lector at Yale University. She has taught foreign languages for thirty-eight years.

**JANE WILLIS** is from Britain but has worked extensively overseas teaching English and French. She has published several prize-winning books, including *A Framework for Task-Based Learning, Challenge and Change in Language Teaching*, with D. Willis, and *English for Primary Teachers*, with Mary Slattery, and she has coedited with Corony Edwards *Teachers Exploring Tasks in English Language Teaching*. She recently retired from Aston University, where she taught in the distance learning master's in TESOL and TESP programs. She continues to work as a writer and ELT consultant and travels widely.

# Index

Page references with a f indicate figures, page references with a t indicate tables.